PSALMSONGS

PSALMSONGS

A Gathering of Psalms

GAYA ARANOFF BERNSTEIN

AN ARTHUR KURZWEIL BOOK
New York/Jerusalem

AN ARTHUR KURZWEIL BOOK
11 Bond Street #456
Great Neck, NY 11021

First edition

Rabbi Adin Even-Israel Steinsaltz's introductory comments on
each psalm (*Tehillim*, Koren Publishers, 2005), translated into
English by G.A. Bernstein, are included in this volume
by permission of the author.

Please note that this volume includes a book of the Bible,
and should be treated accordingly.

Gaya Aranoff Bernstein
Psalmsongs
A Gathering of Psalms

ISBN 978-0-9855658-3-1

for Aryeh

God rules all
but
we can choose
to believe it
or not

הכל בידי שמים חוץ מיראת שמים
Babylonian Talmud
Berachot 33b

PSALMSONGS

A Gathering of Psalms

Table of Contents

Foreword

Psalms are songs.[1] The *Book of Psalms* is part of the Hebrew Scriptures.

Jews draw from the *Book of Psalms*, and read or sing, in a whisper or aloud, the nourishing words that their ancestor, King David, and others, wrote down, recited, and passed on to their children, in prayer, in song, in need.

Christians throughout the world, regardless of affiliation, cherish the *Book of Psalms*.

Muslims know that the *Book of Psalms* was a gift from the Divine. The verse from the Qur'an (4:163) says, "David was given the Psalms."

But you don't have to be religious to find inspiration or comfort in the *Book of Psalms*. You just need to be alive.

The psalmsongs in this book are not English translations of the *words* of the Psalms; they are English translations of their *essences*.

There are 150 psalms. One of them, Psalm 23, begins famously, "The Lord is my shepherd." In other words, *"You lead, I'll follow"* (Psalmsong 23).

The author of *Psalmsongs* explains:
> *Psalmsongs* are interpretations of Psalms, rather than translations. They are psalms through the prism of my soul. I have attempted to be true to each psalm, to convey the passion and timelessness of King David's ancient angst, faith, resilience, and joy. Enemies still plague us; hope still sustains us. One does not have to be religious to try to make some sense of it all.

I open an edition of the *Book of Psalms* to a random page — Psalm 102. It reads:
> *Hear my prayer, O Lord, and let my cry come unto thee.*
> *Hide not thy face from me in the day when I am in trouble;*
> *incline thine ear unto me:*
> *in the day when I call, answer me speedily.*

---

[1] The Hebrew name for the *Book of Psalms* is *Tehillim* ("praises"), while the English word *psalms* is a transliteration of the Greek word for "songs."

I then turn to Psalmsong 102, and I read:

> *Don't make (me) believe*
> *that You don't see me*
> *in my time of need*
>
> *See me   hear me*
> *Answer me*
> *immediately*
> *my time is running out*
> *the sand is racing through the hourglass*

An essential part of the Bible, the *Book of Psalms* has for centuries been published by itself, to serve those who have, since time immemorial, turned to its words for prayerful expressions of the widest range of human emotions.

Psalmsongs opens doors to the *Book of Psalms*. "The author's retellings make the psalms vibrant, fresh, and immediately accessible," explains Rabbi Joseph Telushkin. And, more than simply making the text more tangible, the psalmsongs "represent something between a translation and a reactive commentary," says Rabbi Jonathan Rosenblatt, "challenging the reader to awaken from the lulling drone of traditional liturgical syntax and actually listen to the challenge and the comfort of the Bible's most affecting book, one that, when allowed, enters seldom-explored cavities of the human heart."

In his famous "I Have a Dream" speech on August 28, 1960, the Reverend Martin Luther King alluded to the 30th psalm when he spoke of the abolition of slavery: "It came as a joyous daybreak to end the long night of their captivity."

In Psalmsong 30, our author writes:

> *things change*
> *in a heartbeat*
> *life flips*
> *in a minute*
> *terror of night*
> *can end with day*

Many reggae songs include in their lyrics, "The earth is the Lord's and the fullness thereof." It's from Psalm 24.

Or, as Psalmsong 24 says,
it's all God's
the endless universe
and everything within
belong to Him

One more example, from Psalm 137:
By the rivers of Babylon,
there we sat down and wept.

Or as Psalmsong 137 puts it:
homeless
we sit by the river and weep
remembering Zion

I take *Psalmsongs* with me; it remains available to me when batteries are out of power or when an Internet connection is lost. Inspired by each psalm of the *Book of Psalms*, a book that in thousands of years has never lost its power, *Psalmsongs* has become, for me, the book of choice when I sit alone and I want or need to speak to the Eternal, to find myself. *Psalmsongs* give me the words I need to help locate my feelings, to express the innermost places in my soul, to reach out to the Almighty, to express my deepest fears and hopes, to give words to my prayers.

"The power of these verses is found in their universal understanding of the human condition," says Dr. Jerome Groopman. "None of us moves through life without doubting whether we can persist, and none of us moves through life without experiencing joy. The power of *Psalmsongs* is such that we can be moved back from the edge of despair to a place where we begin to believe again in the future and in the possibility of joy. And that place is where hope resides."

These *psalmsongs* did not come *from* the author; they came *through* her. Praise is due to the Source of All Blessings, for giving the author of *Psalmsongs* the gift to create this book.

And gratitude is due to her for providing us with renewed paths to our own selves, and to Holiness, through these profound, intimate, and exquisite *Psalmsongs*.

— Arthur Kurzweil
Great Neck, NY

Preface

*Because of the limitations of the human soul
and human imagination, the writings of Scripture
have to use anthropomorphic imagery.*
— Rabbi Adin Even-Israel Steinsaltz
The Sustaining Utterance

As I sat in the hospital waiting room shortly after my young daughter was diagnosed with lymphoma, I had a strong visual memory of a woman reading *Psalms*. Her son was my patient, had a brain tumor, and did well. He lived, married. I remembered that when her son was going through medical tests, she always sat silently reading (praying?) from the Hebrew book of *Psalms* (*Tehillim*, ascribed to King David and other biblical psalmists). It had surprised me, because in high heels and slacks, she didn't look the type. I remembered that her son lived, did well. During those socked-in-the-gut first days of my child's diagnosis, I put a book of *Psalms* in my bag and kept it with me. I read *Psalms* during PET scans, during chemo, during insomnia; it was all I could read for months. I read *Psalms* in Hebrew and in English; I tried to make each psalm relevant to my torment. David's enemies were my child's cancer cells, impotent against the Almighty. David's faith in the power of prayer was mine. I found comfort in the psalms, with their raw and unflinching depictions of the human condition, and their intimate first-person conversations with an inconceivable God.

Psalmsongs are psalms through the prism of my soul. They are interpretations of *Psalms*, rather than translations. I have attempted to be true to each psalm, to convey the passion and timelessness of King David's ancient angst, faith, resilience, and joy. Enemies still plague us; hope still sustains us. One does not have to be religious to try to make some sense of it all. My patient and his mother were not the first people in the world to be tested, or to err, or to fall, or to rise, or to be relieved, or to thank God, and neither am I. Millennia have passed since *Psalms* were written, and they remain current. We are still challenged and rewarded by life, still incapable of understanding our own humanity, and forever incapable of comprehending the unfathomable Creator.

This collection would have remained personal and unpublished if not for my husband, Lewis (Aryeh) Bernstein; our friend and publisher, Arthur Kurzweil; and if not for the blessing of Rabbi Adin Steinsaltz. They share in any good that may come of this project; any errors are solely mine. I am grateful to Dr. Jerome Groopman, Rabbi Jonathan Rosenblatt, Rabbi Joseph Telushkin, and Rabbi Avi Weiss for reviewing the manuscript and encouraging its publication. Particular thanks go to Bobby Kurzweil for her unflagging support, and for her subtitle, *A Gathering of Psalms*.

This book is dedicated to my mother (Freda Appleman Aranoff), father (Harry Aranoff, of blessed memory), children (Maya and Noam Silverman, Josh Bernstein, Kyra and Dov Sebrow), grandchildren (Ananya, Shefa, and Erez Silverman, and Nelly Sebrow), and to my sister (Shera Aranoff Tuchman), brother (Jonathan Aranoff), and their families. I am indebted to all of them, as well as to my friends, for being my role models, each in his own unique way.

— Gaya Aranoff Bernstein

Listing of Psalmsongs Based on Content

Although many of the psalmsongs could have been placed in
more than one category, most are listed only in the one
that best characterizes its theme.

Psalmsongs

These are not only poems, they are prayers.

Rabbi Adin Even-Israel Steinsaltz

1

to not get lost
to not get sidetracked
by the expected
by fad or fashion
of the time
to not keep up
with fools, sinners
others

to stay focused
on truth
your truth
God's truth
to yearn for it
day and night

to seek it
night and day
is to find
joy
truelife

like a sapling
near a stream
water for the taking
fruits in season
glistening leaves
growing
rooted

not blown away
a withered leaf
in autumn
an old newspaper
telling
ancient lies

2

stop the noise
Stop it
the idiocy of it
the propaganda
the screaming lying
headlines
Stop them
sightless powers
railing against God
and Israel

we believe in a God
we can't conceive of
but we know
we didn't create
ourselves

God must be amused
at their hubris
they are
out of
control

get real
editors presidents
ministers kings
your emperor
is naked
your castles
sand
your days
human
and God
is
not

3

O God
I am overwhelmed
by the demons
in my heart
at my heels
after me
taunting me
threatening me
aiming at me

but then I sense
You
here
with me
I get out of bed
lift my head
face my life
knowing You know
I'm surrounded

You get them
Kill those bastards
Break their teeth
Bless us

Selah

4

Just God
Answer me when I call
as You did
when things were tight
and I lost my will
to fight
Release me
again

pride-loving sycophants
yesmen
are there for me in my glory
for their glory

We know true love
You feel my tears
the fear and trembling
pounding in my heart
as I lie awake but

trust God
just God
who is
real
truth

I see You
in peace
more sweet
than spoils of war
You're here with me
I lie in bed
and safely sleep
alone

5

O my God I beg You
Hear me wail
see my tears
my cries my fears
O my God my King
my God I start my day
listening for You
waiting
knowing

You don't want evil men
boasting murderous slime
You don't want to look at them
You hate them
You want me
(deserving or not)
You want me
You know I'm waiting
listening always listening
for You
wanting You fearing You
dreaming of knowing You
dreaming of sitting in your palace
intimate old friends
Help me
I'm drugged
by their smooth talk
and twisted words
their wicked fat mouths
like open graves to me

You are my joy
and protection and
those who want to know You
know joy and protection and
song and love and
hope and kindness and
are blessed forever

6

O God don't punish me
don't be angry
have mercy
I am powerless
bereft
sick
spineless

Hear me
Heal me

O God
how long
can this go on
my soul aches
my terrified soul
burns

Free me
let my unworthy body
be   composed
I can't pray sing
praise You
from my grave

every night
my eyes melt
my bed floats on tears
I have aged
I am drained

Pain, depart
God is with me
He hears me

your turn
to be scared

7

O God don't leave me
save me
enemies at my heels
are gaining ground
and I don't know
maybe I deserve
to be ripped to shreds
eaten alive by their lions

if I am guilty
let them
trample my soul
drag it in the dust
kill my name

You be the judge
test my honest heart
my brain
my guts

You be the judge
and test them too
see traps they set
the lying schemes
the pits they dig
for me

I'm trying to
come clean with them
be true to You
O God
expose their treachery
give them their due
as I praise You

8

Awesome Lord of all
I see You
in clods of fertile earth
beneath my feet
in clouds and moon
and stars and sky
above my head
in suckling babies
who can't talk but will grow
to know You
tend Your sheep
and see Your mark
everywhere

why should You
care
about us

who are we
to be crowned
keepers
of Your earth
Your works
Your sheep and cattle
Your birds and fish
and oceans

O great God of all things
You care
we should

9

thank You God thank You God
thank You for this miracle
thank You with all my heart
anyone listening
I'm shouting singing
this miracle was wrought
by God
my enemies are in retreat
trapped in their own nets
drowning in their own slime
sliding into hell
who are they to have
presumed their own power
they control nothing
You rule
terrify them
Show them they die

You searched my heart
heard my case
judged justly
crushed my foes
each one of them
now toothless
swordless
impotent
wiped
out

infinite eternally
Your truth remains
resplendent
and though we are
ephemeral
we seek You
know You are not deaf
to human cries
indefinitely

10

Where are You when I need You
when danger is steadfastly
there for me
where are You
whose side are You on
the evil do evil
and get away with it
thrive prosper
they say You're
not there
not watching
not

Where are You
when they kill children
where are You
in famine and tsunamis
and war
where are You
when the old lady
is raped in her home
and he thinks no one sees

Show Yourself
the humbled can't breathe
when the air is full
of burning flesh
can't breathe
when lions
lick them
can't breathe
when they're drowning

they need to breathe
knowing You
see hear know
everything
knowing You
are just there
and just
here

In God I trust
Don't tell me to take wing
and fly away to safety
what's safety
when arrows can pierce my heart
in flight

In God I trust
to smash the
evil missiles
aimed at me and mine
under cover
of night

In God   I trust
I trust in God
wherever He sits
in celestial glory
infinitely distant
infinitely intimate
to know my thoughts
to see my eyelids
quiver

I trust You God
to rescue me
Demolish all
who seek to harm
Rain sulfur on them
hellfire storms

I trust You God
to notice me
to know my love
to keep me safe

12

Help me God
I've lost my faith
in man

smoothtalkers
spouting lies
doublespeak

bloated by
false pride
convinced
they're their own
masters
convinced
they're ours

Master
of the universe
by Your word
Creator
of the universe
Speak for the weary
the speechless
the humbled
the muted by
life

Your works are Your words
visible in sterling purity
to those not blinded
by their own hot air
engulfed in fog

13

O God
I can't take this much longer
where are You
come out
come out
wherever You are
I can't take this
much longer
Help me

how much longer
can I take this
I can't plan
I'm running
on empty
bereft of ideas
my enemies swift
I see death

look at me
wherever You are
See me
I'm falling
I can't take this
much longer
O show me a light
that my eyes can find
shine on me now
See me

if I die
they'll think they won
they'll dance on my grave
if I live
I'll sing and praise
my God
the only One

14

they say God is dead
then they do as they please
but God sees
everything

He sees them
sit down to dinner
blood on their hands
meat in their teeth
laughing
victorious
as we mourn

we cry
they chew
devouring us
oblivious
to our pain
and God's
presence

He hears us
He sees them
He remembers
everything

we'll get out of this
alive
as God lives

15

who gets You
good God
who gets
to be near
Yourspace
to reach Your
mountaintop
paradise utopia
nirvana eden
wherever
You are
who gets eternal
soulpeace

    prepare
    be there
    with inner life
    always in sync
    with outer life
    in thought
    in speech
    in deed

    be there with love
    be there with fear
    of One
    the only God
    then sure of foot and steadfast
    face steep inclines
    and climb

16

Stay close
You're mine

You're the source
of any good
coming my way

I've inherited You
the boundless wealth
of You
my parents
grandparents
and greats
earned You
and now You're
mine

Help me
guard my legacy
from raiders who
find it worthless
toss it out
raise their glasses
of blood
in empty victory

forgotten
they bequeath
dust

Blessed God
be with me
eternally
guide me rock steady
suffuse me with joy

I know You were
I know You are
I know that You
will be

17

hear me
listen to my thoughts
You know me inside out
I can't deceive
You

You read my heart
all night all day
You know I err
again
and yet I come
to You and cry
Forgive
at least I come to You
O that man   O that I
could pass Your tests
and always do what's right
I try and fail
I fail to try
have mercy

don't use my foes
their weaponry
to mete out punishment
surround me now
with clouds of love
just hide me now
protect me

they lurk like lions
proud and poised
to pounce and make their kill
they have no clue
they're just Your tools

when my time comes
I want to die fulfilled with years
and progeny
I need more time
to purify my soul
my deeds for You

18

I know my King
my rock my source
my strength
thank God
I live

I know You hear
my silent screams
when terror grips
at night
when I lie crouched
in chains in pain
in caves
pursued
You're there

in earth and wind
and fire and hail
and lightning thunder
clouds
You shake your cherubs
from the sky
and angel armies
rally to my aid

unbound by miracle
released
I flee I'm out I'm free
and armed by You
I soar and fly
leave enemies
in my wake

and if they call me
shepherd boy
or call me Israel's king
they know I bow
they know I serve my God
my God alone

19

the sky tells Your story
Your glory speaks
in orbits   planets
night and day
in webs of
space and time
sublime
the heavens express
Your will

each morning in joy
the sun like a groom
leaves its chamber
to start the day
with warmth uncontained
it leaps cross the sky
and radiates heat
light

Your light Your word
are gifts to us
eternally
we have to see
Your constancy
and symmetry
infinity

if only I
could stay the course
that You have set for me
and steep myself
in truth and love
and fear as You dictate
my soul enriched
would overflow

so guide my heart
my head my lips
to sing Your song
and heed You

20

when times are hard
and you are scared
and need and cry
My God! Hear me!
may He

remember when you sang to Him
reached out to Him
with thanks and praise
when times were good

may He
feel your pleading soul
suffuse it with joy

Others gird in armor
find strength in
guns and tanks
or see salvation
by the hands of
man
but metal melts
and metal twists
and man is clothed
in flesh

We know true power
lies in You
we speak Your name
we know You hear
and You renew
the strength of man
so he can stand
to live

21

I, mere king,
hail You my King
this victory is Yours
You read my lips
my silent plea
for life
I prayed
to win this deadly war
You fought for me
and won

a crown of answered prayers
swirl around my head
like golden leaves
encircling me
my path is strewn
with light

We asked to live
and here we are
eternally alive
Daveed melech Yisrael
chai chai vekayam!
David king of Israel
immortal Israel's king!
we're bound to You
in war and peace
and trust
that those who
plot our death
cannot escape Your reach

You'll seek and find them
wipe them out
obliterate their seed
while we
your loyal subjects
praise You
singing   joyous
safe

22

why have You left me
my God
my God so far away
and out of reach
more distant than a morning star
so mute all night
and deaf to all my cries

with mother's milk
for centuries
I learned to call to You
in hunger and in need
to trust the flow of
holy manna
from above

though I am just
an undeserving worm
in pain

come closer now
and hear the howling dogs
the lions roaring in the dark
come see my courage
melt like scalded wax
my fragile bones
exposed and parched
my garments strewn about

come feed me now
and clothe protect
and shelter me and nourish me
and look at me and be with me

I sense that You are
somewhere here
and that You know
my heart and care
and that it matters to You
that I serve and pray
and praise

23

You lead I'll follow
and lack nothing
cushion my falls
softly I'll land in
verdant fields
in calm water
soothe my soul
immerse me in justice
and truth and
in You

leaning on You
I have no fear
I tread lightly
through valleys
and shadows
and nightmares and terror
of doomsday and
death

Your bounty sustains me
I drink my fill
my thirst is quenched
and I empowered
by Your master plan
can face whatever
comes my way
and live my days
in peace

24

it's all God's
the endless universe
and everything within
belong to Him
God set up oceans patterns
galaxies and DNA

so who of us could ever
reach the top
to rise above ourselves
to keep our hearts and deeds
as pure as God's intent

perhaps it's those
who seek to know His ways
they are so blessed
in the endeavor
in the quest to find
and open gates of heaven
to see God
the source of all
unknown

25

I bring myself to You
trusting
You won't turn away
but will accept me
and show me a path
back to You
Remember mercy
forget the sins of my youth
open a door
to awareness of You
an unveiling to calm my soul
I'm trapped in a maze
with a net at my feet
and You
are my only way out

so turn to me hear me
be kind and forgive
I'm poor and alone
and pursued
by enemy forces
beyond my control
I reach out to You
still again

26

look inside the me of me
into my eyes into my soul
and see my love
unwavering
my love for You is real
present if You look or not
there if You care or not

test me if you doubt my love
golden through fire
it will only emerge
refined
unscorched
rekindled

I play by Your rules
not theirs
it's Your light up ahead
that guides my path
I've washed my hands
of things I've done
and stay away from
dirt

I've found myself
my space that's Yours
Your place Your palace
You
and now in found
tranquility
I pray You
keep me there

27

God, with You
lighting my way
shielding me
what could I fear

You've saved me before
I've seen them fall
those who conspire
to devour me
I've seen them
armies of them
weaken and fall
now my heart
has no fear
only desire
for Your ongoing
presence

let me in
to the safety of You
when times get tough
again
open Your gates to me
welcome me
shelter me
nourish me
let me in
I'll get strong and face them
yet again and win again
and let them know
You arm me

I'm orphaned and alone
at war
I need Your arms
I need to trust
to know You're here
lighting my path
giving me hope
and showing me
the way   out

28

if You don't hear me
if You don't listen
I might go straight
to hell
so help me resist
the easy slide
into mire
the pull to deceive
temptation to lie
to myself, others

deception comes easily
I see it all over
how power prestige
can turn some men
into demigods on stilts
heedless of downtrodden
underfoot

payback time
bring them down
and keep them down
stay true to those
who try to live
in truth

redeem Your people
bless Your land
carry us forever
Your truth is what remains
when human power
wanes

when you feel strong
invincible
give God His due
in your honest
inner life
know your power
stems from Him

Hear His voice
in tranquil seas
in crashing waves

Hear His voice
in stormy winds
as limbs of cedars
leap like unicorns
across the sky
their beauty His
unspeakable

Hear His voice
in fire
in silent desert nights
in cries of babies
in the dark

Hear seraphim
in His chambers
whisper holy holy holy
giving credit
where all credit
must be due

know that as the
flood was His
so will the blessed
peace bequeathed
to us
be His
to give

30

I proclaim You most high
You've raised me
from depths unfathomable
lifted me above strife
healed my deadly wounds
carried me out of hell
cleansed my soul
of despair

sing out to God
give thanks and praise
acknowledge Him
remember

things change
in a heartbeat
life flips
in a minute
terror of night
can end with day
security is insecure
Your will controls us all
You are the One
who we must seek
and pray to and beseech
for life and time

bereft of You
we turn to dust
can't breathe
can't think
can't sing

but close to You
with boundless thanks
I'm stepping out of shrouds
embracing life
with holy joy
my dance begins
anew

31

when I lean on You
I'm stable
Be my rock
my fortress my shelter
I'll find my way to You
far from the trap I'm in
I'll place my life
in Your hands
and stop relying on
false guards

O the joy the rapture
to know that You're with me
when I'm left for dead
my hope is with You
not with bodyguards
generals armies and spies

Background noises
plots and whispers
shake my faith
in man
at times in haste
when faced with death
I've also doubted
You

but blessed God
my soul is Yours
my time is Yours to give
I'm not ashamed
to say aloud
I trust in You alone

let prideful babbling foolish men
have shame in arrogance
Lord shine on me
and on all souls who love You
in good faith
and give us strength
and courage
to wait and wait
for You

32

Lucky is he
who doesn't try
to cover up
misdeed
but openly
admits
repents
comes clean
with God and man

for days and heavy nights
my silent sins
gnawed at the marrow
of my bones
and left me
parched

when I reach out to God
in prayer
regretting deeds I never
should have done
He can be kind to me
forgiving
and bestow
upon me mercy
undeserved

don't be an ass an ox a horse
and stand there mute
bedecked with jewels
while in your heart
deceit grows thick
with unchecked sins

cleanse your hands
your soul your heart
and try to make amends
then call to God
in truth and pray
you aren't washed away

33

Sing out to God
O righteous men
and women
Praise Him now!
with music
with a whole new song
with choirs
orchestras!

Proclaim to all
that God controls
the heavens, oceans
 us
that He is truth
that endlessly
He gives

that we are always
in His hands
His thoughts
His plans
and all we are we see we know
arise from His design

His energy empowers
without bounds
and those of us
who can admit
that power stems from Him
can find some
inner peace

how true that human might
is weak
that there are forces
out of our control

but when we trust
have faith in God
while trying hard
to help ourselves
there's hope
we may

34

I will stay aware and thank You
bless You every day
composing prayers
in song and word
so every letter a to z
will speak of You
I'll tell the world
whoever's listening
that You hear
You hear us all

When young and hungry lions
prowled in anger round my camp
I cried and
You sent angels
to my side
to hold my hand
and lead me surely
out of danger
certain death
and when I called You
I somehow
emerged intact

My children
open up your hearts
and let these teachings
enter and take root
and if you want to live and
love your life and face the trials
that will come
be careful with the words
you say and write
stay true to truth
seek peace be kind
and when the need is there
cry out for help to God
who will be with you
always listening
always there

35

Fight for me
aim your arrows
at those who seek my death
speak to me
tell me You're on my side
tell me You're planning
their doom
send me an angel
to keep them at bay
to drive them away
to turn them
to dust

I never saw it coming
they were part of me
I nurtured them
and now they turn around
and try to eat my flesh

I'm crying out to You
come here come now
don't turn away
attention must be paid
they have the strength of lions
see me as their prey
and want to eat me whole

I'm weak they're hungry
only You can change
the course of any war
restore my hope

so fight for me
let me survive
and I'll write poems songs
I'll tell the world
I won't be shy embarrassed coy
to say
You save

36

when sinning dictates
to my heart of hearts
  be brave and stay the course
  no one is watching
schemes I plan
at night
in bed
come easily
slick

but God in clouded distance
reigns and judges all
shows mercy undeserved
to man
and even
beast
and in this knowledge
I find comfort

I can hide beneath
Your wings
find cover
in the gentle mercy
always there
beneath Your wings
and find there
light
and air to breathe
and water for my soul
to be reclaimed
from prideful
lawless power
easy
O so easy
in my hands

so you never shine
and they do
so you're poor and give
and they're rich and don't
you struggle
they thrive
in their careless lives
in their wanton easy lives
don't despair don't compare
they'll be mowed down
like grass
in time they will
and you won't

let your answer be silence
when questions of fairness
worm into and gnaw
at your soul
find joy in the good
and delight in the lot
that is yours to inherit and keep
and trust that God knows
who is just who provides
and whose seed will take root
and survive

and He knows who's a meteor
flash in the pan
evanescent and
brilliant then
gone

38

dear God
dear punishing God
Your arrows
hit their mark
and I can't breathe
with shattered bones
can't run

my sins an evil halo
swirl around my head
land on my shoulders
a yoke
too heavy
to bear

I'm crushed
I'm dust
before I'm dead
I'm mute to all
they can't console

I speak to You alone
and limping wounded
and in pain
and fearing fate I must deserve
I pray
Forgive

39

I wanted to be mute
accept Your will
keep it in
not complain
not erupt and say
what I never
should have said

Tell me
what's my life to You
my speck of dust
of a life
to You
in Your infinite
inconceivable
spacetime

Hear me
Care for me
I'm a guest of Yours
on earth
and I will
silently
accept the fate
that's mine to bear
that's Yours to give
if You only
let me
be me
in peace
before
I have
to go

40

I knew Your will
would be
I hoped Your will
would coincide
with mine
I hoped You'd care
for me

Now here I am
so joyous high
above the quicksand
that was killing me
and flowing from my lips and pen
are songs of praise
of You
O lucky me
and he or she
who put their trust
in You
and stay away
from charlatans
ubiquitous
and lame

What can I ever
give to You
What could You want
from me
I've learned I'm learning
it's not
human sacrifice

I want to follow You
and make Your will
be my desire
the blood and guts of me
and get it out
and publish shout
in God I trust

41

Happy is he who knows
that bad times pass
that things change fast
that you can rise
from a bed drenched
with hopeless blood and tears
that your heart can pour itself
to God
Who cares

when I heard whispers
in the hall
that death is near
but to my face
came lies
that all is well
when optimistic friends
retreated   disappeared
when I had fewer hairs
than pains
when fog obscured my sight
when my heart lacked strength
to beat again
I begged You
to have mercy
and repair
my wretched body
damaged soul

You stay by me
You never go
You're here
You're real
You heal
and I simply
believe in You
Amen
oh man
Amen

42

like a parched doe
near a cool stream
I thirst for the essence
of You
Your water
O my living God
I yearn to know
You

I felt close to You once
I remember the joy
of the presence of You
within me
stability peace
was my daily bread
the holidays Sabbaths
the songs

and now I drink
tears
am bereft
have no clue
cannot fathom
the depth of You

from deep within
I call to the void
in the forest the ocean
the sky
and I search and I wait
as I reach out to You
so desperate
for Your reply

don't cry my soul
just praise my God
He hears me
He'll reply

43

You be my judge
side with me
set me free

Why am I captive
in enemy chains
alone in this vise
despised

Come to me
with angels bearing
light and truth
good news
and lift me high above
this blackened night

and then aloft
unchained
I'll fly
and know
that it was You
and You alone
who got me
out

I'll write You songs
of love and praise
and sing
and play them on my harp
and in my head

44

We've heard
we've learned from history
from fathers Torah
past
that You determine
outcome
it's Your will

that we must try
and we can fight
but if we win
all victories
are Yours
without You
all our swords
are blunt

so now
my fathers' God, and mine
command whatever powers that be
to bend to us
our armies can't prevail alone
and if we triumph
as we did
we always will
give thanks to You

when You turn away from us
we're prey we're lambs
they're wolves
they eat their fill
and scatter our remains

we trust in You
we're killed for this
return to us
dear God return
we never have left
You

45

for the groom

> the ink flows
> from my soul to my pen
> as I write in praise of you
> brave prince among men
> the words from your mouth
> are faceted brilliant jewels
> you are beautiful wise
> and blessed to rise
> above the rest of us
> stay strong stay humble
> vanquish foes
> be fruitful righteous
> grow
> and remain adorned
> and adored for all time
> as you are by your bride
> today

for his bride

> virgin beauties flock in droves
> and he desires your love
> it's time to stand
> beside your man
> and leave your childhood
> home
> to take your place
> and walk with him
> on paths unknown
> as queen
> he sees you precious sparkling
> and bejeweled
> he knows your soul
> and needs you wants you
> for his own alone
> be good to him
> and make his palace
> home
> and live with him and progeny
> forever blessed
> within

46

in the worst of times
it's easiest to find You

when earth and life
turn upside down
foundations quake
and mountains lose control
we're not afraid
we need You
and You're there with us
in silence
through the crash

and though our planet's
rearranged
we focus and we see
the great can fall
the weak can rise
and tranquil rivers
from above
can calm the raging madness
and put out
the fires of war

47

Gather everyone
Applaud!
Sing praise!
Ring bells!
Rejoice!

Blast the shofars
trumpets horns
Proclaim that God is King
and we're His love

He's King
He's chosen us
to watch
to know
that He's in charge
and that He has
the power
to protect

His Kingdom
everything
conceivable
and not

48

God's power
immense
is there
you can see it
in holy Jerusalem
home
in beautiful earth
in mountains
and landscapes
His universe
palaces
fit for
the King

the rulers here
of flesh and blood
all labor and beget
more trembling
mortal flesh
and blood
a breeze a breath
a thought
from God
can crash their ships
against the rocks
or make them
blow away

we hope
imagine
that You will
be true to us
and kind and just
and like the hills
around the mount
of Zion and Jerusalem
You will protect
and cradle us
to the end
of worlds
and time

49

Listen to this
rich man poor man
cave dwellers all
of unstable earth
Listen to the music
of the wisdom
of my heart
and know my song
is true
and know that I don't
live in fear
of death
as some
mortals
do

there's no first class
round trip to the grave
and you can't be
ransomed out
and all of your
power and wealth and fame
count as much in the end
as a pasture does
to a slaughtered
calf

What matters most
what lives beyond
the other side of life
is not of matter
not our bodies
bound for mother earth
and not the moneyed towers
we have built
but deeds we've done
and kindnesses
each one immortal
measured cherished counted
loved by God

50

Great God Speaks
perfection
rises over Zion in the east
and bathes the earth
in beauty and light

thundering judgment
reigns beneath
the brightened sky
and all is known

> *keep your bloody sacrifices*
> *sacred cows and flesh*
> *don't offer Me*
> *what's Mine in any case*
> *you've no control*
> *where matter is concerned*
>
> *come seek Me with*
> *what's in your realm*
> *your soul*
> *your power to choose*
>
> *approach Me*
> *shed deceit*
> *be real*
> *come clean*
>
> *and stand exposed*
> *in My pure light*
> *with every truth*
> *revealed*

51

Show clemency to me
dear God
I've sinned
I see sins in my mirror
filthy potent in my gut
royal
mortal
sins

I'm broken now
in pieces
on the ground
and only You
who formed me
in my mother's womb
know human weakness
is a part
of man
so look away
from what I've done
and take me
as I am
repentant
working on my soul
and get me out of this
alive and clean
and bring me back
the holy joy
of being whole
with You
so I can teach
all sinners
that the sacrifice
You won't reject
is a humbled heart
still true to You
still yearning
to come home

52

Don't pride yourself
on all your wealth
your mouth's your only strength
with its tongue that
thinks and speaks and acts
a sharpened razor
broken glass
feeding on lies
and dealing death
and spouting slander out

You're high on words
but God will bring you
down and break
your wicked tongue
and shatter it
and silence you for good
and wise men seeing this
will nod their heads
and point you out
and know that you're an evil fool
immersed in stealth deceit
and self

I trust in God
live in His house
I'm evergreen
renewed
my olive branches spanning worlds
remain abundant
blessed strong
survive and thrive
by God

53

in silence the villain
says to himself
there is no god
no one is good
I'm not alone
we're all depraved
look at the chosen ones
united in their choice
of sin
conspiring and corrupt
oblivious
to a creator
no one knows
the things
we do

but God
unknowable
keeps track
keeps faith
and listens listens
for a human cry
so that
He can
respond

so call to Him
and may He hear
and send salvation
starting now
from Zion
radiating
to encompass
all of man
and freeing us
from dangers
at our borders
and from demons
deep within

54

I'm calling You by name
almighty God
I beg of You
to hear me
listen closely
if no sound comes out
I pray you
read my lips

the strangers
who are after me
don't know that You
are there for me
to foil their
evil plans

and when You do
I will give thanks
to You
with every
sacrificial
breath
that I
have left

I will
outlast
my foes
but keep
them all
in sight

55

I'm burdened trembling
terrified
and begging of You
not to hide from me
in distant Godly skies
while I'm surrounded
on the ground
by accusations
evil shrieking voices
flinging hatred at me
fast

if only I could rise
above it all
sprout wings
and be alone
with You
in quiet
sheltered
peace

the treachery within my walls
untethered me
and now I doubt
that I can trust
my bosom friends
whose words were
sweet and wise
and soft
convincing
cursed
lies

I'm shedding
sandbags of deceit
for You to judge
they're in Your hands
I'm letting go
to fly

56

O God have mercy
every day
I run away
from hostile hordes
all chasing me
relentlessly
they congregate
and spy on me
and count my steps
and wait

they've caught me now
I'm in a vise
as they compete
for the prize
of my head

I crouch in caves
cry hurricanes
and trust that You
collect each solitary tear
to cleanse
and polish my poor soul

what have I to fear of man
when I still stand
and still can pray
to God
who keeps
my burnished soul
protected
in His light

57

Lord have mercy
take me in
so that the cooling shadows
of Your wings
protect me
and relieve the heat
until this fury passes
and I'm safe

cage the lions
prowling round my cave
tongues and arrows
saber teeth and swords
unite in desire
for my life
as nets of fire
hem me in

awaken, soul
and shake off panic
stifled hope
get up and pray
and sing out loud
take out your harp
and rouse the dawn
and beg the Lord of heavens
to make light
of night
to day

58

How can you be silent
not declare me
innocent
when you have
the power
to help

you must know
right from wrong
but your muted tongue
has a will of its own
and your hands
steeped in blood
have no heart

like a snake
uncharmed
by his master's flute
you remain immobile
deaf
you've earned
and deserve
the silence
of death

God break the wicked
long before their baby teeth
turn into fangs
make them retreat
turn into snails
curl into shells
and make their wombs
their tombs

then the oppressed
will know of God
that justice reigns
that virtue can bear fruit

59

throw me a rope
a straw to grasp
and lift me up and out of here
show me a light
to focus on
as I sit here trapped
and they come in stealth
amassing on the fragile
membrane of my cell

they drool like dogs
and bark their lies
incriminating me
denying You
they circle round
and round
noses to the ground
sniffing for hope
to destroy

redeem your loyal subjects
let the evil rabid dogs
all die like dogs

I raise my sights to heaven
knowing I'm within Your reach
You can find me in a crater
rescue me from any pit
if I just sing to You
You'll hear me
in Your tower
high away

60

Is this a test
did I not do what's right
that now I have to fight
bewildered as a drunk
unclear of why
we were attacked
and here we are again at war
without a better reason than
we
didn't
start
it

we fight and kill
on shaky ground
not knowing
where it all
will end

remember each of us
by name
remember Judah and Menashe
and Ephraim and Gilad
husbands fathers brothers
all beloved sons
and bring us home again
to wives
and
daughters

61

Hear O Lord
as David sings
a prayer to You

From the ends of the earth
I call to You
You take my hand
and lead me to
Your tower fortress
walls of rock
protecting me
no enemy
can reach me now
I want to stay
and hide here
for all time
but I have promises to keep
and miles to go
before I sleep

so give me strength
and give me time
so I can pay my dues
and try to meet
whatever comes
live out my days
with hope sustained
by closeness God
to You

62

Only God
>> knows my silent self
>> true to Him
>> true to me

Only God
>> is my source of hope
>> my anchor
>> when at sea

why would I lean
on a broken fence
when God is a fortress
and strength and reserve
come from Him

Only man
>> delusional
>> puts faith
>> in power
>> money
>> air

Only man
>> a puff of smoke
>> can live a shameless lie
>> and call it true

Only God
>> when judging man
>> determines
>> what he's due

63

My tired body rises
as the sun begins to parch another day
and O my God
I thirst for You

I search for You
through searing light
and dream of knowing You
in holiness
the vision of it
precious
as my life

You're not mirage
You are oasis
always there
I long to cling to You
and drink of You
and sing to You
replenished
never leave
and my reward in reaching You
will far surpass
the sweetest waters
I could find

I know that when I'm on my watch
beneath the stars
deep in the cooling desert nights
I'm not alone
I am at one with You
and those who seek my harm
are doomed to fall
and fail
again

64

it may look as though
I'm mumbling to myself
but I am calling You
so hear me
I am praying
for my life

my foes collaborate
conspire against me
search my files to look for dirt
bury landmines in my path
sharpen teeth and knives and razors
aim to kill

they don't know me
don't know You
don't admit
that in an instant
You can twist
their tongues and guns
their pens and arrows
change the course of war

when You do
all those who can
will see Your hand
in victory
rejoicing
grateful
ever grateful
that You haven't
looked away

65

Wait for us
though silent now
we'll come to you in Zion
singing praise

Keep the heavens open
drench our land
with mist and dew
and when the bounty comes
we'll know it comes
from You

Flocks of sheep
white as clouds
obscure our verdant hills
newborn babies pink and healthy
come with ease into our lives
our fields are ripe and sweet
with fat of land
and salt of earth

Sated
we'll remember You
keep our word
bring You joyous tithes
and tell ourselves we're giving back
but know
that what You really want of us
is just
to search for You
ascend to You

66

Voices from all corners of the earth
sing out in harmony
a symphony of awe and praise
to honor the Creator
of us all

Acknowledge that He rules
and seek Him
in the oceans He has moved
to let your feet
walk on dry land
see Him
in the molecules of water
in the channels
of your cells
find Him in the infinite
infinitesimal

Enter His domain
keep promises you made
when in distress
see Him in the soul of man
the eyes of sacrificial cows
the wings of butterflies
and tails of comets

Search for Him revere Him
even when you may be forced
to walk through fire
and if you somehow manage
to emerge alive intact
as I have done
know
that when you're blessed
it's by the grace
of God

67

keep the blessings coming
rain predictable and gentle
sun to warm our fields and pastures
  and our homes
light our paths
our lives
our seasons
notice everyman
and everyone
will know Your name
and thank You
as we toil and sow and reap
and we harvest
cornucopias
of plenty

68

When God's presence is revealed
and truth prevails
corrupt foundations crack
mountains fall
earthquakes melt golden calves
and righteous men see God's design
in this reordering of power
and rejoice

unrepentant self-made masters
run for cover in the flattened plains
the landscape's changed
to nourish those returning
day by day
each blessed day a gift
as wayward sons
come home
assume their rightful places
under God
bulls and bears and
students housewives
Jew and gentile
visionaries
workers rulers
princes kings
all congregate to sing
Your praise

69

Help me God before I drown
the water's rising to my neck
and I can't breathe or move
I'm trapped in quicksand
enemies metastasizing everywhere
exact their toll
and I have nothing left
to give
Is there a better time than now
for You to hear me cry

don't let those who need You
lose all hope because they think
that You have left me here
to die
You who know me
You who see me broken
You who have forgiven
my past sins

turn Your tide against my foes
Bleed them blot them
from Your book of life
Wipe them out
count their sins

make me an example of Your mercy
and I'll sing so all of earth and heaven hear
that fearing serving loving God
redeems

70

Quickly come to me
my God
and take my side

Shame on them
pity them
stigmatizing me
for curses that befell me
who knows why
they lack pity and compassion
cluck their tongues
as I am shunned
while they secretly are glad
to see me fall

Turn Your back on them
and stand by me
Hasten my recovery
Restore the life that I have known
so all of us who can
will see
that those in need
who seek Your help
will get Your help
and recognize Your greatness
and rejoice in You
and me

71

I still rely on You my God
to keep protecting me

When I was a child
I trusted You
I spoke to You
You answered me
and now I'm old
and weak and needy
don't abandon me

the sharks smell blood
and circle for the kill
emboldened
sensing I'm alone

but You who are eternal
steadfast faithful righteous great
are with me always
never leave me
I still look to You for aid
and though You've tested me
and test me yet again
I cannot help but reach for You
and sing to You and praise You
You are mine
and You are there for me
in old age
as in youth

72

Judge me
God of Israel
but please my Lord
be charitable with my son
my heir
my Solomon

Let his reign
be like the rain
that falls on orchards
sees them blossom
and bear fruit

Make him notice the oppressed
as well as those more blessed
and let his rulings be
compassionate and just

Have kings of other nations
look to him
to emulate and adulate
bathe his life in golden light
and bless his name eternally
his name my name
my prayer
Amen

73

Better men than I
know God is good
but I for one
have had my doubts

I've seen how evildoers
flourish and succeed
I've envied them
their lives of ease
longevity and health
and their cocksuredness
in self
I've heard them speak from lofty places
spewing dirt
negating You
and wondered why I always try
to keep my thoughts and speech and deeds
in check in purity for You
when I am plagued all day all night
with my troubled tortured life
and You don't care

I am anguished mortal clueless
but I somehow sense You
everywhere
and know that You and only You
retain the power
to flip a life
so those on tops of mountains
slip and
in an instant fall
from grace
but I have seen You
just as quickly
lift the righteous to the skies
on angel wings

I trust that You will guide me
hold my hand and not let go
stay by my side be close to me
and hear me pray and speak to You
and know I lean
on You alone

74

Don't forget that
You chose us
long ago in better times
when we were young
You carried us into Your home
made us aware of You
Remember us

With passing time
we've come to see our temple crash
as enemies build idols
in our holy inner spaces
and we know
that they're Your adversaries too

They're burning generations
of Your people
of Your teachings
and their axes
plunder forests of Your trees
we're banished from the homes we built
according to Your plans

We're slaves of man
of lawless beasts
but trust in You
to end this reign
to lift us gently up and out
to handle us with care
and lovingly dispatch us
to the skies You have created
and like homing pigeons
we'll return to You

75

We who try
to know You
reach You
pray You
don't destroy us
in our search
for the sublime

> *your world is fluid*
> *My design*
> *and I will choose*
> *the place and time*
> *to rearrange*
> *the order*
> *up or down*

Stop the haughty sinners
planting flags
in their secure positions
in the desert on the mountains
claiming turf

Show them
You make victors
You decide
who wears the crown
who drinks the wine
and who will sip
the bitter dregs

76

God is known in Judah
and Jerusalem
His name revered in Zion
where He's fought

and though we know
He's everywhere
it's easier to find Him
where He's sought

God of Israel
Source of power
confound plans
to harm Your land
pulverize the weapons
aimed at us
before
they explode
in our homes

Send amoral armies running
scared and scattered
flying backwards
impotent and blind
make their kings
and dictators
stand humbly
as defendants
in Your court
bring them down
to final justice
waiting deep within the earth

77

when I can't speak
but my voice just cries
and cries to You
in pain
when I can't sleep
and my arms are powerless
but reach for You
in vain
when I can't think
but my soul still yearns for You
with doubt

do You hear me
as I thought You did
do You collect my tears
or do they fall into a void
have You abandoned me

when this fear
evokes more terror
than my wounds
I remind my pounding heart
that You are there
I must have faith
I cannot understand
Your plan
but know You can
and will deliver
turn the tide
and send a Moses or an Aaron
lead me to a better place
a milk and honey
promised land

78

Pay attention
to the truth
reread white spaces
between lines
and teach your children
ancient Torah
that you know
or think you know
search for threads
that unify
the tapestry of history
so progeny may bow
to God's design

tell of forefathers
who strayed rejected God
or maybe just forgot
His presence in their lives
tell of wonders supernatural
plagues on Egypt
walls of water standing tall protecting us
and crashing on the heads of Pharaoh's men
tell of manna from the sky
water sprouting in the desert
from a rock

tell of those
who reached for God
when they felt
the need for God
but scorned Him
when they didn't need His help

God turned from those
who turned from Him
and chose instead
the seed of David
loyal shepherd poet king
to carry His inheritance
with pride and love and deed

my God
they've broken into
holy spaces
spreading filth

our corpses lie exposed
and birds are pecking
at our flesh

blood flows freely
in the streets
nations cross the line
to gawk and mock
denying that You care

we've sinned
we know
but how much longer
will You punish us
Unleash Your wrath
on people who deserve it
more

let us heal
have mercy God
avenge us sevenfold
we'll follow You
like sheep
we'll always follow You
and fear and love You
seek You
Praise the Lord

80

Shepherd of Israel
You know love
show Yourself
You who dwell
between the cherubs
You who knew
of Jacob's love
his Rachel love
the children of that love
by name
the Yosef and Menashe
Binyamin Ephraim love

You who can uproot with love
You who took us out of Egypt
brought us home
to nurture us
until we covered Israel
with our vines

keep the hungry boars away
the ones who chew our roots
and trample shoots
come back to Your vineyard
and tend to us
with love again
with clouds of dew
and sun again
and watch us thrive

81

Sing to God
in joy and strength
with harps and violins
with trumpets shofars
saxophones and drums
mark time keep track
of each new moon
and celebrate another chance
another month to live and grow
as Joseph did on foreign soil
knowing God was with him
pit to prison
houseboy
to viceroy

listen closely
try to hear
the song of God
and follow it
though you are deaf
and it is dark
and you are blinded
by your quest for things
that fade

God's music plays for you
and if you seek it
it is there
and if you heed it
it is sweet
and can fulfill
beyond desire

82

In God we trust
to stand for justice
in the courts of man and God
but here on earth
the weak are sentenced
those with power
get off

stretch to reach
the drowning
overwhelmed
unfairly judged
the homeless
and the helpless
and the poor
the all alone
who walk in darkness
with no hope
of ever seeing
any light

In you they trust
though you be mortal
judge or general or king
be godlike fair to all
and pray
that when you die
as they will
you'll find mercy
in the court

83

now is not the time
dear God
for silence or withdrawal
our ancient foes
the Philistines
and sons of Ishmael
from Edom Moav Amalek
Assyria and Tyre
have terrorized Your world
as they collaborate
with modern hate
to stream and form
a river
rushing toward us
in jihad
poison
to obliterate
us all

now's the time
right now's the time
for You to show
that power is Yours
that if You will
a glance a puff
can blow them all away
like straw in wind
like straw in fire
like dung
that returns
to the earth

let them learn
to see the shame
of murder suicide and war
and let them see
You reign
in peace

84

How sweet it could be
to call Your place
my home
to live where You dwell
to know that
my eggs are safe
in Your nest
to have the keys
to get inside
behind Your walls

how lucky are they
who find the strength
to follow You
and praise Your path
even as they walk
through tears
they drink
from springs
of faith

a single day of life
with hope
is better than thousands
without
better than decades
of doubt

please hear me God
and let me in
I know You're home

happy are they
who trust You

85

You wanted us home
in Your land
You brought us back
forgave us
gathered our sins
and Your wrath
and buried them both
that was then
and this is now
we've strayed
and need mercy
again

dwell within us
where we live
let truth and kindness merge
let peace and justice intermingle
and take root in fertile earth
and rain on us
from heaven
gently

step by step
we will return
to be with You
in the place
we know
is home

86

Listen to me
I am needy and bereft
I trust You
to show mercy

all day long
I cry to You
beseeching You
to hear my prayers
to lift my soul
to bring me joy
again
I call to You
when I'm in pain
because I know
You'll answer

nothing can compare
to You Your deeds Your miracles
unify my heart's desires
to seek Your truth
to shed false skin
and still remain protected
to honor You and thank You
for redeeming me
from godless foes
who sought my soul

Look at me
be gracious to me
give me strength to carry on
send me a sign
that You still care
that You're still there
beside me

87

when holiness
is the foundation
bedrock of a soul
or city
Godliness can enter
through the gates

fortunate are those
conceived within

each one precious
from the start
each one counted
and protected
each one nurtured
from the womb
with thoughts
of God

each one special
as is Zion
to the Jews

88

I cried by day
at night
I stood in prayer
my God Almighty
save me

I've had my fill
of trouble
I am ready
for the grave
I'm numb
I've lost all strength
to cope

You've shown me
only wrath
You have abandoned me
I have no friends
You've lowered me
into a pit
I am half dead

every day begins
with prayer
my arms reach up
to You
I hope for miracles
though You are far
and I am suffocating
all alone
and in the dark

89

I sing of the loving
kindness
on which Your world
is built
the heavenly order
that rules

I sing of the promises
You made
to build the house of David
and nourish his seed
for all time

I sing of the oneness
of Adonai
Creator of the sea
and stars and earth
and sky and all
of us

I sing of Your throne
eternal
erected in mercy and truth

lucky are nations
who follow You
Your prophets knew
that David's house
is one that would
and they entreated him
to base his earthly throne
on lovingkindness
too

in time, in turn
as David's children
stay with You
or stray from You
we still are
intertwined with You
remember to
be kind

90

Our ancestors and progeny
all dwell within
the endless time and space
You made
from nothing

mornings noons
and decades
stream by us
relentlessly

You have given
us the power to change
regret the past
and keep our eyes
on present deeds
as we return to You

buds at sunrise
blooms at noon
withered chaff by night
we race through time
and waste our fleeting years

You push us
to the brink
then say
Return
when will You
return to us
sate us with as much
delight
as You have
with sorrow

teach us how
to live our lives
to build immortal souls
with deeds of splendor
that will meet Your expectations of us
lofty though they be

91

He sits hidden somewhere
in shadows of ineffable secrecy
and I tell Him
You are my refuge
my protector
I trust You
keep me safe

He will cover you
He'll shield you
take you under His wing
take a bullet for you
or an arrow
or whatever whizzes past your head
endangering your life
your soul your loves
Lift your eyes
and see the wicked
fall in droves
while you remain intact
He will order angels
to guard you and yours
everywhere
to carry you
when the land gets rough
you'll crush the heads
of snakes and lions
evil will never
befall your house

He knows my name
He knows I'm His
He answers me

> *I am your refuge*
> *your protector*
> *I will be with you*
> *through hard times*
> *you will live*
> *a long good life*

92

it's good to pause
to praise the Lord
and notice all you have
with Sabbath eyes

to take the sofa
off your back
and sit

to start the morning
sing the dawn
and see the work of God

to slow
the pace
of time

to wonder at the colors
and the fragrance of the earth
to look up and
to see cerulean skies

to wait until the stars bring back
inevitable night
and you resume your search
to gather shards
of shattered light

those who never stop
to lift their eyes
can't contemplate
the work
of God

the righteous are renewed by God
like palm trees near a stream
like cedars old and strong
and evergreen

93

God rules
behind the scenes
cloaked in grandeur
and power
and the majesty
of nature

oceans and motion
follow His laws
galaxies
obey
strings of cosmos
heed His word

ever loyal
all bear witness
to eternal
holy
truths

94

God of vengeance God of right
reveal Yourself
and show all those
abusing might
that You give back
what they deserve

nazis cossacks haman satan
terrors of the night
how much longer
will they have
the upper hand
confident
as they devour innocents
at will
randomly destructive
they declare that You don't care

do they not know
that He who made the ear
can hear
that He who formed the eye
can see
that You have access
to their inner thoughts
and know them
to the core

that You're the holy spark of hope
that glows within our breast
that You're the rock we cling to
when endangered and oppressed
that we know You
reverse the course of evil
when You wish

send it somersaulting backward
into infinite oblivion
the nothingness
it's due

95

Let's call to God
when we're joyful
when times are good
and we're singing

Let's sing to God
express our thanks
acknowledge that
we are aware
that He created
oceans mountains
joy and song
and the mystery
of us

Let's try to accept
His dominance
our need to follow Him
and never again
incur His wrath
as we wander for years
on a desert path
of anger and angst
in a futile search
for a golden calf
that can never
lead us
home

96

Sing to God
a different song
a new and ancient
joyous song
Sing like the earth
sing like the whales
so all who try to listen
hear
One God created all

Broadcast news
that God is here
exhort the world
to leave their fragile idols
demigods and lords
One God created all

there's majesty within His court
His gardens all bear gifts
wheat and willow bow to Him
as mountains reaffirm
His righteous reign

Sing out ring bells
of thanks and joy
to God alone
omnipotent
all knowing God
eternal God
the God
who rules
us all

God is King
so earth be glad

myriad islands
in turquoise and green
sparkle in sunlight
and moonlight

God is King
surrounded by clouds
shrouded
in layers
of gray

God is King
His crystal throne
is clear and etched
in precious stone
each facet
glowing truth

iceberg myths
and mountains melt
as idols crash
and burn in the fire
of His gaze

the righteous
sowing seeds of light
dispel the fog

Happy are they
who do no harm
believers
in God
the promise of life
the mercy of
rainbows

98

Another song
a new one now
of miracles
of outstretched arms
that reach for us
and lift us up
with holy strength
unveiled
so doubters clearly see
the hand of God

Blast the shofars
trumpets horns
come mountains
blow your tops
and roar
as rapid rivers
crash and clap
together sing
with all of life
before the King
who comes to us
a righteous judge
His path to us
and ours to Him
forever
unobstructed

99

God is King
He chose us
and we chose Him
and God only knows
which came first

Someday everyone
will choose
and tremble
in awareness of
accountability
to Him

we won't be
the only ones
who see the
inconceivable
cherubic mighty purity
inherent
in His rule

we've been taught
to seek Him
when on mountains
or in valleys
and to find Him
where we are

prophets priests of Israel
Moses Aaron Samuel
called to God
with human angst
and listened
through a fog
to hear His answers
guide their lives

one day everyone
will meet the Maker
hear His voice
exalt His greatness
bow to Him
alone

100

Don't just think it

Speak your mind
and give God thanks
out loud

Sing His praises
serve Him
work with joy

Know that He
created us
that we belong to Him

Come with me
to bless His name
He has been good to us

Let us trust
that He'll continue
to show kindness
to our children
generations of them
always
in good faith

101

this is a song
from me to You
reminding me
that if I want
to be near You
I must act wisely
and be kind

When will You
come to me

I will stay pure
in my thoughts
and heart
in my home
and when
I'm out

I won't eye evil
won't seek trash
and neither
will ever
cling to me

I'll purge my life
of influence
from cheats and sneaks
and liars
steeped in pride

I'll keep my vision
high
surround myself
with upright men
to talk to me
and walk with me
on paths
that lead
to You

102

Don't make (me) believe
that You don't see me
in my time of need

See me hear me
answer me
my time is running out
the sand is racing through the hourglass
I'm withering
I live on ashes air and tears
You have abandoned me

bird on a wire
I stand alone
with a heavy wing
and a broken voice
that cannot sing

I've fallen from my aerie
lie in shadows on the ground
but You are King
of land and sky
Your time is not
my time
Your thoughts are not
my thoughts
and You will see me
from Your holy perch
one day
when Your compassion
reigns

the day has come
for You to rise
expose Your lovingkindness
to the steadfast

Show me mercy
as I need You
now

103

Soul of mine
bless my God
and all He does
remember that you're His
that you'll return to Him

bless Him
for healing
for giving
for distancing us
from our misdeeds
and gifting us
second chances
lives we haven't earned
or even dreamed of

bless Him
for serendipity
for all that we savor
for sightings of eagles
soaring high

bless Him
for teaching us
not to despair
we're human
we err
but we can repair our souls
and He divine
with eternal patience
will wait for us

104

soul of mine
bless my God
Creator boundless
veiled in light
draped with cosmic power

You sail clouds across the sky
make messengers of wind and fire
place ground beneath our feet
surround the earth with atmosphere
suspend it in thin air

You determine boundaries
of every niche unique
goats on a mountaintop
rabbits in a hole
lions on the prowl for prey
streams quench thirst
of cedars and birds
as the moon marks time
and the sun knows when
to set

newborn babies breathe new souls
man makes bread out of the soil
and savors its wine and oil

O the joy when You provide
the terror when You don't

I'll sing to You while there's breath in me
and bless You as I live
aware of You away from sin
Amen
Halleluya

105

Thank God in public
write Him songs
and praise His miracles
seek Him find Him
everywhere
so those in search of meaning
notice patterns
that appear

look at nations over time
some will ascend
survive the climb
some won't
look at sons of Israel
humble roots transplanted
onto foreign soil
in hostile lands
again again
and though like Joseph
they can thrive
diaspora is never home
and transplants
often wither

plagues of war and darkness
come with blood and lice
and freezing rain
and death of sons
yet slaves emerged
miraculously free
sheltered by a cloud each day
guided by fire at night
then carried home
on eagle wings
to flower
in the eastern sun

Thank God
Praise one and only God
who gifted land and law to us
eternal homes of Israel

106

Halleluya
worlds exist by the mercy of
a God we can't conceive of
and those who can suspend the need
to try to understand Him
may live with faith
and sing His praise
happy are they who do

Remember me God
when You dole out joy
so I can be among the blessed
who get to see
that promises You've made
are kept

forget my father's sins and mine
forget the wrongs we've done
negating You as You nourished us
forget that You've seen us
rebellious entitled
cavorting with idols
and steeped in innocent blood
Remember when Moses
our leader defender beseeched You
have mercy forgive
   Adonai Adonai El rachum vechanun
   erech apayim rav chesed emet
Remember You listened
forgave
How far we've strayed
to live in worlds
from which You have
withdrawn

we're ready to
return to You
so gather our remnants
and bring us home
and we'll know You again
and bless You Amen
forever
Halleluya

107

you who have passed through narrow straits
and emerged so far intact
thank God who is good and merciful
thank God who brings you back

you who have wandered in deserts
cloaked in hunger and thirst
crying to God from the depths of despair
then finding a way back home
thank God who is real
works miracles
remember to give back
with your hands and your hope
and your story to tell

you who have known
the razor of loss
and have been left
bereft
abandoned in hospitals nursing homes jails
marking the days toward death
thank God who is good and merciful
thank God who brings you back

you who have lived to
breathe free air
see iron curtains fall
thank God who is One all powerful
thank God who breaks down walls

you who've survived tornadoes
earthquakes tsunamis and war
you who have seen the hand of God
reverse the acid tide
to sweeten springs
and moisten sands
allowing fruit to grow

praise God who ennobles the humbled
bless God who is seen by the wise

108

In glory days
and when in need
my heart is loyal
up at dawn
to sing to You
with harp and strings
a reveille of praise

Arise O nations
congresses and parliaments
to sounds of truth
and hear the music
in the sky
and wake up strong and sure
you are a guest
in God's domain

reach for me God
and hear my psalms
and guide me always
shape my will
to bend to Yours
and keep me able
to sustain
my life my land my people

teach me how
to give and take
while knowing
all is Yours

109

my God   my own exalted God
Do not be silent now
evil spits its filthy lies
and bloody libel
everywhere
it fills the air with poison smoke
that saturates the atmosphere
and chokes the breath of innocents
rewarding trust
with murder

Here on earth now
evil reigns
merciless amoral wicked
crouching at membranes and portals and doors
ready to pounce
and blot out life
and suffocate all prayer
sometimes it wears a human mask
sometimes it hovers in ether or gas

Obliterate eradicate
its name its progeny
Send angels of death
to slaughter its mother
purge its every seed
Be merciless
so there will be no trace of it
no memory no scent
Send Satan himself
to finish the job

and let the humble and oppressed
arise though wounded
stumbling hungry
ravaged hollow dazed
Help them recover so all will see
their bones come alive
the work of Your hands
a phoenix renewed

so help me God exalted God
we will rejoice again

110

God said to you
> *sit on my right*
> *stay close*
> *and wait*

He told you
He would fight for you
place your foes
on their knees
at your feet

that though young
you would rule
in their midst
unafraid

that your people would rally
emerge with the dawn
glistening with dew
bearing gifts for you

He gave you His word
He would never regret
crowning you His
eternally

He chooses who
will reign on earth
which heads will roll
whose tongue will taste
the dust of death
which king will drink
sweet water

111

Halleluya
I will thank God
in my heart of hearts
as I sit among scholars in intimate rooms
as I speak aloud before crowds

His deeds are great
His energy unspeakable
and formidable
giving healing
infinite and just
kind and loving
merciful to us

His name is holy
He is One
we cannot comprehend
but we can pray and question
and have faith
and those who fear Him
only Him
rejoice to see
their terrors lose power
their beasts in shreds

until the end of time and worlds
trials will come from God
to burnish life revealing
what is shining what is real
to help us shed the empty shells
that crumble to dust
when touched

knowledge stems from
the fear of God
and human vulnerability
wise men know
that the unknown x
we yearn to solve
is zero
we are really nothing
next to the infinite
God

112

Happy is he
who's afraid of God
and desperately wants
to please Him
by living a life
based on good deeds
and generosity

Seeds of kindness
sown by him
fall everywhere
on fertile soil
and thrive eternally
he has no need
to fear ill winds
bad news the dark
his path is clear
his heart is light
he's loved
and revered
by the family
of man

those who choose
a selfish life
grasping hoarding
helping none
gnash their teeth
at the end of the day
full of just
regrets

113

Halleluya
think of God
with gratitude
notice those
who serve Him in good faith
emulate the fortunate
who see Him
feel His presence
in the hours
and the minutes
of their lives

greater than
an earthly reign
His kingdom spans
the heavens

who but He
could ever be
in charge of life
and notice me
down here

redeeming me
from poverty
and garbage and filth
to sit among princes
rulers of men
replacing my barrenness
aimlessness hell
with fertile
productive
joy

114

When Israel escaped from Egypt
sons of Jacob fleeing flying
cruelty pursuing
in dead heat
they made it home
to Israel
a holy land
as sovereign people
bowing to God's rule

the raging sea
became a path
to shelter them
and guide them out

the rivers ran upstream
and rocky mountains
leapt like rams
to heed the will
of God

what is real what's miracle
did nature change its course
did mountains leap
did rivers run amok

the Lord of all
creates His laws
and has the power
to bend His laws

to melt a rockhard
cancer mass
converting it
to water

115

When You show the watching world
that You are true and kind to us
it's Your name that is glorified
not ours

Why should nations
look at Jews
and wonder if our God
is powerless
or worse
that He has chosen us
to suffer

You are One
the only God
omnipotent and omnipresent
always in our lives

their gods are manmade mindless idols
speechless dumb with silver tongues
golden eyes that lack all vision
ears immune to human cries
hearts of ice and legs of stone
incapable of change
those who put their faith in matter
share its fragile fate

we the house of Aharon
beseech You
love us back
bless us all
with health with life
be good to us
and to our children
and our aged
we are Yours
and want to please You
with our deeds

we can accomplish nothing
from the grave

116

I love that God
will hear my voice
and know my racing heart
when I find myself
surrounded by death
and maws of waiting graves

God has mercy
on the simple
and the simply helpless
Hell pursued me
roped me in
its tentacles a noose around my neck
and here I walk
untethered free alive

I knew throughout
You had the power
to mercifully
rescue me

how should I
give back to You
knowing You can
partner with man
precious to You
in life and death

shall I raise a glass and toast You
shall I sacrifice a lamb
shall I orchestrate a gala
in Jerusalem
or shall I try to emulate
Your lovingkindness here
and work with You and serve You
with my deeds

117

no matter what
the state of your faith
praise the Maker
of your life

be grateful
be awed
by the truth
of God

118

Give thanks to God
the source of good
His mercy sustains all worlds
Come holy man and common man
God-fearing man and frightened man
Admit within and say aloud
His mercy envelops worlds

I pray confined
to a small dark place
where all I see
is a wall in my face
He answers me from
expanses of light
enabling me to see
He's on my right He's by my side
what have I to fear from man
I trust in God and forge ahead
with reason to be brave
I don't have to wait for noble souls
to notice that I am in need
Armies chase me closing in like swarms of bees
and I'm the one who stings with fire
and comes out singing Halleluya
Listen to the joy the music
coming from a place of faith

Open gates of righteousness
Let me in to walk your paths
These are the gates I want to enter
This is the road I want to take
This is the way I want to thank You
for the gift of life
Here is a block I stumbled on
now stabilizing me
Miraculous reversals
came to be

This is the day God made for us
to celebrate and play
Welcome enter eat with us
and thank the Host who nurtures us
His mercy sustains all worlds

119

First comes honesty with self
pure devotion to the truth
then searching for a way to live
and yearning learning how to live
and following Your way to live
then joy

Your words delight my soul
I love to think of You
and speak of You
Unveil my eyes and let me see
Your deeds Your miracles
Your Torah
is my song my hope
my consolation and my crown

How can a man stay whole stay pure
in thought and speech and deed
Teach me how to live my God
Protect me from all fallacy
I yearn for peace my soul is dry
I need You water me
I am a stranger here on earth
I trust You stay with me

I have been robbed pursued and slandered
tested and maligned
and all my trials just made me stretch
to reach for You
renewed determined
steadfast in my love
You know me You created me
Do not abandon me
I follow the eternal code
You gave to us for life
I rise at midnight and compose
these psalms for You
I love Your law
and want to live out all my days
immersed in truth
and love of You and feel Your presence
close to me as I live
close to You

120

when I was down
I cried to You
You answered me
I need You now
again

this time to keep me
whole despite
the firestorm
consuming me

tongues of arson
taste my soul
set fire to
undying coals
that burn and burn
within

if only I
had stayed away
alone
a nomad
far from here

I've lived too long
immersed in stealth

I yearn for peace
but when I speak
they answer me
with war

121

I lift my eyes
to mountains skies
and wonder where
relief resides
I know that God
made mountains skies
and my belief in Him
abides

my God
the Guard of Israel
will never sleep
won't let me fall
He watches me
protects me from
the midnight moon
the noonday sun

He'll rescue you
from random fate
restore your body
and your soul
He is with you
through birth and death
as you come in
and when you go

122

With joy I joined
a pilgrimage
to walk up to
Jerusalem
home of
the house
of God

Our feet stood at
the very gates
that welcomed
tribes of Israel
millennia ago

Jerusalem
above below
united whole
rebuilt with stones
that saw the thrones
of David's house
and witnessed justice
in the courts
of Solomon the wise

Lovers of Jerusalem
tranquility serenity
seek peace
within her palace walls
find armies of friends
at her gates

I speak for the sake
of brothers and foes
I speak for the sake of man
striving to live
at home with God
for the good of His house
for the good of us all

123

it's You I seek
when I gaze above
with pleading
slavegirl eyes

waiting for grace
trembling with fear
aware of where
power lies

mercy my God
have mercy on us

we've been forcefed
scorn and contempt
our spirit is broken
we're gagging
on bile
we're stuffed
and we're starved
and we're spent

peacocks in uniforms
cruel with pride
peck at what's left
of our souls

124

if You had not
been with us then
when we were prey

if You had not
been there to see
our enemies
prepare to eat us
swallow us
alive

then we would now
be air or water
overcome
dead souls
adrift

thank God
we're not

we slashed their nets
escaped their traps
and flew like birds
to live
and soar

thank God
who made
the earth and skies
bless God
who set us
free

125

those who trust in God
endure
like Zion
like Jerusalem
ringed by hills
forever there
to guard the
magnet core

those who trust in God
don't try
to grasp
the spears of fate
don't live at the edge
of a carousel
don't reach for
unholy grails

the center holds
it won't fly off
we're grounded
by our faith
Be good to the good
who trust You God
let evil go astray

may Israel
find peace endure
believe in You
and be secure

126

things were so bad
and then so good
we thought it all
a dream

we couldn't help
but smile throughout
when talked about
when word got out
when those who heard our story
couldn't help but see
the miracles
and say that God was good to us
and silently hope
He'd be good
to them too

all of us came back
by God
the stragglers
ingathered
mainstream

we carried
our burden
continued to sow
continued to hope
continued to know
that those who plant in tears
but plant
retain a chance
to harvest joy
and bring it home
and taste it

127

in vain
the grandest buildings are built
if there's no life
within

in vain
a fortune is guarded secure
if solely bequeathed
to a vault

in vain
a man may rise at dawn
to bake and bake
amassing bread
that surely will
decay

but sons and daughters
blessed by God
are gifts from God
and can propel
a legacy
of life
into the future

happy are they
who can bravely say
they toiled to nurture life
and aimed their arrows
far ahead
with steady hands
and hope

128

Happy are men
who think and act
with God in mind
they know when they're blessed

their wives are their homes
sweet grapes and wine
vineyards and groves
bearing fruit

daughters and sons
surround their table
saplings in fertile soil
branches that flower
arms that reach up
to gentle and generous skies

what life is richer
more pleasant than this

stay close to God
be blessed live well
and long enough to see
Jerusalem in peace
your children's children
at your feet

129

I've endured so much
from childhood on
I've been tested
again and again

I've been hit from all sides
furrowed and ploughed
but I am still here
now

I believe God is just
sees everything
that He knows
when and whom
to reward

no grass should thrive
in an evil field
no harvest should ever be
reaped
by those who oppress
may they wither
retreat
and never be
never be
blessed

130

I call to You
from the depths of me
I beg You
turn to me

Notice me
Hear me out
Judge me
leniently

I'm counting on
Your mercy
I am waiting
to be tried
No man can stand
before You
confident
of innocence

I wait like a tired
guard in the night
for relief to come with dawn
in darkness I wait
for a glimpse
of a ray
of Your
abundant light

131

I do not have
a haughty heart
my eyes do not
look down
I do not walk
in shoes too big
for me

when I can't have
what I desire
I can be weaned
of that desire
as a babe is weaned
from milk

but I cannot
be weaned
of dreams
I dream as Israel dreams
to be redeemed
from longing
to be close
to God again
intimate recipients
of milk and honey now

132

Remember what I promised
when I suffered
through hard times
that I could never
close my eyes in peace
until I found
a place for You
a sacred holy space
where I could go
to find You
easily

Come with me friends
prepare yourselves
to be aware of truth
to bare your souls
to think to pray to feel
to talk to God
Who knows and hears
your every silent thought
to sense His omnipresence
always real

Remember what You promised
when You chose us chose our seed
to seek You and to learn
a way to live
You promised
if we followed You
You never would withdraw
You'd clothe our priests
in righteousness
You'd feed our needy bread
You'd crown our kings
until the end of days

133

O how good
how sweet to see
a dwelling place
of peace
brothers neighbors
living without strife

like oil that anoints
it sanctifies
like salve like balm
it soothes

like morning dew
like fragrance rising
to perfume the air
like clouds that float
and bless the hills
of Zion

134

those who pray alone
unseen
in the foxholes of the night
mouthing silent holy words
of prayer
beseech and praise
the only God
who hears

bless God who made
the earth and sky
bless all who reach for Him
with open arms

135

Praise God praise the idea of God
praise the name of God

willing servants of the Lord
standing up for Him
praise Him as they do His work
pleasantly they sing
that God is good to them
and finds them precious

I for one
know God
is greater than
all forces and all power
everything He wants to do
He can
sea and sky and earth and fire
thunder dew and zephyr
heed His word

it is God in charge of life
and God in charge of death
of firstborn sons of cattle and of kings

generations come and go
and God presides
eternally the judge
who can be bribed
with our repentance

gold and silver idols
blind to need and deaf to cries
are works of man
it's God who takes
and God who gives us
land and law and life

know Him bless Him
priests and servants
sing out Halleluya
to the One aware
of all the prayers
that saturate the air

136

Come give thanks
for God is good
and endlessly
He gives

Thank God the inconceivable
Creator of the skies
the One who set
the solid earth apart

Thank God the One
who rolled out suns
and planets moons and stars
and space and time
in webs of boundless night

Thank God who cares
remembered us
when we had reached the end
delivered us
with gentle arms
and hope

Thank God the One
who cut our chains
and plucked us up and out
of slavery and misery
and strongarmed the oppressors
who pursued us to the seas

Thank God who never
left our side
in desert wanderings
thank God
who keeps our enemies at bay

Thank God the One
providing bread
that keeps our flesh alive

Thank God
whose lovingkindness
has no end

137

homeless
we sit by the river and weep
remembering Zion
abandoning song
brazen
we balk as tormentors emerge
demanding performance and mirth
as we mourn

I'd rather be struck
dumb by a stroke
feel my right arm go limp
than lose my fragrant memories
of sweet Jerusalem
I long to rise to her in joy

my God
You hear them
taunting chanting
raze her raze her raze
O to be the lucky man
who finds a way
to dash their plans
on unforgiving rock
so we can all return
and sing to You
again

138

I've come to search my soul and pray
and all that I feel
in my heart and my gut
is overwhelming gratitude

I need to bow
I need to kneel before You
prostrate myself on the ground
and weep
in thanks

I cried to You
You heard me
and You showered me with miracles
that drenched my world
and left me breathless
but alive
with newfound strength

earthly kings should sing to You
and listen for Your voice
how great to be able to hear the truth
and be deaf to the noise
of lies

I know if I seek You
You'll hear me You're there
even when I am lost
I know there is nowhere
no battle no front
no place
where You
are not

139

God read my soul
and You will know
my core as You always have
and I never will begin to know
the hows of all Your record keeping
but I am sure
as I am of my breath
that I have no thoughts
unknown to You
and that I can never
hide from You
How terrifying
comforting
and true

You can bring me back
from the edge of space
from the bottom of hell
and I won't know how
and I won't know why
but I have no doubt
that You can

Cover my night
with blankets of light
Enable me to see
Examine my soul
before You
exposed
Determine it worthy
to walk with You
to navigate my world

140

Shield me from
the evil souls
who lie in wait
to fight
like snakes
with pointed arrow
venom tongues
and eyes wide open
searching dirt
for naked heels to strike

and I am barefoot
sidestepping the coils

my gaze is down
my thoughts aloft
You are my only strength

Lure them into
pits of fire
from which they can't escape

so those whose eyes
look up to You
can walk the earth
and sing Your praise

141

Accept the prayers
from my mouth
like incense
like a sacrifice
smoke ascending
through a veil of clouds

Rain protection
on my soul
anoint my head
with holy oils
the guidance and the words
of righteous men

Let evil counsel
crash on rocks
distant from my path
an avalanche afar
that does no harm

I know, in time, my bones will lie
abandoned white as chalk
in time all flesh returns
to earth

yet I still need
to move to breathe
and I still need to hope
and I still look to You
for life

142

I know You hear
my voice my thoughts
the howling pain
within
when black moods come

I hide
but I have not a friend
who cares
to seek

I weep
You hear my tears
and as I live
and as I change
You are my constant
You remain

listen for the spark
within me
free it lift me
rescue me
whirl me
out of shrouds
that now envelop me
enable me
to wear a crown
of righteousness
that fits

143

Hear me
Listen
Answer me
with mercy
as no human
can be guiltless
in Your court

an enemy attacked me
ground me down
to almost dead

my heart in shock
remembered days
when my thoughts
were of You
and my speech
was of miracles
wrought by Your hands
and my hands
reached for You
and my soul wanted drink
from the water of You
as a parched earth
thirsts

my breath is shallow
don't turn from me now
as my steps close in
to the grave
let morning come
with compassion from You
send currents of air
on which I'll soar
to safely land
on paths swept clean
of torturers and murderers

don't judge me now
just help me find a compass
that will lead me back
to You

144

Blessed is God
my rock my core
my guide in peace
my shield in war
my rescuer
my King

What am I
what's man to You
a shadow fleeting
passing through
beseeching You
beseeching You

Reach from heaven
rip the sky
move mountains oceans
terrify
the hostile armies
liars thieves
poised to strike and kill

Make them turn retreat and fall
I'll lift my lyre
and sing so all
can hear of peace
that will endure

O to live in lands of bounty
ruled by men of tolerance
youth surviving growing planting
harvesting their dreams
blessed are those
who live this way
and know that
God is King

145

I'll extol You endlessly
my God my Lord my King
and bless Your name
each day each year
while there is breath
in me

Your sovereignty
extends to worlds
and generations
we can't know
but I have seen
Your miracles
and I will speak
and teach of You
ineffable in majesty
unreachable yet close enough
to intimately love

I have seen
Your kindness boundless
tolerance of man

we stoop and lean
we fall and cry
we look to You for food
and You
with open palms
provide
a niche for every soul

in time when air
is breathed in peace
when evil is expunged
all life will sing
and echo words of praise
now on my lips

146

as I inspire
as I expire
I sing my songs
to God

don't look for mortal
benefactors
destined as we all are
for the grave

fortunate are those
who seek support
from their Creator
from the One
who owns the earth
and air and water

the One
who metes out justice
feeds the starved
and frees the bonded
lifts the broken
loves the righteous
reaches out
to widows orphans
guides the weak
away from danger
and lets evil
self-destruct

generations
come and go
but God is King
eternally
sing Halleluya
praise His endless reign

147

it feels good to sing to God
our praise becomes Him

He who built Jerusalem
on high and here on earth
with golden light
and fragrant air
restorative to souls

He who knows the stars by name
each lost forgotten lonely star
each sun
He who lifts the humble
turns His back when wicked fall
Acknowledge Him
and answer
when He calls

He who turns the clouds
to fountains
making mountains
emerald green
sails the snowflakes
on the wind
to drape the hills in white

He who feeds the beast and raven
owns the bounty that we hunt
He who sends the arrows
and the hail

He who doesn't need our strength
but wants our love and fear
What man can stand alone
without His shield

Sing Halleluya sing to God
Who gave us life
and laws of truth
How fortunate are we

148

Halleluya
from above
seraphim sing
where angels fly
in choruses of light

Halleluya over skies
where dazzling milky
constellations
flow through heaven's night

Halleluya
in their presence
praise the One
who made them

Halleluya
from below
where hellfires burn
and ice winds blow
at His command

Halleluya
from the deep
where oceans house
unknowns

Halleluya
from the hills
where trees bear fruit
for bird and beast

earthly lords and presidents
judges and celebrities
sages idols prodigies
commoners and kings
sing Halleluya in your sleep
and when you are awake
thank God for land you walk on
thank God for air you breathe
thank God whose banner
always waves
for human righteous deeds

149

Halleluya

sing to God
a different song
not just help me God
when you are down

multitudes of righteous souls
look to Him
as life unfolds
rejoicing in ongoing gifts
of time

God gave us
bodies with our souls
hearts and guts
and flesh and bone
He must want us to sing
and love and dance and play
and live in ways
that honor Him
and bring us joy

when all pleasure
stems from power
grabbed or self-ordained
people fall
or even jump
from towers they have made

eternal laws
foresee the falls
and see the falls sustained
by justice
splendor of the wise
who reign with words
of God

150

Praise God's holiness
unknowable
Praise His deeds
magnificent
try to praise
what language
can't describe

Praise like a shofar
piercing the sky
Praise Him
with violins
Praise with your heart
Pound like a drum
Praise Him
with dancing limbs
Praise Him
with winds and bells and chimes
Praise Him
with prayers and dreams

Praise Him
with breath
that repeats like a song
like a psalm
each time
you breathe

In the end
what's left of me
may only be
a psalm

Index of First Lines

THE BOOK OF PSALMS

With introductory comments by
Rabbi Adin Even-Israel Steinsaltz

This English translation of the *Book of Psalms* is based on the *New American Standard Bible* version, with revisions (by G.A. Bernstein) based on comparisons to the *New King James Version* and to *Tehillim* in Hebrew. Rabbi Steinsaltz's introductory comments are presented in italics before each psalm.

This is a poem for contemplation of the happiness that ensues when a person chooses to walk in God's ways. A person who lives righteously has hope and endures; he is unlike the wicked, whose existence is fleeting and whose end is dissolution and death.

1 Blessed is the man who has not walked in the counsel of the wicked, has not stood on the ground of sinners, and has not sat in the company of scorners. 2 But whose delight is the law of the Lord, and whose mind is on it day and night. 3 He shall be like a tree planted by rivers of water, which brings forth its fruit in season, and whose leaf shall not wither; whatever he does shall prosper. 4 The wicked are not so, but are like chaff that wind blows away. 5 Therefore the wicked shall not stand up in judgment, and evildoers shall have no place among the upright. 6 For the Lord knows the way of the righteous, but the way of the wicked shall perish.

This is a victory poem for a regal savior. Despite war on all fronts, and rebellion against him, all of the wishes of the king's heart, including the one for absolute victory over all of his enemies, are fulfilled by God.

2 Why do nations rage, and people think only of vanities? 2 The kings of the earth have taken their place, and rulers are aligned in their purpose against the Lord and against His anointed, saying 3 Let their chains be broken, and their bindings be taken off of us. 4 He whose seat is in heaven will laugh; my Master shall make sport of them. 5 Then His angry words shall reach their ears, and they shall be troubled by His wrath. 6 "But I have anointed my king on Zion, my holy mountain." 7 I shall make the Lord's decision clear; He has given me life, called me His creation; 8 "Make your request of Me, and I shall make nations your heritage; the ends of earth shall be in your hands. 9 They shall be ruled by you with an iron rod, broken like a potter's vessel." 10 So now, kings, be wise; take instruction, judges of the earth. 11 Serve the Lord with fear, tremble with joy. 12 Prostrate yourselves lest He be angry and you be lost, even if His anger burns only slightly. Happy are all who rely on Him.

Although the psalmist is pursued, surrounded by enemies on all sides, and perceived by all as devoid of hope, he has faith that God will rescue him from all of his enemies, and bring him victory and peace.

3 A psalm of David when he fled from Absalom his son. 2 Lord, how numerous are my tormentors; great numbers of them rise up against me. 3 Many tell my soul there is no salvation in God, Selah. 4 But Your strength, O Lord, surrounds me; You are my glory; You lift my head. 5 I cried to the

Lord with my voice and He heard me from His holy mount, Selah. 6 I lay down and slept, and awoke because the Lord sustains me. 7 I shall have no fear, though ten thousand people surround me and are against me. 8 Arise O Lord; keep me safe, O my God; for You have given all who hate me blows on the cheekbone; You have broken the teeth of the wicked. 9 Salvation belongs to the Lord; Your blessing is on Your people, Selah.

In this poem of supplication, the psalmist, unjustly attacked by adversaries who defile his name and conspire to destroy him, prays to God, Who exposes the schemes of evil men, and is the Savior of the pursued.

4 For the chief musician; on stringed instruments, a psalm of David. 2 Answer me when I call, O God of my righteousness. You have relieved me in my distress; be gracious to me and hear my prayer. 3 O sons of men, how long will you shame my honor, love vanity, seek deception? Selah. 4 Know that the Lord has set apart the devoted for Himself; the Lord hears when I call to Him. 5 Tremble and do not sin; meditate in your heart, upon your bed, and be still, Selah. 6 Offer sacrifices of righteousness, and trust in the Lord. 7 Many are saying, who will show us any good? Lift up the light of Your countenance upon us, O Lord! 8 You have put gladness in my heart, more than when grain and new wine abound. 9 In peace I will both lie down and sleep, for You alone, O Lord, allow me to dwell in safety.

This prayer is directed against the wicked, whom the psalmist says are not worthy of God's mercy. He prays that his own righteousness be evident, and that deliverance come to him and to all those worthy of it.

5 For the chief musician; for flute accompaniment, a psalm of David. 2 Give ear to my words, O Lord; consider my meditation. 3 Listen to the voice of my cry, my King and my God, for to You I pray. 4 In the morning, O Lord, You will hear my voice; in the morning I shall direct my prayer to You and I will look up. 5 For You are not a god who takes pleasure in wickedness; no evil dwells with You. 6 The foolish shall not stand before Your eyes; You hate all evildoers. 7 You destroy those who speak falsehood; the Lord abhors a man of bloodshed and deceit. 8 But as for me, through Your abundant lovingkindness, I shall enter Your house; at Your holy temple I will bow in reverence for You. 9 Lead me, O Lord, in Your righteousness, because of my foes; make Your way straight before me. 10 There is nothing reliable in what they say; their inner thought is deceit, their throat is an open grave, they flatter with their tongue. 11 Condemn them, O God; let them fall by their own devices. Cast them out into their legion transgressions, for they have rebelled against You. 12 But let all those who put their trust in You rejoice; let them sing for joy forever, and You will shelter them. Those who love Your name will exult in You. 13 For it is You who blesses the righteous man, O Lord. You surround him with favor, as with a shield.

This is the supplication of someone who is ill, pursued, suffering, and in tears, entreating God to show mercy and hear his prayers.

6 For the chief musician on stringed instruments, with an eight-stringed harp, a psalm of David. 2 O Lord, rebuke me not in Your anger, nor chasten me in the heat of Your displeasure. 3 Have mercy on me, O Lord, for I am weak; heal me, O Lord, for my bones are frightened. 4 My soul is also frightened. And You, O Lord, how long? 5 Return, O Lord. Free my soul, save me for mercy's sake. 6 For in death, there is no memory of You; in the grave, who can give You thanks? 7 I am depleted by my groaning; every night I cause my bed to swim, I drench my couch with my tears. 8 My eye wastes away because of grief, it ages because of all of my enemies. 9 Depart from me, all you workers of iniquity, for the Lord has heard the voice of my weeping. 10 The Lord has heard my supplication and the Lord will receive my prayer. 11 Let all my enemies be ashamed and terrified; they will retreat, suddenly put to shame.

In this prayer the psalmist, falsely accused and falsely pursued, prays to God to see his innocence and to take vengeance on his enemies.

7 A meditation of David; a song which he sang to God concerning the words of Cush the Benjamite. 2 O Lord, I put my faith in You; deliver me from all of my pursuers and rescue me 3 Lest he tear my soul like a lion, rending it in pieces, while there is no one to be my savior. 4 O Lord, my God, if I have done this, if my hands have done any wrong 5 If I have repaid my friends with evil, or plundered my enemy without cause 6 Let the enemy persecute my soul and take it. Let my life be crushed to the earth, and my honor to the dust, Selah. 7 Arise, O Lord, in Your anger; lift Yourself up against my enemies, awaken for me. Give orders for the judgment that You have commanded. 8 Congregations of nations will surround You; take Your seat over them, on high. 9 The Lord will be the judge of the peoples; judge me O Lord, according to my righteousness, and according to my integrity. 10 Let the evil of the evildoers come to an end, but give strength to the upright, for men's minds and hearts are tested by the God of righteousness. 11 God, the savior of the upright of heart, is my breastplate. 12 God is a righteous judge, and the Almighty is angered every day. 13 If a man does not turn from evil, He will sharpen His sword; His bow is bent and ready. 14 He has prepared deadly weapons for him, with arrows that can reach the swift. 15 Behold how he works in evil, conceives iniquity and brings forth deceit. 16 He has dug a hole deep in the earth, and fell into the pit he dug. 17 His wrongdoing will come back to him; his violent behavior will come down on his head. 18 I will praise the Lord for His righteousness; I will sing to the name of Lord, most high.

This is a song thanking God for selecting humanity. Despite His greatness and sovereignty over all worlds and all existence, God chose to give special attention to human beings. For this, gratitude is expressed.

8 For the chief musician on the Gittith, a psalm of David. 2 O Lord, our Master, whose glory is higher than the heavens, how noble is Your name in all the earth! 3 Even out of the mouths of babes at breast You have established strength, to stop the cruel and violent men, those who are against you. 4 When I see Your heavens, the work of Your fingers, the moon and the stars, which You have put in place 5 What is man, that You keep him in mind, a human being, that You take him into account? 6 For You have made him only a little less than divine, crowning him with glory and honor. 7 You have made him ruler over the works of Your hands; You have put all things at his feet 8 All sheep and oxen, all the beasts of the field 9 The birds of the air and the fish of the sea, and whatever passes through deep waters of the seas. 10 O Lord, our God, how noble is Your name over all the earth.

In this poem the psalmist, who has been rescued from his foes and granted victory, expresses gratitude to God. His prayer continues with an entreaty to God, to come to his aid in the future, as he is still at war with other adversaries.

9 For the chief musician, on the death of Labain, a psalm of David. 2 I will give You praise O Lord, with all my heart. I will make clear all the wonder of Your works. 3 I will be glad and delight in You. I will make a song of praise to Your name, O Most High. 4 When my enemies are turned back, they shall fall and perish before You. 5 For You have maintained my right and my cause; You sat on Your throne, judging in righteousness. 6 You have rebuked the nations, You have sent destruction to the sinners, You have blotted out their name forever and ever. 7 You have destroyed their cities; the memory of them is gone; they have become waste forever. 8 But the Lord shall endure forever; He has prepared His throne for judgment. 9 And He will judge the world in righteousness; He will minister judgment to the people with equity. 10 The Lord will be a fortress for the oppressed, a fortress in times of trouble. 11 And those who know Your name will put their faith in You, because You, O Lord, have not forsaken those who seek

You. 12 Sing to the Lord, whose house is in Zion; make His deeds clear to the people. 13 When He avenges blood, He remembers them; He doesn't forget the cries of the poor. 14 Have mercy on me, O Lord; see how I am impoverished by my enemies. You lift me up from the gates of death 15 So I may speak Your praise at the gates of the daughter of Zion. I will rejoice in Your salvation. 16 The nations have drowned in the pit they have dug; their feet have been trapped in the nets they have hidden. 17 The Lord has made Himself known through the judgments He executes; the evildoer is snared in the work of his hands. Reflect upon this, Selah. 18 The sinners and all nations who have no memory of the Lord will be directed to hell. 19 For the needy will not always be forgotten; the hopes of the poor will not be crushed forever. 20 Arise O Lord; do not let man prevail; let the nations be judged in Your sight. 21 Put them in fear, O Lord, so that the nations may see that they are only men. Selah.

This is a prayer for a time when evil is rampant and triumphant. The psalmist describes the acts of the wicked, who are confident that there is no law, no judge, and that any abomination can be performed with impunity. He begs God to show Himself, and extinguish iniquity.

10 Why do You stand far off, O Lord? Why do You hide Yourself in times of trouble? 2 With pride, the wicked fervently pursue the afflicted. Let them be caught in the plots which they have devised. 3 For the wicked boasts of his heart's desire, and the greedy man curses and spurns the Lord. 4 The wicked, with his proud countenance, does not seek God; God is not his thoughts. 5 His ways always prosper; Your judgments are on high, out of his sight. As for his adversaries, he snorts at them. 6 He has said in his heart, I shall not be moved; throughout generations I shall never be in adversity. 7 His mouth is full of curses and deceit and oppression. Under his tongue is mischief and wickedness. 8 He sits lurking in hiding places of villages where he murders the innocent, his eyes stealthily set against the poor. 9 He lurks in a hiding place like a lion in his lair; he lurks to catch the afflicted. He catches the afflicted and draws him into his net. 10 He crouches, he bows down, and the unfortunate fall into his might. 11 He says to himself: The Almighty has forgotten, He has hidden His face, He will never see. 12 Arise O Lord God! Raise Your hand; do not forget the afflicted. 13 Why has the wicked mocked the Lord, by saying to himself, You will not seek revenge? 14 You have seen it; You have beheld mischief and anger and You have the power to let it be. The poor rely on You; You have helped the orphan. 15 Break the arm of the wicked and evildoer; purge his wickedness until You can find none. 16 The Lord is King forever and ever; nations have perished from His land. 17 O Lord, You have heard the desire of the humble; You will strengthen their heart, You will incline Your ear 18 To vindicate the orphan and the oppressed, so that man who is of the earth will no longer cause terror.

This is a poem for contemplation of the evil in the world. Wicked men scheme against the righteous in private and openly, and lie in ambush, poised to attack. They are not aware that God is in charge of the world, that He sees everything, and that He will punish them as they deserve to be punished.

11 For the chief musician, a psalm of David. In the Lord I take refuge. How can you say to my soul, flee as a bird to your mountain? 2 For, behold, the wicked bend the bow; they have made ready their arrow on the string, to shoot in darkness at the upright of heart. 3 If the foundations are destroyed, what can the righteous do? 4 The Lord is in His holy temple, the Lord's throne is in heaven. His eyes behold, His eyelids examine the sons of men. 5 The Lord tests the righteous and the wicked. 6 He will rain snares upon the wicked; fire and brimstone and burning wind is the portion of their cup. 7 For the Lord is righteous; He loves righteousness. The upright will behold His countenance.

This poem of supplication is a prayer beseeching God to protect all those who choose to walk in a righteous path, from evil men who triumph in the world despite their deceitful words and harmful actions.

12 For the chief musician, on eight-stringed harp, a psalm of David. 2 Help, Lord, for the godly man is no more, for the faithful disappear from among sons of men. 3 They speak falsehood to one another; they speak with flattering lips and a double heart. 4 May the Lord cut off all flattering lips, and the tongue that speaks haughtily. 5 They who have said, with our tongue we will prevail, our lips are our own, who is lord over us? 6 "Because of the devastation of the afflicted, because of the groaning of the needy, now I will arise," says the Lord. "I will grant him deliverance," says He. 7 The words of the Lord are pure words, like silver purified in the furnace of the earth, refined seven times. 8 You, O Lord will preserve them; You will keep them secure from such a generation forever. 9 The wicked wander, sidelined, when the scorned are exalted among the sons of men.

In this supplication the psalmist, in dire straits, thinks that God is turning away from him and delivering him into the hands of his enemies. He pleads for redemption, and for the revelation of God's mercy.

13 For the chief musician, a psalm of David. 2 For how long, O Lord? Will You forget me forever? How long will You hide Your face from me? 3 How long must I devise plans in my soul, have sorrow in my heart all day? For how long will my enemies tower over me? 4 Observe and answer me, my Lord; bring light to my eyes or I will sleep in death. 5 Lest my enemy say, I have overcome him, lest my adversaries rejoice when I am shaken. 6 But I trust in Your lovingkindness; my heart shall rejoice in Your salvation. I will sing to the Lord, for He has dealt kindly with me.

This is a psalm of contemplation of the wicked of the world, nonbelievers who have no fear of God. Their lack of fear frees them to behave immorally, and creates a world full of evil and cruelty. The psalmist prays for relief and support from God in this time of suffering.

14 For the chief musician, a psalm of David. A fool says in his heart, there is no God. All are corrupt, they act abominably; there is no one who does good. 2 The Lord looks down from heaven upon the children of men, to see if there are any men of understanding who seek God. 3 They all went astray, together became corrupt; there are none who do good, not even one. 4 Have all the workers of iniquity no knowledge? They, who eat up my people as they eat bread, and do not call out to the Lord. 5 There they are, in great fear, for God is with the righteous of the generation. 6 You shame the defender of the poor, but the Lord is his refuge. 7 O that the salvation of Israel would emerge from Zion! When the Lord brings back the captives of His people, Jacob will rejoice, and Israel will be glad.

This poem instructs and clarifies how one can become deserving of closeness to God. It lists the moral human characteristics that make a man worthy of intimacy with and protection by God. It addresses mainly those characteristics that are manifest in relationships between man and his fellow man.

15 A psalm of David. O Lord, who may abide in Your tent? Who may dwell on Your holy mountain? 2 He who walks with integrity, and does righteous works, and speaks the truth in his heart. 3 He who does not slander with his tongue, nor does evil to his neighbor, nor disgraces his fellow man. 4 In his eyes a vile person is despised, but he honors those who fear the Lord. He abides by his oaths, even if they cause him harm. 5 He does not lend with usury, nor does he take bribes against the innocent. Whoever does these things shall abide forever.

This song gives thanks to God for guiding the psalmist toward the right path, and for bringing him the joy that ensues from feeling close to God.

16 An instruction of David. Almighty, preserve me, for I take refuge in You. 2 I said to the Lord, You are my master; I have no goodness without You. 3 As for the holy of the earth, they are the majestic ones; all my desires are with them. 4 The sorrows of those who have traded for another god will be multiplied; I will not pour their libations of blood, nor carry their names on my lips. 5 The Lord is my inheritance, the portion of my cup, sustainer of my fate. 6 The borders that have fallen to me are in pleasant places; my inheritance is beautiful to me. 7 I will bless the Lord, Who has counseled me, even on nights when my thoughts are tortured. 8 I have set the Lord before me always. Because He is on my right, I am secure in my place. 9 Because of this my heart is glad, my honor is glorified, my body rests securely. 10 For You will not abandon my soul to the grave; You will not allow Your devoted one to see doom. 11 You will show me the path of life; in Your presence is fullness and joy; eternal pleasure is at Your right hand.

In this prayer the psalmist requests that God watch over those who walk in His ways, rescue them from their nemeses, and bring them the joy and the privilege of being close to Him in this world.

17 A prayer of David. Hear O Lord, what is right; listen to my cry; give ear to my prayer, which does not come from deceitful lips. 2 Let my judgment come forth from Your presence; let Your eyes see uprightness. 3 You have examined my heart, remembered nights when I was tested and nothing was found; transgressions will not pass my lips. 4 Regarding deeds of men and the word of Your lips, I have preserved my soul, avoiding the paths of those who destroy. 5 Secure my steps to Your path so my feet will not slip. 6 I have called upon You, for You will answer me, Almighty. Incline Your ear to me, hear my speech. 7 Your wondrous mercy redeems those who rely on You from those who rise up against Your right hand. 8 Guard me like the pupil of an eye; hide me in the shadow of Your wings 9 From the wicked who oppress me, enemies of the soul who surround me. 10 They are encased in their fat; their mouths speak with pride. 11 They now surround us as we step; they set their eyes on the earth 12 Like a lion greedy to tear his prey, like a lion cub lurking in secret. 13 Arise, O Lord, subdue him, bring him to his knees, rescue my soul from the wicked who are Your sword. 14 Rather, give me death by Your hand, O Lord; death like men whose lot is with this life, with its hidden treasures. You fill their bellies, satisfy them with children, bequeath their inheritance to their offspring. 15 I shall see Your face in righteousness. Awake, I will be filled with Your presence.

This hymn expresses thanksgiving to God for rescuing King David. God's power, greatness, and glory are manifest in all worlds. God relieved David of every misery, supported him in war, and brought him victory and sovereignty.

18 To the chief musician, by David, servant of the Lord, who spoke the words of this song to the Lord on the day the Lord saved him from the hands of all his enemies and from the hand of Saul. 2 And he said, I love You, O Lord, my strength. 3 The Lord is my rock, my fortress, my redeemer. My Almighty, my rock, I take refuge in Him, my shield, the source of my salvation. 4 With praise I call to the Lord and I am delivered from my enemies. 5 I was surrounded by throes of death; floods of destruction terrified me. 6 Bonds of hell encircled me; snares of death confronted me. 7 In my distress I called to the Lord, cried out to God. From His dwelling place He heard my voice, and my wailing cries reached His ears. 8 The earth shook and quaked, mountains trembled, shaken because of His anger. 9 Smoke arose from His nostrils, a consuming fire from His mouth, burning coals emerged from Him. 10 He bent the heavens and came down, clouds beneath His feet. 11 He rode on a cherub and flew, soaring on wings of wind. 12 He made darkness His secret place, His sheltered surroundings, darkness of waters, clouds of the skies. 13 To the brightness before Him, His clouds brought hailstones and coals of fire. 14 And God thundered in the heavens, the Most High gave voice to hailstones and coals of fire. 15 And He sent His arrows and dispersed the enemy; lightning rods confounded them. 16 Then streams of water appeared, and the foundations of the world were laid bare at Your rebuke, O Lord, from the blast of the breath of Your nostrils. 17 He sent from above and He took me; He drew me out of many waters. 18 He delivered me from my mighty enemy, from those who hated me, for they were too strong for me. 19 When they confronted me on the day of my calamity, God was a support to me. 20 He brought me out into an open space; He rescued me because He delighted in me. 21 God has rewarded me for my righteousness; He gave me what I deserved, based on the purity of my hands. 22 For I have kept the ways of the Lord, and have not wickedly departed from my God. 23 For all His judgments were before me, and I did not dismiss his statutes. 24 I was upright with Him, and guarded myself from my iniquity. 25 And the Lord recompensed me according to my righteousness in His eyes, according to the cleanliness of my hands. 26 With the merciful You act mercifully, with the blameless You will show Yourself to be blameless. 27 With the pure, You will show Yourself pure, with the devious you will show Yourself shrewd. 28 For You will rescue the poor, but abase those with haughty looks. 29 For You light my lamp, Lord God, illuminate my darkness. 30 For with You

I can run down troops, with God I can leap over a wall. 31 The Almighty's way is blameless, the word of God is purity; He is a shield to all who take refuge in Him. 32 For who is God, but the Lord? And who is a rock, except our God? 33 The Almighty girds me with strength, and gives me a faultless path. 34 He makes my feet as swift as hinds', and sets me in high places. 35 He trains my hands for battle so that my arms can bend a bow of bronze. 36 You have given me the shield of Your salvation; Your right hand upholds me; Your humility makes me great. 37 You have widened my stride and my feet have not slipped. 38 I pursued my enemies and overtook them, and I did not turn back until they were consumed. 39 I shattered them, so they were unable to rise; they fell under my feet. 40 For You have girded me with strength for battle; You have subdued, under me, those who rose up against me. 41 You have also made my enemies turn their backs to me, and I destroyed those who hated me. 42 They cried for help, even to God, Who did not answer; there was no one to save. 43 Then I beat them as fine as dust in the wind; I poured them out like slop in the streets. 44 You have delivered me from contentious people; You have placed me at the head of nations. A people whom I have not known serve me. 45 As soon as they hear, they obey me; sons of strangers submit to me. 46 Sons of strangers fade away, and come trembling out of their fortresses. 47 The Lord lives; blessed is my rock. Exalted be the God of my salvation 48 The Almighty who executes vengeance for me, and subdues peoples under me 49 Rescues me from enemies, lifts me above those who rise up against me, saves me from men of violence. 50 Because of this I will give thanks to You among the nations, O Lord, and to Your name I will sing praises. 51 He gives great deliverance to His king, shows lovingkindness to His anointed, to David and to his descendants, eternally.

There are three parts to this song: the world, the Torah, and man. All glorify God. The world, its universe, and patterns are all essentially a silent expression of God's glory; the Torah contains myriad facets of God's glory within; and man, who has the capacity to regret sin and change for the good, glorifies God with repentance.

19 To the chief musician, a psalm of David. 2 The heavens declare the glory of God, the skies show the work of His hands. 3 Day by day expressions of speech, night by night demonstrations of wisdom. 4 There is no talk, nor are there words; their voice is never heard. 5 Their horizon extends to the ends of the earth, their utterances to the end of the world; in a tent within, He placed the sun 6 Which, like a bridegroom leaving his chamber, rejoices with strength to run his course. 7 It rises from one end of the heavens, coursing the skies to the other end; nothing escapes its heat. 8 The Torah of the Lord is perfect, restoring the soul; the testimony of Lord can be trusted; it makes the simple, wise. 9 The precepts of the Lord are upright, and gladden the heart; the commandments of the Lord are clear, enlighten the eyes. 10 Fear of the Lord is pure, and endures forever; the judgments of the Lord are true and altogether righteous. 11 They are more desirable than gold, than quantities of fine gold, and sweeter than honey and the drippings of the honeycomb. 12 Even your servant is mindful of them; in keeping them there is great reward. 13 Who can discern his own errors? Acquit me of hidden faults. 14 Also keep Your servant far from conscious sins; let them not have dominion over me. Then I will be blameless, and cleansed of great transgression. 15 Let the words of my mouth and the meditation of my heart be acceptable in Your sight, O Lord, my rock and my redeemer.

The song begins with a prayer for God's deliverance in a time of trouble and war, and with a request that God rescue those who rely on Him. It ends with words of thanks for victory in this war.

20 To the chief musician, a psalm of David. 2 May the Lord answer you on a day of trouble; may the name of the God of Jacob fortify you. 3 May He send you help from the sanctuary, and support you from Zion. 4 May He remember all your offerings and accept your burnt sacrifice, Selah. 5 May He grant you your heart's desire and fulfill all your plans. 6 We will sing with joy at your victory, and raise banners in the name of our God. May the Lord fulfill all of your wishes. 7 Now I know that the Lord rescues His anointed; He will answer him from His holy heavens, with the mighty strength of His right hand. 8 Some rely on chariots and some on horses, but we rely on the name of the Lord our God. 9 They have bowed down and fallen, but we have risen to stand upright. 10 Deliver us, O Lord! The King will answer us on the day we call.

This song is one of praise and glory on the occasion of a king's victory. It is a poem of triumph, telling of a righteous king who trusts in God, and who is rewarded with the ability to overcome his foes. The poem essentially gives honor to God, as He is the one who determines victory.

21 To the chief musician, a psalm of David. 2 The king shall have joy in Your strength, O Lord; in Your salvation how greatly shall he rejoice. 3 You have given him his heart's desire, and have not denied the request of his lips, Selah. 4 You set before him the blessings of the good; You set a crown of pure gold upon his head. 5 He asked You for life; You gave it to him, length of days forever and ever. 6 His glory is great in Your salvation; You place splendor and majesty upon him. 7 For You make him most blessed forever; You make him exceedingly joyous in Your presence. 8 For the king trusts in the Lord; in the lovingkindness of the Most High he will not be toppled. 9 Your hand will find all of Your enemies; Your right hand will find those who hate You. 10 You will make them like a fiery oven in the time of your anger; the Lord will consume them with His wrath, and let fire devour them. 11 You will destroy their offspring from the earth, and their descendants from among the sons of men. 12 Though they intended evil against You, and devised a plot, they will not succeed. 13 For You will make them turn back; You will aim Your bowstring at their faces. 14 Be exalted, O Lord in Your strength; we will sing and praise Your power.

This song begins with a supplication, a call for help by the psalmist who prays alone, surrounded by many foes. It ends with a poem of praise for God's deliverance, which has become evident to all.

22 To the chief musician on Ayelet Hashachar, a psalm of David. 2 My God, my God, why have You forsaken me so far from my deliverance, from the words that I cry? 3 My God, I cry by day, but You do not answer; by night I have no rest. 4 Yet You are holy, enthroned in the praises of Israel. 5 Our fathers trusted in You; they trusted, and You delivered them. 6 They cried out to You and were delivered; they trusted You and were not disappointed. 7 But I am a worm and not a man, scorn of man and despised by people. 8 All who see me sneer at me, rejecting me with a curled lip and a wag of the head, saying 9 Let him commit himself to the Lord, let Him save him, let Him rescue him for He delights in him. 10 For You brought me forth from the womb; You made me secure at my mother's breast. 11 I have been cast on You from birth; from my mother's womb You have been my Almighty. 12 Be not far from me, for trouble is near, and there is no one to help. 13 Many bulls have surrounded me; strong bulls of Bashan have encircled me. 14 They open their mouths wide at me, like ravenous and roaring lions. 15 I am poured out like water, all my bones are disjointed; my heart is like wax, melted within me. 16 My strength is dried up like baked clay, my tongue cleaves to my mouth; You have brought me to the dust of death. 17 For dogs have surrounded me, a band of evildoers have encircled me like lions at my hands and feet. 18 They look and stare at me as I count all my bones. 19 They divide my garments among them, and they cast lots for my clothing. 20 But You, O Lord, be not far off; my strength, hasten to help me. 21 Deliver my soul from the sword, my only life from the power of the dog. 22 Save me from the lion's mouth. From the horns of the wild oxen, You answer me. 23 I will tell of Your name to my brothers; in the midst of the assembly I will praise You. 24 You, who fear the Lord, praise Him, all of you, the seed of Jacob, glorify Him, and stand in awe of Him. All praise You. 24 You who fear the Lord, praise Him, all of you, the seed of Jacob, glorify Him. And stand in awe of Him, all of you, seed of Israel. 25 For He has not despised and not abhorred the poverty of the poor, nor has He hidden His face from him; when he cried to Him, He heard. 26 My praise shall be of You, in the great assembly; I will pay my vows in the presence of those who fear Him. 27 The humble will eat and be satisfied; those who seek Him will praise the Lord; may your hearts live forever. 28 All the ends of the earth will remember and return to the Lord; all the families of nations will bow down before You. 29 For kingship belongs to the Lord; He rules over nations. 30 All the prosperous of the earth who have eaten will bow down before Him; all those who return to the dust, even he who cannot keep his soul alive, will kneel before Him. 31 Posterity will serve Him; coming generations will be told of the Lord. 32 They will come and declare His righteousness, his works, to a newborn people.

This is a poem of devotion to God, in which the psalmist compares himself to a little lamb who relies on and trusts the loyal shepherd to lead him on a secure path, and to guide him to a place of rest, well-being, and peace.

23 A psalm of David. The Lord is my shepherd, I shall not want. 2 He makes me lie down in green pastures; He leads me beside still waters. 3 He restores my soul; He leads me in a path of righteousness, for His name's sake. 4 Though I walk through the valley of the shadow of death, I shall fear no evil, for You are with me; Your rod and Your staff, they comfort me. 5 You prepare a table before me, in the presence of my enemies. You anoint my head with oil; my cup runs over. 6 Surely goodness and kindness shall pursue me all the days of my life, and I will dwell in the house of the Lord forever.

This hymn on the revelation of God speaks of God's greatness in the world, and describes how His majesty and glory are revealed in His holy chamber. Those with pure hearts and unsullied hands are worthy of being with Him when He is revealed.

24 By David, a psalm. The earth is the Lord's, as is everything within it, the world, and all of its inhabitants. 2 For He founded it upon the seas, and established it upon the waters. 3 Who may ascend the mountain of the Lord? Who may stand in His holy place? 4 He who has clean hands and a pure heart, he who has not carried his soul with vanity, nor sworn deceitfully. 5 He shall receive the blessing of the Lord, and righteousness from the God of his deliverance. 6 This generation of Jacob is of those who seek Him, those who seek Your presence, Selah. 7 Lift up your heads, gates; be uplifted, entrances of the world, so that the King of glory may enter. 8 Who is this King of glory? The Lord, strong and mighty, the Lord, mighty in battle. 9 Lift up your heads, gates, and lift up the entrances of the world, so that the King of glory may enter. 10 Who is He, this King of glory? The Lord of hosts, He is the King of glory, Selah.

This song, meant to educate, is a prayer entreating God to teach and help the penitent find the best way to return to the right path. It expresses trust that God will help and protect those who walk in his ways.

25 A psalm of David. To You, Lord, I lift up my soul. 2 My God, in You I trust; do not let me be shamed, do not let my enemies triumph over me. 3 Indeed, those who hope for You will not be ashamed. Those who deal treacherously without cause will be ashamed. 4 Show me Your ways, O Lord; teach me Your path. 5 Lead me in Your truth and teach me, for You are the God of my salvation; for You I hope all day. 6 Remember, O Lord, Your compassion and lovingkindness, for they have existed forever. 7 Do not remember the sins of my youth nor my transgressions; remember me with Your mercy, for Your goodness' sake, O Lord. 8 Good and upright is the Lord; that is why He instructs sinners in the way. 9 He guides the humble with justice, and He teaches the humble His way. 10 All the paths of the Lord are mercy and truth, for those who keep His covenant and His testimonies. 11 For the sake of Your name, O Lord, pardon my iniquity, for it is great. 12 Who is the man who fears the Lord? He will instruct him in the way he should choose. 13 His soul will abide in prosperity, and his descendants shall inherit the earth. 14 The secret of Lord is with those who fear Him; He will make them know His covenant. 15 My eyes are ever toward the Lord, for He shall pluck my feet out of the net. 16 Turn to me and be gracious to me, for I am lonely and afflicted. 17 The troubles of my heart have spread; bring me out of my distresses. 18 See my affliction and my pain and forgive all my sins. 19 See my enemies, for they are many; they hate me with violent hatred. 20 Guard my soul and deliver me; do not let me be ashamed, for I take refuge in You. 21 Let integrity and uprightness preserve me, for I wait for You. 22 O God, redeem Israel from all its troubles.

In this song of prayer the psalmist is trying to choose the right path, both with respect to his personal religious behavior, and with respect to the company he keeps. He requests that God watch over and protect him so that he won't be harmed by falling into the company of sinners.

26 By David. Vindicate me, O Lord, for I have walked in my integrity, and I have trusted in the Lord without wavering. 2 Examine me, O Lord, and try me; test my mind and my heart. 3 For Your lovingkindness is before my eyes, and I have walked in Your truth. 4 I have not sat with deceitful men, nor will I go with those who sin secretly. 5 I hate the assembly of evildoers, and I will not sit with the wicked. 6 I will wash my hands in innocence, and I will encircle Your altar, O Lord 7 So that I may proclaim with the voice of thanksgiving and tell of all Your wonders. 8 O Lord, I love the habitation of Your house, the place where Your glory dwells. 9 Do not gather my soul with sinners, or my life with men of bloodshed 10 In whose hands is a sinister scheme, and whose right hand is full of bribes. 11 As for me, I will walk in my integrity; redeem me and be gracious to me. 12 My foot stands on a straight path; in the congregations, I will bless the Lord.

Although this song begins with the psalmist in dire straits, his devotion to God fills him with trust in God. He is aware that in his inner life, what matters to him more than anything in the whole world is to strive to attain pure devotion to God.

27 By David. The Lord is my light and my salvation; whom shall I fear? The Lord is the defense of my life; whom shall I dread? 2 When evildoers came upon me to devour my flesh, they, my adversaries and my enemies, stumbled and fell. 3 Though an army may encamp against me, my heart shall not fear; though war may rise against me, in this I shall be confident. 4 One thing I have asked of the Lord, that I shall seek, is that I may dwell in the house of the Lord all the days of my life, to behold the beauty of the Lord and to meditate in His temple. 5 For in the time of trouble He will shelter me in His tabernacle, in the secret place of His tent He will hide me. He will set me high upon on a rock. 6 And now my head shall be lifted up above my enemies around me, and I will offer sacrifices in His tent with cries of joy. I will sing, yes, I will sing praises to the Lord. 7 Hear, O Lord, when I cry with my voice. Be gracious to me and answer me. 8 To You, my heart said, seek me; Your presence, O Lord, I seek. 9 Do not hide Your face from me; do not turn Your servant away in anger. You have been my help; do not abandon me nor forsake me, O God of my salvation. 10 When my father and my mother forsake me, the Lord will gather me up. 11 Teach me Your way, O Lord, and lead me on a level path because of my foes. 12 Do not deliver me over to the desires of my adversaries. False witnesses who breathe violence would have destroyed me 13 Had I not believed that I would see the goodness of the Lord in the land of the living. 14 Wait for the Lord; be strong and let your heart take courage, yes, wait for the Lord.

This song begins with words of supplication by the psalmist, who beseeches God to save him from enemies who seek his destruction and death. It continues with words of thanksgiving for victory and success, which do come, in the end.

28 By David. To You, O Lord, I call; my rock, do not be deaf unto me. For if You are silent to me I become like those who go down to the pit. 2 Hear the voice of my supplications when I cry to You for help, when I lift up my hands toward Your holy sanctuary. 3 Do not drag me away with the wicked, and with those who work iniquity, who speak peace with their neighbors when evil is in their hearts. 4 Requite them according to their deeds and according to the evil of their practices. Give back to them what their hands have done; render to them what they deserve. 5 For they do not regard the works of the Lord, nor the deeds of His hands; He will tear them down and not build them up. 6 Blessed be the Lord, for He has heard the voice of my supplication. 7 The Lord is my strength and my shield; my heart trusts in Him, and I am helped. Because of this my heart exults, and with my song I will praise Him. 8 The Lord is strength to them; He is the saving refuge of His anointed. 9 Deliver Your people and bless Your inheritance; shepherd them and carry them forever.

This hymn on Divine revelation (referred to in this song as "the voice of God"), describes how all of creation has its own unique reaction to God's presence and manifestation in this world. God is the supreme King; He rules over His world and endows it with stability.

29 A Psalm of David. Give unto the Lord, sons of the mighty, give unto the Lord glory and strength. 2 Give unto the Lord, the glory due His name; worship the Lord in holy splendor. 3 The voice of the Lord is over the waters; the glory of God thunders; the Lord is upon many waters. 4 The voice of the Lord is powerful; the voice of the Lord is majestic. 5 The voice of the Lord breaks cedars; the Lord splinters the cedars of Lebanon. 6 He makes them skip like a calf, Lebanon and Sirion like a young wild ox. 7 The voice of the Lord hews out flames of fire. 8 The voice of the Lord makes the desert tremble; the Lord shakes the desert of Kadesh. 9 The voice of the Lord causes deer to calve, and strips the forests bare. In His temple all proclaim His glory. 10 The Lord sat enthroned at the flood; the Lord sits as King forever. 11 The Lord will give strength to His people; the Lord will bless His people with peace.

This is a song of thanksgiving by the psalmist, whose well-being has been obliterated suddenly, by great trouble or illness; his whole life has been darkened. When he prays to God for help, he is blessed with a complete recovery, and is restored to his former state of strength.

30 A psalm, a song for the dedication of the temple, by David. 2 I will extol You, O Lord, for You have lifted me up, and have not let my enemies rejoice over me. 3 O Lord, my God, I cried out to You and You healed me. 4 O Lord, You have lifted my soul out of hell, You have kept me alive, kept me from going down to the pit. 5 Sing praise to the Lord, you, His godly ones, and give thanks to His holy name. 6 For His anger is but for a moment, His favor is for life. At night one may weep, but joy comes in the morning. 7 As for me, I said in my prosperity, I shall never be moved. 8 O Lord, by Your favor, You made my mountain stand strong; You hid Your face, and I was troubled. 9 To You, O Lord, I called; I prayed to my Master. 10 What benefit is there in my blood, if I go down to the pit? Will the dust praise You? Will it declare Your truth? 11 Hear me O Lord, and have mercy on me; Lord help me. 12 You have turned my mourning into dancing, you have loosened my sackcloth and clothed me with joy 13 So that my soul may sing praise to You and not be silent. O Lord, my God, I will give thanks to You forever.

In this poem the psalmist expresses faith in God and praises God, as He protects those who trust Him. Yet even though he has professed his faith in God, the psalmist admits despair, as he is surrounded by adversaries who attack him from all sides. He beseeches God for deliverance and protection.

31 To the chief musician, a psalm of David. 2 In You, O Lord, I place my trust; let me never be ashamed. In Your righteousness, let me escape. 3 Incline Your ear to me; rescue me quickly. Be my rock of refuge, a stronghold to save me. 4 For You are my rock and my fortress. For Your name's sake You will lead me and guide me. 5 Pull me out of the net which they have laid for me in secret, for You are my strength. 6 Into Your hand I commit my spirit; You have redeemed me, O Lord, God of truth. 7 I have hated those who cherish worthless vanities; as for me, I trust in the Lord. 8 I will rejoice and be glad in Your mercy, for You have seen my affliction, You know my troubled soul. 9 And You have not given me over into the hand of the enemy; You have set my feet in open space. 10 Be gracious to me, O Lord, for I am in distress; my eye wastes away with grief, my soul, my body also. 11 For my life is spent in sorrow, and my years in sighing. My strength fails, because of my iniquity, and my bones have wasted away. 12 Because of all my adversaries, I have been disgraced, an object of dread to my acquaintances, especially to my neighbors. Those who see me in the street flee from me. 13 I am as forgotten as a dead man; I am like an abandoned vessel. 14 For I have heard the slander of many, terror from every side. They counseled together against me; they schemed to take away my life. 15 But as for me, I trust in You, O Lord; I declare You are my Lord. 16 My times are in Your hand. Deliver me from the hand of my enemies and from those who persecute me. 17 Shine your countenance on Your servant; deliver me for Your mercies' sake. 18 Let me not be put to shame, O Lord, for I call upon You. Let the wicked be put to shame; let them be silent in the grave. 19 Let lying lips that speak arrogance, pride, and contempt against the righteous be muted. 20 How great is Your goodness, which You have preserved for those who fear You, which You have given to those who take refuge in You, in the presence of the sons of men. 21 You hide them in the secret place of Your presence, away from the conspiracies of men. You keep them secretly secure from the strife of tongues. 22 Blessed is the Lord, for the wondrous lovingkindness He has shown me in a besieged city. 23 And I had said in my panic, I am cut off from Your vision. Still, You heard the voice of my prayers when I cried out to You. 24 Love the Lord, all who are His devoted ones. The Lord preserves the faithful, and recompenses with exactness those who act haughtily. 25 Be strong and let your hearts have courage, all of you who hope in the Lord.

In this song the psalmist confesses his sins and faults to God. He admonishes others of the importance of feeling a basic connection to God. Because of the psalmist's belief in this connection, he is certain that God will rescue him from all difficulties.

32 A contemplation, by David. Blessed is he whose transgression is forgiven, whose sin is pardoned. 2 Blessed is the man to whom the Lord does not impute iniquity, and in whose spirit there is no deceit. 3 When I kept silent about my sin, my body wasted away, through my groaning all day long. 4 For day and night Your hand was heavy upon me; my marrow was parched as if by drought of summer, Selah. 5 I acknowledged my sin to You; I did not hide my iniquity. I said, I will confess my transgressions to the Lord, and You forgave the guilt of my sin, Selah. 6 Like this, all who are devoted to You should pray at a time when You may be found; then, surely, mighty threatening waters shall not reach them. 7 You are my hiding place, You preserve me from disaster, You surround me with songs of deliverance, Selah. 8 I will instruct you and teach you in the path you should take; I will advise you, with my eye on your benefit. 9 Do not be like a horse or a mule with no understanding, that with bit and bridle must be restrained when approached. 10 Many are the sorrows of the wicked, but mercy surrounds he who trusts in the Lord. 11 Rejoice in the Lord, and be glad, you righteous ones; shout for joy, all whose hearts are upright.

This song glorifies God; He alone has the power to rescue. Without God's help, all forces are extraneous and indeterminate. One can only count on God.

33 Rejoice in the Lord, righteous ones! Praise is becoming to the upright. 2 Give thanks to the Lord with the lyre; sing praises to Him with a ten-stringed harp. 3 Sing Him a new song; play skillfully with shouts of joy. 4 For the word of the Lord is upright, and all his work is done faithfully. 5 He loves righteousness and justice; the earth is full of the goodness of the Lord. 6 The heavens were made by the word of the Lord, by the breath of His mouth, all their hosts. 7 He gathers the waters of the seas as if in a flask; he treasures the deep waters in vaults. 8 Fear the Lord, all the earth; stand in awe of Him, all inhabitants of the world. 9 For He spoke and it was done; He commanded, and it stood fast. 10 The Lord nullifies the counsel of nations; He frustrates the plans of peoples. 11 The counsel of the Lord stands forever, the plans of His heart from generation to generation. 12 Blessed is the nation whose God is the Lord, the people He chose as His heritage. 13 The Lord looks from heaven; He sees all the sons of men. 14 From His dwelling place He looks out on all the inhabitants of the earth. 15 He fashions their hearts individually; He understands all their works. 16 No king is saved by a mighty army; no warrior is rescued by his own strength. 17 A horse is false hope for victory; it does not provide escape with its great strength. 18 The eye of the Lord is on those who fear Him, on those who hope for his mercy 19 To deliver their soul from death and to keep them alive in famine. 20 Our soul waits for the Lord; He is our help and our shield. 21 For our heart rejoices in Him, because we trust in His holy name. 22 Let Your mercy, O Lord, be upon us, as we have waited for You.

This poem teaches of the paths that are good for a man to follow. Those who choose these paths are worthy of God's help and protection.

34 By David, when he pretended madness before Avimelech, who drove him away, and he left. 2. I will bless the Lord at all times; His praise shall continually be in my mouth. 3 My soul shall take pride in the Lord; the humble shall hear this and rejoice. 4 Declare the greatness of the Lord with me; let us exalt His name together. 5 I sought the Lord and He answered me; He delivered me from all of my fears. 6 Those who look to Him are enlightened; their faces shall never be ashamed. 7 This poor man cried, and the Lord heard him, and saved him from all his troubles. 8 The angel of the Lord encamps around those who fear Him, and rescues them. 9 Taste and see that the Lord is good; how blessed is the man who takes refuge in Him. 10 Fear the Lord, you His holy ones, for those who fear Him lack nothing. 11 Even young lions suffer hunger, but those who seek the Lord will lack no good thing. 12 Come, children, and listen to me; I will teach you to fear the Lord. 13 Who is the man who desires life, and loves his days, and desires to see good? 14 Guard your tongue from evil and your lips from speaking deceit. 15 Turn away from evil, and do good; seek peace and pursue it. 16 The eyes of the Lord are on the righteous, and His ears are open to their cry. 17 The face of the Lord turns against evildoers, to excise their memory from the earth. 18 When the righteous and repentant cry, the

Lord hears them, and delivers them from all their troubles. 19 The Lord is close to the brokenhearted, and saves those whose spirit is crushed. 20 Many evils afflict a righteous man, but the Lord delivers him from them all. 21 He preserves all his bones, not one of them is broken. 22 Evil causes the death of the wicked; those who hate the righteous will be condemned. 23 The Lord redeems the souls of His servants; none who take refuge in Him shall be condemned.

This is a prayer asking for God's help against adversaries. The psalmist prays to God for deliverance from, and vengeance against, outright and clandestine enemies, traitors, and ingrates who use every means within their power, to cause harm.

35 By David. Strive, O Lord, against those who strive against me. Fight against those who fight against me. 2 Take hold of shield and armor and rise up to help me. 3 Draw also spear and battle axe to stop those who pursue me; say to my soul, I am your salvation. 4 Let those who seek my life be ashamed and dishonored; let those who devise evil against me be turned back and humiliated. 5 Let them be like chaff in the wind, with the angel of the Lord driving them off. 6 Let their way be dark and slippery, and let the angel of the Lord pursue them. 7 Without cause they have buried nets to trap me; without cause they dug a pit for my soul. 8 Let destruction come upon him unawares; let the net which he buried, trap him. Into that very destruction let him fall. 9 And my soul will rejoice in the Lord; it will exult in His salvation. 10 All my bones will say, O Lord, who is like You, who delivers the afflicted from those who are too strong for him, the poor and the needy from the robber? 11 Malicious witnesses rise up; they ask of me things I do not know. 12 They repay me evil for good, to the bereavement of my soul. 13 But as for me, when they were sick, my clothing was a sackcloth, I humbled my soul with fasting, and prayers returned to my breast. 14 I paced about as if he were my friend or bother; I bowed down in mourning, as one who grieves for a mother. 15 But when I stumbled, they came together and rejoiced; even the lame I did not know joined in against me, slandering me without ceasing. 16 Like godless jesters at a feast, they gnashed me with their teeth. 17 O Lord, how long will You look on? Rescue my soul from their ravages, my only life from the lions. 18 I will thank You in the great congregation; I will praise You among a mighty throng. 19 Do not let those who are wrongfully against me hate me and rejoice over me; do not let those who hate me without cause wink maliciously. 20 For they do not speak of peace; they devise deceitful words against those who keep quiet in the land. 21 They open their mouth wide against me, saying, aha, aha, our eyes have seen it all. 22 You have seen it, God; do not keep silent; O God, do not be far from me. 23 Rise up and wake to my cause, my Lord and Master. 24 Vindicate me, O Lord, my God, according to Your righteousness; do not let them rejoice over me. 25 Do not let them say in their heart, aha, our desire has been gratified; do not let them say we have swallowed him up. 26 Let those who rejoice at my distress be ashamed and humiliated altogether; let those who magnify themselves at my expense be clothed in shame and dishonor. 27 Let those who want to see me vindicated shout with joy and rejoice; let them say continually, great is the Lord who delights in the prosperity of His servant. 28 My tongue will speak of Your righteousness, and of Your praise, all the day long.

This song compares the wicked to the righteous. A wicked person's lack of faith results in his sinking lower and lower into iniquity. A righteous person's great fortune is devotion and closeness to God. The psalmist prays for the fall of the wicked and the ascent of the righteous.

36 For the chief musician, by David, servant of the Lord, 2 A discourse from within my heart, on the transgression of the wicked, in whose eyes there is no fear of the Lord. 3 It smooths the way for him to accept his hateful iniquity, in his own eyes. 4 The words of his mouth are wickedness and deceit; he has ceased to be wise and do good. 5 He plots wicked deeds on his bed; he sets himself on a path of no good; he does not abhor evil. 6 Your mercy, O Lord, extends to the heavens; Your faithfulness reaches the skies. 7 Your righteousness is like mighty mountains, Your judgments great and unfathomable; O Lord, You redeem man and beast. 8 How precious is Your lovingkindness, O Lord; the children of man take refuge in the shadow of Your wings. 9 They drink their abundant fill in Your house; You offer them drink from the river of Your delights. 10 For with You is the fountain of life; in Your light we see light. 11 Continue to show lovingkindness to those who know You; show righteousness to the upright of heart. 12 Let not the foot of pride overtake me, and let not the hand of the wicked rattle me. 13 There the workers of iniquity have fallen, cast down and unable to rise.

This song teaches that the ways of the wicked are doomed to failure and impermanence. In contrast, the path of the righteous, even if initially difficult, results in security and deliverance that lasts for generations.

37 A psalm of David. Do not fret because of evildoers, nor be envious of the workers of iniquity. 2 They shall soon be cut down like grass, wither like the green herb. 3 Trust in the Lord and do good; dwell on the land and cultivate faithfulness. 4 Delight in the Lord and He will give you the desires of your heart. 5 Commit your way to the Lord; trust in Him and He shall bring it to pass. 6 He shall bring your righteousness to light, your judgment bright as noon. 7 Be silent before the Lord and wait patiently for Him; do not fret when those with evil schemes prosper. 8 Cease from anger and forsake wrath; do not fret, it leads only to evildoing. 9 Evildoers shall be cut off, but those who wait for the Lord shall inherit the earth. 10 In a short while the wicked shall be no more; you will look closely at his place and he will not be there. 11 But the meek shall inherit the earth and shall delight in an abundant peace. 12 The wicked plot against the righteous, gnash at them with their teeth. 13 The Lord laughs; He sees their day coming. 14 The wicked have drawn swords and bent their bows to cast down the afflicted and the needy, to slay those who are upright in conduct. 15 Their swords shall enter their own hearts; their bows shall be broken. 16 A little, for the righteous man, is better than abundance for many wicked men. 17 For the arms of the wicked shall be broken, but the Lord upholds the righteous. 18 The Lord knows the days of the blameless; their inheritance will last forever. 19 They will not be humiliated in times of evil; in days of famine they shall be satisfied. 20 But the wicked will perish, and the enemies of the Lord shall be consumed by flames. They shall vanish into smoke, like the fat of rams. 21 The wicked borrow and do not repay; the righteous are gracious and give. 22 Those blessed by Him shall inherit the earth; those cursed by Him shall be cut off. 23 The Lord establishes the footsteps of man; He desires that man walk in His ways. 24 When he falls he will not remain cast down, because the Lord holds his hand. 25 I have been young, and now I am old, and I have not seen the righteous forsaken, nor his descendants begging for bread. 26 Ever merciful all his days, his seed is blessed. 27 Depart from evil and do good, and dwell securely forever. 28 The Lord loves justice and does not forsake His devoted ones; they are guarded forever. The descendants of the wicked shall be cut off. 29 The righteous shall inherit the earth and dwell in it forever. 30 The mouth of the righteous utters wisdom, and his tongue speaks justice. 31 The law of the Lord is in his heart; his steps do not slip. 32 The wicked spies on the righteous and seeks to kill him. 33 The Lord shall not let go of his hand nor let him be condemned when judged. 34 Place your hope in the Lord and keep His ways, and He will exalt you to inherit the earth; the wicked are cut off, you shall see. 35 I have seen a wicked violent man spread himself like a luxuriant tree in its native soil. 36 He passed away and was no more; I looked for him but he was nowhere. 37 Observe the blameless man, behold the upright; the man of peace has a future. 38 But transgressors shall be completely destroyed; the descendants of the wicked shall be cut off. 39 The salvation of the righteous is from the Lord; He is their strength in times of trouble. 40 The Lord helps them and delivers them; He shall deliver them from the wicked, because they take refuge in Him.

In this supplication the psalmist is suffering physically and emotionally. He has been abandoned, delivered into the hands of enemies and traitors. He admits his own faults and confesses his sins. All that he has left in his world is God. Because he has leaned on Him throughout his life, he entreats God again, now, to relieve him of current misfortune.

38 A psalm of David, to bring remembrance. 2 O Lord, do not rebuke me with your wrath; do not chasten me with Your burning anger. 3 Your arrows have pierced me deeply; Your hand has pressed down upon me. 4 There is no unmarred spot on my flesh because of Your anger, nor any health in my bones because of my sin. 5 I am over my head in iniquities; like an onerous burden, they are too heavy for me. 6 My wounds grow foul and fester because of my folly. 7 I am bent over and greatly diminished; I walk about, melancholy all day long. 8 My thoughts are filled with futility, my flesh has no rest. 9 I am numb and badly crushed; I groan with agitation in my heart. 10 O Lord, I desire only You; my sighing is not hidden from You. 11 My heart throbs, my strength fails me; even the light of my eyes has gone from me. 12 My loved ones and friends stand aloof from my plague; my relatives stand far off. 13 Those who seek my life lay snares for me; those who seek to harm me threaten destruction; they devise treacherous plans all day long. 14 I am like a deaf man; I do not hear. I am like a mute man; I do not open my mouth. 15 Yes, I am like a man who does not hear, a man in whose mouth there are no arguments. 16 I hope in You, my Lord. You will answer, my God and my Master. 17 For I said, hear me, so they will not rejoice when my foot slips, so they will not glorify themselves at my expense. 18 I am ready to stumble; my sorrows are continually before me. 19 I confess my iniquity; I am anxious because of my sins. 20 My enemies are vigorous and strong; many are those who hate me wrongfully. 21 Those who render evil for good, oppose me because I pursue what is good. 22 Do not forsake me O Lord; O my God, do not be far from me. 23 Make haste to help me, Master of my deliverance.

This poem, contemplating the brevity and difficulty of human life, is a prayer to God, the only One who can deliver the psalmist from adversaries and illness.

39 For the chief musician, for Yedutun, a psalm of David. 2 I will guard my ways lest I sin with my tongue; I will guard my mouth, as if it were muzzled, while the wicked are in my presence. 3 I was mute and silent; I refrained even from good, but my sorrow grew worse. 4 My heart was hot within me; while I was musing the fire burned, then I spoke with my tongue. 5 O Lord, let me know my end; what will be the measure of my days; let me know how transient I am. 6 See the handbreadth of my days; my life is nothing in Your sight. All is nothingness, all of mankind's stability, Selah. 7 Surely man walks around as a shadow, surely he is in turmoil, for nothing, amassing riches, not knowing who will gather them. 8 And now, O Lord, what do I wait for? My hope is in You. 9 Deliver me from all my transgressions; do not make me a disgrace among the degenerate. 10 I have become mute, I do not open my mouth; it is You who have done it. 11 Remove Your plague from me; I am perishing because Your hand is against me. 12 With reproof, You chasten a man for his sin; You consume what is precious to him, like a flame consumes a moth. Surely man is mere nothingness, Selah. 13 Hear my prayer, O Lord, and listen to my cry; do not be silent at my tears. I am a stranger with You, a sojourner, as all my fathers were. 14 Let me be, so I may regain strength, before I depart and am no more.

This is a poem of thanksgiving. God had delivered the psalmist from many difficulties, but most recently and critically, from enemies during war. The psalmist admits his own past transgressions, and states that because he received the punishment he deserved, he is now worthy of God's deliverance. He publicly declares that God has shown him lovingkindness.

40 For the chief musician, a psalm of David. 2 I had hoped and hoped for the Lord, and He turned to me and heard my cry. 3 He brought me out of the pit of destruction, out of the swamp of clay, and He set my feet upon a rock, and firmly established my steps. 4 He put a new song in my mouth, a song of praise for our God. Many will see, and fear and trust in the Lord. 5 Blessed is the man who puts his trust in the Lord, and has not turned to the proud and the false. 6 Many things, O Lord my God, have You done; Your wondrous works and thoughts are toward us. There is nothing that compares to You. I declare and speak of Your miraculous deeds, but they are too numerous to count. 7 You do not desire sacrifice or meal offerings. You have opened my ears. You do not require burnt offerings or sin offerings. 8 So I said, I have come here with the scroll of Your book, 9 I delight in doing Your will, my God; Your law is within my heart. 10 I have proclaimed righteousness with joy in the great assembly; I shall not restrain my lips, my Lord, as You know. 11 I have not concealed Your righteousness within my heart; I have spoken of Your faithfulness and Your salvation. I have not concealed Your lovingkindness and Your truth from the great assembly. 12 You, my Lord, will not withhold Your compassion from me; Your lovingkindness and Your truth shall continually preserve me. 13 For innumerable evils surround me. My iniquities, more numerous than the hairs on my head, have overtaken me, so that I cannot see. My heart has failed me. 14 Please, my Lord, deliver me; make haste to help me. 15 Let those who seek my life, to destroy it, be ashamed and humiliated together. Let those who delight in my misfortune fall back and be disgraced. 16 Let those who say, aha, aha to me, be confounded because of their shame. 17 Let all who seek You rejoice and be glad in You; let those who love Your salvation say continually, the Lord be magnified. 18 As I am afflicted, and needy, may my Master be mindful of me; You are my help and my savior; my God, do not delay.

This song of thanksgiving to God is by a great man (of wealth, or a king) who has recovered from a deadly illness. It first describes his abandonment by relatives and friends, who were only close to him in his glory. It then describes his great relief at deliverance, his complete recovery, and the restoration of his former stature.

41 For the chief musician, a psalm of David. 2 Blessed is he who considers the helpless; the Lord will deliver him in times of trouble. 3 The Lord will preserve him and keep him alive; he shall be blessed on earth. You will not give him over to the will of his enemies. 4 The Lord will heal him on his sickbed; You restore him to health when ill. 5 As for me, I said, O Lord, be gracious to me, heal my soul for I have sinned against You. 6 My enemies speak evil against me, saying, when will he die, and his name perish? 7 When he comes to see me, he speaks falsely; his heart contains wickedness; he goes outside and speaks of it. 8 All who hate me whisper together against me; they devise to hurt me, and say, 9 Bad things have befallen him; now that he lays may he rise no more. 10 Even my friend, whom I trusted, who ate my bread, has lifted his heel against me. 11 But You, O Lord, be gracious to me and raise me up, so I may repay them. 12 Then I will know that You care for me, because my enemy will not shout in triumph over me. 13 As for me, You have kept me unblemished, stable before You forever. 14 Blessed is the Lord God of Israel, from everlasting to everlasting, Amen and Amen.

In this poem of longing and supplication, the psalmist is in exile, alone, hunted and hated. He knows that only God can save him from all of the difficulties engulfing him.

42 For the chief musician, a contemplation of the sons of Korach. 2 As the deer pants for brooks of water, my soul pants for You, O God. 3 My soul thirsts for God, the living God. When will I come and appear before God? 4 My tears have been my food, day and night. All day long they say to me, where is your God? 5 When I remember these things I pour out my soul within. I used to go with the throngs, with the multitudes keeping the festival, leading them in procession to the house of God, with a voice of joy and thanksgiving. 6 Why do you despair, O my soul? Why are you disquieted within me? Hope in God, for I shall praise Him again for the help of His presence. 7 My God, my soul despairs within me; I remember You from the land of the Jordan, from the peaks of Hermon, form Mount Mizar. 8 Depth calling depth are the sounds of Your waterfalls; all of your breakers and waves have gone over me. 9 The Lord will command His lovingkindness by day, His song will be with me by night, a prayer to the God of my life. 10 I will say to God, my rock, why have You forgotten me? Why am I mourning, oppressed by the enemy? 11 The taunts of my adversaries slaughter my bones, when all day they say to me, where is your Lord? 12 Why do you despair, my soul? Why are you disturbed within me? Hope in God, for I shall yet thank Him, for He is my deliverance, the light of my countenance, and my God.

This poem is a continuation of the preceding one. The psalmist entreats God to relieve his plight and bring him home from exile, so that he can give thanksgiving to God in His holy temple.

43 Vindicate me, O God, and plead my cause, against a nation without kindness. Protect me from the deceitful and unjust man. 2 For You are the God of my strength. Why have You forsaken me? Why do I mourn, oppressed by my enemy? 3 Send Your light and Your truth; let them lead me, let them bring me to Your holy mountain sanctuary, and to Your dwelling place. 4 Then I will come to the altar of the God, to the Almighty, in my exceeding joy; I will praise You upon the harp, O God, my God. 5 Why are you in despair, my soul? Why are you disquieted within me? Hope in God, for I will yet thank Him, my savior, the light of my countenance, and my God.

This prayer is a supplication as well as a complaint to God about the dire straits of the people of Israel. Foreign powers rule Israel, defame and besiege its people. The psalmist recounts the golden eras of Israel, when God was our redeemer, always with us. Israel was ascendant then, not because of its own strength, but because it was God's will. Even if Israel now has sinned, punishment meted out by foreign powers is unjust, as Israel is made to suffer specifically because we remain close to God.

44 To the chief musician, a contemplation of the sons of Korach. 2 We have heard with our ears, O God. Our fathers have told us of the deeds You did in their day, in days of old. 3 You, with Your hand, drove out nations, then You planted them. You afflicted nations and drove them away. 4 For not by their own swords did they inherit the land; their own arms did not deliver them. It was Your right hand and Your arm and the light of Your countenance, because You favored them. 5 You are my King, O God. Command victories for Jacob. 6 Through You we will gore our adversaries; through Your name we will trample those who rise up against us. 7 For I do not put trust in my bow; nor shall my sword save me. 8 But You have delivered us from our adversaries and have put to shame those who hate us. 9 In God we glory, all day long, and praise Your name forever, Selah, 10 Even though You have rejected and disgraced us, and have not accompanied our armies. 11 You made us retreat from our adversaries; those who hate us have taken spoils for themselves. 12 You gave us up like sheep to be eaten, and have scattered us among the nations. 13 You sold Your people cheaply; You did not set their value high. 14 You humiliated us to our neighbors, made us scorned, a derision to those around us. 15 You made an example of us among nations, a cause for nations to shake their heads. 16 All day long my dishonor is before me; the shame of my face has covered me 17 Because of sounds of reproach and blasphemy, in the presence of enemies and avengers. 18 All this has befallen us, but we have not forgotten You; we have not dealt falsely with Your covenant. 19 Our hearts have not turned back; our steps have not deviated from Your way. 20 Yet You have crushed us in a place of reptiles, and covered us with the shadow of death. 21 Have we forgotten the name of our God, or reached out our hands to a strange god? 22 Would God not know? He knows the secrets of the heart. 23 It is for Your sake we are killed all day long; we are taken like sheep to the slaughter. 24 Arise, why do You sleep, O Lord? Awake, do not reject us forever. 25 Why do You hide Your face, and forget our affliction and our oppression? 26 Our soul has sunk down into the dust; our body cleaves to the earth. 27 Arise, help us, redeem us for Your mercies' sake.

This is a wedding song, really a song to honor the groom, who is like a great king about to be married. The song speaks of the wedding of a king, but its exalted descriptions and praise pertain to every groom, each of whom is like a king on his wedding day.

45 For the chief musician, on Shoshanim, a contemplation of the sons of Korach, a song of love. 2 My heart overflows with good words; I address my verses to the king. My tongue is the pen of a dexterous writer. 3 You are fairer than sons of men; grace pours from your lips; God has blessed you forever. 4 Gird your sword to your thigh, mighty one, in splendor and majesty. 5 Ride victoriously in majesty for the cause of truth, humility, and righteousness. Let your right hand teach you awe. 6 Your arrows are sharp; people fall under you; your arrows reach the hearts of the king's enemies. 7 Your lordly reign will last forever; the scepter of righteousness is the scepter of your kingdom. 8 You love righteousness and hate wickedness. Because of this,

God, your God, has anointed you with the oil of joy, placed you above your fellows. 9 All your garments are like myrrh, aloes, and cassia from ivory palaces, to make you glad. 10 The daughters of kings are among your honored friends; at your right hand stands the queen, in gold from Ophir. 11 Listen, O daughter, and pay attention; incline your ear. Forget your people and your father's house 12 So the king will desire your beauty. He is your master, bow to him. 13 The daughter of Tyre will come with gifts; the rich among the people will seek your favor. 14 The princess within is all honor, her dress interwoven with gold. 15 In embroidered clothing she will be led to the king; her virgin companions will follow her, escorting her to you. 16 They will be led forth with gladness and rejoicing to enter the palace of the king. 17 In place of your fathers shall be your sons; you will make them princes all over the earth. 18 Your name will be remembered from generation to generation; nations will praise you forever.

This poem praises God, thanking Him for deliverance, after victory in a war that was almost lost; God's intervention changed the course of events. Terror and devastation ended; peace and tranquility were restored.

46 For the chief musician, of the sons of Korach, a song on Alamot. 2 God is our refuge and our strength, very present help in times of trouble. 3 Therefore we will not fear, though the earth change, though mountains slip into the heart of the sea. 4 Though waters roar and foam, though mountains quake before His glory, Selah. 5 There is a river whose streams gladden the city of the God, the holy dwelling place of the Most High. 6 God is in her midst; she shall not be moved; God shall help her at the break of day. 7 Nations raged, kingdoms tottered; He raised His voice and the earth melted. 8 The Lord of hosts is with us; the God of Jacob is our stronghold, Selah. 9 Come behold the works of the Lord, Who has made desolations on the earth. 10 He causes wars to cease throughout the earth; He breaks bows and cuts spears in two; He will burn chariots in fire. 11 "Desist, and know that I am God; I will be exalted among nations, I will be exalted on earth." 12 The Lord of hosts is with us; the God of Jacob is our stronghold, Selah.

This is a short hymn extolling God's revelation. More specifically, it is a poem proclaiming His kingship over the whole world. Nations gather to proclaim and praise God's sovereignty; they are accompanied by musical instruments and the blasts of rams' horns. All of mankind participate in the celebration and in singing God's praise. (It is for this reason that Psalm 47 is recited on Rosh Hashana, the New Year.)

47 For the chief musician, a psalm of the sons of Korach. 2 All people, clap your hands; shout to God with the voice of joy. 3 For the Lord most high is awesome, a great King over all the earth. 4 He subdues peoples under us; nations are at our feet. 5 He chose our inheritance, the pride of Jacob, whom He loves, Selah. 6 God has ascended with a blast, the Lord, with the sound of a shofar. 7 Sing praises to the God, sing praises. Sing praises to our King, sing praises. 8 For God is King of all the earth; sing praises, composed with skill. 9 God reigns over all nations; God sits on His holy throne. 10 Princes of peoples have assembled with the people of the God of Abraham. The shields of the earth belong to the Almighty; He is greatly exalted.

This is a song about the glory of the city of Jerusalem. The psalmist praises Jerusalem's exalted status. It is recited by pilgrims who visit the city and exult in her glory, as they see the beauty, holiness, and greatness of everything within.

48 A song, a psalm of the sons of Korach. 2 The Lord is great and greatly to be praised in the city of our God, on His holy mountain. 3 Beautiful in its views, a joy of the whole earth, with Mount Zion in the high north, it is the city of the great King. 4 God is in her palaces; He is known as a stronghold. 5 Behold, kings assembled, and passed there together. 6 They saw it and were amazed; they were terrified, they fled in alarm. 7 Panic seized them there; they were as anguished as a woman giving birth. 8 You can break the ships of Tarshish with the east wind. 9 As we had heard, so we have seen, in the city of the Lord of hosts, in the city of our God; may God establish it forever, Selah. 10 We have meditated on Your lovingkindness in the midst of Your sanctuary. 11 Like Your name, O God, praise of You extends to the end of the earth; Your right hand is full of righteousness. 12 Let Mount Zion be glad; let daughters of Judah rejoice because of Your judgments. 13 Rally around Zion and encircle her; count her towers. 14 Consider her ramparts; go through her palaces, so you may recount, to the last generation, 15 That God is our God, forever and ever. He will guide us beyond death.

This hymn about death teaches that everything that happens to a man in this life – failure or success – disappears and ends with death. Death is the great equalizer. It doesn't differentiate between old, young, smart, or foolish; there is no escape from it. The only thing that provides hope, not only in this world, but also for an existence after death, is devotion to God. One should learn about devotion to God, and occupy oneself with this alone.

49 For the chief musician, a psalm of the sons of Korach. 2 Hear this, all people; listen, inhabitants of a decaying world. 3 Sons of Adam, all sons of men, rich and poor together. 4 My mouth shall speak wisdom, the meditation of my heart, understanding. 5 I shall incline my ear to a parable; I shall open the question to the accompaniment of a harp. 6 Why should I fear in days of adversity, when the evil I have trod on surrounds me? 7 Those who trust in their wealth take great pride in their riches. 8 A man cannot redeem his brother nor give God a ransom for him. 9 The redemption of his soul is too costly; it shall cease to be forever. 10 Can man live forever? Can he not undergo decay? 11 He sees that wise men die; the foolish and the senseless alike, perish and leave their wealth to others. 12 Their inner thought is that their houses will last forever, their dwelling places for all generations; they call lands after their own names. 13 But man in his pomp will not endure; he is likened to silenced beasts. 14 This is the way of the foolish, and of followers who agree with their speech, Selah. 15 Like sheep, they are destined for the grave; death shall be their shepherd; the upright shall rule over them in the morning. Their form will be consumed in the grave, far from their dwelling. 16 But God will redeem my soul from the power of the grave; He shall take me in, Selah. 17 Do not fear a man who becomes rich, when the glory of his house is increased. 18 For when he dies he shall take nothing with him; his glory shall not descend after him. 19 Though while alive, he blesses his soul, as you are praised when fortunate, 20 He shall go to generations of his fathers who preceded him, and never see the light. 21 Man, with all his pomp, does not understand that he is likened to silenced beasts.

This poem explains our relationship to sacrifice, and teaches that God does not need sacrifices. Man is granted the privilege of bringing a sacrifice to God, as a way to show gratitude or to fulfill a vow. Having said this, the psalmist stresses that the only recourse for someone who has behaved badly, either in speech or deed, is to repent. Only after repentance is a sacrifice to God accepted.

50 A psalm of Asaph. The Almighty God the Lord has spoken and called to the earth, from the rising of the sun to its setting. 2 Out of Zion, the perfection of beauty, God shines forth. 3 God shall come and shall not keep silent. Fire consumes before Him, it surrounds Him with fury. 4 He summons the heavens above, and earth, to judge His people. 5 "Gather my devoted ones to Me, those who have made a covenant with Me by sacrifice." 6 The heavens declare His righteousness, for God Himself is judge, Selah. 7 "Hear, my people, and I will speak, O Israel, I will testify against you. I am God, your God. 8 I do not rebuke you for your sacrifices, or your burnt offerings which are continually before Me. 9 I will not take a young bull from your house, or a male goat from your corral. 10 For every beast of the forest is Mine, as are the cattle on a thousand hills. 11 I know every bird of the mountains, and everything that moves in the field is Mine. 12 If I were hungry, I would not tell you, for the world and all it contains is Mine. 13 Shall I eat the flesh of bulls or drink the blood of male goats? 14 Offer God a sacrifice of thanksgiving, and pay your vows to the Most High. 15 Call on Me in the day of trouble; I will rescue you and you will honor Me." 16 But to the wicked, the Lord says, "What right have you to speak of My statutes and to have words of My covenant on your lips? 17 For you hate discipline, and you cast My words behind you. 18 When you see a thief, you are pleased with him; you associate with adulterers. 19 You lips are loose with evil, and your tongue frames deceit. 20 You sit and speak against your brother; you slander your own mother's son. 21 You have done these things and I kept silent; did you think I was like you? I will reprove you and set things straight in your eyes. 22 Now consider this, you who have forgotten God, lest I will tear you to pieces, and there will be no one to rescue you. 23 He whose offering is one of thanksgiving honors Me, and prepares the way. I will show him the salvation of God."

This song of confession is also a request for forgiveness. The sinner acknowledges his transgression, admits his guilt, and prays for God's forgiveness and for the privilege of having a pure soul. He beseeches God to restore the lovingkindness God showed him prior to his sin. He promises to do penance and to help others, by making his repentance a model for theirs.

51 For the chief musician, a psalm by David 2 When Nathan the prophet came to him after he had been with Batsheva. 3 Be gracious to me, O God; show lovingkindness, in accordance with the greatness of Your compassion; blot out my transgressions. 4 Cleanse me thoroughly from my iniquity, and wash away my sin. 5 I know my transgressions; my sin is always before me. 6 Against You alone I have sinned; I have done that which is evil in Your eyes. You are justified when You speak, and blameless in Your verdict. 7 I was formed in iniquity; in sin my mother conceived me. 8 You desire innermost truth; with hiddenness You have shown me wisdom. 9 Purify me with hyssop and I will be clean; wash me so I will be whiter than snow. 10 Make me hear joy and gladness; let the bones which You have broken, rejoice. 11 Hide Your face from my sins, and blot out all of my iniquities. 12 Create a clean heart within me, O God, and renew a steadfast spirit within me. 13 Do not cast me away from Your presence, and do not take Your holy spirit from me. 14 Restore the joy of Your salvation to me; sustain me with a willing spirit. 15 I will teach Your ways to transgressors; sinners will return to You. 16 Save me from bloodshed, O God, God of my salvation; my tongue will joyfully sing of Your righteousness. 17 O Lord, open my lips so my mouth may declare Your praise. 18 For You do not delight in sacrifice, otherwise I would give it. You are not pleased with a burnt offering. 19 A sacrifice to God is a broken spirit; You will not despise a broken and contrite heart, O God. 20 By Your favor, be good to Zion; rebuild the walls of Jerusalem. 21 Then You will delight in righteous sacrifices, in burnt offerings and whole burnt offerings; then young bulls will be offered on Your altar.

This is a prayer against liars and informers. There are times when it seems that deceivers are close to achieving their goals and carrying out their deception. In the end, the lie and its inventor are exposed and lose power; the honest man benefits from God's protection, tranquility, and security.

52 For the chief musician, an instruction of David 2 When Doeg the Edomite came and told Saul that David had come to the house of Achimelech. 3 Why do you boast of evil, mighty man; the lovingkindness of God endures all day long. 4 Worker of deceit, your tongue plans destruction, and is as sharp as a razor. 5 You love evil more than good, falsehood more than honest speech, Selah. 6 You love all devouring words and tongues of deceit. 7 But the Almighty will break you down forever; He will snatch you up and tear you away from your tent, and uproot you from the land of the living, Selah. 8 And the righteous will see and fear, and will laugh, saying 9 Behold the man who would not make God his refuge, but instead trusted in the abundance of his riches, and was haughty in his wickedness. 10 But as for me, I am like a green olive tree in the house of God; I trust in the lovingkindness of God forever and ever. 11 I will give thanks to You forever, for what You have done, and I will place my hope in Your name, for You are good to your devoted ones.

This contemplative song about the evils of this world, proposes that iniquity stems from a lack of faith in God, Who is protective of the world. It is self-delusion to believe that the world has been abandoned to the powerful and amoral. God watches over and guards His world, and punishes the wicked.

53 For the chief musician, on the Mahalath, an instruction of David. 2 The fool has said in his heart, there is no God. They are corrupt, and have committed abominable injustices; there is no one who does good. 3 God looks down from heaven on the sons of men, to see if there is anyone with understanding, who seeks God. 4 Every one of them has turned aside; together they have become corrupt; there is no one who does good, not even one. 5 Do the workers of iniquity have no knowledge? They who eat up my people like they eat bread, they who have not called upon God 6 They were there in great fear, a fear like no other, for God scattered the bones of those who encamped against you. You put them to shame because God despised them. 7 O, that salvation of Israel would come out of Zion. When God restores His captive people, let Jacob rejoice, let Israel be glad.

This prayer against the wicked is an expression of trust in God. The psalmist believes that God will save him from the hands of enemies who are out to destroy him, and that God will punish them as they deserve to be punished.

54 For the chief musician on stringed instruments, an instruction, a psalm by David 2 When the Ziphites came and said to Saul, behold, David is hiding himself among us. 3 O God, by Your name, save me, and vindicate me by Your power. 4 O God, hear my prayer; listen to the words of my mouth. 5 For strangers have risen against me, and violent men have sought my life; they have not placed God before them, Selah. 6 Behold, God is my helper; the Lord sustains my soul. 7 He will repay evil to my foes; in faithfulness, You will destroy them. 8 Willingly I will sacrifice to You; I will give thanks to Your name, O Lord, for it is good. 9 For He has delivered me from all troubles. I have prevailed, and my eyes have looked upon my enemies.

This prayer is by a man who is surrounded by enemies, some of whom are former friends who have betrayed him. All he has left is the faith that he may be worthy of God's help. God alone has the power to punish the traitors and deceivers.

55 For the chief musician on stringed instruments, an instruction by David. 2 Listen to my prayer, O God; do not hide Yourself from my supplication. 3 Heed me and answer me; I am restless with complaint and agitation 4 Because of the voice of the enemy, because of the oppression of the wicked, for they bring down trouble upon me, and in wrath they hate me. 5 My heart is in anguish within me; terrors of death have descended upon me. 6 Fear and trembling come upon me, and horror has overwhelmed me. 7 I said, O that I may have wings of a dove, I would fly away and be at rest. 8 I would wander far away to live in the wilderness, Selah. 9 I would hurry to my place of refuge from the stormy wind and tempest. 10 Confuse them, O Lord, divide their tongues, for I have seen violence and strife in the city. 11 Day and night they go around her on her walls; iniquity and mischief are in her midst. 12 Destruction is in her midst; oppression and deceit do not depart from her streets. 13 For it is not an enemy who reproaches me; then I could bear it. Nor is it one who hates me who has exalted himself against me; then I could hide myself from him. 14 But it is you, a man, my equal, my companion and familiar friend. 15 We had sweet fellowship together; we walked in throngs to the house of God. 16 Let death come upon them with deceit; let them go down to living hell; evil is in their dwelling, in their midst. 17 As for me, I will call upon God; the Lord will save me. 18 Evening and morning, and at noontime, I will pray and cry aloud, and He will hear my voice. 19 He will redeem my soul in peace from my battle ahead; many are on my side. 20 God will hear and answer them. He abides from days of old, Selah. They will not change, they do not fear the Lord 21 Those who raised arms against friends, violated his covenant. 22 His speech was smoother than butter, but his heart was at war. His words were softer than oil, yet they were drawn swords. 23 Cast your burden upon the Lord, and He shall sustain you; He will never allow the righteous to be shaken. 24 You, O God, will bring them down to the pit of destruction. Men of bloodshed and deceit will not live out half their days, but I will trust in You.

This song begins with the prayer that God rescue the psalmist from the hands of surrounding enemies, but it is essentially a song about belief in God. One who trusts in God does not fear adversity or danger.

56 For the chief musician, on the silent and distanced dove; an instruction by David, when the Philistines seized him in Gath. 2 Be gracious to me O God, for man has trampled on me; fighting all day, he oppresses me. 3 My foes have trampled on me all day long; many fight proudly against me. 4 When I am afraid, I will put my trust in You. 5 In God whose words I praise, in God I have put my trust. I will not be afraid; what can man do to me? 6 All day long they distort my words; all their thoughts are against me and evil. 7 They attack, they lurk, they watch my steps as they wait to take my life. 8 Cast them out because of their wickedness. In anger, cast down the nations, O God. 9 You have counted my wanderings. Put my tears in Your bottle; have You counted them? 10 Then my enemies will turn back, on the day I call. This I know, that God is with me. 11 God's words I praise; the Lord's words I praise. 12 In God I have put my trust; I will not be afraid; what can man do to me? 13 The vows I have made to You are binding; I will render thanksgiving offerings to You. 14 For You have delivered my soul from death, my feet from stumbling, so that I may walk before God in the light of the living.

The psalmist, in dire straits, turns to God in prayer. Despite the fact that he is surrounded by foes, he has complete faith that God will come to his aid and destroy his enemies. He expresses gratitude to God for help he believes will be imminent.

57 For the chief musician, do not destroy, an instruction of David, when he fled from Saul to the cave. 2 Be merciful to me O God, be merciful to me, for my soul takes refuge in You. And in the shadow of Your wings I will take refuge, until destruction passes by. 3 I will cry out to God most high, to God who accomplishes all things for me. 4 He shall send from heaven and save me; He reproaches those who trample on me, Selah. God will send forth His mercy and His truth. 5 My soul is among lions; I must lie among those who breathe fire, among sons of men whose teeth are spears and arrows and tongues a sharp sword. 6 Be exalted above the heavens, O God; let Your glory be above all the earth. 7 They have prepared a net for my steps; my soul is bowed down. They dug a pit before me; they have fallen into it, Selah. 8 My heart is steadfast, O God, my heart is steadfast. I will sing, yes, I will sing praises. 9 Awaken, my glory! Awaken, harp and lyre. I will wake the dawn. 10 I will give thanks to you, O Lord, among the people; I will sing Your praises to the nations. 11 For Your mercy reaches unto the heavens; Your truth spans all the clouds. 12 Be exalted above the heavens, O God; let Your glory be above all the earth.

This prayer is against wicked people, who are filled with evil thoughts. The psalmist beseeches God to destroy evil and wipe it out completely, so there will be no trace of it left in this world.

58 For the chief musician, do not destroy, an instruction of David. 2 Do you speak with righteousness, or indeed, do you remain mute when you should judge sons of man honestly? 3 No, your heart carries out wrongful deeds in the land; you measure the violence wrought by your hands. 4 The wicked go astray from the womb; deceivers are estranged from birth. 5 They have venom like the venom of a serpent, like a deaf cobra that will not hear. 6 It does not hear the voice of charmers, skillful casters of spells. 7 O God, shatter their teeth in their mouths; break the fangs of the young lions, O Lord. 8 Let them melt away like the runoff of water; when He aims His arrows let them be cut down. 9 Let them be like snails that melt away as they go along, like a stillborn that has never seen the sun. 10 Before your shoots understand that they can be thorns, He will sweep them away with His living wrath, like a whirlwind. 11 The righteous will rejoice to see vengeance; he will wash his feet in the blood of the wicked. 12 And man will say, surely there is a reward for the righteous; surely there is a God who judges on earth.

The psalmist begins this psalm with a prayer to God to rescue him from adversaries who are out to destroy him, despite his innocence. He continues by expressing faith that God will not let his enemies overcome him. He believes that after his adversaries fall, they will acknowledge their transgressions. The psalmist will then be able to thank God with a full heart.

59 For the chief musician, do not destroy; an instruction of David, when Saul sent men and they watched the house in order to kill him. 2 Deliver me from my enemies, O my God. Make me secure, high above those who rise up against me. 3 Deliver me from the workers of iniquity; save me from men of bloodshed. 4 Behold, they have set an ambush for my life. Fierce men launch an attack against me, not because I have transgressed or sinned, O Lord. 5 They run to set themselves against me, through no fault of mine. 6 And You, O Lord, God of hosts, God of Israel, awaken and punish all the nations. Do not be merciful to any wicked transgressors, Selah. 7 Toward evening they return to howl like a dog, and surround the city. 8 See how they bark with their mouths, swords for their lips, saying, who hears? 9 But You, O Lord, laugh at them; You scoff at all the nations. 10 I will wait for You; Your strength, my God, sustains me. 11 My God of lovingkindness will precede me; God will let me look upon my foes. 12 Do not slay them, as my people will forget; scatter them by Your power and bring them down, O Lord, our shield. 13 Because of the sin of their mouths, the words of their lips, the curses and lies that they utter, let them be caught in their pride. 14 Destroy them in wrath; destroy them that they may be no more, that men may know that God rules in Jacob, to the ends of the earth, Selah. 15 And they return toward evening to howl like a dog, and surround the city. 16 They wander about for food and growl if they are not satisfied. 17 But as for me, I will sing of your strength. Yes, I shall joyfully sing of Your lovingkindness in the morning, for You have been my stronghold, and a refuge in the day of my distress. 18 My strength comes from You; I will sing praises to You; for God is my defense, my God of mercy.

This is a poem of thanksgiving for a glorious victory. The song begins with a description of past hardship, times of failure, and downfall. The psalmist then proceeds to express gratitude for the brilliant victory over all of his surrounding enemies. He acknowledges that everything – the bad as well as the good – is meted out by the hand of God.

60 For the chief musician, on a rose of testimony, an instruction of David, to teach 2 When he struggled with Aram-naharaim and with Aram-zobah, and Joab returned, and smote twelve thousand of Edom in the Valley of Salt. 3 O God, You have rejected us. You have broken us. You have been angry with us. Restore us. 4 You have made the land quake, You have split it open; heal its breaches, for it totters. 5 You have made Your people experience hardship; You have given us poison wine to drink. 6 You have tested those who fear You, so that the truth can become evident, Selah. 7 So that Your loved ones may be released, save us with Your right hand, answer us. 8 God has spoken in holiness, saying, I will exult, I will divide Shechem and measure out the valley of Succoth. 9 Gilead is mine, and

Menashe is mine; Ephraim is the stronghold of my head; Judah is my law-giver. 10 Moav is my washbowl; over Edom I will throw my shoe. Join forces with me, Philistia. 11 Who will bring me into the besieged city, who will lead me to Edom? 12 Have You, O God, rejected us? Will You not go forth with our armies, O God? 13 Give us help against the adversary, for deliverance by man is in vain. 14 Through God we will prevail valiantly; it is He who will tread down upon our adversaries.

In this poem of thanksgiving the psalmist expresses gratitude to God for shielding him and helping him in times of trouble. He feels secure and fortunate, sheltered under the protective wings of God.

61 For the chief musician, on a musical instrument, by David. 2 Hear my singing, O God, attend to my prayer. 3 From the end of the earth I will call to You, when my heart is overwhelmed; lead me to a rock that is higher than I am. 4 For You have been a refuge to me, a tower of strength against the enemy. 5 Let me dwell in Your tent forever; let me take refuge in the shelter of Your wings, Selah. 6 For You, O God, have heard my vows; You have given me the heritage of those who fear Your name. 7 You will prolong the king's life, his years for many generations. 8 He will abide before the Lord forever. Make his portion kindness and truth, that they may preserve him. 9 Yes, I will sing praise to Your name forever, that I may pay my vows day by day.

In this contemplative poem, the psalmist compares the lives of the wicked, whose speech and deeds are evil, to the lives of those who are devoted to God. The comparison makes clear that, in the end, those who rely on their own powers and schemes succeed only fleetingly. Those who trust in God and have faith in Him remain connected to the eternal.

62 For the chief musician, on Yedutun, a psalm by David. 2 My soul waits in silence for God alone; my salvation is from Him. 3 Only He is my rock and my salvation, my stronghold; I will not be greatly shaken. 4 How long will you assail a man? You shall be slain, all of you, like a leaning wall and a tottering fence. 5 They have advised him only to thrust him down from his high position. They delight in falsehood. They bless with their mouth, but inwardly they curse, Selah. 6 My soul, wait in silence for God alone; my hope is from Him. 7 He alone is my rock and my salvation, my stronghold; I will not be shaken. 8 My salvation and my glory rest with God, rock of my strength; my refuge is in God. 9 Trust in Him at all times, O people. Pour out your heart before Him; God is a refuge for us, Selah. 10 Lowly sons of man are nothing, as are men of rank. On the scales they rise, lighter than breath. 11 Do not trust in oppression; do not vainly hope in robbery; if wealth increases, do not take it to heart. 12 Once God has spoken, I hear His words again. Power belongs to God. 13 Mercy is Yours, O Lord, for You render to every man according to his deeds.

This is a song of devotion to God. While in the desert, a place of deprivation and thirst, the psalmist describes a thirst that is greater than the thirst for water: a yearning for closeness to God. The ecstasy of achieving closeness to God brings the greatest possible gratification. Inevitably, one is confronted by obstacles on all sides, but it is their fate to be overcome. When one is devoted to God, great happiness is a consequence of that devotion.

63 A psalm by David, when he was in the wilderness of Judah. 2 O God, You are my Almighty, I will seek You earnestly; my soul thirsts for You, my flesh yearns for You in a dry and weary land where there is no water. 3 Yes, in the sanctuary I have seen You, seen Your power and Your glory. 4 For Your lovingkindness is better than life; my lips will praise You. 5 So I will bless You as long as I live; I will lift up my hands in Your name. 6 My soul will be as satisfied as with fat and marrow; my mouth offers praises with joyful lips. 7 As I remember You on my bed, I meditate on You in the night watches. 8 For You have been my help, and in the shadow of Your wings I sing for joy. 9 My soul clings to You; Your right hand supports me. 10 But those who seek to destroy my life will go into the depths of the earth. 11 They will be delivered to the power of the sword; they will be prey for foxes. 12 But the king will rejoice in God. Everyone who swears by Him will be glorified. The mouths of those who speak lies will be closed.

This is an entreaty to God. Hemmed in by overt and covert enemies who use every means available to cause harm, the psalmist pleads with God to protect him, and to destroy his foes.

64 For the chief musician, a psalm by David. 2 Hear my voice, O God, in my prayer; preserve my life from the terror of the enemy. 3 Hide me from the secret counsel of the wicked, from the gathering of workers of iniquity 4 Who whet their tongue like a sword, aim their arrows, bitter words 5 To shoot in secret at the innocent. Suddenly they shoot him, and do not fear. 6 They encourage themselves to do evil matters; they speak of laying hidden snares, and say, who will see them? 7 They seek out iniquities. Both the inward thought and the heart of man are deep. 8 But the Lord will shoot them with an arrow; suddenly they will be wounded. 9 They were made to fall upon themselves by their own tongues; all who see them shake their heads. 10 And all men feared and declared it the work of God;

---

they understood it to be His doing. 11 The righteous will rejoice in the Lord and trust in Him, and all the upright in heart shall glory.

This song glorifies God, Who forgives sinners and embraces the penitent; He imbues the world with goodness, tranquility, and abundant beneficence.

65 For the chief musician, a psalm by David, a song. 2 For You, O God, praise awaits in Zion; to You vows will be paid. 3 You who hear prayer, to You all men come. 4 Iniquities overwhelm me; You forgive our transgressions. 5 Fortunate is the one You choose to bring near to You, to dwell in Your sanctuary. We will be satisfied in the goodness of Your house, in Your holy temple. 6 By awesome deeds You answer us, in righteousness, O God of our salvation, You, who are the confidence of the ends of the earth and the farthest sea 7 Who establishes mountains by His strength, girded with might 8 Who stills the roaring of the seas, the roaring of their waves, and the tumult of the people. 9 They who dwell to the ends of the earth stand in awe of Your signs; You make the dawn and the sunset shout with joy. 10 You remember the earth and water it, enriching it greatly; the streams of God are full of water. You prepare the grain, for this You prepare the earth. 11 You water its furrows abundantly; You settle its ridges; You soften it with showers; You bless its growth. 12 You crown the year with your goodness and Your paths drip with abundance. 13 The pastures of the wilderness drip with abundance; the hills gird themselves with joyousness. 14 The meadows are covered with flocks of sheep; the valleys are wrapped in grain. They shout for joy, yes, they sing.

In this poem about the glory of God, the psalmist tells of God's revelation in general and specific terms. He cites the revelation at Sinai and the exodus from Egypt. He recounts triumphs and tribulations of the people of Israel throughout history. By acknowledging at the end that he is aware of the hand of God in his own life, the psalmist's prayer is personalized.

66 For the chief musician, a song, a psalm. All the earth, shout with joy to God. 2 Sing the glory of His name; make His praise glorious. 3 Say to God, how awesome are Your works. Because of Your great power Your enemies feign obedience to You. 4 The entire earth will bow down to You, will sing praises to You, will sing praises to Your name; Selah. 5 Come and see the works of God, awe-inspiring acts for the sons of men. 6 He turned the sea into dry land; they passed through the river on foot. There we shall rejoice in Him. 7 He rules the world with His might; His eyes keep watch on the nations. The rebellious should not exalt themselves, Selah. 8 Bless our God, O people, and sound His praise abroad. 9 He who gives life to our souls, and does not allow our feet to slip. 10 For You have tested us, O God; You have refined us as silver is refined. 11 You brought us into the net; You constrained our loins. 12 You made men ride over our heads. We went through fire and water, but You brought us out to abundance. 13 I will come to Your house with burnt offerings; I will pay You my vows 14 Which my lips uttered and my mouth spoke when I was in distress. 15 I will offer You the burnt offerings of fat animals, the burning of rams; I will offer bulls and male goats, Selah. 16 Come and hear, all who fear God, and I will tell of what He has done for my soul. 17 I called to Him with my mouth, and He was extolled with my tongue. 18 If I see wickedness in my heart, the Lord does not attend to it. 19 But God listens and attends to the sound of my prayer. 20 Blessed be God, who has not turned away my prayer, nor His mercy from me.

This song glorifies God, who rules with mercy that is manifest in the world; human beings are obligated to express gratitude.

67 For the chief musician, a psalm with instrumental music, a song. 2 God will favor us and bless us and shine His countenance upon us, Selah 3 So that Your way become known on earth, Your salvation within all nations. 4 Nations will thank God; all nations will praise You. 5 Let the people be glad and sing for joy, for You will judge all nations justly, and guide the people of the earth, Selah. 6 The nations will thank You, God; all the nations will thank You. 7 The earth has yielded its produce; God, our own God, shall bless us. 8 God shall bless us, and all will fear Him, to the ends of the earth.

This hymn of glory, about God's revelation at Mount Sinai, describes the unique and specific ways in which nations, individuals, and all of creation, animate and inanimate, experience the revelation and give honor to God.

68 For the chief musician, a psalm of David, a song. 2 Let God arise; let His enemies be scattered and let those who hate Him flee before Him. 3 Drive them away as smoke is driven away; as wax melts before the fire, let the wicked perish before God. 4 But let the righteous be glad; let them exult before God; yes, let them rejoice in gladness. 5 Sing to God; sing hymns to His name. Extol Him, He of the unfathomable name, who rides the heavens. Be joyous before Him. 6 A father of orphans and judge for widows is God in His holy dwelling. 7 God brings home the lonely, He leads prisoners to prosperity; only the rebellious dwell in a parched land. 8 O God, when You went forth before Your people, when You marched through the wilderness, Selah, 9 The earth quaked, the heavens dropped at the presence of God. Sinai itself quaked in the presence of God, the God of Israel. 10 You poured generous rain on Your land when it was weary; You established it solidly. 11 Your flock settled in it. In Your goodness You provided for the poor, O God. 12 My Master gives word, announced by His great hosts, and 13 Kings of armies flee, they flee, and she who remains steadfast at home distributes the spoils. 14 Though you lie within boundaries, wings of the dove are covered with silver, its pinions with burnished gold. 15 Shaddai scattered the kings like snowflakes in Tzalmon. 16 A mountain of God, is Mount Bashan; a mountain of peaks, Mount Bashan. 17 Why do you envy, mountains of peaks, the mount that God desired for His abode, as the Lord will surely dwell forever. 18 The chariots of God are myriad, thousands upon thousands. The Lord is with them, as with Sinai, in holiness. 19 You have ascended on high; You have captured the captive, You have received gifts among men. Even among rebels, the unfathomable God may dwell. 20 Blessed be my Master, day by day. Even as He burdens us, the Almighty delivers us, Selah. 21 The Almighty to us is the Almighty of deliverances; through the Lord, my Master, there are escapes from death. 22 Surely God will shatter the head of His enemies, the hairy crown of him who goes on with his guilty deeds. 23 My Master said, I will bring them back from Bashan, I will bring them back from the depths of the sea 24 So that your foot can wade in their blood, and the tongue of your dogs have a portion of your enemies. 25 They have seen Your sanctuary, O God, the procession of the Almighty, my King, in holiness. 26 First the singers, followed by musicians, in the midst of maidens playing tambourines. 27 Choruses, bless God, my Master, the fount of Israel. 28 There is Benjamin, the youngest, ruling them; the princes of Judah in the throng; the princes of Zevulun, the princes of Naphtali. 29 Your God has commanded your strength. Show Yourself strong, O God, for You have acted on our behalf. 30 To Your temple in Jerusalem, kings will bring gifts to You. 31 Rebuke the beasts in the reeds, the assembly of bulls among the calves of the nations, who trample for pieces of silver, and desire battles in foreign nations. 32 Noblemen will arrive from Egypt; Ethiopia will reach out to God. 33 Sing to God, kingdoms of the earth; sing praises to my Master, Selah. 34 To the rider upon the highest of ancient heavens, He who speaks with His voice, a mighty voice. 35 Ascribe strength to God; His majesty is over Israel, His strength in the distant skies. 36 Awesome is God. From Your sanctuary, the Almighty of Israel gives strength and power to the people. Blessed be God.

This is a poem of supplication and prayer, said by one who has chosen to live a life devoted exclusively to serving God. He is surrounded by people who hate him, specifically because of this devotion to God. The psalmist knows that he is imperfect, and that he, too, has sinned before God. Still, he prays for salvation, for the sake of his own life, and also for the honor of God, because the psalmist's life is seen as an example of consummate devotion to God.

69 For the chief musician, on Shoshanim, by David. 2 Rescue me, God, for the waters have reached up to my breath. 3 I am sinking in deep mire, and have no foothold. I am in deep waters, and a flood overflows me. 4 I am weary with my crying; my throat is parched. My eyes fail as I wait for my God. 5 Those who hate me without cause are more plentiful than the hairs on my head. Those who want to destroy me are plentiful, and are wrongfully my enemies. Mighty are the enemies who lie, and who want to cut me off. I must restore that which I did not steal. 6 O God, You know my folly; my wrongs are not hidden from You. 7 May those who wait for You not be ashamed through me, my Master, Lord of hosts. May those who seek You not be dishonored through me, God of Israel. 8 For Your sake I have borne reproach; disgrace has covered my face. 9 I have become estranged from my brothers, an alien to my mother's sons. 10 Zealotry for Your house has consumed me. Indignities toward You fall on me. 11 My soul cried and fasted without regard for my dignity. 12 When I made a sackcloth for my clothing, I became an example for them. 13 Those who sit at the gate talk about me; I am the song of the drunkards. 14 But as for me, my prayer to You, O Lord, is a time of favor. O God, in the greatness of Your mercy, answer me with the truth of Your deliverance. 15 Deliver me from the mire, and do not let me sink. May I be delivered from my foes and from the deep waters. 16 May the flood of water not flow over me, nor the deep swallow me up, nor the pit close its mouth over me. 17 Answer me, O Lord, for your lovingkindness is good. Turn to me with an abundance of Your compassion. 18 Do not hide Your face from Your servant, for I am in distress; answer me quickly. 19 Draw near to my soul and redeem it; ransom me from my enemies. 20 You know my disgrace and my shame and my dishonor; all my adversaries are before You. 21 Humiliation has broken my heart, and I am very sick; I hoped for sympathy but there was none; for consolers, but I found none. 22 They put poison in my food, and gave me vinegar to drink. 23 May their table turn into a snare before them; when they are at peace, may it become a trap. 24 May their eyes grow dim so that they cannot see; make their loins shake continuously. 25 Pour out Your wrath on them; let the fierceness of Your anger overtake them. 26 May their camp be desolate; may none dwell in their tents. 27 For they have pursued those whom You have smitten, and they tell of the pain of Your wounded. 28 Add iniquity to their iniquities, so they may not enjoy Your righteousness. 29 May they be blotted out of the book of life; may they not be recorded with the righteous. 30 But I am afflicted and in pain; may Your salvation, O God, strengthen me. 31 I will praise the name of God in song, and magnify Him with thanksgiving. 32 And it will please the Lord more than a bull with horns and hoofs. 33 The humble will see it and be glad; You who seek God, let your hearts be revived. 34 For the Lord hears the needy, and does not despise His prisoners. 35 Let heaven and earth, the seas and everything moving within, praise Him. 36 For God will save Zion and build the cities of Judah, and they will settle there and possess it. 37 The descendants of His servants will inherit it, and those who love His name will dwell in it.

This supplication is by a man surrounded by enemies who not only want to harm him, but also to celebrate his downfall. The psalmist understands that he can rely on God alone for kindness and redemption.

70 For the chief musician, a memorial, by David. 2 God save me; O Lord, hasten to help me. 3 Let those who seek my life be ashamed and humiliated; let those who delight in hurting me be turned back and dishonored. 4 Let those who say, aha, aha, be turned back in shame. 5 Let all who seek You rejoice and find joy in You; let those who love deliverance by You keep saying, let God be magnified. 6 But I am afflicted and needy; hurry to me, O God. You are my help and my rescuer; O Lord, do not delay.

This song of supplication is by an old man, who has lived a life of connectedness and devotion to God. At the end of his life, he finds himself surrounded by adversaries, who are convinced that he will never rise again. He pleads with God not to abandon him, and to give him the strength to regain his former stature.

71 In You, O Lord, I have taken refuge; let me never be ashamed. 2 Deliver me and rescue me in Your mercy; incline Your ear to me and rescue me. 3 Be a rock, a shelter for me to enter at all times. You have given commandments to save me; You are my rock and my fortress. 4 O God, rescue me from the hand of the wicked, from the grasp of the wrongdoer and ruthless man. 5 For You are my hope, my Master, O Lord, in whom I have trusted from my youth. 6 I have been sustained by You from birth; You brought me out of my mother's womb. My praise is continually of You. 7 I have been an example for many, and You are my mighty refuge. 8 My mouth is filled with praise for You, for Your glory, all day long. 9 Do not cast me off in the time of old age; do not forsake me when my strength fails. 10 For my enemies have spoken against me; those who keep watch on my soul have conspired together 11 Saying, God has forsaken him; pursue and seize him, for there is no one to rescue him. 12 O God, do not be distant from me; O God, hasten to help me. 13 Let those who are adversaries of my soul be ashamed and consumed; let those who seek to injure me be covered with reproach and dishonor. 14 But as for me, I will hope continually, and will praise You more and more. 15 My mouth will tell of Your righteousness and of Your salvation, all day long; I do not know their limits. 16 I will assert the mighty acts of my Master, the Lord; I will tell of Your righteousness, Yours alone. 17 O God, You have taught me from my youth, and I still declare Your wondrous deeds. 18 Until I am old and gray, O God, do not leave me; until I tell of Your strength to this generation and of Your power to all who are to come. 19 For Your righteousness, O God, reaches the heavens. You have done great things. O God, who is comparable to You? 20 You, who have shown me many troubles and distresses, will revive me again, and bring me up again from the depths of the earth. 21 May You increase my greatness and turn to comfort me. 22 I will praise You on a harp; I will sing praises of Your truth, O my God, on a lyre, O Holy One of Israel. 23 My lips, and my soul, which You have redeemed, will shout for joy when I sing praises to You. 24 My tongue will speak of Your righteousness all day long. Those who seek to harm me will be confounded and brought to shame.

This is a song of encouragement, hope, and blessing for the savior king. It describes an ideal kingdom of Israel, one in which king and country are in their glory. The kingdom is blessed internally and externally with economic abundance, peace, stability, and strength, and positioned to provide leadership to other nations.

72 A psalm for Solomon. Endow the king with Your justice, O God, Your righteousness for the king's son. 2 May he judge Your people with righteousness, and the poor with justice. 3 May the mountains bring peace to the people, and the hills, charity. 4 May he vindicate the afflicted of the people, save the children of the needy, and crush the oppressor. 5 Let them fear You as long as the sun and moon endure, throughout all generations. 6 May he descend like rain on mown grass, like showers that water the earth. 7 May the righteous flourish in his days; may peace be abundant until the moon is no more. 8 May he also rule from sea to sea, from the river to the ends of the earth. 9 Let the nomads of the desert bow before him; let his enemies lick the dust. 10 Let the kings of Tarshish and of the islands bring presents; the kings of Sheba and Seva offer gifts. 11 And let all kings bow down before him, all nations serve him. 12 For he will deliver the needy who cry for help, and the poor who have no one to help. 13 He will have compassion on the poor and needy, and he will save the lives of the needy. 14 He will rescue their lives from oppression and violence, and their blood will be precious in his sight. 15 So may he live. And may the gold of Sheba be given to him. Let them pray for him continually; let them bless him all day long. 16 May there be abundance of grain in the earth on top of the mountains. Its fruit will rustle like in Lebanon. May it blossom in the city like grass of the earth. 17 May his name endure forever. May his name be magnified as long as the sun shines. Let men bless themselves by him. Let all nations call him blessed. 18 Blessed be the Lord God, the God of Israel, who alone works wonders. 19 And blessed be His glorious name forever; may the whole earth be filled with His glory, Amen and amen. 20 The prayers of David, the son of Jesse, are ended.

In this poem of contemplation the psalmist sees evil on the rise. He sees the success of the wicked in the world, and finds it baffling and hurtful. With deeper understanding, it becomes clear to him that the rewards of the wicked are temporary and fleeting; devotion to God is an incentive in itself, capable of bringing immeasurable bliss.

73 A psalm by Asaph. Surely God is good to Israel, to those pure of heart. 2 But as for me, my feet came close to stumbling; my steps had almost slipped. 3 For I was jealous of the arrogant, and I saw the prosperity of the wicked. 4 For there is no suffering as they die, and their bodies are fat. 5 They are not as troubled as other men, nor are they plagued like mankind. 6 Therefore, pride is their necklace; a garment of violence covers them. 7 Their eye bulges from fatness; the imaginations of their heart run riot. 8 They mock, and speak wickedly of oppression; they speak from on high. 9 They have set their mouth against heaven; their tongue parades through the earth. 10 Therefore His people return here, to drink from abundant waters. 11 They say, how does God know, is there knowledge in the Most High? 12 Behold, these are the ungodly, always at ease in the great wealth they have attained. 13 Surely, in vain I have kept my heart pure, and washed my innocent hands. 14 For I have been stricken all day long, and chastened every morning. 15 If I had said, I will speak of this, I would have betrayed generations of Your children. 16 When I pondered to understand this, it was troublesome in my sight. 17 Until I came into the sanctuary of the Lord; then I perceived their end. 18 Surely You have set them on slippery slopes; You cast them down to destruction. 19 How they are destroyed in a moment, utterly swept away by sudden terrors. 20 Like a waking dream; O Lord, when You are aroused, their image will be despised in the city. 21 When my heart was bitter, and I was pierced within. 22 I was senseless and ignorant; I was like a beast before You. 23 Yet I am continually with You; You have held my right hand. 24 You will guide me with Your counsel, and afterward receive me in glory. 25 Who have I in heaven but You? I desire nothing on earth. 26 My flesh and my heart may fail, but God is the strength of my heart and my portion forever. 27 See that those who are distant from you will perish; You destroy all who are unfaithful to You. 28 But for me, nearness to God is good; I have put my trust in the Lord God, so I may tell of all Your works.

This supplication, by the people of Israel, is for hard times when they are overwhelmed by enemies. It is a prayer for God's redemption and for miracles, like those performed by Him for Israel in olden days. When Israel is redeemed, God is honored, as its people have a covenant with God; His name is a part of them.

74 An instruction by Asaph. O God, why have You rejected us forever? Why does Your anger against the sheep of Your pasture continue to smolder? 2 Remember Your congregation, which You acquired of old, which You redeemed to be the tribe of Your inheritance. And remember Mount Zion, where You have dwelt. 3 Turn Your footsteps toward the perpetual ruins; the enemy has damaged everything within the sanctuary. 4 Your adversaries roared within Your meeting place, and have set up their own standards as signs. 5 It looks as if one lifted his axe in a forest of trees. 6 Now all of its carved work they smash with hatchet and hammers. 7 They have burned Your sanctuary to the ground; they have defiled the dwelling place of Your name. 8 They said in their heart, let us completely subdue them. They have burned all the meeting places of God in the land. 9 We cannot see our signs; there is no longer any prophet. Nor is there any among us who knows for how long. 10 How long, O God, will the adversary revile; will the enemy spurn Your name forever? 11 Why do You withdraw Your hand, Your right hand within Your bosom? Destroy them. 12 God is my King, who performs acts of deliverance on earth, from times of old. 13 You divided the sea with Your strength; You broke the heads of sea monsters within the waters. 14 You crushed the heads of Leviathan; You fed him to creatures of the wilderness. 15 You broke open springs and torrents, dried up ever-flowing streams. 16 The day is Yours, and Yours is the night. You prepared light and the sun. 17 You established all the boundaries on earth; You made summer and winter. 18 Remember this, O Lord, that the enemy, a foolish people, has reviled and spurned Your name. 19 Do not deliver the soul of Your turtledove to the wild beast. Do not forget the lives of Your afflicted, forever. 20 Consider the covenant. The dark places of the land are full of habitations of violence. 21 Do not let the oppressed return dishonored. Let the afflicted and needy praise Your name. 22 Arise, O God, and plead Your own cause. Remember how the foolish man reproaches you all day long. 23 Do not forget the voice of your adversaries, the continuous ascending uproar of those who rise against You.

This is poem of thanksgiving for the defeat of the wicked. Even though it appeared initially that evil would triumph, it did not. The Judge of the earth avenges, and in the end, evil is punished as it deserves to be punished, with inevitable downfall.

75 For the chief musician, do not destroy, a psalm by Asaph, a song. 2 We give thanks to You, O God, we give thanks, for Your wondrous works declare that Your name is near. 3 At the appointed time, it is I who will judge with equity. 4 When the earth and all who dwell within melt, it is I who firmly set its pillars, Selah. 5 I said to the boastful, do not boast, and to the wicked, do not flaunt your grants. 6 Do not lift high that which has been granted to you; do not speak with insolent pride. 7 For exaltation does not come from the east or from the west or from the desert. 8 But God is the judge; He humbles this one and raises up that one. 9 For the cup is in the hand of God; He mixes it well and pours out of it. The wicked of the earth will drain and drink only of its dregs. 10 But as for me, I will declare forever, sing praises to the God of Jacob. 11 All of the grants of the wicked will be cut off, and the grants of the righteous will be made greater.

This is a poem of thanksgiving for victory over enemies. Israel is besieged, at war, surrounded. God reveals His infinite power by completely destroying Israel's foes, within sight of the people of Israel, who seize the opportunity to give thanks to Him.

76 For the chief musician, on stringed instruments, a psalm of Asaph, a song. 2 God is known in Judah; His name is great in Israel. 3 His tabernacle is in Salem; His dwelling place is in Zion. 4 There He broke the flaming arrows, the shield and the sword and the weapons of war, Selah. 5 You are resplendent, and mightier than terrifying mountains. 6 The stout-hearted were stupefied, they sank into sleep; soldiers could not use their hands. 7 At Your rebuke, O God of Jacob, both chariot and horse were cast into a deep sleep. 8 You, You are to be feared. Who may stand in Your presence once You are angry? 9 You caused Your sentence to be heard from the heavens; the earth feared and was still 10 When the Lord arose in judgment, to save all of the humble of the earth, Selah. 11 For wrathful man will come to praise You, and You will restrain the residue of Your wrath. 12 Make vows to God the Lord and fulfill them; let all who are around Him bring gifts to Him, the One to be feared. 13 He can cut down the spirit of princes; He is feared by the kings of the earth.

This contemplative song recounts Israel's miraculous exodus from Egypt and subsequent exceptional journey. It serves as a source of reassurance and inspiration during difficult present times.

77 For the chief musician, for Yedutun, a psalm by Asaph. 2 I will lift my voice to God and cry and He will listen to me. 3 In the day of my trouble I sought the Lord; in the night my hand was stretched out without getting weary, but my soul refused to be comforted. 4 When I remember God, I moan; I pray and my spirit is faint, Selah. 5 You have kept my eyelids open; I am so troubled I cannot speak. 6 I pondered the days of old, the years of ancient times. 7 I shall remember my song in the night; I shall meditate with my heart. My spirit ponders. 8 Will my Master reject forever? Will He never find favor in me again? 9 Has His mercy ceased forever? Has His promise come to an end, for generations to come? 10 Has He forgotten to be gracious, or has He withdrawn His compassion in anger? Selah. 11 Then I said, it is to frighten me that the right hand of the Most High has changed. 12 I will remember the deeds of the unfathomable Lord; I will remember Your ancient wonders. 13 I will meditate on all of Your work and muse on Your deeds. 14 Your path, O God, is holy; what power is great as God? 15 You are the Almighty who works wonders; You have made Your strength known among the people. 16 By Your power, You have redeemed Your people, the sons of Jacob and Joseph, Selah. 17 The waters saw you, O God; the waters saw You and were in anguish; the deep also trembled. 18 The clouds poured out water, the skies rumbled with noise, Your arrows flashed here and there. 19 The sound of Your thunder was in a whirlwind; the lightening lit up the world; the earth trembled and shook. 20 Your way was in the sea; Your paths in the mighty waters, though Your footprints were not to be known. 21 You led Your people like a flock of sheep, by the hands of Moses and Aaron.

This hymn recounting the history of Israel starts with the ten plagues and the exodus from Egypt (the beginning of the redemption), continues through Israel's desert wandering and conquest of the land of Israel, and ends with the monarchy of King David. Despite the sins of the people of Israel, which this hymn does not attempt to conceal, God protects Israel from harm, forgives its transgressions, and ultimately grants it tranquility and greatness.

78 An instruction by Asaph. Listen, my people, to my laws. Lend an ear to the instruction of my mouth. 2 I will open my mouth with an example; I will utter riddles from ancient times. 3 That which we have heard and known, that which our fathers have taught us 4 We will not conceal from the children. Tell the generation to come the praises of the Lord, of His might and of the wonders that He has done. 5 He established a testimony in Jacob and appointed law in Israel, which He commanded our fathers to teach to their children. 6 So generations, even of children not yet born, would come to know, so they might rise and tell their own children 7 That they should put their confidence in God and not forget the works of God, but keep His commandments, 8 Not like their fathers, a stubborn and rebellious generation that did not prepare its heart and whose spirit was not faithful to the Almighty. 9 The sons of Ephraim were archers equipped with bows, yet they turned back in the day of battle. 10 They did not keep the covenant of God, and refused to walk in His law. 11 They forgot His deeds and the miracles that He had shown them. 12 He wrought wonders before their fathers in the land of Egypt, in the field of Zoan. 13 He divided the sea and allowed them to pass through; He made the waters stand up like a heap. 14 Then He led them with a cloud by day, and all night with a light of fire. 15 He split the rocks in the wilderness, and gave them drink, abundant like the depths of the ocean. 16 He also brought forth streams from the rock and caused waters to run down like rivers. 17 Yet they still continued to sin against Him, to rebel against the Most High, in the desert. 18 In their hearts they put the Almighty to the test by asking for foods they desired. 19 Then they spoke against God, saying, can the Almighty prepare a table in the wilderness? 20 Behold, He struck the rock so that waters gushed out, and streams were overflowing. Can He provide bread also? Will He provide meat for His people? 21 The Lord was enraged because He heard this, and a fire was kindled against Jacob, and anger also mounted against Israel 22 Because they did not believe in God, and did not trust in His deliverance. 23 Still, He commanded the clouds above and opened the doors of heaven. 24 He rained down manna upon them to eat, and gave them food from heaven. 25 Man ate the bread of angels; He sent them provisions in abundance. 26 He caused the east wind to blow in the heavens, and by His power he directed the south wind. 27 He rained meat upon them like the dust, winged fowl like the sand by the seas. 28 He let it fall in the midst of their camp, round about their dwellings. 29 So they ate and were filled; He gave them their desire. 30 While the food was still in their mouths, before they had satisfied their desire, 31 The anger of the Lord rose against them and killed some of their stoutest ones, subduing choice men of Israel. 32 In spite of all this they still sinned, and did not believe in His wonderful works. 33 Therefore their days He consumed in futility, and their years in terror. 34 When He slew them, then they sought Him, and returned to search diligently for the Almighty. 35 They remembered that God was their rock, the Most High Almighty their redeemer. 36 But they deceived Him with their mouth, and lied to Him with their tongue. 37 For their heart was not steadfast toward Him, nor were they faithful to His covenant. 38 But He, being compassionate, forgave their iniquity and did not destroy them. He often restrained His anger, and did not arouse all of His wrath. 39 He remembered that they were but flesh, a passing breeze that does not return. 40 How often they rebelled against Him in the wilderness and grieved Him in the desert. 41 Again and again they tested the Almighty; they asked for a sign from the Holy One of Israel. 42 They did not remember the strength of His hand the day He redeemed them from their adversaries 43 When He performed His signs in Egypt and His marvels in the field of Zoan 44 And turned their rivers and their streams to blood and they could not drink. 45 He sent swarms of flies among them, which devoured them, and frogs, which destroyed them. 46 He also gave their crops to grasshoppers, and the product of their labors to locusts. 47 He destroyed their vines with hailstones, and their sycamore trees with frost.

48 He also gave their cattle over to hailstones, and their herds to bolts of lightning. 49 He sent them His burning anger, fury, indignation, and trouble, a band of destroying angels. 50 He cleared a path for His anger; He did not spare their souls from death, but gave their lives over to the plague 51 And smote all the firstborns in Egypt, the first issue of their virility in their tents of heat. 52 But He led forth His own people like sheep, and guided them in the wilderness like a flock. 53 He led them safely, so they did not fear, but the sea engulfed their enemies. 54 He brought them to the boundary of His holiness, to the mountain attained by His right hand. 55 He drove out the nations before them, measuring out their apportioned inheritance. He made the tribes of Israel dwell in their tents. 56 Yet they tempted Him and rebelled against God Most High, and they did not keep His testimonies. 57 They turned back and acted treacherously, like their fathers; they turned bad like a warped bow. 58 They provoked Him with their altars in high places, and aroused His jealousy with their graven images. 59 God heard, and was filled with wrath and greatly abhorred Israel 60 He abandoned the dwelling place at Shiloh, the tent which He had pitched among men. 61 He sent His strength into captivity, His glory into the hand of the adversary. 62 He delivered His people to the sword, and was filled with anger toward His inheritance. 63 Fire devoured His young men, and His virgins had no wedding songs. 64 His priests fell by the sword, and His widows could not weep. 65 Then my Master awoke as if from sleep, like a warrior who had been overcome by wine. 66 He drove His adversaries backward and bestowed on them eternal humiliation. 67 He also rejected the tent of Joseph and did not choose the tribe of Ephraim 68 But chose the tribe of Judah, and Mount Zion which He loved. 69 And like the heights of heaven, like the earth which He has founded forever, He built His sanctuary. 70 He chose David, His servant, and took him from the sheep 71 From caring for ewes and suckling lambs He brought him to shepherd Jacob, His people, and Israel, His inheritance. 72 He shepherded them with a pure heart and led them with skillful hands.

This supplication, a prayer said in time of defeat, is also a poem on the devastation of war and the wreckage it leaves in its wake. It is an entreaty to God to take vengeance on the enemies of Israel.

79 A psalm by Asaph. O Lord, the nations have invaded Your inheritance; they have defiled Your holy temple. They have laid Jerusalem in ruins. 2 They have fed the corpses of Your servants to birds of the heavens, the flesh of Your godly ones to the beasts of the earth. 3 They spilled blood like water around Jerusalem, and there was no one to bury the dead. 4 We were humiliated in public, derided and scoffed at by those around us. 5 How long, O Lord. Will You be angry forever? Will Your jealousy burn like fire? 6 Pour out Your wrath on nations who do not know You, and on king-doms that do not call Your name. 7 For they have devoured Jacob and laid waste to his habitation. 8 Do not remember, or hold the iniquities of our forefathers against us. Let Your compassion come to us quickly, for we have been brought very low. 9 Help us, O God of our salvation, for the glory of Your name; deliver us and forgive our sins for Your name's sake. 10 Why should nations say, where is their God? Let it be known among nations, let us see vengeance for the spilt blood of Your servants. 11 Let the groaning of prisoners reach You. Preserve, with the greatness of Your power, those who are doomed to die. 12 Give back, to the bosom of our neighbors, seven times the scorn with which they scorned You, my Master 13 So that we, Your people, the sheep of Your pasture, will give thanks to You forever; generation to generation, recounting Your praise.

This song begins with a recounting of the glory and power that were Israel's when they left Egypt, and continues with the victorious journey that brought them to the land of Israel. That era is contrasted with current difficult times. The psalmist ends with the prayer that God return to show us the miraculous lovingkindness he has shown in the past.

80 For the chief musician, to Shoshanim, a testimony, a psalm by Asaph. 2 Shepherd of Israel, listen. Appear to us, You who led Joseph like a flock, You who are enthroned above the cherubs. 3 Stir up Your power, before Ephraim and Benjamin and Menashe, and come to save us. 4 Restore us, O God, shine Your face on us and we will be saved. 5 O Lord God of hosts, for how long will you be angry with the prayer of Your people? 6 You have fed them the bread of tears; You have made them drink triple por-tions of tears. 7 You have made us a target of our neighbors; our enemies mock us. 8 Restore us, O God of hosts, shine Your face on us and we will be saved. 9 You uprooted a vine from Egypt, drove out the nations and planted it. 10 You cleared space for it, and it took root deeply, and filled the land. 11 The mountains were covered with its shadow, the cedars of God with its boughs. 12 It sent out its branches to the sea, and its shoots to the river. 13 Why have You broken its fences, so that all who pass can pick its fruit? 14 A boar from the forest eats at it; whatever moves in the field feeds on it. 15 O God of hosts, turn to us again, now, we beseech You. Look down from heaven and see us; take care of this vine. 16 And take care of the stem which Your right hand has planted, and of the prog-eny which You Yourself have nurtured. 17 They have been burned with fire and cut down, perishing at the rebuke You have shown them. 18 Let Your hand assist the man on Your right, the man You chose to strengthen. 19 We will not turn back from You; revive us, and we will call Your name.

20 O Lord God of hosts, restore us. Shine Your countenance on us and we shall be saved.

This song of glory, recited on the New Year (Rosh Hashana), proclaims God's magnificence in general, and His steadfast lovingkindness toward the people of Israel in particular. It specifically emphasizes that when the people of Israel walk in God's ways, they deserve God's lovingkindness, which brings abundant material and spiritual fulfillment to their lives.

81 For the chief musician, on Gittith, a psalm by Asaph. 2 Sing for joy to God, our strength; shout with joy to the God of Jacob. 3 Take up hymns, sound the drums, a pleasant harp, and lute. 4 Blow the shofar at the time of the new moon, the appointed time of our holiday. 5 For it is a statute for Israel, a law of the God of Jacob. 6 He established it as a testimony for Joseph who left Egypt, a land with a language foreign to me. 7 I removed a burden from his back; freed his hands from the basket. 8 When you called, in trouble, I strengthened you; I answered you with hidden thunder; I tested you at the waters of Merivah, Selah. 9 Listen, my people; I will testify for you, Israel, if you will listen to me. 10 Let there be no strange god among you; you shall not worship any foreign god. 11 I am the Lord your God who brought you up from the land of Egypt; open your mouth wide, and I will fill it. 12 But my people did not listen to my voice; Israel did not want me. 13 I sent them to follow their hearts' desires, to walk in their own counsel. 14 O that my people would listen to me, that Israel would walk in my ways. 15 I would subdue their enemies quickly, and turn my hand against their adversaries. 16 Those who hate the Lord feign obedience to Him; their punishment will last forever. 17 He would have fed them the finest of wheat; He would have satisfied them with honey from the rock.

This poem serves as a warning to judges. In it, the psalmist reminds them of the importance of their task, and of their responsibility to judge justly. When they do not perform their mission with integrity, the people have no recourse but to appeal to God to reveal Himself, judge the world, and mete out justice.

82 God stands within the congregation of the Almighty; in the midst of the judges He gives judgment. 2 For how long will you judge unjustly, and show partiality to the wicked? Selah. 3 Vindicate the weak and the fatherless; be just to the afflicted and destitute. 4 Deliver the poor and needy; free them from the hands of the wicked. 5 They do not know and they do not understand; they walk about in darkness. All of the foundations of the earth are shaken. 6 I said, you are godlike, and all of you are children of the

Most High. 7 But you shall die like men, and fall like any prince must. 8 Arise, O God, and judge the earth, for You shall inherit all nations.

This poem is a prayer, recited at a time when Israel is terrorized by war in its own land. It is a war with not just one, but with multiple enemies attacking from all sides simultaneously. Their common objective is to obliterate Israel completely. This prayer beseeches God to bring about the downfall of Israel's enemies, and to protect and save Israel, because Israel bears God's name.

83 A song, a psalm by Asaph. 2 O God, do not remain quiet, do not be silent; O God, do not be still. 3 See your enemies in an uproar; those who hate You have exalted themselves. 4 They plot deceitfully against Your people, conspire together against Your treasured ones. 5 They said come, let us wipe them out as a nation, so that the name of Israel will be remembered no more. 6 They have conspired together with one mind; they make pacts against You. 7 The tents of Edom and the Ishmaelites, Moav and the Hagrites, 8 Gebal and Ammon and Amalek, Philistia with the inhabitants of Tyre 9 Assyria has also joined them; they assist the children of Lot, Selah. 10 Deal with them as with Midian, as with Sisera and Jabin at the torrent of Kishon. 11 Destroyed at Ein Dor, they became dung for the ground. 12 Make their nobles like Oreb and Zeeb, all their princes like Zebah and Zalmuna, 13 Who said, let us take the pastures of God for ourselves. 14 O my God, make them like whirling dust, like chaff before the wind. 15 Like fire that burns in the forest, like flames that set mountains on fire. 16 Pursue them with Your tempest; terrify them with Your storm. 17 Fill their faces with shame, and they will seek Your name, O Lord. 18 They will be ashamed and dismayed forever; let them be humiliated, and perish. 19 So they will know that You, whose name is the Lord, are alone the Most High over all of the earth.

This song is a poem of devotion and gratitude. The psalmist describes the outcome of putting one's trust in God. Spiritual and physical happiness ensue – closeness to God, dwelling in His holy temple, protection, and security.

84 For the chief musician, on Gittith, a psalm for the sons of Korach. 2 How beloved are Your dwelling places, O Lord of hosts. 3 My soul longs and even pines for the courtyards of the Lord; my heart and my flesh sing with joy to the living Almighty. 4 Even a bird found a house, and the swallow a nest for herself, where she may lay her young at Your altars, Lord of hosts, my King and my God. 5 How blessed are those who dwell in Your house; may they continue to praise You, Selah. 6 How blessed is the man who finds his strength in You, and whose heart follows upright paths. 7

Though they pass through a valley of tears, they make it into a spring that covers them with blessings like the first rains. 8 They go from strength to strength, and appear before the Almighty God in Zion. 9 O Lord God of hosts, hear my prayer; listen, O God of Jacob, Selah. 10 See our shield, O God; look at the face of your anointed. 11 One day in Your courtyard is better than a thousand; I would rather stand at the threshold of the house of my God than dwell in tents of wickedness. 12 For the Lord God is a sun and a shield; the Lord gives grace and glory. He withholds no good thing from those who walk uprightly. 13 O Lord of hosts, blessed is the man who trusts in You.

This poem expresses gratitude for the tranquility and equanimity that follow great hardship. The psalmist describes a time when the blessing of peace is accompanied by numerous other good things, all of which interconnect to form a blessed whole.

85 For the chief musician, a psalm for the sons of Korach. 2 Lord, You showed favor to Your land; You returned Jacob from captivity. 3 You forgave the iniquity of Your people; You pardoned all of their sins, Selah. 4 You withdrew all of Your fury; You turned away from Your burning anger. 5 Return to us, O God of our salvation, and annul the anger You have toward us. 6 Will Your anger toward us last forever? Will You prolong Your anger for generations? 7 Will You Yourself not revive us again, so that Your people may rejoice in You? 8 Show us Your mercy, O Lord, and grant us Your salvation. 9 I will hear what God the Lord will say, for He will speak peace to His people, to His godly ones. Let them not turn back to folly. 10 Surely His salvation is near for those who fear Him, so that glory may dwell in our land. 11 Mercy and truth have combined; righteousness and peace have kissed. 12 Truth springs from the earth, and righteousness looks down from heaven. 13 And the Lord will give what is good; our land will yield its produce. 14 Righteousness will go before Him, and shall make His footsteps our path.

In this poem of supplication the psalmist entreats God to reach out to him in his time of trouble, and relieve him of his miseries, so that he will be able to continue to follow a righteous path. The psalmist beseeches God to come to his aid in the future, as He has in the past.

86 A prayer by David. Listen to me O Lord, answer me, for I am afflicted and needy. 2 Guard my soul, for I am devoted; You are my God; save your servant, who trusts in You. 3 Be gracious to me, my Master, as I cry to You all day long. 4 Make the soul of Your servant glad, for to You, O Lord, I lift up my soul. 5 For Lord, You are good, and ready to forgive, and abundant in mercy to all who call You. 6 Listen, God, to my prayer, hear the voice of my supplications. 7 In the day of my trouble I will call to You, for you will answer me. 8 There is no god like You, my Master; there are no works like yours. 9 You made all nations, and they shall come and worship before you, my Master; they shall glorify Your name. 10 For You are great and do wondrous deeds; You alone are the Lord. 11 Teach me Your way, O Lord, so that I may walk in Your truth. Make my whole heart fear Your name. 12 I will give thanks to You, O Lord, my Master, with all my heart, and I will glorify Your name forever. 13 For Your mercy toward me is great; You have delivered my soul from the depths of Sheol. 14 O God, arrogant men have risen up against me; a band of violent men have sought my life. They have not set You before them. 15 But You, O Lord, are Almighty, full of compassion and gracious, longsuffering and abundant in mercy and truth. 16 Turn to me and have mercy on me. Grant Your strength to Your servant; save the son of Your handmaid. 17 Give me a good sign, so that those who hate me may see it and be ashamed, because You, O Lord, have helped me and comforted me.

The psalmist compares the holy city of Jerusalem to other places, and attributes the intrinsic superiority of Jerusalem to its holiness.

87 A song, a psalm for the sons of Korach. Its foundation is in the holy mountains. 2 The Lord loves the gates of Zion more than all dwelling places of Jacob. 3 Glorious things are spoken of you, O city of God, Selah. 4 To those who know me, I will mention Rahab and Babylon, and behold Philistia and Tyre and Ethiopia; this one was born there. 5 But of Zion it shall be said, this one and that one were born in her; He will establish her on high. 6 When He chronicles peoples, the Lord will note this one was born there, Selah. 7 And singers and dancers alike will say, all of my innermost thoughts are of You.

This is the supplication of a person suffering from a devastating illness. Because of the nature of the disease, even friends and family have distanced themselves from him. He appeals to God to heal him and to restore his good health.

88 A song, a psalm for the sons of Korach; for the chief musician, on Machalat Leanot, an instruction of Heiman the Ezrachi. 2 O Lord, God of my salvation, I cried by day and in the night for You. 3 Let my prayer be accepted by You; listen to my cry. 4 For my soul has had enough trouble, and my life has drawn near to the grave. 5 I am like those who have descended into a pit; I have become like a man with no strength, 6 Like the forsaken dead, like the slain who lie in a grave, cut off from Your hand, remembered by You no more. 7 You have put me in the lowest pit, in the depths of dark places. 8 Your wrath has come to rest on me; You have afflicted me with all Your tidal waves, Selah. 9 You have estranged me far from my friends; You have made me an object of loathing to them. I am shut in and cannot go out. 10 My eyes are wasted from my misery. O Lord, I have called to You every day; I have stretched out my hands to You. 11 Will You perform wonders for the dead? Shall departed spirits rise and praise You, Selah? 12 Shall Your mercy be recounted from the grave? Your faithfulness in the place of destruction? 13 Shall Your wonders be made known in darkness? Your righteousness in a land of oblivion? 14 Yet I, Lord, have cried out to You for help, and my prayer is before You in the morning. 15 O Lord, why do You reject my soul? Why do You hide Your face from me? 16 I have been afflicted and near death from youth; I suffer terrors from You. I am overcome. 17 Your burning anger overwhelms me; Your terrors destroy me. 18 They have surrounded me like water all day long; they have encompassed me altogether. 19 You have distanced friend and lover from me; those who know me have left me in darkness.

This song of grievance begins by enumerating the virtues of the house of David, when God's greatness was revealed in the world. It reminds God of His promise to secure the reign of David's descendants for generations. It ends in protest at the fall of the house of David, and with a prayer that God return it to ascendancy and power.

89 An instruction of Etan the Ezrachi. 2 I will sing of the mercy of the Lord forever. To all generations I will make Your faithfulness known with my mouth. 3 For I have said, mercy will build worlds, just as You established faithfulness in the heavens. 4 I have made a covenant with my chosen ones; I have sworn to David my servant. 5 I will establish your seed forever, build up your throne for all generations, Selah. 6 The heavens will praise Your wonders, O Lord, Your faithfulness praised in the assembly of holy ones. 7 For who in the skies compares to the Lord? Who among sons of the mighty are like the Lord? 8 God is revered in the secrets of holiness, and is awed above all His surroundings. 9 O Lord God of hosts , who is like You, O mighty Lord? Faithfulness surrounds You. 10 You rule the swelling sea; when its waves rise, You still them. 11 You Yourself crushed Rahab like a corpse; with Your arm's strength You scattered Your enemies. 12 The heavens are Yours; the earth also is Yours; You founded the world and all it contains. 13 You created the north and the south. Tabor and Hermon shout with joy at Your name. 14 Your arm is strong and Your hand is mighty, Your right hand, exalted. 15 Righteousness and justice are the foundations of Your throne; mercy and truth precede Your presence. 16 How fortunate are people who understand the call of the Lord; they walk in the light of Your countenance. 17 They rejoice in Your name all day; they are exalted by Your righteousness. 18 For You are the glory of their strength; by Your favor our grants are exalted. 19 For the Lord is our shield; our King is the Holy One of Israel. 20 Once, You spoke in a vision to Your devoted ones and said, I have aided a mighty one, I have exalted one chosen from the people. 21 I have found David, my servant; I have anointed him with my holy oil. 22 My hand will be established through him; My arm will strengthen him. 23 The enemy will not deceive him, nor will the sons of wickedness afflict him. 24 I will crush his adversaries before him and strike those who hate him. 25 My faithfulness and mercy will be with him, and in My name his grants will be exalted. 26 I will set his hand upon the seas, his right hand on the rivers. 27 He will call to Me, You are my father, my God, the rock of my salvation. 28 I will make him the first and the highest of the kings of the earth. 29 I will keep my mercy for him forever; My covenant will be steadfast with him. 30 I will establish his descendants on his throne forever, as in heavenly days. 31 If his sons forsake My law and do not walk in My judgments 32 If they violate My statutes and do not keep My commandments 33 I will punish their transgressions with a rod, and their iniquity with lashes. 34 But I will not remove My kindness from him; I will not lie about My faithfulness. 35 I will not violate My covenant, nor alter the utterance of My lips. 36 Once I have sworn by My holiness, I will not lie to David. 37 His descendants will endure forever, and his throne will be as the sun before Me. 38 It will be established to last forever, like the moon; the witness in the sky is faithful, Selah. 39 Yet, You have cast off and rejected; You have been full of wrath against Your anointed. 40 You have spurned the covenant of Your servant; You have profaned his crown in the land. 41 You have broken down all of his walls; You have brought his stronghold to ruin. 42 All who pass along the way can chew him; he has become a humiliation to his neighbors. 43 You have exalted the right hand of his adversaries; You have made all of his enemies rejoice. 44 You even turned back the edge of his sword, and have not sustained him in battle. 45 You have let his splendor end, cast his throne to the ground. 46 You have shortened the days of his youth, and have covered him with shame, Selah. 47 How long, O Lord? Will You hide Yourself forever? Will Your wrath burn like fire? 48 Remember the brevity of my lifespan. For what futility did You create all of the sons of man? 49 What man can live and not see death? Can he deliver his own soul from the power of the grave? Selah. 50 Where are Your former acts of mercy, O Lord, which You swore to David in faithfulness? 51 Remember, O Lord, the humiliation of Your servants, that I bear in my bosom for so many people. 52 Your enemies shamed us, O Lord; they shamed the footsteps of Your anointed. 53 Blessed be the Lord forever, Amen and Amen.

This song of reflection, prayer, and also partially of grievance, is about the brevity of human life. Death causes a loss of significance of everything man works for during his lifetime. The psalmist's chief complaint is that life is too short and too difficult for man to reach the spiritual heights that he may be capable of, and that are expected of him. He prays for greater awareness of his own evanescence, and at the same time, for a life without spiritual and physical torment.

90 A prayer of Moses the man of God. Lord, You have been a dwelling place for us from generation to generation. 2 You are Almighty, from before the time that mountains were born, from before You gave birth to the earth and the world, from time everlasting to time everlasting. 3 You push man until he is crushed, and then You say, return, children of men. 4 A thousand years in Your eyes are like yesterday that passes by, or like a night's watch duty. 5 They are swept away into sleep and in the morning they have been transformed into new grass. 6 In the morning it flourishes and sprouts anew, and toward evening it fades and withers away. 7 We are consumed by Your anger, we are terrified of Your rage. 8 You have placed our transgressions before You, the sins of our youth before the light of Your countenance. 9 All of our days defer to Your wrath, our years are ended like a sigh. 10 The days of our lives are seventy years, or with strength, eighty years, yet they are mostly toil and sorrow, then gone, and we fly away. 11 Who understands the power of Your anger? Your fury is great, as is the fear due to You. 12 So teach us to count each of our days, so we will acquire a heart of wisdom. 13 Return to us, O Lord; how long will it take? Comfort Your servants. 14 Satisfy us with Your mercy in the morning, so that we may sing for joy and be glad throughout our days. 15 Make the days of our joy as longlasting as the days of our affliction, and as the years we have seen evil. 16 Let Your deeds be seen by Your servants, Your majesty by their children. 17 May the pleasantness of the Lord our God be upon us, and may it establish the work of our hands, and yes, establish the work of our hands.

This choral hymn praises those who have faith in God. The song describes how God protects them from hidden as well as evident dangers, from any and all harm. The song has several voices: that of the chorus, praising the person who has faith in God; that of the faithful; and that of God, Who promises to guard and watch over His faithful.

91 He who dwells in the shelter of the Most High shall abide in the shadow of the Almighty. 2 I will say of the Lord, He is my refuge and my fortress, God in whom I trust 3 For it is He who delivers you from the snare of the trapper, and from deadly pestilence. 4 He will cover you with His feathers; you will find refuge under His wings; His truth is a shield and a bulwark. 5 You will not fear the terror of night, nor the arrow that flies by day 6 Nor the pestilence that stalks in darkness, nor the destruction that lays waste at noon. 7 A thousand may fall at your side, and ten thousand at your right hand, but it will not approach you. 8 Just look with your eyes and see the punishment of the wicked. 9 For you say, the Lord is my refuge; you have also made the Supreme One your dwelling place. 10 No evil will befall you, nor will any plague come near your tent. 11 For He will charge his angels concerning you, to guard you in all your ways. 12 They will carry you in their hands, so that you do not strike your foot against a stone. 13 You will tread upon the lion and the cobra; you will trample on the young lion and the serpent. 14 I will deliver him because he has loved Me; I will set him securely on high, because he has known My name. 15 He will call upon Me and I will answer him; I will be with him in times of trouble; I will rescue him and honor him. 16 I will satisfy him with long life, and show him My salvation.

This song is not only a reflection on the Sabbath day, but also on everything that transpires in the world. It is a grand accounting of all that is good and bad, success and failure. The song reflects on the "Sabbath of the world" – a future era when everything will be in its right place. At that time, it will be evident that the successes of the wicked of this world are fleeting; they harbor seeds of failure and self-destruction. The righteous will be proven to be stable with longstanding, fruitful prosperity.

92 A psalm, a song for the Sabbath day. 2 It is good to give thanks to the Lord, and to sing praises to Your name, O Most High. 3 To declare Your mercy in the morning and Your truth in the nights 4 With the ten-stringed lute and with the harp, with resounding music on the lyre. 5 For You O Lord, have made me glad by what You have done; I will sing for joy at the work of Your hands. 6 How great are Your works, O Lord; how profound Your thoughts. 7 A man without sense cannot know this, nor a fool understand 8 That when the wicked sprouted like grass, and all who were sinful flourished, it was only so that they might be destroyed forever. 9 But You, O Lord, are on high forever. 10 See Your enemies, O Lord; see that Your enemies will perish , and all who do iniquity will be scattered. 11 But You have increased my strength to be like that of a wild ox; I am saturated with fresh oil. 12 My eye sees those who spy on me; my ears hear the wicked who plot against me. 13 The righteous man will flourish like a palm tree; he will grow like a cedar in Lebanon. 14 Planted in the house of the Lord, they will blossom in the courts of our God. 15 They will still yield fruit in old age; they will be fresh and full of sap 16 And declare that the Lord is upright; He is my rock, and devoid of injustice.

This is a hymn on the revelation of God. All of existence is filled with poetry when God is revealed in His world. All become aware of how God rules His world; all can see Him revealed in His chamber.

93 The Lord reigns; He is clothed in majesty; the Lord has clothed and girded Himself with strength. The world is firmly established so that it will not fall. 2 Your throne is established from of old; You are everlasting. 3 The rivers rose up, O Lord, the rivers rose and raised their voices; the rivers swelled with their raging waves. 4 Greater than the sounds of many waters, than the mighty waves of the sea, is the greatness of the Lord on high. 5 Your testimonies are very sure; holiness adorns Your house, O Lord, forever.

This prayer is for contemplation of God's vengeance against the wicked, who are convinced that there is no law, no judge, and that there are no consequences to their evil deeds. The psalmist knows that God watches over those who are close to Him, that their troubles are a means of atonement and that, in the end, the wicked inevitably fail.

94 O Lord God, to whom vengeance belongs, O God, to whom vengeance belongs, shine forth. 2 Arise, judge of the earth, repay the arrogant with their just reward. 3 How long will the wicked, O Lord, how long will the wicked exult? 4 They express themselves speaking with arrogance; all evildoers are boastful. 5 They crush Your people, O Lord, and oppress Your heritage. 6 They slay the widow and the stranger and murder the orphans. 7 They say, the Lord does not see, the God of Jacob is not concerned. 8 Understand this, senseless among the people; fools, when will you become wise? 9 He who planted the ear, shall He not hear? He who formed the eye, shall He not see? 10 He who chastises nations, He who teaches man knowledge, shall He not rebuke? 11 The Lord knows the thoughts of men, that they are vanity. 12 Blessed is the man whom You chastise, O Lord, whom You guide with Your laws 13 To grant him relief in the days of adversity, until a pit is dug for the wicked. 14 For the Lord will not abandon His people, nor will He forsake His inheritance. 15 Judgment will again be righteous, and all of the upright of heart will follow it. 16 Who will rise up for me against the wicked? Who will take a stand for me against the evildoers? 17 If the Lord had not helped me, my soul, in an instant, would have dwelt in silence. 18 If I should say my foot has slipped, Your mercy, O Lord, would hold me up. 19 When my anxious thoughts multiply within me, Your consolations delight my soul. 20 Can a throne of destruction, one which devises mischief by decree, be allied with You? 21 They band themselves together against the lives of the righteous, and condemn the innocent to death. 22 The Lord has been my stronghold; God, the rock of my refuge. 23 He has brought their own wickedness upon them, and will destroy them in their own evil. The Lord our God shall cut them off.

This is a song glorifying the oneness and greatness of God, thanking Him for His kindness and greatness. It also serves as a warning against ingratitude, citing our forefathers when they left Egypt, as an example.

95 Come and let us sing for joy to the Lord; let us shout joyfully to the rock of our salvation. 2 Let us greet Him with thanksgiving; let us shout joyfully to Him with psalms. 3 For the Lord is a great God, a great King, above all gods. 4 The depths of the earth are in His hand; mountain peaks are also His. 5 The sea is His, for it was He who made it; His hands formed the dry land. 6 Come, let us worship and bow down; let us kneel before the Lord our Maker. 7 For He is our God, and we are the people of His pasture and the flock led by His hand, even today, if you would hear His voice. 8 Do not harden your hearts, as you did at Merivah, as in the days of the trek through the wilderness. 9 When your fathers tested Me, they tried Me, though they had seen My work. 10 For forty years I quarreled with that generation; I said they are a people who err in their hearts, they do not know My ways. 11 In anger I swore that they will not enter My resting place.

This hymn is a call to all of the inhabitants of the earth to show gratitude to God as He is revealed, and to proclaim His greatness to the entire world.

96 O, sing to the Lord a new song; sing to the Lord, all the earth. 2 Sing to the Lord, bless His name; proclaim the good tidings of His salvation day by day. 3 Tell of His glory among the nations, His wonderful deeds among all peoples. 4 For the Lord is great, and greatly to be praised; He is to be feared above all gods. 5 For all gods of the peoples are idols, but the Lord made the heavens. 5 Splendor and majesty are before Him; strength and beauty are in His sanctuary. 6 Give to the Lord, O families of the peoples, give to the Lord, glory and strength. 8 Give to the Lord the glory due His name; bring an offering, and come into His courts. 9 Worship the Lord in holy attire; tremble before Him, all of the earth. 10 Say among the nations that the Lord reigns, that His world is firmly established and cannot be moved, that He will judge the people with uprightness. 11 Let the heavens be glad, and let the earth rejoice. Let the sea and all it contains roar. 12 Let the fields and all they contain exult, and all the trees of the woods will rejoice 13 Before the Lord, for He is coming, for He is coming to judge the earth. He will judge the world with righteousness, and the people with His truth.

This hymn depicts the joy and excitement felt by the righteous, and the shame and downfall suffered by idol worshippers, at the revelation of God.

97 The Lord reigns; let the earth rejoice; let the many islands be glad. 2 Clouds and thick darkness surround Him. Righteousness and justice are the foundations of his throne. 3 Fire precedes Him and burns around His adversaries. 4 His lightning illuminates the world; the earth sees and trembles. 5 Mountains melt like wax at the presence of the Lord, before the Master of all the earth. 6 The heavens declare His righteousness; all the people have seen His glory. 7 All who serve graven images, who boast of idols, will be ashamed; all gods bow down before Him. 8 Zion hears this and is glad; the daughters of Judah rejoice because of Your judgments, O Lord. 9 For You are the Lord Most High over all the earth; You are exalted above all gods. 10 Haters of evil, love the Lord, who preserves the souls of His godly ones; He delivers them from the hand of the wicked. 11 Light is sown for the righteous, and gladness for the upright of heart. 12 Rejoice, righteous ones, and give thanks at the remembrance of His holy name.

This hymn is a call to the people of Israel, and to the entire world, to use music and harmony to express their gratitude to God for His sovereignty, and for His revelation in the world.

98 A psalm. Sing to the Lord a new song, for He has done wonderful things; His right hand and His holy arm have gained victory for Him. 2 The Lord has made known His salvation; He has revealed His justice within sight of nations. 3 He remembered His mercy and His faithfulness to the house of Israel. All the ends of the earth have seen the salvation of our God. 4 All of earth, raise your voices with joy to the Lord. Break forth and sing for joy; sing praises. 5 Sing to the Lord with the harp, with the harp and the sound of a psalm. 6 With trumpets and the sound of the shofar, shout joyfully before the Lord the King. 7 Let the sea and all its fullness roar, the world and all those who dwell in it. 8 Let the rivers clap their hands, let the hills sing together for joy 9 Before the Lord, for He is coming to judge the earth. He will judge the earth with righteousness, and the people in truth.

This hymn is one of gratitude to God for His revelation at Mount Sinai and in the holy temple. It is a call to the people to join His prophets and sages in thanksgiving and praise.

99 The Lord reigns, and the people tremble. He sits with cherubs; the earth quakes. 2 The Lord is great in Zion, exalted above all the peoples. 3 They will acknowledge Your great and awesome name, as it is holy. 4 The King's strength also loves justice. You have established equity; You have executed justice and righteousness in Jacob. 5 Exalt the Lord our God, and worship at His footstool; He is holy. 6 Moses and Aaron were among his priests, and Samuel among those who called His name; they called to the Lord and He answered them. 7 He spoke to them in a pillar of cloud; they kept his testimonies, and the statutes He gave them. 8 O Lord our God, You answered them; You were a forgiving Almighty to them, yet You took vengeance on their misdeeds. 9 Exalt the Lord our God, and prostrate yourselves at His holy mountain, for the Lord our God is holy.

This poem of thanksgiving and praise calls for the people to come to the house of God to show gratitude for all of His kindnesses – especially for choosing Israel as His people.

100 A psalm of thanksgiving. Shout for joy to the Lord, everyone on earth! 2 Serve the Lord with joy; come before him with exaltation. 3 Know that the Lord Himself is God; it is He who made us, not we ourselves. We are his people and the flock of His pasture. 4 Enter His gates with thanksgiving, and His courts with praise. Give thanks to Him; bless His name. 5 For the Lord is good. His mercy is eternal, His faithfulness everlasting from generation to generation.

This poem is written to teach, in a poetic way, how people can become close to and loved by God, and how they can become distanced, far from Him.

101 I will sing of mercy and justice. To You, O Lord, I will sing praises. 2 With forethought, I will follow a path of simple purity. When will You come to me? I will walk within my house with a pure heart. 3 I will set nothing wicked before my eyes. I hate the work of those who have gone astray; it will not take hold of me. 4 A perverse heart will be estranged from me; I will know no evil. 5 Whoever secretly slanders his neighbor shall be cut down by me; I will endure no one who has a haughty look and an arrogant heart. 6 My eyes will be on the faithful in the land; they shall dwell with me. He who walks blamelessly is the one who will minister to me. 7 He who practices deceit will not dwell within my house; he who speaks falsehood will not maintain a position with me. 8 Every morning I will cut down all of the wicked of the land, to cut off from the city of God all those who do evil.

This is the supplication of a person whose entire life is overwhelmed by poverty, illness, misery, and suffering. The psalmist affirms his belief that God comes to the aid of His people and provides salvation to all who suffer. He praises God, the omnipotent Creator.

102 A prayer of the poor man, who, when steeped in affliction, pours out his complaints before the Lord. 2 Hear my prayer, O Lord, and let my cry for help reach You. 3 Do not hide Your face from me in the day of my distress; listen to me. In the day when I call, answer me. 4 For my days are consumed in smoke, and my bones are as scorched as a hearth. 5 My heart has been smitten like grass and has withered away; I even forget to eat my bread. 6 My bones cling to my flesh, to the sound of my sighing. 7 I resemble a pelican of the wilderness; I have become like an owl of the wasteland. 8 I lie awake; I have become like a lonely bird on a rooftop. 9 My enemies taunt me all day long; those who mock me swear at me. 10 I have eaten ashes like bread, and have mixed my drink with tears 11 Because of Your indignation and Your wrath. You lifted me up and cast me away. 12 My days are like a lengthened shadow, and I wither away like grass. 13 But You, O Lord, Your name abides, remembered forever, from generation to generation. 14 You shall arise and have compassion for Zion, for it is time to be gracious to her; the appointed time has come. 15 For Your servants take pleasure in her stones and feel pity for her dust. 16 Nations shall fear the name of the Lord, and all kings of the earth Your glory. 17 When the Lord builds up Zion, His glory is apparent. 18 He turned to the prayer of the lonely one, did not despise his prayer. 19 This shall be written for the generation to come, so that people not yet created may praise the Lord. 20 He looked down from His holy height; from heaven the Lord gazed upon the earth 21 To hear the groaning of the prisoner, to set free those who were doomed to death 22 So that men may speak the name of the Lord in Zion, His praise in Jerusalem 23 When peoples are gathered together and kingdoms come to serve the Lord. 24 Along the way, He weakened my strength, He shortened my days. 25 I said, O my God, do not take me away in the midst of my days; Your years last forever, from generation to generation. 26 You laid the foundations of the earth; the heavens are the work of Your hands. 27 Even they will perish, but You endure; they all will wear out like a garment. You change them, and, like clothing, they will be changed. 28 But You are the same; Your years will never come to an end. 29 The children of Your servants will be secure, and their descendants will be established before You.

This is a song of praise and thanksgiving to God, Who forgives individuals as well as whole congregations of sinners. By doing so, God renews their lives, gives them hope, and proves that He is loyal to those devoted to Him. Because of this, it behooves all who live on earth to join in this song of praise.

103 Bless the Lord, O my soul, and all that is within me, bless His holy name. 2 Bless the Lord, O my soul; forget none of His beneficial deeds. 3 It is He who forgives all of your iniquities and heals all of your diseases. 4 He redeems your life from the pit, and crowns you with kindness and compassion 5 He satisfies and adorns you with good, so that your youth is renewed like a phoenix. 6 The Lord performs deeds of righteousness and justice to all of the oppressed. 7 He made His ways known to Moses, His deeds to the sons of Israel. 8 The Lord is compassionate and gracious, slow to anger and abounding in mercy. 9 He will not argue with us forever, nor shall he stay angry forever. 10 He has not dealt with us as we deserved, for our sins, and He has not paid us back as we deserved, for our iniquity. 11 For as high as the heavens are above the earth, so high is His mercy toward those who fear Him. 12 As far as the east is from the west, that is how far He has removed our transgressions from us. 13 As a father has compassion for his children, so the Lord has compassion for those who fear Him. 14 He himself knows our nature; He is mindful that we are but dust. 15 As for man, his days are like grass; he flourishes like a flower in the field. 16 When a deadly wind passes over it, it is no more; it no longer has a place. 17 But the mercy of the Lord, to those who fear Him, endures from world to world; His righteousness endures to children's children 18 For those who keep His covenant and remember to act on His precepts. 19 The Lord has established His throne in the heavens; His sovereignty rules over all. 20 Bless the Lord, His angels, mighty in strength, who perform His word, and obey the call of His word. 21 Bless the Lord, all His hosts, you who serve Him, doing His will. 22 Bless the Lord, all of His works, in all places of His dominion. Bless the Lord, O my soul.

This is a hymn about creation, a grand poem about the world and everything within, large and small, earth and skies and seas. It depicts the diverse lives of all creatures, and the great, far-reaching cycle of life, which includes death and resurrection.

104 Bless the Lord, O my soul; O Lord, my God, You are greatly exalted. You are clothed in splendor and majesty. 2 Wrapped in light as in a cloak, He spreads out the heavens like a curtain. 3 He lays the beams of His upper chambers in the waters, He makes clouds His chariot; He walks upon the wings of the wind. 4 He makes the winds His messengers, the flaming fires His ministers. 5 He established the earth on its foundations, so that it shall never ever be unstable. 6 He covered the depths as with a garment, made waters stand above mountains. 7 At Your rebuke they fled; at the sound of Your thunder they hurried away. 8 The mountains rose, the valleys sank down to the place You established for them. 9 You set a boundary they could not cross, so they shall not return to cover the earth. 10 He sends springs to the valleys; they flow between mountains. 11 They give drink to every beast of the field; wild donkeys quench their thirst. 12 Birds of the heavens dwell beside them, and lift their voices among branches. 13 He waters the mountains from His upper chambers; the earth is satisfied with the fruit of His works. 14 He makes the grass grow for the cattle, vegetation for the labor of man, so that he may bring forth bread from the earth, 15 And wine, which makes man's heart glad, and oil to make his face glisten, and food which sustains man's heart. 16 The Lord's trees, cedars of Lebanon, which He planted, drink their fill. 17 There the birds, and the stork, whose home is the fir tree, build their nests. 18 The high mountains are for the wild goats, the cliffs are a refuge for hares. 19 He made the moon for the seasons; the sun knows the place to set. 20 You appoint darkness, and it becomes night, when the beasts of the forest prowl about. 21 The young lions roar after their prey, and seek their food from the Almighty. 22 When the sun rises they withdraw, and lie down in their dens. 23 Man goes out to his work, and labors until the evening. 24 O Lord, how many are Your deeds. You have made them all in wisdom. The earth is full of Your possessions. 25 There is the sea, great and broad, in which there are swarms, animals both great and small, without number. 26 There the ships move along, and the Leviathan, which You created to play with. 27 They all wait for You to give them their food at the right time. 28 When You give it to them, they gather it up; when You open Your hand, they are satisfied with good. 29 When You hide Your face, they are dismayed; You take away their spirit, they expire and return to dust. 30 When You send forth Your spirit, they are created; You renew the face of the land. 31 Let the glory of the Lord endure forever; let the Lord be glad with His works. 32 He looks at the earth, and it trembles; He touches the mountains, and they smoke. 33 I will sing to the Lord as long as I live; I will sing praise to my God while I still am alive. 34 May my meditation please Him. As for me, I rejoice in the Lord. 35 May sin be excised from the earth, may evil be no more. Bless the Lord, O my soul, praise the Lord.

This song teaches of the history of Israel. It poetically summarizes Israel's past, from the time of our forefather Abraham, through the lives of his descendants and Israel's redemption from Egypt and entrance into the land of Israel. The purpose of recounting this history in poetic form is to arouse feelings of gratitude and praise for the Almighty, for the benevolence He has shown to His people throughout history.

105 Give thanks to the Lord, proclaim His name. Make His deeds known among the people. 2 Sing to Him, sing praises to Him; speak of all His wonders. 3 Glory is His holy name; let the hearts of those who seek the Lord be glad. 4 Seek the Lord, and His strength; seek His presence continually. 5 Remember the wonders which He has done, His marvels, and the judgments uttered by His mouth. 6 O seed of Abraham, His servant, O sons of Jacob, His chosen ones 7 He is the Lord our God; the entire earth is governed by His laws. 8 He remembers His covenant, the words He has commanded to a thousand generations, forever. 9 He made the covenant with Abraham, gave His oath to Isaac. 10 Then He confirmed it to Jacob as a statute, to Israel as an everlasting covenant 11 Saying, to you I will give the land of Canaan as the portion of your inheritance. 12 They were only a few men in number, very few, and strangers to it. 13 They wandered about from nation to nation, from one kingdom to another people. 14 He permitted no man to oppress them, and He reproved kings for their sakes. 15 Do not touch my anointed ones; do my prophets no harm. 16 He called for a famine upon the land; He broke every supply of bread. 17 He sent Joseph, the man who was sold as a slave, before them. 18 They tortured his feet with chains; an iron chain was laid on his soul. 19 The word of the Lord tested him, until the time His words came to pass 20 The king sent for him and released him; the ruler of people set him free. 21 He made him master of his house and ruler of all his possessions 22 To endear his soul to his princes, to teach his elders wisdom. 23 And Israel came to Egypt, and Jacob resided in the land of Ham. 24 He made his people very fruitful, and He made them stronger than their adversaries. 25 He turned their hearts to hate His people, to conspire against His servants. 26 He sent Moses, His servant, and Aaron, whom He had chosen. 27 They performed His wondrous acts among them, miracles in the land of Ham. 28 He sent the darkness and made it dark; they did not rebel against His words. 29 He turned their waters into blood and made their fish die. 30 Their land swarmed with frogs, even in the chambers of their kings. 31 He spoke, and swarms of flies came, and gnats appeared all over their territories. 32 He gave them hail for rain, flaming fire in their land. 33 He struck down their vines and their fig trees also; He shattered the trees of their territory. 34 He spoke, and locusts came, young locusts without number. 35 They ate up all the vegetation in their land, and ate up the fruits of their ground. 36 He struck down all of the firstborns in their land, the first fruits of all their vigor. 37 Then He brought them out with silver and gold, and among His tribes there was not one who stumbled. 38 Egypt was glad when they departed, for the dread of them had fallen on them. 39 He spread out a cover of clouds, and fire to illuminate the night. 40 They asked, and He brought quail, and satisfied them with the bread of heavens. 41 He opened a rock and water flowed out; it ran in dry places like a river. 42 For He remembered His holy word to Abraham, His servant.

42 And He brought out His people with joy, His chosen ones with joyous song. 44 And He gave them the lands of nations, to inherit the fruits of their labors 45 So that they might keep His statutes and observe His laws. Halleluya.

This poem is also meant to teach, though it is a prayer for help from God to rescue Israel from surrounding belligerent enemies. The song poetically enumerates all of the past sins and punishments of the people of Israel in order to make God's lovingkindness tangible. Despite all of Israel's sins during their desert wanderings and after their arrival in the land of Israel, God continued to accompany them, and to show them mercy, compassion, and total forgiveness.

106 Halleluya; give thanks to the Lord, for He is good, for His mercy is everlasting. 2 Who can recount the mighty deeds of the Lord, or praise Him enough to make it understood? 3 Fortunate are those who keep justice, who practice righteousness at all times. 4 Remember me, O Lord, when You favor Your people; guard me with Your salvation, 5 So that I may see the prosperity of Your chosen ones, so that I may rejoice in the gladness of Your nation, so that I may glory in Your inheritance. 6 We have sinned like our fathers; we have committed iniquity; we have behaved wickedly. 7 Our fathers in Egypt did not understand Your wonders; they did not remember Your abundant kindnesses. They rebelled by the sea, the Red Sea. 8 And He delivered them for His name's sake, so that He might make His power known. 9 And He rebuked the Red Sea and it dried up; He led them through the deep, as if through a wilderness. 10 He saved them from the hands of those who hated them, redeemed them from the hand of the enemy. 11 The waters covered their adversaries; not one of them was left. 12 Then they believed in His words; they sang His praise. 13 They quickly forgot His works; they did not wait for His counsel, 14 But lusted exceedingly in the wilderness, and tested the Almighty in the desert. 15 He gave them their request, but sent emaciation to their souls. 16 In the camp, when they became envious of Moses and Aaron, the holy ones of the Lord, 17 The earth opened and swallowed Datan, and engulfed the company of Aviram. 18 A fire blazed in their company; the flames consumed the wicked. 19 They made a calf in Horev, and worshiped a molten image. 20 They traded their glory for the image of an ox that eats grass. 21 They forgot their Almighty savior who had done great things in Egypt, 22 Wonders in the land of Ham and awesome deeds by the Red Sea. 23 He spoke to destroy them, had not Moses, His chosen one, stood in the breach before Him to turn back His wrath from destruction. 24 And they despised the pleasant land; they did not believe His word. 25 They grumbled in their tents; they did not listen to the voice of the Lord. 26 And He raised His hand against them, to cast them down in the desert, 27 To cast down their seed among nations, and scatter them in the lands. 28 They clung to Baal Peor and ate sacrifices offered to the dead. 29 They provoked His anger with their deeds; a plague broke out among them. 30 Pinchas stood up and wrought judgment, and the plague ceased. 31 For this, he is thought to be righteous, by all generations to come, forever. 32 They provoked Him to wrath at the waters of Merivah; because of them, Moses suffered badly. 33 Because they were rebellious against His spirit, he swore with his lips. 34 They did not destroy the people as the Lord commanded them to, 35 But mingled with the nations and learned their practices 36 And served their idols, which became a snare for them. 37 They even sacrificed their sons and their daughters to demons 38 And shed innocent blood, the blood of their sons and their daughters whom they sacrificed to the idols of Canaan. The land was polluted with blood. 39 And they were defiled by their practices, prostituting themselves with their deeds. 40 And the Lord's fury blazed against His people; He abhorred His inheritance. 41 He delivered them into the hands of the nations; those who hated them ruled over them. 42 Their enemies oppressed them; they were subdued under their power. 43 He rescued them many times, but they were rebellious in their counsel, and sank deep into their iniquity. 44 But He saw their distress when He heard their cry 45 And He remembered His covenant for their sake, and relented in accordance with the greatness of His mercy. 46 He caused them to be pitied by their captors. 47 Save us, O Lord our God, and gather us in from among the nations, so we can give thanks to Your holy name and glory in Your praise. 48 Blessed be the Lord God of Israel, forever and forever. Let all people say Amen, Halleluya.

This song of gratitude is by people who were in dire straits, and who were saved by the grace of God. It describes four circumstances in detail: being imprisoned, ill, lost in a desert, or lost at sea. All are situations of constraint, trouble, hardship, and danger, and all ended well with relief, peace, and tranquility. Those who were saved join in the recitation of this poem of thanksgiving.

107 Give thanks to the Lord, for He is good, for His mercy is everlasting. 2 Let those redeemed by the Lord say it, those He has redeemed from the hand of the adversary 3 And gathered in from the lands, from the east and from the west, from the north and from the south. 4 They wandered in the wilderness of the desert; they did not find their way to an inhabited city. 5 Hungry and thirsty, their souls fainted within them. 6 They cried out to the Lord in their trouble; He delivered them out of their distress. 7 He led them on a straight path to an inhabited city. 8 Let them thank the Lord for His mercy, and for His wonders to the sons of men. 9 For He has satisfied the thirsty soul, and filled the hungry soul with goodness. 10

Those who dwelt in darkness and in the shadow of death, prisoners in misery and chains 11 Because they had rebelled against the word of the Almighty and spurned the counsel of the Most High 12 Were humbled to their hearts with labor. They stumbled, and there was no one to help. 13 They cried out to the Lord in their trouble; He rescued them from distress. 14 He brought them out of darkness and the shadow of death, and broke their chains. 15 Let them give thanks to the Lord for His mercy, and for His wonders to the sons of men. 16 He has shattered gates of bronze, and cut apart iron bars. 17 They are fools, because their rebellious ways and their iniquities cause their own affliction. 18 Their souls abhorred all kinds of nourishment, and they drew near to the gates of death. 19 Then they cried out to the Lord in their distress, and He delivered them from their anguish. 20 He sent His word, and healed them, and delivered them from destruction. 21 Let them thank the Lord for His mercy, and for His wonders to the sons of men. 22 Let them offer sacrifices of thanksgiving, and tell of His works with joyful singing. 23 Those who go down to the seas in ships, and do business on great waters 24 Have seen the works of the Lord, His wonders in the deep. 25 He spoke, and storm winds stood and lifted its waves. 26 They rose up to the heavens, they went down to the depths. Their souls melted in misery. 27 They reeled and staggered like drunken men, and were at their wit's end. 28 They cried to the Lord in their trouble, and He brought them out of their distress. 29 He caused the storm to be still so that the waves of the sea were hushed. 30 They were joyful with the quiet; He guided them to the haven they desired. 31 Let them thank the Lord for His mercy, and for His wonders to the sons of men. 32 Let them extol Him in the congregation of people, and praise Him where wise men converge. 33 He changes rivers into wilderness, springs of water into thirsty land, 34 A fruitful land into a salty waste, because of those who dwell on it. 35 He changed the wilderness into a pool of water and dry land into springs of water 36 And brought the hungry to dwell there, so they could establish an inhabited city 37 And sow fields and plant vineyards and gather a fruitful harvest. 38 He blessed them and they multiplied greatly; He did not let their cattle diminish. 39 But when they were diminished and brought low through oppression, misery, and sorrow, 40 He poured contempt upon princes and made them wander in a pathless wasteland. 41 He lifted the needy high away from affliction; He made families His flock. 42 The upright see this and are glad; the mouth of iniquity will be shut. 43 Whoever is wise will understand these things, and meditate on the mercy of the Lord.

This poem expresses thanksgiving to God for victory in a major battle against multiple enemies. It is similar to Psalm 60, emphasizing feelings of gratitude, as God alone determines who is triumphant in war.

108 A song, a psalm by David. 2 My heart is steadfast, O God. I will sing and I will offer hymns, and my glory also. 3 Awake, harp and lyre; I will awaken the dawn. 4 I will give thanks to You, O Lord, among the people; I will sing Your praises among the nations. 5 For Your mercy is greater than the heavens; Your truth reaches the skies. 6 Be exalted above the heavens, O God; Your glory is above all of the earth. 7 Deliver me with your right hand, and answer me, so that Your loved ones may be released. 8 God spoke in His holiness, saying, I will exult; I will divide Shechem and portion out the valley of Succoth. 9 Gilead is mine, Menashe is mine, Ephraim is the helmet of my head, and Judah is my scepter. 10 Moav is my washbasin; I will throw my shoe over Edom; I will thunder over Philistia. 11 Who will bring me to the besieged city? Who will lead me to Edom? 12 Has God forsaken us? Has God declined to go out with our armies? 13 Give us help against our adversaries; help from man is futile. 14 Through God we will be valiant; He will trample our enemies.

These words of supplication are by a person in danger, who has just learned that people, whom he has never harmed, have turned against him, defaming him, cursing him, shaming him. He knows that God is his only shelter. God knows the truth, and has the power to do him justice.

109 O God of my praise, do not keep silent. 2 For the mouths of the wicked and the mouths of the deceitful are opened against me. They have spoken against me with lying tongues. 3 Hateful words surrounded me. They fought against me without cause. 4 In return for my love they demonized me. I am all prayer. 5 They repaid my good with evil, my love with hatred. 6 Appoint over him a wicked man; let an accuser stand at his right hand. 7 When he is judged, let him be guilty; let his prayer be turned into sin. 8 May his days be few; let another take his position. 9 Let his children be fatherless, and his wife a widow. 10 Let his children wander and beg; let them search among their ruins. 11 Let creditors seize all he has; let strangers plunder the product of his labor. 12 Let there be no one to extend kindness to him, no one to be gracious to his fatherless children. 13 Let his posterity be cut off. Let their name be blotted out from future generations. 14 Let the iniquity of his fathers be remembered by the Lord; do not erase the sins of his mother. 15 Let them be before the Lord continually. May He erase their memory from the earth 16 Because he did not remember to show kindness, but persecuted a poor, needy, and broken-hearted man unto death. 17 He loved curses, so they came to him; he hated blessing, so it is far from him. 18 He clothed himself in curses like a garment; they entered his body like water, like oil into his bones. 19 Let them be for him like a garment with which he covers himself, like a belt with which he constantly girds himself. 20 This is the reward that the Lord gives to my adversaries for their deeds against me, for their words of evil to my soul. 21 But You, O God, my Master, deal with me for Your name's sake; deliver me, because Your mercy is good. 22 For I am afflicted and needy, and my heart is wounded within me. 23 I am fading like a lengthening shadow; I am as shaken off as a locust. 24 My knees are weak from fasting; my flesh has grown lean, without fat. 25 I have become a disgrace to them; they see me and shake their heads. 26 Help me, O Lord my God; deliver me with Your mercy. 27 And they will know that it is Your hand, that You, O Lord, have done it. 28 They may curse, but You bless. They rose, but they will be humiliated, and Your servant will be glad. 29 Let my accusers be clothed in dishonor; let them wear their own shame like a robe. 30 With my mouth, I will give abundant thanks to the Lord; in the midst of multitudes I will praise Him. 31 For He stands at the right hand of the needy, to deliver him from those who judge his soul.

This is a poem by King David, at a time when David's throne was secure, and he was blessed. God was by his side as he reigned in triumph over all of his enemies.

110 A psalm by David. The Lord said to my master, sit on my right until I make your enemies a footstool for your feet. 2 The Lord shall extend the scepter of your strength out from Zion to rule in the midst of your enemies. 3 In the days of your campaign, your people shall willingly volunteer to serve in holy splendor; you possess the dew of youth that you had from dawn in the womb. 4 The Lord has sworn, and will not rescind; you are a priest forever, according to the word of my King of justice. 5 My Master is at your right hand; He shall shatter kings in the day of His wrath. 6 He shall judge the nations and fill them with corpses. He shall break the leaders of many lands. 7 And then he shall drink from the brook by the way and lift his head high.

This poem teaches about the glory of God, His truth, and His power. It describes how He comes to the aid of all those who fear Him, and how He particularly watches over and rescues the people of Israel.

111 Halleluya. I will thank the Lord with all my heart, in the council of the upright and in the assembly. 2 Great are the works of the Lord; they are studied by all who delight in them. 3 Splendid and majestic is His work; His righteousness endures forever. 4 He has made His wonders memorable; the Lord is gracious and compassionate. 5 He gave food to those who feared Him; He will remember His covenant forever. 6 He has made the power of His works known to His people, by giving them the heritage of the nations. 7 The works of His hands are truth and justice; all of His precepts are true. 8 They are ordained forever and ever; they are conceived in truth and uprightness. 9 He sent redemption to His people; He has ordained His covenant forever. Holy and awesome is His name. 10 Fear of the Lord is the basis of wisdom; those who act on it are of a good mind. His praise endures forever.

This song teaches of the reward that comes to those who fear God and walk in His ways. A person who is exceedingly charitable and kind benefits from God's protection and from its rewards — success and happiness in life.

112 Halleluya. Fortunate is the man who fears the Lord, and who greatly delights in his commandments. 2 His descendants will be mighty on earth; the generation of the upright will be blessed. 3 Wealth and riches are in his house, and his righteousness endures forever. 4 For the upright, light shines in the darkness, for He is gracious and compassionate and righteous. 5 It is good for man to be gracious and lend, and conduct his affairs with justice. 6 He will never be shaken; the righteous are remembered forever. 7 He will not fear evil tidings; his heart is steadfast in trust in the Lord. 8 His heart is steadfast and will not fear, even before he sees the fall of his adversaries. 9 He has given widely to the poor; his righteousness endures forever. He will be granted exalted honors. 10 A wicked person, seeing this, will be vexed and grind his teeth. Desire melts away; the desire of the wicked shall perish.

This poem glorifying God depicts God's attribute of omnipresent greatness, in juxtaposition to His attribute of concern and lovingkindness toward unfortunate, suffering individuals.

113 Halleluya. Praise, servants of the Lord; praise the name of the Lord. 2 Blessed be the name of the Lord from now until forever. 3 From sunrise in the east, to sunset, the name of the Lord is to be praised. 4 The Lord is high above all nations; His glory is above the heavens. 5 Who is like the Lord, our God, who dwells on high 6 Yet humbles Himself to watch over heaven and earth. 7 He raises the poor from the dust, lifts the needy from the ash heap, 8 To seat them among nobles, the nobility of His people. 9 He returns a barren woman home, to live as a joyful mother of children. Halleluya.

This poem of glory and thanksgiving describes God's revelation when Israel left Egypt. The miracles that occurred are nature's way of expressing joy at the revelation of God.

114 When Israel went out of Egypt, the house of Jacob from a foreign-language people, 2 Judah became His holy nation, Israel, His dominion. 3 The sea looked, and fled; the Jordan turned back. 4 The mountains skipped like rams, the hills like lambs. 5 What troubles you, sea, that you flee, Jordan, that you turn back 6 Mountains, that you skip like rams, hills, like lambs? 7 Tremble, earth, before the Master, before the God of Jacob 8 Who turns the rock into a pool of water, the flint into a fountain of water.

This prayer, recited by those who fear God, is a hymn showing the contrast between nations who worship idols and the people of Israel, who believe in God. It contains a supplication that those who fear God be rewarded with success, and flourish, so they will be able to continue to bless God's name.

115 Not to us, O Lord, not to us, but to Your name give glory, because of Your mercy, because of Your truth. 2 Why should nations say please, where is their Lord? 3 When our God is in the heavens and does whatever He desires. 4 Their idols are silver and gold, the work of man's hands. 5 They have mouths, but cannot speak. They have eyes, but cannot see. 6 They have ears, but cannot hear. They have noses, but cannot smell. 7 They have hands, but cannot feel. They have feet, but cannot walk. They cannot make a sound with their throat. 8 Those who make them, everyone who trusts in them, will become like them. 9 Israel trusts in the Lord; He is their help and their shield. 10 The house of Aaron trusts in the Lord; He is their help and their shield. 11 Those who fear the Lord trust in the Lord; He is their help and their shield. 12 The Lord remembers us and will bless us. He will bless the house of Israel, He will bless the house of Aaron. 13 He will bless the small and the great, all those who fear the Lord. 14 May the Lord add to you and to your children. 15 Blessed are you to the Lord, the Maker of heaven and earth. 16 The heavens are the heavens of the Lord, but He has given the earth to the sons of men. 17 The dead cannot praise the Lord, nor can any who go down into silent graves. 18 But we will bless the Lord, from now until forever. Praise the Lord.

This is a poem of thanksgiving and praise for God's salvation. The psalmist describes in detail how he was steeped in trouble, illness, and loneliness. He thanks God for relieving him of all his miseries, and vows to continue to serve God and to declare His name to all.

116 I love when the Lord hears my voice and my supplications. 2 Because He hears me, I will call, all my days. 3 Throes of death encompassed me, terrors of the grave came to me; I found distress and sorrow. 4 I call the name of the Lord saying, I beseech You, save my life. 5 The Lord is gracious and righteous, and our God is compassionate. 6 The Lord protects the simple. I was brought low, and He saved me. 7 Return, O my soul, to restfulness, for the Lord has rewarded you bountifully. 8 For You have rescued my soul from death, my eyes from tears, my feet from stumbling. 9 I will walk before the Lord in the land of the living. 10 I believed, even when I said I suffer greatly. 11 In my haste, I said all men are liars. 12 What shall I give to the Lord in return for all the benefits He bestowed on me? 13 I will lift a cup of salvation, and call the name of the Lord. 14 I will fulfill my vows to the Lord in the presence of all of His people. 15 Precious, in the eyes of the Lord, is the death of His pious ones. 16 Please, O Lord, I am Your servant, the son of Your handmaid; You have loosened my bonds. 17 I will offer a sacrifice of thanksgiving to You, and call the name of the Lord. 18 I will fulfill my vows to the Lord in the presence of all of His people 19 In the courtyards of the house of the Lord, in Your midst, in Jerusalem. Praise the Lord.

This short poem of praise calls for everyone to thank and praise God for the kindnesses He has shown to the people of Israel.

117 Praise the Lord, all nations. Extol Him, all peoples. 2 For his mercy is great toward us, and the truth of the Lord is everlasting. Praise the Lord.

This is a song of thanksgiving and praise for God's salvation. After finding himself in grave danger, surrounded on all sides by enemies and terrorists, the psalmist is rescued by God, Who destroys all of his adversaries. He promises to make a pilgrimage to God's temple to thank Him for His mercies, and to give others the opportunity to join in thanksgiving to God.

118 Give thanks to the Lord, for He is good; His mercy is everlasting. 2 Let Israel say, His mercy is everlasting. 3 Let the house of Aaron say, His mercy is everlasting. 4 Let those who fear the Lord say, His mercy is everlasting. 5 From the narrow straits of distress I called to the Lord and the Lord answered me with Divine expanse. 6 The Lord is with me; I shall not fear. What can man do to me? 7 The Lord is with me, with those who help me; I will see to my enemies. 8 It is better to take refuge in the Lord than to trust in man. 9 It is better to take refuge in the Lord than to trust in princes. 10 All nations surround me; in the name of the Lord, I will cut them down. 11 They surrounded me, they surround me. In the name of the Lord, I cut them down. 12 They surrounded me like bees; they were extinguished as thorns in a fire. In the name of the Lord, I cut them down. 13 You pushed and pushed me to fall, but the Lord helped me. 14 The strength and retribution of the Lord was deliverance to me. 15 The sound of joy and deliverance emerges from the tents of the righteous; the right hand of the Lord performs valorous deeds. 16 The right hand of the Lord is exalted; the right hand of the Lord performs valorous deeds. 17 I will not die, but live to tell of the work of the Lord. 18 The Lord disciplined me severely, but He has not given me over to death. 19 Open gates of righteousness for me; I will enter through them. I will give thanks to the Lord. 20 This is the gate to the Lord; the righteous enter through it. 21 I will give thanks to You, for You have answered me; You have been my salvation. 22 The stone that the builders rejected has become the chief cornerstone. 23 This is the Lord's doing; it is marvelous in our eyes. 24 This is the day the Lord made, we will rejoice and be glad in it. 25 O Lord, save us; we beseech You. O Lord, let us succeed; we beseech You. 26 Blessed be the one who comes in the name of the Lord; we bless you from the house of the Lord. 27 The Lord is God; He has given us light. Bind the festival sacrifice with cords to the horns of the altar. 28 You are my Almighty, and I give thanks to You. My God, I will exalt You. 29 Give thanks to the Lord, for He is good, for His mercy is everlasting.

In this long didactic poem, sentences follow an alphabetical pattern (eight for each letter). Consecutive sentences are not always related to each other; each sentence is a saying that can stand alone. The sentences in this psalm are connected in various ways by topic, for example. Some of the topics addressed are devotion to God, His Torah, and observance of His commandments, despite internal resistance and external obstacles to doing so. The psalmist beseeches God to continue to provide help and salvation, so that he will be able to continue to follow a righteous path.

119 Blessed are they of simple paths, who walk in the law of the Lord. 2 Blessed are they who observe His laws, and seek Him with a full heart. 3 They not only abstain from unrighteousness, but also walk in His ways. 4 You commanded that we should keep Your precepts diligently. 5 I wish that my ways would be firmly established to keep Your statutes. 6 Then I will not be ashamed, when I observe all of Your commandments. 7 I will give thanks to You with an upright heart when I learn of Your righteous judgments. 8 I will keep Your statutes. Do not forsake me completely. 9 How can a young man keep his way pure? By guarding it according to Your word. 10 I have sought You with all my heart; keep me from mistakes in Your commandments. 11 I treasure Your word in my heart, so I may not sin against You. 12 Blessed are You, O Lord; teach me Your statutes. 13 With my lips I have told of all of the ordinances of Your mouth. 14 I have rejoiced in Your path, as if with riches. 15 I will meditate on Your precepts and regard Your ways. 16 I will delight in Your statutes; I will not forget Your words. 17 Deal bountifully with Your servant, so I may live and keep

Your word. 18 Open my eyes to see wonderful things from Your law. 19 I am a stranger on earth; do not hide Your commandments from me. 20 My soul is crushed from its desire to immerse in Your mandates at all times. 21 You rebuke the arrogant, the cursed, who wander from Your commandments. 22 Remove contempt and reproach from me, for I observe Your testimonies. 23 Even as princes sit and talk against me, Your servant meditates on Your statutes. 24 Your testimonies are my delight, and my counselors. 25 My soul cleaves to the dust; revive me with Your word. 26 I told of my ways, and You answered me. Teach me Your statutes. 27 Make me understand the way of Your precepts, and I will meditate on Your wonders. 28 My soul weeps with grief; strengthen me with Your word. 29 Remove falsity from me; grant me Your law graciously. 30 I have chosen the way of faith; I have placed Your ordinances before me. 31 I cling to Your testimonies; O Lord, do not put me to shame. 32 I will run to the path of Your commandments, for You have expanded my heart. 33 Teach me, O Lord, the way of Your statutes, and I will observe it to the end. 34 Give me understanding, so I may observe Your law and keep it with all my heart. 35 Make we walk in the path of Your commandments, for I delight in it. 36 Incline my heart toward Your testimonies, not to material gain. 37 Turn my eyes away from looking at vanity; revive me in Your ways. 38 Fulfill the promise You made to Your servant, who fears You. 39 Let my humiliation, which I dread, pass away, for Your ordinances are good. 40 Here, I long for Your precepts; revive me through Your righteousness. 41 May Your mercy and salvation come to me, O Lord, according to Your word. 42 Then I will have an answer for him who taunts me, for I trust in Your word. 43 Do not let words of complete truth be removed from my mouth; I wait for Your mandates. 44 I will keep Your law continually, forever and ever. 45 I will walk about openly, because I have sought Your precepts. 46 I will speak of Your testimony before kings, and not be ashamed. 47 I will delight in Your commandments, which I love. 48 I will lift my hands to Your commandments, which I love, and meditate on Your statutes. 49 Remember the word to Your servant, in which You gave me hope. 50 This is my comfort in my affliction; Your word revives me. 51 Sinners deride me, utterly; I do not turn away from Your laws. 52 I remember Your ancient ordinances, O Lord, and comfort myself. 53 I am seized by burning indignation toward the wicked who forsake Your laws. 54 Your statutes were songs to me in the house where I sojourn. 55 O Lord, I remember Your name in the night, and keep Your laws. 56 This has become mine, the observance of Your precepts. 57 The Lord is my portion; I promise to keep Your words. 58 I sought Your favor with all my heart; be gracious to me, according to Your word. 59 I considered my ways, and turned my feet toward Your testimonies. 60 I rushed, did not delay to keep Your commandments. 61 Bands of the wicked have encircled me, but I have not forgotten Your laws. 62 At midnight, I will rise to give thanks to You, because of Your righteous ordinances.

63 I am a companion to all who fear You, to those who keep Your precepts. 64 The earth is full of Your mercy, O Lord; teach me Your statutes. 65 You have dealt well with Your servant, O Lord, according to Your word. 66 Teach me knowledge to discern well, for I believe in Your commandments. 67 Before, I was afflicted and went astray, but now I keep Your word. 68 You are good, and do good; teach me Your statutes. 69 Arrogant sinners slandered me falsely. With all my heart I will observe Your precepts. 70 Their heart is covered with fat; I delight in Your law. 71 It is good for me that I was afflicted, so I may learn Your statutes. 72 The laws of Your mouth are better for me than thousands of gold and silver pieces. 73 Your hands made and fashioned me. Give me understanding, so I may learn Your commandments. 74 May those who fear You see me and be glad, because I wait for Your word. 75 I know, O Lord, that Your judgments are righteous, and that You afflicted me in faithfulness. 76 May Your mercy comfort me, according to Your word to Your servant. 77 May Your compassion come to me so I might live; Your law is my delight. 78 May arrogant sinners be ashamed, for they subvert me with lies. I will meditate on Your precepts. 79 May those who fear You, even those who know Your testimonies, turn to me. 80 May my heart be blameless in observance of Your statutes, so that I will not be ashamed. 81 My soul languishes for Your salvation; I wait for Your word. 82 My eyes fail with longing for Your word; they say, when will You comfort me. 83 Even though I have become like leather in an oven, I do not forget Your statutes. 84 How many days has Your servant? When will You judge my pursuers? 85 Sinners, who are not in accordance with Your law, dig pits for me. 86 They pursue me falsely. All of Your commandments are faithful. Save me! 87 They almost wiped me off the earth, but as for me, I did not forsake Your precepts. 88 Revive me, according to Your lovingkindness, so that I may keep the testimony of Your mouth 89 Forever, O Lord; Your word stands in the heavens. 90 Your faithfulness is throughout all generations; You established the earth, and it endures. 91 To this day, they endure by Your judgment; all things are Your servants. 92 If Your law had not been my delight, I would have perished in my affliction. 93 I will never forget Your precepts, for by them You have revived me. 94 I am Yours; save me, for I have sought Your precepts. 95 The wicked wait for me, to destroy me; I diligently meditate on Your testimonies. 96 I see the limits of all perfection; Your commandments are exceedingly broad. 97 How I love Your law; I meditate on it all day. 98 Your commandments are always with me; they make me wiser than my enemies. 99 I have gained insight from all of my teachers; Your testimonies are my meditation. 100 I understand more than my elders, for I have kept Your precepts. 101 I have restrained my feet from every evil way, so that I may keep Your word. 102 I have not turned away from Your ordinances; You Yourself have taught me. 103 How sweet are Your words to my taste, sweeter, yes, than honey to the mouth. 104 I gain understanding from Your precepts; I hate

every false way. 105 Your word is a lamp to my feet and a light to my path. 106 I have sworn, and I confirm, that I will keep Your righteous ordinances. 107 I am exceedingly afflicted. Revive me, O Lord, according to Your word. 108 Accept the free will offerings of my mouth, O Lord, and teach me Your ordinances. 109 My life is continually in my hand, yet I do not forget Your laws. 110 The wicked have laid a snare for me, yet I have not strayed from Your precepts. 111 I have inherited Your testimonies forever; they are the joy of my heart. 112 I have inclined my heart to perform Your statutes forever, to the end. 113 I hate those who are of two minds. I love Your laws. 114 You are my hiding place and my shield; I wait for Your word. 115 Depart from me, evildoers, so I may observe the commandments of my God. 116 Sustain me according to Your word, so I may live. Do not let me be ashamed of my hope. 117 Support me, so I may be safe, so I may regard Your statutes continually. 118 You have rejected all those who stray from Your statutes; their deceitfulness is useless. 119 You have nullified the wicked of the earth like ashes; I love Your testimonies. 120 My flesh trembles in fear of You; I am afraid of Your judgments. 121 I have acted with justice and righteousness; do not leave me to my oppressors. 122 Ransom Your servant, for good. Do not let me be oppressed by sinners. 123 My exhausted eyes seek Your deliverance and righteous sayings. 124 Treat Your servant according to Your mercy; teach me Your statutes. 125 I am Your servant; give me understanding so I may know Your testimonies. 126 It is time for the Lord to act, for they have broken Your law. 127 Yes, I love Your commandments more than gold, more than pure gold. 128 Yes, I esteem all of Your precepts, concerning everything. I hate every false way. 129 Your testimonies are wonderful; yes, my soul observes them. 130 Your words unfold and give light, give understanding to the simple. 131 I opened my mouth wide, panting, longing for Your commandments. 132 Turn to me and be gracious to me, as is Your manner with those who love Your name. 133 Establish my footsteps in Your world. Do not let any iniquity have dominion over me. 134 Redeem me from the oppression of man, so I may keep Your precepts. 135 Shine Your face on Your servant, and teach me Your statutes. 136 My eyes shed streams of water because they do not keep Your laws. 137 You are righteous, O Lord, and upright in Your judgments. 138 You have commanded Your testimonies in righteousness and exceeding faithfulness. 139 My zeal has consumed me, as Your adversaries have forgotten Your words. 140 Your word is very pure; that is why Your servant loves it. 141 I am small and despised, but I do not forget Your precepts. 142 Your righteousness is an everlasting righteousness, and Your law is truth. 143 Trouble and anguish have come to me; Your commandments are my delight. 144 Your testimonies are righteous forever. Give me understanding, so I may live. 145 I cried with all my heart; answer me, O Lord. I will observe Your statutes. 146 I cried to You, save me, and I will keep Your testimonies. 147 I rise before dawn, and cry for help; I wait for

Your words. 148 My eyes anticipate night watches so I may meditate on Your word. 149 Hear my voice, as befits Your mercy; revive me, O Lord, as befit Your ordinances. 150 Followers of wickedness draw near; they are distant from Your law. 151 You are near, O Lord, and all of Your commandments are truth. 152 From the outset, from Your testimonies, I knew that You founded them to be eternal. 153 Look on my affliction, and rescue me, for I do not forget Your laws. 154 Plead my cause and redeem me; revive me as befits Your word. 155 Salvation is far from the wicked; they do not seek Your statutes. 156 Great are Your mercies, O Lord; revive me according to Your ordinances. 157 My persecutors and adversaries are numerous, yet I do not turn away from Your testimonies. 158 I see the treacherous and loathe them because they do not keep Your word. 159 See how I love Your precepts; revive me, O Lord, according to Your mercy. 160 The sum of Your word is truth; every one of Your righteous ordinances is everlasting. 161 Princes persecute me without cause, but my heart stands in awe of Your words. 162 I rejoice at Your word, as one who has found great spoils. 163 I hate and despise falsehood; I love Your laws. 164 Seven times a day I praise You, because of Your righteous ordinances. 165 Those who love Your laws know great peace; nothing causes them to stumble. 166 I hope for Your salvation, O Lord, and to perform Your commandments. 167 My soul keeps Your testimonies; I love them exceedingly. 168 I keep Your precepts and Your testimonies; all my ways are before You. 169 Let my cry come before You, O Lord; give me understanding, according to Your word. 170 Let my supplication come before You; deliver me according to Your word. 171 Let my lips utter praise as You teach me Your statutes. 172 Let my tongue sing of Your word, for all Your commandments are righteousness. 173 Let Your hand be ready to help me, for I have chosen Your precepts. 174 I long for Your salvation, O Lord; Your law is my delight. 175 Let my soul live, so it may praise You; let Your ordinances help me. 176 I have gone astray like a lost sheep. Seek Your servant, for I do not forget Your commandments.

This is a condemnation of people who slander and malign. It shows how dreadful and dangerous they can be to people of peace. They can cause harm even when they have nothing to gain from their own malice.

120 A song of ascents. In my distress I cried to the Lord and He answered me. 2 Deliver my soul, O Lord, from lying lips, from a deceitful tongue. 3 What will He give you, what else will He give to a deceitful tongue? 4 Sharp arrows of the warrior, burning coals of a broom. 5 Woe is me, that I dwell in Meshech, and that I reside among the tents of Kedar. 6 My soul has dwelled for too long with those who hate peace. 7 I am for peace, but when I speak, they are for war.

This poem is about faith in God. Even one who appears to be completely vulnerable and insecure can trust in God's protection. God watches over all men, and protects them from all forms of misfortune, apparent or unseen.

121 A song of ascents. I will lift up my eyes to the hills. From whence comes my help? 2 My help is from the Lord, Maker of heaven and earth. 3 He will not allow your foot to slip. He who keeps You will not slumber. 4 Behold, the Guardian of Israel will neither slumber nor sleep. 5 The Lord is your keeper. The Lord is your shelter, at your right hand. 6 The sun shall not strike you by day, nor the moon by night. 7 The Lord shall protect you from all evil; He shall protect your soul. 8 The Lord shall guide your going out and your coming in, from now until forever.

This poem, sung by pilgrims, tells of the glory and greatness of Jerusalem. It describes an era when all of the tribes of Israel were unified, and Jerusalem was the site of the holy temple and the epicenter of Judean sovereignty.

122 A song of ascents, by David. I rejoiced when they said to me, let us go to the house of the Lord. 2 Our feet stood within your gates, Jerusalem. 3 Jerusalem, built as a city of binding togetherness. 4 There our tribes, the tribes of the Lord, went up to give thanks to the name of the Lord, as a testimony of Israel. 5 Thrones were set there for judgment, thrones of the house of David. 6 Pray for the peace of Jerusalem; those who love you will find serenity. 7 May peace be within your walls, serenity within your palaces. 8 For the sake of my brothers and my friends, I will say, peace be with you. 9 For the sake of the house of the Lord our God, I will seek your good.

This is a poem of supplication. The psalmist, immobilized, bereft of good deeds, depressed and suffering, turns to God for mercy. Though unworthy, he is completely reliant on the benevolence and compassion of God to save him from those who defame and wound him.

123 A song of ascents. I lift my eyes to You, who dwell in heaven. 2 Here, as the eyes of servants are to the hand of their master, as the eyes of a maid are to the hand of her mistress, so are our eyes to the Lord, our God, until He is gracious to us. 3 Be gracious to us, O Lord; be gracious to us, for we are fully satiated with humiliation. 4 Our soul is overfilled with the scorn of those who are at ease, with humiliation by proud pigeons.

This is a song of thanksgiving to God, who rescued His servants from danger during a time of trouble and adversity, when it seemed to them that all hope was lost.

124 A song of ascents, by David. Let Israel now say, had it not been for the Lord, who was with us 2 Had it not been for God, who was with us, when men rose up against us, 3 They would have swallowed us alive, as their anger was kindled against us. 4 The waters would have engulfed us; the stream would have swept over our soul. 5 The raging waters would have swept over our soul. 6 Blessed be the Lord, who did not give us as prey to their teeth. 7 Our soul escaped like a bird out of the snare of a trapper. The snare is broken, and we have escaped. 8 Our help is in the name of the Lord, who created heaven and earth.

Those who trust in God can rely on His help, knowing that no evil will befall them. In the end, the wicked fail and are destroyed.

125 A song of ascents. Those who trust in the Lord are as Mount Zion, which cannot be moved, but abides forever. 3 The scepter of wickedness shall not rest on the land allotted to the righteous, lest the righteous use their hands to do wrong. 4 The Lord will be good to the good, to the upright of heart. 5 But as for those who turn aside to their crooked ways, the Lord shall lead them away with the doers of iniquity. Peace be upon Israel.

This is a song celebrating an era of redemption to come. When it arrives, the past, with all of its tribulations, will seem like only a dream. The suddenness and surprise of redemption will make true joy and laughter possible. The past will be seen in a new light, revealed as just a preparatory phase of labor that precedes the reward.

126 A song of ascents. When the Lord brought back the captivity of Zion, we were like those who dream. 2 Then our mouths filled with laughter, and our tongues with joyful song. Then the nations said, the Lord has done great things for them. 3 The Lord had done great things for us; we were joyful. 4 O Lord, bring our captives back home, like streams to the desert. 5 Those who sow in tears shall reap in joy. 6 He who weeps as he walks to and fro, carrying his bag of seed, will surely return, in joyous song, bringing his sheaves with him.

This song teaches that those who think success in life is solely a result of man's interest, effort, and determination are mistaken. Wealth, success, security, and each and every blessing comes to man only with the help of God. The greatest of God's blessings are children who remain close and provide continuity.

127 A song of ascents by Solomon. Unless the Lord builds a house, those who build it labor in vain. Unless the Lord guards a city, the watchman stays awake in vain. 2 It is in vain for you to rise up early and retire late to eat the bread of painful labor; He will surely give sustenance, and sleep, to his loved ones. 3 Children are a heritage from the Lord; the fruit of the womb is a reward. 4 Like arrows in the hand of a warrior, so are the children of one's youth. 5 How blessed is the man whose quiver is full of them. They shall not be ashamed when they speak with their enemies at the gate.

This song glorifies the joyous life of one who walks in the way of God. It specifically describes the essential happiness of family life. A man who walks in God's ways, and is sustained by the work of his own hands, enjoys the basic, simple joy of being surrounded by a loving family, a wife, sons and daughters, who are close to him.

128 A song of ascents. Blessed are all who fear the Lord, who walk in His ways. 2 When You eat the labor of your hands you shall be happy, and it shall be well with you. 3 Your wife shall be like a fruitful vine within your house; your children surround your table like young olive trees. 4 This is how a man who fears the Lord is blessed. 5 May the Lord bless you from Zion; may you see the prosperity of Jerusalem all the days of your life, 6 And yes, may you see the children of your children. Peace be upon Israel.

This is a song of thanksgiving and entreaty. The people of Israel, who have always been surrounded by enemies, thank God for saving them from their adversaries. Israel is compared to plowed earth, Israel's enemies to plants that grow rapidly and dry out rapidly: They are not a blessing; they are of no use.

129 A song of ascents. Let Israel now say they have persecuted me many times. 2 They have persecuted me many times, from my youth on, yet they have not prevailed against me. 3 The plowers plowed on my back; they lengthened their furrows. 4 The Lord is righteous. He has cut the cords of the wicked. 5 May all who hate Zion be put to shame and be turned backward. 6 Let them be like grass that withers before it springs up on the roof. 7 May the reaper not fill his hand with it, nor the binder of sheaths fill his arms with it. 8 And may those who pass by them not say, the blessing of the Lord be with you, we bless you in the name of the Lord.

This is a poem of heartfelt repentance, requesting forgiveness from God. Mercy and compassion from God only add to man's feelings of awe and fear of God.

130 A song of ascents. Out of the depths I have cried to You, O Lord. 2 O Lord, hear my voice; let Your ears be attentive to the voice of my supplications. 3 If You, O Lord, should mark our iniquities, who could survive? 4 But there is forgiveness with You, that You may be feared. 5 I wait for the Lord; I hope in His word, and my soul waits. 6 My soul waits for the Lord, more than those who watch for the morning, more than those who watch for the morning. 7 Israel, hope in the Lord, for with the Lord there is mercy, and with Him is abundant redemption. 8 He will redeem Israel from all its iniquities.

This is a poem of essential devotion to God, on a most intimate level. The psalmist compares himself to an infant who has been weaned from the breast, but who clings to his mother out of pure love, happy just to be close to and devoted to her.

131 A song of ascents, by David. Lord, my heart is not haughty, nor my eyes lofty, and I did not concern myself with things too great or too wonderful for me. 2 Have I not composed and quieted my soul, like a child weaned from his mother? My soul is like a weaned child within me. 3 Israel, wait for the Lord, from now until forever.

This is a poem of thanksgiving, glorifying King David for the work and effort he expended in preparing a place for the holy temple.

132 A song of ascents. O Lord, remember David and all his afflictions. 2 How he swore to the Lord and vowed to the Mighty One of Jacob, 3 I will not enter my house nor lie on my bed, 4 I will not give sleep to my eyes nor slumber to my eyelids 5 Until I find a place for the Lord, a dwelling place for the Mighty One of Jacob. 6 We heard it in Ephrata; we found it in the fields of the forest. 7 Let us go to His dwelling place; let us worship at His footstool. 8 Arise, O Lord, to Your resting place, You and the ark of Your strength. 9 Let Your priests be clothed in righteousness; let Your godly ones sing for joy. 10 For the sake of David, Your servant, do not turn away the face of Your anointed. 11 To David, the Lord has vowed a truth from which He will never turn back. I will set upon your throne the fruit of your loins. 12 If your sons will keep My covenant and My testimony, which I will teach them, their sons will also sit upon your throne forever. 13 For the Lord has chosen Zion; He desired it for His habitation. 14 This is My resting place forever; here I will dwell, for I have desired it. 15 I will bless her provision abundantly; I will satisfy her needy with bread. 16 I will also clothe her priests with salvation; her godly ones will sing aloud for joy. 17 I will cause the rays of David to shine forth from there; I have prepared a lamp for My anointed. 18 I will clothe his enemies in humiliation, but on him, a crown will shine.

This is a poem honoring the priests, who sit together in brotherhood and with mutual respect, in the holy temple a place overflowing with tranquility and blessing.

133 Behold how good and how pleasant it is for brothers to dwell together in unity. 2 It is like precious oil on the head, running down the beard, like the beard of Aaron, dripping to the edge of his garments. 3 It is like the dew of Hermon descending upon the mountains of Zion, for there the Lord commanded the blessing of life, forever.

This is a poem glorifying and honoring not only God's priests, but all God-fearing people who come to the holy temple at night to pray and to show devotion to His divine spirit.

134 A song of ascents. Behold, bless the Lord, servants of the Lord, who serve by night in the house of the Lord. 2 Lift up your hands to the sanctuary and bless the Lord. 3 The Lord who made heaven and earth will bless you from Zion.

This poem glorifies the greatness of God in His world, specifically the lovingkindness that He showed to Israel when they left Egypt and entered the land of Israel. It calls to all of God's servants to join in His praise.

135 Praise the Lord, praise the name of the Lord; praise Him, servants of the Lord. 2 You who stand in the house of the Lord, in the courts of the house of our Lord 3 Praise the Lord, for the Lord is good. Sing praises to His name, for it is pleasant. 4 For the Lord has chosen Jacob for Himself, Israel as His treasure. 5 For I know that the Lord is great, and that our Master is above all gods. 6 Whatever the Lord desires to do, He has done in heaven and on earth, in the seas and in all depths. 7 He makes clouds ascend from the ends of the earth; He makes lightning for the rain, brings out winds from His vaults. 8 He struck down the firstborn of both man and beast in Egypt. 9 He sent signs and wonders into the midst of Egypt, Pharaoh, and all his servants. 10 He smote many nations and slew mighty kings, 11 Sichon, king of the Amorites, and Og, king of Bashan, and all of the kingdoms of Canaan. 12 And He gave their lands as an inheritance, an inheritance to Israel, His people. 13 O Lord, Your name is everlasting; the Lord is to be remembered from generation to generation. 14 For the Lord will judge His people, and will have compassion on His servants. 15 The idols of the nations are silver and gold, the work of man's hands. 16 They have mouths, but do not speak; they have eyes, but do not see. 17 They have ears, but do not hear. 18 Those who make them, and yes, everyone who trusts in them, will be like them. 19 House of Israel, bless the Lord; House of Aaron, bless the Lord. 20 House of Levi, bless the Lord; you who revere the Lord, bless the Lord. 21 Blessed be the Lord from Zion; He dwells in Jerusalem, Halleluya.

This is a song for chorus; every stanza has a choral refrain. The theme is praise for God, His greatness in the world, and the mercies He shows to all. It also praises God specifically for the miracles of the exodus from Egypt and conquest of the land of Israel.

136 Give thanks to the Lord, for He is good, for His mercy endures forever. 2 Give thanks to the God of gods, for His mercy endures forever. 3 Give thanks to the Master of masters, for His mercy endures forever. 4 He, who alone does great wonders, for His mercy endures forever. 5 He, who made the heavens with skill, for His mercy endures forever. 6 He, who spread out the earth above the waters, for His mercy endures forever. 7 He, who made the great lights, for His mercy endures forever. 8 The sun to rule by day, for His mercy endures forever. 9 The moon and stars to rule by night, for His mercy endures forever. 10 He, who smote Egypt through their firstborn, for His mercy endures forever. 11 And brought Israel out from their midst, for His mercy endures forever. 12 With a strong hand and an outstretched arm, for His mercy endures forever. 13 He, who divided the Red Sea asunder, for His mercy endures forever. 14 And made Israel pass through the midst of it, for His mercy endures forever. 15 But He churned Pharaoh and his army in the Red Sea, for His mercy endures forever. 16 He, who led His people through the wilderness, for His mercy endures forever. 17 He, who smote great kings, for His mercy endures forever. 18 And slew mighty kings, for His mercy endures forever. 19 Sichon, king of the Amorites, for His mercy endures forever. 20 And Og, king of Bashan, for His mercy endures forever. 21 And gave their land as an inheritance, for His mercy endures forever. 22 An inheritance to Israel, His servant, for His mercy endures forever. 23 In our lowliness, He remembered us, for His mercy endures forever. 24 And He freed us from our oppressors, for His mercy endures forever. 25 He gives food to all flesh, for His mercy endures forever. 26 Give thanks to the Almighty of heaven, for His mercy endures forever.

This is a lamentation on exile, and the pain it causes the soul. Memories of the past are so vivid that they preclude the possibility of joy or poetry in exile.

137 By the rivers of Babylon, there we sat down and yea, we wept when we remembered Zion. 2 Upon the willows, in their midst, we hung our harps. 3 For there our captors demanded songs of us, our tormentors mirth, saying, sing us of the songs of Zion. 4 How can we sing the song of the Lord on foreign soil? 5 If I forget you, O Jerusalem, let my right hand be disabled. 6 My tongue will cleave to my palate if I do not remember you, if I do not place you above my chief joy. 7 Remember, O Lord, the Jerusalem day when the sons of Edom said, raze, raze, to its very foundation. 8 O daughter of Babylon, it is you who are the annihilated one. Fortunate is the one who will repay you for what you have done to us. 9 Fortunate is he who will seize and dash your little ones against the rock.

This is a poem of thanksgiving and entreaty. The psalmist thanks God for past kindnesses, which in themselves glorify His name, and requests that God continue to show him lovingkindness in the future.

138 A psalm by David. I will praise You with all my heart; I will sing praises to You before gods. 2 I will prostrate myself toward Your holy sanctuary and give thanks to Your name, for Your mercy and Your truth; for You have made Your word far greater than even Your name. 3 On the day that I called, You answered me; You made me bold, and made my soul strong. 4 All the kings of the earth will give thanks to You, O Lord, when they hear the words of Your mouth. 5 They will sing of the ways of the Lord, for the glory of the Lord is great. 6 Though the Lord is exalted, He regards the lowly; the haughty He knows from afar. 7 Though I walk in the midst of trouble, You will revive me; You will stretch out Your hand against my enemy's wrath; Your right hand will save me. 8 The Lord will finish this for me; Your mercy, God, is everlasting; do not forsake the work of Your hands.

This is a song of introspection and devotion. The psalmist cleaves to God, aware that God is omnipresent in all situations, in darkness and in light, from the beginning of life until its end. Continual and all-encompassing closeness to God is the basis of devotion. In this song, the psalmist identifies with God, expressing love for those beloved by God, and hatred for His enemies.

139 For the chief musician, a psalm by David. O Lord, You have searched me, and know me. 2 You know when I sit down and when I rise up; You understand my thoughts from afar. 3 You encompass my journeys and my rests; You know all my ways. 4 There is no word on my tongue, yet You know it all. 5 You created the front and back of me; You formed me with Your hand. 6 This knowledge is too wonderful for me; it is above me. I cannot attain it. 7 Where could I go from Your spirit? Where could I flee from Your presence? 8 If I ascend to heaven, You are there; if I make my bed in a netherworld, You are there. 9 If I traveled on the wings of the dawn, if I dwelled in the most remote sea, 10 Even there Your hand would lead me, Your right hand would hold me. 11 If I say darkness will surely envelop me; light around me will turn to night 12 Even darkness is not dark to You, and the night is as bright as day. Darkness and light are alike to You. 13 For You formed my organs; You sheltered me in my mother's womb. 14 I will give thanks to You, for I have been formed by Your awesome and wonderful deeds. Wonderful are Your works; my soul knows this well. 15 My essence was not hidden from You when I was made in secret, wrought from the depths of earth. 16 Your eyes saw my unformed substance. And in Your book were written all the days created for me, as well as the one that is His. 17 How precious to me are thoughts of You, O God. How vast the sum of them. 18 If I tried to count them, they would outnumber the sand. If I were I to finish, I would still be with You. 19 If only You, my God, would slay the wicked, remove from me men of bloodshed 20 Enemies who speak Your name profanely, and in vain. 21 Do I not hate those who hate You, and loathe those who rise up against You? 22 I hate them with the utmost hatred; they have become my enemies. 23 Search me, O God, and know my heart; test me and know my thoughts. 24 And see if there is any wicked way in me. Lead me on an everlasting path.

This is an entreaty to God to rescue the psalmist from evil adversaries, who betray him in secret and use all of the means in their power to carry out their evil treason. The psalmist prays to see their downfall.

140 For the chief musician, a psalm by David. 2 Rescue me, O Lord, from an evil man; preserve me from a violent man 2 And from men who devise evil things in their hearts, and continually stir up wars. 3 They sharpen their tongues like serpents; viper's venom is under their lips, Selah. 4 Keep me, O Lord, from the hands of the wicked; preserve me from a violent man who conspires to trip my feet. 5 The haughty have hidden a trap for me; they have spread a net with ropes by the wayside, and set snares for me, Selah. 6 I said to the Lord, You are my Lord, listen, O Lord, to the voice of my supplications. 7 O God, my Lord, strength of my deliverance, You have protected my head in the day of battle. 8 O Lord, do not grant the desires of the wicked. Do not promote his aspirations, so that they can exalt themselves, Selah. 10 As for the heads of those who surround me, may the mischief of their own lips cover them. 11 Let burning coals fall on them. May they be cast into the fire, into deep pits from which they cannot rise. 12 A slanderer will not be established on the earth. An evil violent man will be pushed into his own traps. 13 I know that the Lord will do justice to the poor and be just to the needy. 14 The righteous will surely give thanks to Your name; the upright will dwell in Your presence.

This is a poem of supplication for rescue from the hands of the wicked, and from evil itself. The psalmist pleads to God to help him withstand the seductions of the wicked and their evil ways; he pleads to be rescued from their hands as they become his enemies.

141 A psalm of David. O Lord, I have called out to You; hurry to help me. Listen to my voice as I call out to You. 2 Let my prayer be as an offering of incense before You, the lifting of my hands as an evening offering. 3 Place a guard, O Lord, at my mouth; watch over the door to my lips. 4 Do not incline my heart to any evil thing, to practice deeds of wickedness with men of iniquity. Do not let me eat of their delicacies. 5 Let the righteous men smite me in kindness to reprove me; it is oil upon my head. Do not let me refuse it. My prayer is against wicked deeds. 6 They are cast on the rocks by their judges, who hear my words, for they are pleasing. 7 Our bones have been scattered at the mouth of the grave, as if the earth had been plowed and broken up. 8 My eyes look to You, O Lord, my Master; in You I take refuge. Do not leave me defenseless. 9 Keep me from the jaws of the trap that they have set for me, from the snares of the doers of evil. 10 Let the wicked fall together into their own nets, until I pass by.

This is a supplication by one who is alone, surrounded on all sides by hatred and enemies. He prays to be rescued from all of the malevolence.

142 An instruction, a prayer, by David when he was in the cave. 2 I cry to the Lord with my voice; I plead to the Lord with my voice. 3 I pour out my prayer before Him; I speak of my troubles to His face. 4 When my moods engulfed me, You knew my way. They have hidden a trap for me. 5 Look to the right and see; there is no one who acknowledges me. No one cares for my soul. 6 I cried out to You, O Lord, and said You are my refuge, my lot in the land of the living. 7 Listen to my cry, for I have been brought very low. Deliver me from my persecutors; they are too strong for me. 8 Bring my soul out of prison, so that I may give thanks to Your name. The righteous will surround me, for You will deal bountifully with me.

This is a song of supplication that has a dual request: a spiritual one, to be worthy of God's forgiveness for past sins and for help in choosing the right path in the future, and a material one, to be worthy of immediate redemption from enemies and adversaries.

143 A psalm by David. O Lord, hear my prayer, listen to my supplications. Answer me in Your faithfulness, in Your righteousness. 2 And do not enter into judgment of Your servant, for no life can be justified before You. 3 The enemy has pursued my soul, crushed my life to the ground, placed me in dark places, like the eternally dead. 4 My mood envelops me; my heart is appalled within me. 5 I remember the days of old. I meditate on all Your doings; I muse on the work of Your hands. 6 I stretch out my hands to You. My soul, like a parched land, longs for You, Selah. 7 Answer me quickly, O Lord; my spirit fails. Do not hide Your face from me, or I will become like those who descend to a pit. 8 Let me hear Your mercy in the morning, for I trust in You. Let me know the way in which I should walk, for I lift up my soul to You. 9 Deliver me, O Lord, from my enemies; I take refuge in You. 10 Teach me to do Your will, for You are my God. Let Your good spirit lead me to level ground. 11 Revive me, for the sake of Your name, O Lord. In Your righteousness, bring my soul out of trouble. 12 And in Your mercy, cut off my enemies, and destroy all of the oppressors of my soul, for I am Your servant.

This poem of glory and victory enlightens about war and the peace that follows. It is a poem about the thankfulness of the victor, who attributes his triumph not to his own bravery but to God's salvation. God saved him from evil enemies, which enabled him, in the end, to give wholehearted thanks for the tranquility, peacefulness, and expansive happiness that have come to all.

144 A psalm by David. Blessed is the Lord, my rock, who trains my hands for war, my fingers for battle. 2 My mercy and my fortress, my stronghold and my deliverer, my shield, is He in whom I take refuge, who subdues people under me. 3 O Lord, what is man that You should acknowledge him, the son of man that You should think of him? Man is like vapor, his days like a passing shadow. 5 O Lord, bend Your heavens and descend; touch the mountains and they will smoke. 6 Flash lightning and scatter them; send Your arrows and stun them. 7 Stretch out Your hand from above; deliver and rescue me from powerful waters, from the hand of strangers 8 Whose mouths speak deceit, whose right hand is a hand of falsehood. 9 I will sing a new song to You, God. On a harp of ten strings I will sing praises to You, 10 Who give salvation to kings, who rescue David, His servant, from the evil sword. 11 Rescue me and deliver me out of the hands of strangers, whose mouths speak deceit, whose right hand is the right hand of falsehood. 12 Let our sons be like plants nourished from youth, and our daughters like corner pillars fashioned for a palace 13 And our garners, full, with every kind of produce, our flocks increasing by the thousands and ten thousands in our fields 14 Our leaders tolerated without rebellion or revolt and without outcries in the streets. 15 Fortunate is a nation like this; fortunate are the people whose Lord is God.

This poem of glory teaches of God's greatness, specifically of His mercy and lovingkindness. It is a poem of thanksgiving and praise, recited by those who acknowledge God's greatness and praise Him for the kindness He shows to all who are in need – the suffering, the hungry, and all who call out to Him in truth.

145 A psalm of praise, by David. I will extol You, my God, the King, and I will bless Your name forever and ever. 2 Every day I will bless You, and I will praise Your name forever and ever. 3 The Lord is great, and highly extolled; His greatness is unfathomable. 4 From generation to generation Your works will be praised; they will declare Your mighty acts. 5 I will meditate on the splendor of your glorious majesty, and on the words of Your wonders. 6 They speak of the power of Your awesome acts. I will tell of Your greatness. 7 They will express remembrance of Your bountifulness, and exultation of Your righteousness. 8 The Lord is gracious and merciful, slow to anger and great in lovingkindness. 9 The Lord is good to all; His mercy extends to all of His works. 10 All of Your works will thank You, O Lord, and Your pious ones will bless You. 11 They will speak of the glory of Your kingdom, and speak of Your power 12 To make Your mighty acts, and the glory of the majesty of Your kingdom, known to the sons of men. 13 Your kingdom is a kingdom of all worlds; Your reign endures from generation to generation. 14 The Lord supports all who fall, and straightens all who are bowed down. 15 All eyes look to You, and You give them their food in its time. 16 You open Your hand and satisfy the desire of every living thing. 17 The Lord is righteous in all His ways, and kind in all His deeds. 18 The Lord is near to all who call Him, to all who call Him in truth. 19 He grants the wishes of those who fear Him; He hears their cry and delivers them. 20 He watches over all who love Him, and destroys all the wicked. 21 My mouth will speak praise of the Lord, and all flesh will bless His holy name forever and ever.

This is a poem of introspection and praise. Man should not depend on promises made by others, no matter who they are, because even the strongest and most charitable human beings can disappear. But man can rely on God's help. God helps everyone, especially the miserable, who have no true relief, except from God.

146 Halleluya. My soul praises the Lord. 2 I will praise the Lord while I live; I will sing praises to the Lord while I am alive. 3 Do not put trust in princes, in mortal man, in whom there is no salvation. 4 His spirit departs; he returns to the earth. On that day his plans perish. 5 Fortunate is he whose help is from the God of Jacob, whose hope is in the Lord his God 6 Who made heaven and earth, the sea and all that is in it, who guards truth forever. 7 Who executes justice for the oppressed, who gives bread to the hungry. The Lord releases the imprisoned. 8 The Lord restores sight to the blind; the Lord straightens the bent. The Lord loves the righteous. 9 The Lord protects strangers. He encourages orphan and widow. He thwarts the way of the wicked. 10 The Lord will reign forever, your Lord, Zion, from generation to generation, Halleluya.

This poem of glory speaks, on one hand, of God's power, revealed in various acts of nature, and on the other hand, of God's involvement in the lives of all those in need of help, especially the people of Israel, whom God embraces and supports.

147 Halleluya, for it is good to sing to our God, for praise is befitting and pleasant. 2 The Lord builds Jerusalem, and will gather the banished ones of Israel. 3 He heals the brokenhearted and binds their wounds. 4 He fixes the number of stars, and calls them all by name. 5 The Lord is great and abundant in strength; His understanding is infinite. 6 The Lord encourages the humble, and brings the wicked down to the ground. 7 Sing to the Lord with thanksgiving; sing praises on the lyre to our God 8 Who covers the heavens with clouds, provides rain for the earth, and makes grass grow on the mountains. 9 He gives food to the beasts and to young ravens when they call. 10 He does not desire the strength of horses, or want the strong muscles of man. 11 The Lord wants those who fear him and those who wait for His mercy. 12 Praise the Lord, Jerusalem. Praise your God, Zion. 13 For He has strengthened the bars of your gates; He has blessed your sons within. 14 He makes peace at your borders; He satisfies you with the finest wheat. 15 He sends His commands to earth; His word races swiftly. 16 He sends snow like fleece, scatters frost like ashes. 17 Who can withstand His cold? He hurls ice in pieces. 18 He sends word and melts them; He makes His wind blow, and they flow like water. 19 He declares His word to Jacob, His statutes and laws to Israel. 20 He has not done so with any other nation; they have not known His laws. Halleluya.

This is a choral poem, a call for everyone to join in praise of God. In this poem the world is divided (as is the song) into two parts. The first part speaks of celestial creations, the heavens and all they contain (spiritual beings and angels). The second part speaks of the inhabitants of the earth: creatures large and small, natural forces, animal and vegetative life, and all of humanity. The song ends with praise of people of Israel, who acknowledge and exalt God for everything.

148 Halleluya. Praise the Lord from the heavens, Halleluya from the heights. 2 Praise Him, all of His angels; praise Him, all of his legions. 3 Praise Him, sun and moon; praise Him all the stars of light. 4 Praise Him, highest heavens, and the waters that are above the heavens. 5 They will praise the name of the Lord, for He commanded and they were created. 6 He established them for all time; it is a decree that will not be altered. 7 Praise the Lord from the earth, sea creatures and all that is deep 8 Fire and hail, snow and clouds, stormy wind fulfilling His word. 9 Mountains and all the hills, fruit trees and all the cedars 10 Beasts and all cattle, creeping things and winged fowl, 11 Kings of the earth and all peoples, princes and all judges on earth, 12 Young men and virgins, old men and children 13 They all praise the name of the Lord, for His name alone is exalted. His glory is above earth and heaven. 14 He will raise the stature of His people, bring praise for all His pious ones, for the children of Israel, the people near to Him, Halleluya.

This is a poem of glory and of war. God is exalted and glorified by a community of the righteous who are eager to fight God's battles. Those who love God and are devoted to Him are not satisfied to serve Him only with words of praise. Even if weapons are needed, they actively fight evil, and are victorious.

149 Halleluya. Sing to the Lord, a new song; Praise Him in a congregation of the devoted. 2 Israel will rejoice in its Creator; the sons of Zion will rejoice in their King. 3 They will praise His name with dance; with drum and harp they will sing to Him. 4 For the Lord desires His people; He will adorn the humble with salvation. 5 His devoted ones will rejoice in honor; they will sing for joy on their beds. 6 High praise for the Almighty will be in their throats, and a double-edged sword in their hand 7 To avenge nations and punish peoples 8 To bind their kings with chains and their nobles with iron fetters. 9 This is an honor for His pious ones, to carry out judgment written for them. Halleluya.

This is a poem for chorus. Its central theme is that glorification and praise of God can be expressed by all means and in all ways. His greatness and magnitude are communicated by instruments that blast and trumpet their sounds, as well as by instruments with refined, delicate resonance. Just as all of the different instruments express praise of God, so do all souls. "Let every soul praise the Lord" not only means all different types of souls, but also all parts of every soul.

150 Halleluya. Praise the Almighty in His sanctuary; praise Him in the heaven of His might. 2 Praise Him for His mighty deeds; praise Him in accord with the abundance of His greatness. 3 Praise Him with the blowing of the shofar; praise Him with lyre and harp. 4 Praise Him with drum and dance; praise Him with stringed instruments and flute. 5 Praise Him with resounding cymbals; praise Him with bursts of cymbals. 6 Let every soul praise the Lord. Halleluya.

ספר תהילים

א: אַשְׁרֵי הָאִישׁ אֲשֶׁר לֹא הָלַךְ בַּעֲצַת רְשָׁעִים וּבְדֶרֶךְ חַטָּאִים לֹא עָמָד וּבְמוֹשַׁב לֵצִים לֹא יָשָׁב:

ב: כִּי אִם בְּתוֹרַת יְהוָה חֶפְצוֹ וּבְתוֹרָתוֹ יֶהְגֶּה יוֹמָם וָלָיְלָה:

ג: וְהָיָה כְּעֵץ שָׁתוּל עַל פַּלְגֵי מָיִם אֲשֶׁר פִּרְיוֹ יִתֵּן בְּעִתּוֹ וְעָלֵהוּ לֹא יִבּוֹל וְכֹל אֲשֶׁר יַעֲשֶׂה יַצְלִיחַ:

ד: לֹא כֵן הָרְשָׁעִים כִּי אִם כַּמֹּץ אֲשֶׁר תִּדְּפֶנּוּ רוּחַ:

ה: עַל כֵּן לֹא יָקֻמוּ רְשָׁעִים בַּמִּשְׁפָּט וְחַטָּאִים בַּעֲדַת צַדִּיקִים:

ו: כִּי יוֹדֵעַ יְהוָה דֶּרֶךְ צַדִּיקִים וְדֶרֶךְ רְשָׁעִים תֹּאבֵד:

פרק ב

א: לָמָּה רָגְשׁוּ גוֹיִם וּלְאֻמִּים יֶהְגּוּ רִיק:

ב: יִתְיַצְּבוּ מַלְכֵי אֶרֶץ וְרוֹזְנִים נוֹסְדוּ יָחַד עַל יְהוָה וְעַל מְשִׁיחוֹ:

ג: נְנַתְּקָה אֶת מוֹסְרוֹתֵימוֹ וְנַשְׁלִיכָה מִמֶּנּוּ עֲבֹתֵימוֹ:

ד: יוֹשֵׁב בַּשָּׁמַיִם יִשְׂחָק אֲדֹנָי יִלְעַג לָמוֹ:

ה: אָז יְדַבֵּר אֵלֵימוֹ בְאַפּוֹ וּבַחֲרוֹנוֹ יְבַהֲלֵמוֹ:

ו: וַאֲנִי נָסַכְתִּי מַלְכִּי עַל צִיּוֹן הַר קָדְשִׁי:

ז: אֲסַפְּרָה אֶל חֹק יְהוָה אָמַר אֵלַי בְּנִי אַתָּה אֲנִי הַיּוֹם יְלִדְתִּיךָ:

ח: שְׁאַל מִמֶּנִּי וְאֶתְּנָה גוֹיִם נַחֲלָתֶךָ וַאֲחֻזָּתְךָ אַפְסֵי אָרֶץ:

ט: תְּרֹעֵם בְּשֵׁבֶט בַּרְזֶל כִּכְלִי יוֹצֵר תְּנַפְּצֵם:

י: וְעַתָּה מְלָכִים הַשְׂכִּילוּ הִוָּסְרוּ שֹׁפְטֵי אָרֶץ:

יא: עִבְדוּ אֶת יְהוָה בְּיִרְאָה וְגִילוּ בִּרְעָדָה:

יב: נַשְּׁקוּ בַר פֶּן יֶאֱנַף וְתֹאבְדוּ דֶרֶךְ כִּי יִבְעַר כִּמְעַט אַפּוֹ אַשְׁרֵי כָּל חוֹסֵי בוֹ:

פרק ג

א: מִזְמוֹר לְדָוִד בְּבָרְחוֹ מִפְּנֵי אַבְשָׁלוֹם בְּנוֹ:

ב: יְהוָה מָה רַבּוּ צָרָי רַבִּים קָמִים עָלָי:

ג: רַבִּים אֹמְרִים לְנַפְשִׁי אֵין יְשׁוּעָתָה לּוֹ בֵאלֹהִים סֶלָה:

ד: וְאַתָּה יְהוָה מָגֵן בַּעֲדִי כְּבוֹדִי וּמֵרִים רֹאשִׁי:

ה: קוֹלִי אֶל יְהוָה אֶקְרָא וַיַּעֲנֵנִי מֵהַר קָדְשׁוֹ סֶלָה:

ו: אֲנִי שָׁכַבְתִּי וָאִישָׁנָה הֱקִיצוֹתִי כִּי יְהוָה יִסְמְכֵנִי:

ז: לֹא אִירָא מֵרִבְבוֹת עָם אֲשֶׁר סָבִיב שָׁתוּ עָלָי:

ח: קוּמָה יְהוָה הוֹשִׁיעֵנִי אֱלֹהַי כִּי הִכִּיתָ אֶת כָּל אֹיְבַי לֶחִי שִׁנֵּי רְשָׁעִים שִׁבַּרְתָּ:

ט: לַיהוָה הַיְשׁוּעָה עַל עַמְּךָ בִרְכָתֶךָ סֶּלָה:

פרק ד

א: לַמְנַצֵּחַ בִּנְגִינוֹת מִזְמוֹר לְדָוִד:

ב: בְּקָרְאִי עֲנֵנִי אֱלֹהֵי צִדְקִי בַּצָּר הִרְחַבְתָּ לִּי חָנֵּנִי וּשְׁמַע תְּפִלָּתִי:

ג: בְּנֵי אִישׁ עַד מֶה כְבוֹדִי לִכְלִמָּה תֶּאֱהָבוּן רִיק תְּבַקְשׁוּ כָזָב סֶלָה:

ד: וּדְעוּ כִּי הִפְלָה יְהוָה חָסִיד לוֹ יְהוָה יִשְׁמַע בְּקָרְאִי אֵלָיו:

ה: רִגְזוּ וְאַל תֶּחֱטָאוּ אִמְרוּ בִלְבַבְכֶם עַל מִשְׁכַּבְכֶם וְדֹמּוּ סֶלָה:

ו: זִבְחוּ זִבְחֵי צֶדֶק וּבִטְחוּ אֶל יְהוָה:

ז: רַבִּים אֹמְרִים מִי יַרְאֵנוּ טוֹב נְסָה עָלֵינוּ אוֹר פָּנֶיךָ יְהוָה:

ח: נָתַתָּה שִׂמְחָה בְלִבִּי מֵעֵת דְּגָנָם וְתִירוֹשָׁם רָבּוּ:

ט: בְּשָׁלוֹם יַחְדָּו אֶשְׁכְּבָה וְאִישָׁן כִּי אַתָּה יְהוָה לְבָדָד לָבֶטַח תּוֹשִׁיבֵנִי:

פרק ה

א: לַמְנַצֵּחַ אֶל הַנְּחִילוֹת מִזְמוֹר לְדָוִד:

ב: אֲמָרַי הַאֲזִינָה יְהוָה בִּינָה הֲגִיגִי:

ג: הַקְשִׁיבָה לְקוֹל שַׁוְעִי מַלְכִּי וֵאלֹהָי כִּי אֵלֶיךָ אֶתְפַּלָּל:

ד: יְהוָה בֹּקֶר תִּשְׁמַע קוֹלִי בֹּקֶר אֶעֱרָךְ לְךָ וַאֲצַפֶּה:

ה: כִּי לֹא אֵל חָפֵץ רֶשַׁע אָתָּה לֹא יְגֻרְךָ רָע:

ו: לֹא יִתְיַצְּבוּ הוֹלְלִים לְנֶגֶד עֵינֶיךָ שָׂנֵאתָ כָּל פֹּעֲלֵי אָוֶן:

ז: תְּאַבֵּד דֹּבְרֵי כָזָב אִישׁ דָּמִים וּמִרְמָה יְתָעֵב יְהוָה:

ח: וַאֲנִי בְּרֹב חַסְדְּךָ אָבוֹא בֵיתֶךָ אֶשְׁתַּחֲוֶה אֶל הֵיכַל קָדְשְׁךָ בְּיִרְאָתֶךָ:

ט: יְהוָה נְחֵנִי בְצִדְקָתֶךָ לְמַעַן שׁוֹרְרָי הושר {הַיְשַׁר} לְפָנַי דַּרְכֶּךָ:

י: כִּי אֵין בְּפִיהוּ נְכוֹנָה קִרְבָּם הַוּוֹת קֶבֶר פָּתוּחַ גְּרוֹנָם לְשׁוֹנָם יַחֲלִיקוּן:

יא: הַאֲשִׁימֵם אֱלֹהִים יִפְּלוּ מִמֹּעֲצוֹתֵיהֶם בְּרֹב פִּשְׁעֵיהֶם הַדִּיחֵמוֹ כִּי מָרוּ בָךְ:

יב: וְיִשְׂמְחוּ כָל חוֹסֵי בָךְ לְעוֹלָם יְרַנֵּנוּ וְתָסֵךְ עָלֵימוֹ וְיַעְלְצוּ בְךָ אֹהֲבֵי שְׁמֶךָ:

יג: כִּי אַתָּה תְּבָרֵךְ צַדִּיק יְהוָה כַּצִּנָּה רָצוֹן תַּעְטְרֶנּוּ:

פרק ו

א: לַמְנַצֵּחַ בִּנְגִינוֹת עַל הַשְּׁמִינִית מִזְמוֹר לְדָוִד:

ב: יְהוָה אַל בְּאַפְּךָ תוֹכִיחֵנִי וְאַל בַּחֲמָתְךָ תְיַסְּרֵנִי:

ג: חָנֵּנִי יְהוָה כִּי אֻמְלַל אָנִי רְפָאֵנִי יְהוָה כִּי נִבְהֲלוּ עֲצָמָי:

ד: וְנַפְשִׁי נִבְהֲלָה מְאֹד וְאַתָּה יְהוָה עַד מָתָי:

ה: שׁוּבָה יְהוָה חַלְּצָה נַפְשִׁי הוֹשִׁיעֵנִי לְמַעַן חַסְדֶּךָ:

ו: כִּי אֵין בַּמָּוֶת זִכְרֶךָ בִּשְׁאוֹל מִי יוֹדֶה לָּךְ:

ז: יָגַעְתִּי בְּאַנְחָתִי אַשְׂחֶה בְכָל לַיְלָה מִטָּתִי בְּדִמְעָתִי עַרְשִׂי אַמְסֶה:

ח: עָשְׁשָׁה מִכַּעַס עֵינִי עָתְקָה בְּכָל צוֹרְרָי:

ט: סוּרוּ מִמֶּנִּי כָּל פֹּעֲלֵי אָוֶן כִּי שָׁמַע יְהוָה קוֹל בִּכְיִי:

י: שָׁמַע יְהוָה תְּחִנָּתִי יְהוָה תְּפִלָּתִי יִקָּח:

יא: יֵבֹשׁוּ וְיִבָּהֲלוּ מְאֹד כָּל אֹיְבָי יָשֻׁבוּ יֵבֹשׁוּ רָגַע:

פרק ז

א: שִׁגָּיוֹן לְדָוִד אֲשֶׁר שָׁר לַיהוָה עַל דִּבְרֵי כוּשׁ בֶּן יְמִינִי:

ב: יְהוָה אֱלֹהַי בְּךָ חָסִיתִי הוֹשִׁיעֵנִי מִכָּל רֹדְפַי וְהַצִּילֵנִי:

ג: פֶּן יִטְרֹף כְּאַרְיֵה נַפְשִׁי פֹּרֵק וְאֵין מַצִּיל:

ד: יְהוָה אֱלֹהַי אִם עָשִׂיתִי זֹאת אִם יֶשׁ עָוֶל בְּכַפָּי:

ה: אִם גָּמַלְתִּי שׁוֹלְמִי רָע וָאֲחַלְּצָה צוֹרְרִי רֵיקָם:

ו: יִרַדֹּף אוֹיֵב נַפְשִׁי וְיַשֵּׂג וְיִרְמֹס לָאָרֶץ חַיָּי וּכְבוֹדִי לֶעָפָר יַשְׁכֵּן סֶלָה:

ז: קוּמָה יְהוָה בְּאַפֶּךָ הִנָּשֵׂא בְּעַבְרוֹת צוֹרְרָי וְעוּרָה אֵלַי מִשְׁפָּט צִוִּיתָ:

ח: וַעֲדַת לְאֻמִּים תְּסוֹבְבֶךָּ וְעָלֶיהָ לַמָּרוֹם שׁוּבָה:

ט: יְהוָה יָדִין עַמִּים שָׁפְטֵנִי יְהוָה כְּצִדְקִי וּכְתֻמִּי עָלָי:

י: יִגְמָר נָא רַע רְשָׁעִים וּתְכוֹנֵן צַדִּיק וּבֹחֵן לִבּוֹת וּכְלָיוֹת אֱלֹהִים צַדִּיק:

יא: מָגִנִּי עַל אֱלֹהִים מוֹשִׁיעַ יִשְׁרֵי לֵב:

יב: אֱלֹהִים שׁוֹפֵט צַדִּיק וְאֵל זֹעֵם בְּכָל יוֹם:

יג: אִם לֹא יָשׁוּב חַרְבּוֹ יִלְטוֹשׁ קַשְׁתּוֹ דָרַךְ וַיְכוֹנְנֶהָ:

יד: וְלוֹ הֵכִין כְּלֵי מָוֶת חִצָּיו לְדֹלְקִים יִפְעָל:

טו: הִנֵּה יְחַבֶּל אָוֶן וְהָרָה עָמָל וְיָלַד שָׁקֶר:

טז: בּוֹר כָּרָה וַיַּחְפְּרֵהוּ וַיִּפֹּל בְּשַׁחַת יִפְעָל:

יז: יָשׁוּב עֲמָלוֹ בְרֹאשׁוֹ וְעַל קָדְקֳדוֹ חֲמָסוֹ יֵרֵד:

יח: אוֹדֶה יְהוָה כְּצִדְקוֹ וַאֲזַמְּרָה שֵׁם יְהוָה עֶלְיוֹן:

פרק ח

א: לַמְנַצֵּחַ עַל הַגִּתִּית מִזְמוֹר לְדָוִד:

ב: יְהוָה אֲדֹנֵינוּ מָה אַדִּיר שִׁמְךָ בְּכָל הָאָרֶץ אֲשֶׁר תְּנָה הוֹדְךָ עַל הַשָּׁמָיִם:

ג: מִפִּי עוֹלְלִים וְיֹנְקִים יִסַּדְתָּ עֹז לְמַעַן צוֹרְרֶיךָ לְהַשְׁבִּית אוֹיֵב וּמִתְנַקֵּם:

ד: כִּי אֶרְאֶה שָׁמֶיךָ מַעֲשֵׂה אֶצְבְּעֹתֶיךָ יָרֵחַ וְכוֹכָבִים אֲשֶׁר כּוֹנָנְתָּה:

ה: מָה אֱנוֹשׁ כִּי תִזְכְּרֶנּוּ וּבֶן אָדָם כִּי תִפְקְדֶנּוּ:

ו: וַתְּחַסְּרֵהוּ מְּעַט מֵאֱלֹהִים וְכָבוֹד וְהָדָר תְּעַטְּרֵהוּ:

ז: תַּמְשִׁילֵהוּ בְּמַעֲשֵׂי יָדֶיךָ כֹּל שַׁתָּה תַחַת רַגְלָיו:

ח: צֹנֶה וַאֲלָפִים כֻּלָּם וְגַם בַּהֲמוֹת שָׂדָי:

ט: צִפּוֹר שָׁמַיִם וּדְגֵי הַיָּם עֹבֵר אָרְחוֹת יַמִּים:

י: יְהוָה אֲדֹנֵינוּ מָה אַדִּיר שִׁמְךָ בְּכָל הָאָרֶץ:

פרק ט

א: לַמְנַצֵּחַ עַל מוּת לַבֵּן מִזְמוֹר לְדָוִד:

ב: אוֹדֶה יְהוָה בְּכָל לִבִּי אֲסַפְּרָה כָּל נִפְלְאוֹתֶיךָ:

ג: אֶשְׂמְחָה וְאֶעֶלְצָה בָךְ אֲזַמְּרָה שִׁמְךָ עֶלְיוֹן:

ד: בְּשׁוּב אוֹיְבַי אָחוֹר יִכָּשְׁלוּ וְיֹאבְדוּ מִפָּנֶיךָ:

ה: כִּי עָשִׂיתָ מִשְׁפָּטִי וְדִינִי יָשַׁבְתָּ לְכִסֵּא שׁוֹפֵט צֶדֶק:

ו: גָּעַרְתָּ גוֹיִם אִבַּדְתָּ רָשָׁע שְׁמָם מָחִיתָ לְעוֹלָם וָעֶד:

ז: הָאוֹיֵב תַּמּוּ חֳרָבוֹת לָנֶצַח וְעָרִים נָתַשְׁתָּ אָבַד זִכְרָם הֵמָּה:

ח: וַיהוָה לְעוֹלָם יֵשֵׁב כּוֹנֵן לַמִּשְׁפָּט כִּסְאוֹ:

ט: וְהוּא יִשְׁפֹּט תֵּבֵל בְּצֶדֶק יָדִין לְאֻמִּים בְּמֵישָׁרִים:

י: וִיהִי יְהוָה מִשְׂגָּב לַדָּךְ מִשְׂגָּב לְעִתּוֹת בַּצָּרָה:

יא: וְיִבְטְחוּ בְךָ יוֹדְעֵי שְׁמֶךָ כִּי לֹא עָזַבְתָּ דֹרְשֶׁיךָ יְהוָה:

יב: זַמְּרוּ לַיהוָה יֹשֵׁב צִיּוֹן הַגִּידוּ בָעַמִּים עֲלִילוֹתָיו:

יג: כִּי דֹרֵשׁ דָּמִים אוֹתָם זָכָר לֹא שָׁכַח צַעֲקַת עֲנִיִּים {עֲנָוִים}:

יד: חָנְנֵנִי יְהוָה רְאֵה עָנְיִי מִשֹּׂנְאָי מְרוֹמְמִי מִשַּׁעֲרֵי מָוֶת:

טו: לְמַעַן אֲסַפְּרָה כָּל תְּהִלָּתֶיךָ בְּשַׁעֲרֵי בַת צִיּוֹן אָגִילָה בִּישׁוּעָתֶךָ:

טז: טָבְעוּ גוֹיִם בְּשַׁחַת עָשׂוּ בְּרֶשֶׁת זוּ טָמָנוּ נִלְכְּדָה רַגְלָם:

יז: נוֹדַע יְהוָה מִשְׁפָּט עָשָׂה בְּפֹעַל כַּפָּיו נוֹקֵשׁ רָשָׁע הִגָּיוֹן סֶלָה:

יח: יָשׁוּבוּ רְשָׁעִים לִשְׁאוֹלָה כָּל גּוֹיִם שְׁכֵחֵי אֱלֹהִים:

יט: כִּי לֹא לָנֶצַח יִשָּׁכַח אֶבְיוֹן תִּקְוַת עֲנָוִים {עֲנִיִּים} תֹּאבַד לָעַד:

כ: קוּמָה יְהוָה אַל יָעֹז אֱנוֹשׁ יִשָּׁפְטוּ גוֹיִם עַל פָּנֶיךָ:

כא: שִׁיתָה יְהוָה מוֹרָה לָהֶם יֵדְעוּ גוֹיִם אֱנוֹשׁ הֵמָּה סֶלָה:

פרק י

א: לָמָה יְהוָה תַּעֲמֹד בְּרָחוֹק תַּעְלִים לְעִתּוֹת בַּצָּרָה:

ב: בְּגַאֲוַת רָשָׁע יִדְלַק עָנִי יִתָּפְשׂוּ בִּמְזִמּוֹת זוּ חָשָׁבוּ:

ג: כִּי הִלֵּל רָשָׁע עַל תַּאֲוַת נַפְשׁוֹ וּבֹצֵעַ בֵּרֵךְ נִאֵץ יְהוָה:

ד: רָשָׁע כְּגֹבַהּ אַפּוֹ בַּל יִדְרֹשׁ אֵין אֱלֹהִים כָּל מְזִמּוֹתָיו:

ה: יָחִילוּ דְרָכָו בְּכָל עֵת מָרוֹם מִשְׁפָּטֶיךָ מִנֶּגְדּוֹ כָּל צוֹרְרָיו יָפִיחַ בָּהֶם:

ו: אָמַר בְּלִבּוֹ בַּל אֶמּוֹט לְדֹר וָדֹר אֲשֶׁר לֹא בְרָע:

ז: אָלָה פִּיהוּ מָלֵא וּמִרְמוֹת וָתֹךְ תַּחַת לְשׁוֹנוֹ עָמָל וָאָוֶן:

ח: יֵשֵׁב בְּמַאְרַב חֲצֵרִים בַּמִּסְתָּרִים יַהֲרֹג נָקִי עֵינָיו לְחֵלְכָה יִצְפֹּנוּ:

ט: יֶאֱרֹב בַּמִּסְתָּר כְּאַרְיֵה בְסֻכֹּה יֶאֱרֹב לַחֲטוֹף עָנִי יַחְטֹף עָנִי בְּמָשְׁכוֹ בְרִשְׁתּוֹ:

י: דכה {וְדָכָה} יָשֹׁחַ וְנָפַל בַּעֲצוּמָיו חלכאים {חֵיל כָּאִים}:

יא: אָמַר בְּלִבּוֹ שָׁכַח אֵל הִסְתִּיר פָּנָיו בַּל רָאָה לָנֶצַח:

יב: קוּמָה יְהוָה אֵל נְשָׂא יָדֶךָ אַל תִּשְׁכַּח עֲנָוִים {עֲנִיִּים}:

יג: עַל מֶה נִאֵץ רָשָׁע אֱלֹהִים אָמַר בְּלִבּוֹ לֹא תִדְרֹשׁ:

יד: רָאִיתָה כִּי אַתָּה עָמָל וָכַעַס תַּבִּיט לָתֵת בְּיָדֶךָ עָלֶיךָ יַעֲזֹב חֵלְכָה יָתוֹם אַתָּה הָיִיתָ עוֹזֵר:

טו: שְׁבֹר זְרוֹעַ רָשָׁע וָרָע תִּדְרוֹשׁ רִשְׁעוֹ בַל תִּמְצָא:

טז: יְהוָה מֶלֶךְ עוֹלָם וָעֶד אָבְדוּ גוֹיִם מֵאַרְצוֹ:

יז: תַּאֲוַת עֲנָוִים שָׁמַעְתָּ יְהוָה תָּכִין לִבָּם תַּקְשִׁיב אָזְנֶךָ:

יח: לִשְׁפֹּט יָתוֹם וָדָךְ בַּל יוֹסִיף עוֹד לַעֲרֹץ אֱנוֹשׁ מִן הָאָרֶץ:

פרק יא

א: לַמְנַצֵּחַ לְדָוִד בַּיהוָה חָסִיתִי אֵיךְ תֹּאמְרוּ לְנַפְשִׁי נודו {נֻדִי} הַרְכֶם צִפּוֹר:

ב: כִּי הִנֵּה הָרְשָׁעִים יִדְרְכוּן קֶשֶׁת כּוֹנְנוּ חִצָּם עַל יֶתֶר לִירוֹת בְּמוֹ אֹפֶל לְיִשְׁרֵי לֵב:

ג: כִּי הַשָּׁתוֹת יֵהָרֵסוּן צַדִּיק מַה פָּעָל:

ד: יְהוָה בְּהֵיכַל קָדְשׁוֹ יְהוָה בַּשָּׁמַיִם כִּסְאוֹ עֵינָיו יֶחֱזוּ עַפְעַפָּיו יִבְחֲנוּ בְּנֵי אָדָם:

ה: יְהוָה צַדִּיק יִבְחָן וְרָשָׁע וְאֹהֵב חָמָס שָׂנְאָה נַפְשׁוֹ:

ו: יַמְטֵר עַל רְשָׁעִים פַּחִים אֵשׁ וְגָפְרִית וְרוּחַ זִלְעָפוֹת מְנָת כּוֹסָם:

ז: כִּי צַדִּיק יְהוָה צְדָקוֹת אָהֵב יָשָׁר יֶחֱזוּ פָנֵימוֹ:

פרק יב

א: לַמְנַצֵּחַ עַל הַשְּׁמִינִית מִזְמוֹר לְדָוִד:

ב: הוֹשִׁיעָה יְהוָה כִּי גָמַר חָסִיד כִּי פַסּוּ אֱמוּנִים מִבְּנֵי אָדָם:

ג: שָׁוְא יְדַבְּרוּ אִישׁ אֶת רֵעֵהוּ שְׂפַת חֲלָקוֹת בְּלֵב וָלֵב יְדַבֵּרוּ:

ד: יַכְרֵת יְהוָה כָּל שִׂפְתֵי חֲלָקוֹת לָשׁוֹן מְדַבֶּרֶת גְּדֹלוֹת:

ה: אֲשֶׁר אָמְרוּ לִלְשֹׁנֵנוּ נַגְבִּיר שְׂפָתֵינוּ אִתָּנוּ מִי אָדוֹן לָנוּ:

ו: מִשֹּׁד עֲנִיִּים מֵאֶנְקַת אֶבְיוֹנִים עַתָּה אָקוּם יֹאמַר יְהוָה אָשִׁית בְּיֵשַׁע יָפִיחַ לוֹ:

ז: אִמְרוֹת יְהוָה אֲמָרוֹת טְהֹרוֹת כֶּסֶף צָרוּף בַּעֲלִיל לָאָרֶץ מְזֻקָּק שִׁבְעָתָיִם:

ח: אַתָּה יְהוָה תִּשְׁמְרֵם תִּצְּרֶנּוּ מִן הַדּוֹר זוּ לְעוֹלָם:

ט: סָבִיב רְשָׁעִים יִתְהַלָּכוּן כְּרֻם זֻלּוּת לִבְנֵי אָדָם:

פרק יג

א: לַמְנַצֵּחַ מִזְמוֹר לְדָוִד:

ב: עַד אָנָה יְהוָה תִּשְׁכָּחֵנִי נֶצַח עַד אָנָה תַּסְתִּיר אֶת פָּנֶיךָ מִמֶּנִּי:

ג: עַד אָנָה אָשִׁית עֵצוֹת בְּנַפְשִׁי יָגוֹן בִּלְבָבִי יוֹמָם עַד אָנָה יָרוּם אֹיְבִי עָלָי:

ד: הַבִּיטָה עֲנֵנִי יְהוָה אֱלֹהָי הָאִירָה עֵינַי פֶּן אִישַׁן הַמָּוֶת:

ה: פֶּן יֹאמַר אֹיְבִי יְכָלְתִּיו צָרַי יָגִילוּ כִּי אֶמּוֹט:

ו: וַאֲנִי בְּחַסְדְּךָ בָטַחְתִּי יָגֵל לִבִּי בִּישׁוּעָתֶךָ אָשִׁירָה לַיהוָה כִּי גָמַל עָלָי:

פרק יד

א: לַמְנַצֵּחַ לְדָוִד אָמַר נָבָל בְּלִבּוֹ אֵין אֱלֹהִים הִשְׁחִיתוּ הִתְעִיבוּ עֲלִילָה אֵין עֹשֵׂה טוֹב:

ב: יְהוָה מִשָּׁמַיִם הִשְׁקִיף עַל בְּנֵי אָדָם לִרְאוֹת הֲיֵשׁ מַשְׂכִּיל דֹּרֵשׁ אֶת אֱלֹהִים:

ג: הַכֹּל סָר יַחְדָּו נֶאֱלָחוּ אֵין עֹשֵׂה טוֹב אֵין גַּם אֶחָד:

ד: הֲלֹא יָדְעוּ כָּל פֹּעֲלֵי אָוֶן אֹכְלֵי עַמִּי אָכְלוּ לֶחֶם יְהוָה לֹא קָרָאוּ:

ה: שָׁם פָּחֲדוּ פָחַד כִּי אֱלֹהִים בְּדוֹר צַדִּיק:

ו: עֲצַת עָנִי תָבִישׁוּ כִּי יְהוָה מַחְסֵהוּ:

ז: מִי יִתֵּן מִצִּיּוֹן יְשׁוּעַת יִשְׂרָאֵל בְּשׁוּב יְהוָה שְׁבוּת עַמּוֹ יָגֵל יַעֲקֹב יִשְׂמַח יִשְׂרָאֵל:

פרק טו

א: מִזְמוֹר לְדָוִד יְהוָה מִי יָגוּר בְּאָהֳלֶךָ מִי יִשְׁכֹּן בְּהַר קָדְשֶׁךָ:

ב: הוֹלֵךְ תָּמִים וּפֹעֵל צֶדֶק וְדֹבֵר אֱמֶת בִּלְבָבוֹ:

ג: לֹא רָגַל עַל לְשֹׁנוֹ לֹא עָשָׂה לְרֵעֵהוּ רָעָה וְחֶרְפָּה לֹא נָשָׂא עַל קְרֹבוֹ:

ד: נִבְזֶה בְּעֵינָיו נִמְאָס וְאֶת יִרְאֵי יְהוָה יְכַבֵּד נִשְׁבַּע לְהָרַע וְלֹא יָמִר:

ה: כַּסְפּוֹ לֹא נָתַן בְּנֶשֶׁךְ וְשֹׁחַד עַל נָקִי לֹא לָקָח עֹשֵׂה אֵלֶּה לֹא יִמּוֹט לְעוֹלָם:

פרק טז

א: מִכְתָּם לְדָוִד שָׁמְרֵנִי אֵל כִּי חָסִיתִי בָךְ:

ב: אָמַרְתְּ לַיהוָה אֲדֹנָי אָתָּה טוֹבָתִי בַּל עָלֶיךָ:

ג: לִקְדוֹשִׁים אֲשֶׁר בָּאָרֶץ הֵמָּה וְאַדִּירֵי כָּל חֶפְצִי בָם:

ד: יִרְבּוּ עַצְּבוֹתָם אַחֵר מָהָרוּ בַּל אַסִּיךְ נִסְכֵּיהֶם מִדָּם וּבַל אֶשָּׂא אֶת שְׁמוֹתָם עַל שְׂפָתָי:

ה: יְהוָה מְנָת חֶלְקִי וְכוֹסִי אַתָּה תּוֹמִיךְ גּוֹרָלִי:

ו: חֲבָלִים נָפְלוּ לִי בַּנְּעִמִים אַף נַחֲלָת שָׁפְרָה עָלָי:

ז: אֲבָרֵךְ אֶת יְהוָה אֲשֶׁר יְעָצָנִי אַף לֵילוֹת יִסְּרוּנִי כִלְיוֹתָי:

ח: שִׁוִּיתִי יְהוָה לְנֶגְדִּי תָמִיד כִּי מִימִינִי בַּל אֶמּוֹט:

ט: לָכֵן שָׂמַח לִבִּי וַיָּגֶל כְּבוֹדִי אַף בְּשָׂרִי יִשְׁכֹּן לָבֶטַח:

י: כִּי לֹא תַעֲזֹב נַפְשִׁי לִשְׁאוֹל לֹא תִתֵּן חֲסִידְךָ לִרְאוֹת שָׁחַת:

יא: תּוֹדִיעֵנִי אֹרַח חַיִּים שֹׂבַע שְׂמָחוֹת אֶת פָּנֶיךָ נְעִמוֹת בִּימִינְךָ נֶצַח:

פרק יז

א: תְּפִלָּה לְדָוִד שִׁמְעָה יְהוָה צֶדֶק הַקְשִׁיבָה רִנָּתִי הַאֲזִינָה תְפִלָּתִי בְּלֹא שִׂפְתֵי מִרְמָה:

ב: מִלְּפָנֶיךָ מִשְׁפָּטִי יֵצֵא עֵינֶיךָ תֶּחֱזֶינָה מֵישָׁרִים:

ג: בָּחַנְתָּ לִבִּי פָּקַדְתָּ לַּיְלָה צְרַפְתַּנִי בַל תִּמְצָא זַמֹּתִי בַּל יַעֲבָר פִּי:

ד: לִפְעֻלּוֹת אָדָם בִּדְבַר שְׂפָתֶיךָ אֲנִי שָׁמַרְתִּי אָרְחוֹת פָּרִיץ:

ה: תָּמֹךְ אֲשֻׁרַי בְּמַעְגְּלוֹתֶיךָ בַּל נָמוֹטּוּ פְעָמָי:

ו: אֲנִי קְרָאתִיךָ כִי תַעֲנֵנִי אֵל הַט אָזְנְךָ לִי שְׁמַע אִמְרָתִי:

ז: הַפְלֵה חֲסָדֶיךָ מוֹשִׁיעַ חוֹסִים מִמִּתְקוֹמְמִים בִּימִינֶךָ:

ח: שָׁמְרֵנִי כְּאִישׁוֹן בַּת עָיִן בְּצֵל כְּנָפֶיךָ תַּסְתִּירֵנִי:

ט: מִפְּנֵי רְשָׁעִים זוּ שַׁדּוּנִי אֹיְבַי בְּנֶפֶשׁ יַקִּיפוּ עָלָי:

י: חֶלְבָּמוֹ סָגְרוּ פִּימוֹ דִּבְּרוּ בְגֵאוּת:

יא: אַשֻּׁרֵינוּ עַתָּה סבבוני {סְבָבוּנוּ} עֵינֵיהֶם יָשִׁיתוּ לִנְטוֹת בָּאָרֶץ:

יב: דִּמְיֹנוֹ כְּאַרְיֵה יִכְסוֹף לִטְרוֹף וְכִכְפִיר יֹשֵׁב בְּמִסְתָּרִים:

יג: קוּמָה יְהוָה קַדְּמָה פָנָיו הַכְרִיעֵהוּ פַּלְּטָה נַפְשִׁי מֵרָשָׁע חַרְבֶּךָ:

יד: מִמְתִים יָדְךָ יְהוָה מִמְתִים מֵחֶלֶד חֶלְקָם בַּחַיִּים וצפינך {וּצְפוּנְךָ} תְּמַלֵּא בִטְנָם יִשְׂבְּעוּ בָנִים וְהִנִּיחוּ יִתְרָם לְעוֹלְלֵיהֶם:

טו: אֲנִי בְּצֶדֶק אֶחֱזֶה פָנֶיךָ אֶשְׂבְּעָה בְהָקִיץ תְּמוּנָתֶךָ:

פרק יח

א: לַמְנַצֵּחַ לְעֶבֶד יְהוָה לְדָוִד אֲשֶׁר דִּבֶּר לַיהוָה אֶת דִּבְרֵי הַשִּׁירָה הַזֹּאת בְּיוֹם הִצִּיל יְהוָה אוֹתוֹ מִכַּף כָּל אֹיְבָיו וּמִיַּד שָׁאוּל:

ב: וַיֹּאמַר אֶרְחָמְךָ יְהוָה חִזְקִי:

ג: יְהוָה סַלְעִי וּמְצוּדָתִי וּמְפַלְטִי אֵלִי צוּרִי אֶחֱסֶה בּוֹ מָגִנִּי וְקֶרֶן יִשְׁעִי מִשְׂגַּבִּי:

ד: מְהֻלָּל אֶקְרָא יְהוָה וּמִן אֹיְבַי אִוָּשֵׁעַ:

ה: אֲפָפוּנִי חֶבְלֵי מָוֶת וְנַחֲלֵי בְלִיַּעַל יְבַעֲתוּנִי:

ו: חֶבְלֵי שְׁאוֹל סְבָבוּנִי קִדְּמוּנִי מוֹקְשֵׁי מָוֶת:

ז: בַּצַּר לִי אֶקְרָא יְהוָה וְאֶל אֱלֹהַי אֲשַׁוֵּעַ יִשְׁמַע מֵהֵיכָלוֹ קוֹלִי וְשַׁוְעָתִי לְפָנָיו תָּבוֹא בְאָזְנָיו:

ח: וַתִּגְעַשׁ וַתִּרְעַשׁ הָאָרֶץ וּמוֹסְדֵי הָרִים יִרְגָּזוּ וַיִּתְגָּעֲשׁוּ כִּי חָרָה לוֹ:

ט: עָלָה עָשָׁן בְּאַפּוֹ וְאֵשׁ מִפִּיו תֹּאכֵל גֶּחָלִים בָּעֲרוּ מִמֶּנּוּ:

י: וַיֵּט שָׁמַיִם וַיֵּרַד וַעֲרָפֶל תַּחַת רַגְלָיו:

יא: וַיִּרְכַּב עַל כְּרוּב וַיָּעֹף וַיֵּדֶא עַל כַּנְפֵי רוּחַ:

יב: יָשֶׁת חֹשֶׁךְ סִתְרוֹ סְבִיבוֹתָיו סֻכָּתוֹ חֶשְׁכַת מַיִם עָבֵי שְׁחָקִים:

יג: מִנֹּגַהּ נֶגְדּוֹ עָבָיו עָבְרוּ בָּרָד וְגַחֲלֵי אֵשׁ:

יד: וַיַּרְעֵם בַּשָּׁמַיִם יְהוָה וְעֶלְיוֹן יִתֵּן קֹלוֹ בָּרָד וְגַחֲלֵי אֵשׁ:

טו: וַיִּשְׁלַח חִצָּיו וַיְפִיצֵם וּבְרָקִים רָב וַיְהֻמֵּם:

טז: וַיֵּרָאוּ אֲפִיקֵי מַיִם וַיִּגָּלוּ מוֹסְדוֹת תֵּבֵל מִגַּעֲרָתְךָ יְהוָה מִנִּשְׁמַת רוּחַ אַפֶּךָ:

יז: יִשְׁלַח מִמָּרוֹם יִקָּחֵנִי יַמְשֵׁנִי מִמַּיִם רַבִּים:

יח: יַצִּילֵנִי מֵאֹיְבִי עָז וּמִשֹּׂנְאַי כִּי אָמְצוּ מִמֶּנִּי:

יט: יְקַדְּמוּנִי בְיוֹם אֵידִי וַיְהִי יְהוָה לְמִשְׁעָן לִי:

כ: וַיּוֹצִיאֵנִי לַמֶּרְחָב יְחַלְּצֵנִי כִּי חָפֵץ בִּי:

כא: יִגְמְלֵנִי יְהוָה כְּצִדְקִי כְּבֹר יָדַי יָשִׁיב לִי:

כב: כִּי שָׁמַרְתִּי דַּרְכֵי יְהוָה וְלֹא רָשַׁעְתִּי מֵאֱלֹהָי:

כג: כִּי כָל מִשְׁפָּטָיו לְנֶגְדִּי וְחֻקֹּתָיו לֹא אָסִיר מֶנִּי:

כד: וָאֱהִי תָמִים עִמּוֹ וָאֶשְׁתַּמֵּר מֵעֲוֺנִי:

כה: וַיָּשֶׁב יְהוָה לִי כְצִדְקִי כְּבֹר יָדַי לְנֶגֶד עֵינָיו:

כו: עִם חָסִיד תִּתְחַסָּד עִם גְּבַר תָּמִים תִּתַּמָּם:

כז: עִם נָבָר תִּתְבָּרָר וְעִם עִקֵּשׁ תִּתְפַּתָּל:

כח: כִּי אַתָּה עַם עָנִי תוֹשִׁיעַ וְעֵינַיִם רָמוֹת תַּשְׁפִּיל:

כט: כִּי אַתָּה תָּאִיר נֵרִי יְהוָה אֱלֹהַי יַגִּיהַּ חָשְׁכִּי:

ל: כִּי בְךָ אָרֻץ גְּדוּד וּבֵאלֹהַי אֲדַלֶּג שׁוּר:

לא: הָאֵל תָּמִים דַּרְכּוֹ אִמְרַת יְהוָה צְרוּפָה מָגֵן הוּא לְכֹל הַחֹסִים בּוֹ:

לב: כִּי מִי אֱלוֹהַּ מִבַּלְעֲדֵי יְהוָה וּמִי צוּר זוּלָתִי אֱלֹהֵינוּ:

לג: הָאֵל הַמְאַזְּרֵנִי חָיִל וַיִּתֵּן תָּמִים דַּרְכִּי:

לד: מְשַׁוֶּה רַגְלַי כָּאַיָּלוֹת וְעַל בָּמֹתַי יַעֲמִידֵנִי:

לה: מְלַמֵּד יָדַי לַמִּלְחָמָה וְנִחֲתָה קֶשֶׁת נְחוּשָׁה זְרוֹעֹתָי:

לו: וַתִּתֶּן לִי מָגֵן יִשְׁעֶךָ וִימִינְךָ תִסְעָדֵנִי וְעַנְוַתְךָ תַרְבֵּנִי:

לז: תַּרְחִיב צַעֲדִי תַחְתָּי וְלֹא מָעֲדוּ קַרְסֻלָּי:

לח: אֶרְדּוֹף אוֹיְבַי וְאַשִּׂיגֵם וְלֹא אָשׁוּב עַד כַּלּוֹתָם:

לט: אֶמְחָצֵם וְלֹא יֻכְלוּ קוּם יִפְּלוּ תַּחַת רַגְלָי:

מ: וַתְּאַזְּרֵנִי חַיִל לַמִּלְחָמָה תַּכְרִיעַ קָמַי תַּחְתָּי:

מא: וְאֹיְבַי נָתַתָּה לִּי עֹרֶף וּמְשַׂנְאַי אַצְמִיתֵם:

מב: יְשַׁוְּעוּ וְאֵין מוֹשִׁיעַ עַל יְהוָה וְלֹא עָנָם:

מג: וְאֶשְׁחָקֵם כְּעָפָר עַל פְּנֵי רוּחַ כְּטִיט חוּצוֹת אֲרִיקֵם:

מד: תְּפַלְּטֵנִי מֵרִיבֵי עָם תְּשִׂימֵנִי לְרֹאשׁ גּוֹיִם עַם לֹא יָדַעְתִּי יַעַבְדוּנִי:

מה: לְשֵׁמַע אֹזֶן יִשָּׁמְעוּ לִי בְּנֵי נֵכָר יְכַחֲשׁוּ לִי:

מו: בְּנֵי נֵכָר יִבֹּלוּ וְיַחְרְגוּ מִמִּסְגְּרוֹתֵיהֶם:

מז: חַי יְהוָה וּבָרוּךְ צוּרִי וְיָרוּם אֱלֹהֵי יִשְׁעִי:

מח: הָאֵל הַנּוֹתֵן נְקָמוֹת לִי וַיַּדְבֵּר עַמִּים תַּחְתָּי:

מט: מְפַלְּטִי מֵאֹיְבָי אַף מִן קָמַי תְּרוֹמְמֵנִי מֵאִישׁ חָמָס תַּצִּילֵנִי:

נ: עַל כֵּן אוֹדְךָ בַגּוֹיִם יְהוָה וּלְשִׁמְךָ אֲזַמֵּרָה:

נא: מַגְדִּל יְשׁוּעוֹת מַלְכּוֹ וְעֹשֶׂה חֶסֶד לִמְשִׁיחוֹ לְדָוִד וּלְזַרְעוֹ עַד עוֹלָם:

פרק יט

א: לַמְנַצֵּחַ מִזְמוֹר לְדָוִד:

ב: הַשָּׁמַיִם מְסַפְּרִים כְּבוֹד אֵל וּמַעֲשֵׂה יָדָיו מַגִּיד הָרָקִיעַ:

ג: יוֹם לְיוֹם יַבִּיעַ אֹמֶר וְלַיְלָה לְּלַיְלָה יְחַוֶּה דָּעַת:

ד: אֵין אֹמֶר וְאֵין דְּבָרִים בְּלִי נִשְׁמָע קוֹלָם:

ה: בְּכָל הָאָרֶץ יָצָא קַוָּם וּבִקְצֵה תֵבֵל מִלֵּיהֶם לַשֶּׁמֶשׁ שָׂם אֹהֶל בָּהֶם:

ו. וְהוּא כְּחָתָן יֹצֵא מֵחֻפָּתוֹ יָשִׂישׂ כְּגִבּוֹר לָרוּץ אֹרַח:
ז. מִקְצֵה הַשָּׁמַיִם מוֹצָאוֹ וּתְקוּפָתוֹ עַל קְצוֹתָם וְאֵין נִסְתָּר מֵחַמָּתוֹ:
ח. תּוֹרַת יְהֹוָה תְּמִימָה מְשִׁיבַת נָפֶשׁ עֵדוּת יְהֹוָה נֶאֱמָנָה מַחְכִּימַת פֶּתִי:
ט. פִּקּוּדֵי יְהֹוָה יְשָׁרִים מְשַׂמְּחֵי לֵב מִצְוַת יְהֹוָה בָּרָה מְאִירַת עֵינָיִם:
י. יִרְאַת יְהֹוָה טְהוֹרָה עוֹמֶדֶת לָעַד מִשְׁפְּטֵי יְהֹוָה אֱמֶת צָדְקוּ יַחְדָּו:
יא. הַנֶּחֱמָדִים מִזָּהָב וּמִפַּז רָב וּמְתוּקִים מִדְּבַשׁ וְנֹפֶת צוּפִים:
יב. גַּם עַבְדְּךָ נִזְהָר בָּהֶם בְּשָׁמְרָם עֵקֶב רָב:
יג. שְׁגִיאוֹת מִי יָבִין מִנִּסְתָּרוֹת נַקֵּנִי:
יד. גַּם מִזֵּדִים חֲשֹׂךְ עַבְדֶּךָ אַל יִמְשְׁלוּ בִי אָז אֵיתָם וְנִקֵּיתִי מִפֶּשַׁע רָב:
טו. יִהְיוּ לְרָצוֹן אִמְרֵי פִי וְהֶגְיוֹן לִבִּי לְפָנֶיךָ יְהֹוָה צוּרִי וְגֹאֲלִי:

פרק כ

א. לַמְנַצֵּחַ מִזְמוֹר לְדָוִד:
ב. יַעַנְךָ יְהֹוָה בְּיוֹם צָרָה יְשַׂגֶּבְךָ שֵׁם אֱלֹהֵי יַעֲקֹב:
ג. יִשְׁלַח עֶזְרְךָ מִקֹּדֶשׁ וּמִצִּיּוֹן יִסְעָדֶךָּ:
ד. יִזְכֹּר כָּל מִנְחֹתֶךָ וְעוֹלָתְךָ יְדַשְּׁנֶה סֶלָה:
ה. יִתֶּן לְךָ כִלְבָבֶךָ וְכָל עֲצָתְךָ יְמַלֵּא:
ו. נְרַנְּנָה בִּישׁוּעָתֶךָ וּבְשֵׁם אֱלֹהֵינוּ נִדְגֹּל יְמַלֵּא יְהֹוָה כָּל מִשְׁאֲלוֹתֶיךָ:
ז. עַתָּה יָדַעְתִּי כִּי הוֹשִׁיעַ יְהֹוָה מְשִׁיחוֹ יַעֲנֵהוּ מִשְּׁמֵי קָדְשׁוֹ בִּגְבֻרוֹת יֵשַׁע יְמִינוֹ:
ח. אֵלֶּה בָרֶכֶב וְאֵלֶּה בַסּוּסִים וַאֲנַחְנוּ בְּשֵׁם יְהֹוָה אֱלֹהֵינוּ נַזְכִּיר:
ט. הֵמָּה כָּרְעוּ וְנָפָלוּ וַאֲנַחְנוּ קַּמְנוּ וַנִּתְעוֹדָד:
י. יְהֹוָה הוֹשִׁיעָה הַמֶּלֶךְ יַעֲנֵנוּ בְיוֹם קָרְאֵנוּ:

פרק כא

א. לַמְנַצֵּחַ מִזְמוֹר לְדָוִד:
ב. יְהֹוָה בְּעָזְּךָ יִשְׂמַח מֶלֶךְ וּבִישׁוּעָתְךָ מַה יָּגֶל {יָגִיל} מְאֹד:
ג. תַּאֲוַת לִבּוֹ נָתַתָּה לּוֹ וַאֲרֶשֶׁת שְׂפָתָיו בַּל מָנַעְתָּ סֶּלָה:
ד. כִּי תְקַדְּמֶנּוּ בִּרְכוֹת טוֹב תָּשִׁית לְרֹאשׁוֹ עֲטֶרֶת פָּז:
ה. חַיִּים שָׁאַל מִמְּךָ נָתַתָּה לּוֹ אֹרֶךְ יָמִים עוֹלָם וָעֶד:
ו. גָּדוֹל כְּבוֹדוֹ בִּישׁוּעָתֶךָ הוֹד וְהָדָר תְּשַׁוֶּה עָלָיו:
ז. כִּי תְשִׁיתֵהוּ בְרָכוֹת לָעַד תְּחַדֵּהוּ בְשִׂמְחָה אֶת פָּנֶיךָ:
ח. כִּי הַמֶּלֶךְ בֹּטֵחַ בַּיהֹוָה וּבְחֶסֶד עֶלְיוֹן בַּל יִמּוֹט:
ט. תִּמְצָא יָדְךָ לְכָל אֹיְבֶיךָ יְמִינְךָ תִּמְצָא שֹׂנְאֶיךָ:
י. תְּשִׁיתֵמוֹ כְּתַנּוּר אֵשׁ לְעֵת פָּנֶיךָ יְהֹוָה בְּאַפּוֹ יְבַלְּעֵם וְתֹאכְלֵם אֵשׁ:
יא. פִּרְיָמוֹ מֵאֶרֶץ תְּאַבֵּד וְזַרְעָם מִבְּנֵי אָדָם:
יב. כִּי נָטוּ עָלֶיךָ רָעָה חָשְׁבוּ מְזִמָּה בַּל יוּכָלוּ:
יג. כִּי תְּשִׁיתֵמוֹ שֶׁכֶם בְּמֵיתָרֶיךָ תְּכוֹנֵן עַל פְּנֵיהֶם:
יד. רוּמָה יְהֹוָה בְעֻזֶּךָ נָשִׁירָה וּנְזַמְּרָה גְּבוּרָתֶךָ:

פרק כב

א. לַמְנַצֵּחַ עַל אַיֶּלֶת הַשַּׁחַר מִזְמוֹר לְדָוִד:
ב. אֵלִי אֵלִי לָמָה עֲזַבְתָּנִי רָחוֹק מִישׁוּעָתִי דִּבְרֵי שַׁאֲגָתִי:
ג. אֱלֹהַי אֶקְרָא יוֹמָם וְלֹא תַעֲנֶה וְלַיְלָה וְלֹא דֻמִיָּה לִי:
ד. וְאַתָּה קָדוֹשׁ יוֹשֵׁב תְּהִלּוֹת יִשְׂרָאֵל:
ה. בְּךָ בָּטְחוּ אֲבֹתֵינוּ בָּטְחוּ וַתְּפַלְּטֵמוֹ:
ו. אֵלֶיךָ זָעֲקוּ וְנִמְלָטוּ בְּךָ בָטְחוּ וְלֹא בוֹשׁוּ:
ז. וְאָנֹכִי תוֹלַעַת וְלֹא אִישׁ חֶרְפַּת אָדָם וּבְזוּי עָם:

ח: כָּל רֹאַי יַלְעִגוּ לִי יַפְטִירוּ בְשָׂפָה יָנִיעוּ רֹאשׁ:

ט: גֹּל אֶל יְהוָה יְפַלְּטֵהוּ יַצִּילֵהוּ כִּי חָפֵץ בּוֹ:

י: כִּי אַתָּה גֹחִי מִבָּטֶן מַבְטִיחִי עַל שְׁדֵי אִמִּי:

יא: עָלֶיךָ הָשְׁלַכְתִּי מֵרָחֶם מִבֶּטֶן אִמִּי אֵלִי אָתָּה:

יב: אַל תִּרְחַק מִמֶּנִּי כִּי צָרָה קְרוֹבָה כִּי אֵין עוֹזֵר:

יג: סְבָבוּנִי פָּרִים רַבִּים אַבִּירֵי בָשָׁן כִּתְּרוּנִי:

יד: פָּצוּ עָלַי פִּיהֶם אַרְיֵה טֹרֵף וְשֹׁאֵג:

טו: כַּמַּיִם נִשְׁפַּכְתִּי וְהִתְפָּרְדוּ כָּל עַצְמוֹתָי הָיָה לִבִּי כַּדּוֹנָג נָמֵס בְּתוֹךְ מֵעָי:

טז: יָבֵשׁ כַּחֶרֶשׂ כֹּחִי וּלְשׁוֹנִי מֻדְבָּק מַלְקוֹחָי וְלַעֲפַר מָוֶת תִּשְׁפְּתֵנִי:

יז: כִּי סְבָבוּנִי כְּלָבִים עֲדַת מְרֵעִים הִקִּיפוּנִי כָּאֲרִי יָדַי וְרַגְלָי:

יח: אֲסַפֵּר כָּל עַצְמוֹתָי הֵמָּה יַבִּיטוּ יִרְאוּ בִי:

יט: יְחַלְּקוּ בְגָדַי לָהֶם וְעַל לְבוּשִׁי יַפִּילוּ גוֹרָל:

כ: וְאַתָּה יְהוָה אַל תִּרְחָק אֱיָלוּתִי לְעֶזְרָתִי חוּשָׁה:

כא: הַצִּילָה מֵחֶרֶב נַפְשִׁי מִיַּד כֶּלֶב יְחִידָתִי:

כב: הוֹשִׁיעֵנִי מִפִּי אַרְיֵה וּמִקַּרְנֵי רֵמִים עֲנִיתָנִי:

כג: אֲסַפְּרָה שִׁמְךָ לְאֶחָי בְּתוֹךְ קָהָל אֲהַלְלֶךָּ:

כד: יִרְאֵי יְהוָה הַלְלוּהוּ כָּל זֶרַע יַעֲקֹב כַּבְּדוּהוּ וְגוּרוּ מִמֶּנּוּ כָּל זֶרַע יִשְׂרָאֵל:

כה: כִּי לֹא בָזָה וְלֹא שִׁקַּץ עֱנוּת עָנִי וְלֹא הִסְתִּיר פָּנָיו מִמֶּנּוּ וּבְשַׁוְּעוֹ אֵלָיו שָׁמֵעַ:

כו: מֵאִתְּךָ תְהִלָּתִי בְּקָהָל רָב נְדָרַי אֲשַׁלֵּם נֶגֶד יְרֵאָיו:

כז: יֹאכְלוּ עֲנָוִים וְיִשְׂבָּעוּ יְהַלְלוּ יְהוָה דֹּרְשָׁיו יְחִי לְבַבְכֶם לָעַד:

כח: יִזְכְּרוּ וְיָשֻׁבוּ אֶל יְהוָה כָּל אַפְסֵי אָרֶץ וְיִשְׁתַּחֲווּ לְפָנֶיךָ כָּל מִשְׁפְּחוֹת גּוֹיִם:

כט: כִּי לַיהוָה הַמְּלוּכָה וּמֹשֵׁל בַּגּוֹיִם:

ל: אָכְלוּ וַיִּשְׁתַּחֲווּ כָּל דִּשְׁנֵי אֶרֶץ לְפָנָיו יִכְרְעוּ כָּל יוֹרְדֵי עָפָר וְנַפְשׁוֹ לֹא חִיָּה:

לא: זֶרַע יַעַבְדֶנּוּ יְסֻפַּר לַאדֹנָי לַדּוֹר:

לב: יָבֹאוּ וְיַגִּידוּ צִדְקָתוֹ לְעַם נוֹלָד כִּי עָשָׂה:

פרק כג

א: מִזְמוֹר לְדָוִד יְהוָה רֹעִי לֹא אֶחְסָר:

ב: בִּנְאוֹת דֶּשֶׁא יַרְבִּיצֵנִי עַל מֵי מְנֻחוֹת יְנַהֲלֵנִי:

ג: נַפְשִׁי יְשׁוֹבֵב יַנְחֵנִי בְמַעְגְּלֵי צֶדֶק לְמַעַן שְׁמוֹ:

ד: גַּם כִּי אֵלֵךְ בְּגֵיא צַלְמָוֶת לֹא אִירָא רָע כִּי אַתָּה עִמָּדִי שִׁבְטְךָ וּמִשְׁעַנְתֶּךָ הֵמָּה יְנַחֲמֻנִי:

ה: תַּעֲרֹךְ לְפָנַי שֻׁלְחָן נֶגֶד צֹרְרָי דִּשַּׁנְתָּ בַשֶּׁמֶן רֹאשִׁי כּוֹסִי רְוָיָה:

ו: אַךְ טוֹב וָחֶסֶד יִרְדְּפוּנִי כָּל יְמֵי חַיָּי וְשַׁבְתִּי בְּבֵית יְהוָה לְאֹרֶךְ יָמִים:

פרק כד

א: לְדָוִד מִזְמוֹר לַיהוָה הָאָרֶץ וּמְלוֹאָהּ תֵּבֵל וְיֹשְׁבֵי בָהּ:

ב: כִּי הוּא עַל יַמִּים יְסָדָהּ וְעַל נְהָרוֹת יְכוֹנְנֶהָ:

ג: מִי יַעֲלֶה בְהַר יְהוָה וּמִי יָקוּם בִּמְקוֹם קָדְשׁוֹ:

ד: נְקִי כַפַּיִם וּבַר לֵבָב אֲשֶׁר לֹא נָשָׂא לַשָּׁוְא נַפְשִׁי וְלֹא נִשְׁבַּע לְמִרְמָה:

ה: יִשָּׂא בְרָכָה מֵאֵת יְהוָה וּצְדָקָה מֵאֱלֹהֵי יִשְׁעוֹ:

ו: זֶה דּוֹר דֹּרְשָׁיו מְבַקְשֵׁי פָנֶיךָ יַעֲקֹב סֶלָה:

ז: שְׂאוּ שְׁעָרִים רָאשֵׁיכֶם וְהִנָּשְׂאוּ פִּתְחֵי עוֹלָם וְיָבוֹא מֶלֶךְ הַכָּבוֹד:

ח: מִי זֶה מֶלֶךְ הַכָּבוֹד יְהוָה עִזּוּז וְגִבּוֹר יְהוָה גִּבּוֹר מִלְחָמָה:

ט: שְׂאוּ שְׁעָרִים רָאשֵׁיכֶם וּשְׂאוּ פִּתְחֵי עוֹלָם וְיָבֹא מֶלֶךְ הַכָּבוֹד:

י: מִי הוּא זֶה מֶלֶךְ הַכָּבוֹד יְהוָה צְבָאוֹת הוּא מֶלֶךְ הַכָּבוֹד סֶלָה:

פרק כה

א: לְדָוִד אֵלֶיךָ יְהוָה נַפְשִׁי אֶשָּׂא:

ב: אֱלֹהַי בְּךָ בָטַחְתִּי אַל אֵבוֹשָׁה אַל יַעַלְצוּ אֹיְבַי לִי:

ג: גַּם כָּל קֹוֶיךָ לֹא יֵבֹשׁוּ יֵבֹשׁוּ הַבּוֹגְדִים רֵיקָם:

ד: דְּרָכֶיךָ יְהוָה הוֹדִיעֵנִי אֹרְחוֹתֶיךָ לַמְּדֵנִי:

ה: הַדְרִיכֵנִי בַאֲמִתֶּךָ וְלַמְּדֵנִי כִּי אַתָּה אֱלֹהֵי יִשְׁעִי אוֹתְךָ קִוִּיתִי כָּל הַיּוֹם:

ו: זְכֹר רַחֲמֶיךָ יְהוָה וַחֲסָדֶיךָ כִּי מֵעוֹלָם הֵמָּה:

ז: חַטֹּאות נְעוּרַי וּפְשָׁעַי אַל תִּזְכֹּר כְּחַסְדְּךָ זְכָר לִי אַתָּה לְמַעַן טוּבְךָ יְהוָה:

ח: טוֹב וְיָשָׁר יְהוָה עַל כֵּן יוֹרֶה חַטָּאִים בַּדָּרֶךְ:

ט: יַדְרֵךְ עֲנָוִים בַּמִּשְׁפָּט וִילַמֵּד עֲנָוִים דַּרְכּוֹ:

י: כָּל אָרְחוֹת יְהוָה חֶסֶד וֶאֱמֶת לְנֹצְרֵי בְרִיתוֹ וְעֵדֹתָיו:

יא: לְמַעַן שִׁמְךָ יְהוָה וְסָלַחְתָּ לַעֲוֹנִי כִּי רַב הוּא:

יב: מִי זֶה הָאִישׁ יְרֵא יְהוָה יוֹרֶנּוּ בְּדֶרֶךְ יִבְחָר:

יג: נַפְשׁוֹ בְּטוֹב תָּלִין וְזַרְעוֹ יִירַשׁ אָרֶץ:

יד: סוֹד יְהוָה לִירֵאָיו וּבְרִיתוֹ לְהוֹדִיעָם:

טו: עֵינַי תָּמִיד אֶל יְהוָה כִּי הוּא יוֹצִיא מֵרֶשֶׁת רַגְלָי:

טז: פְּנֵה אֵלַי וְחָנֵּנִי כִּי יָחִיד וְעָנִי אָנִי:

יז: צָרוֹת לְבָבִי הִרְחִיבוּ מִמְּצוּקוֹתַי הוֹצִיאֵנִי:

יח: רְאֵה עָנְיִי וַעֲמָלִי וְשָׂא לְכָל חַטֹּאותָי:

יט: רְאֵה אֹיְבַי כִּי רָבּוּ וְשִׂנְאַת חָמָס שְׂנֵאוּנִי:

כ: שָׁמְרָה נַפְשִׁי וְהַצִּילֵנִי אַל אֵבוֹשׁ כִּי חָסִיתִי בָךְ:

כא: תֹּם וָיֹשֶׁר יִצְּרוּנִי כִּי קִוִּיתִיךָ:

כב: פְּדֵה אֱלֹהִים אֶת יִשְׂרָאֵל מִכֹּל צָרוֹתָיו:

פרק כו

א: לְדָוִד שָׁפְטֵנִי יְהוָה כִּי אֲנִי בְּתֻמִּי הָלַכְתִּי וּבַיהוָה בָּטַחְתִּי לֹא אֶמְעָד:

ב: בְּחָנֵנִי יְהוָה וְנַסֵּנִי צָרָופָה {צְרָופָה} כִלְיוֹתַי וְלִבִּי:

ג: כִּי חַסְדְּךָ לְנֶגֶד עֵינָי וְהִתְהַלַּכְתִּי בַּאֲמִתֶּךָ:

ד: לֹא יָשַׁבְתִּי עִם מְתֵי שָׁוְא וְעִם נַעֲלָמִים לֹא אָבוֹא:

ה: שָׂנֵאתִי קְהַל מְרֵעִים וְעִם רְשָׁעִים לֹא אֵשֵׁב:

ו: אֶרְחַץ בְּנִקָּיוֹן כַּפָּי וַאֲסֹבְבָה אֶת מִזְבַּחֲךָ יְהוָה:

ז: לַשְׁמִעַ בְּקוֹל תּוֹדָה וּלְסַפֵּר כָּל נִפְלְאוֹתֶיךָ:

ח: יְהוָה אָהַבְתִּי מְעוֹן בֵּיתֶךָ וּמְקוֹם מִשְׁכַּן כְּבוֹדֶךָ:

ט: אַל תֶּאֱסֹף עִם חַטָּאִים נַפְשִׁי וְעִם אַנְשֵׁי דָמִים חַיָּי:

י: אֲשֶׁר בִּידֵיהֶם זִמָּה וִימִינָם מָלְאָה שֹּׁחַד:

יא: וַאֲנִי בְּתֻמִּי אֵלֵךְ פְּדֵנִי וְחָנֵּנִי:

יב: רַגְלִי עָמְדָה בְמִישׁוֹר בְּמַקְהֵלִים אֲבָרֵךְ יְהוָה:

פרק כז

א: לְדָוִד יְהוָה אוֹרִי וְיִשְׁעִי מִמִּי אִירָא יְהוָה מָעוֹז חַיַּי מִמִּי אֶפְחָד:

ב: בִּקְרֹב עָלַי מְרֵעִים לֶאֱכֹל אֶת בְּשָׂרִי צָרַי וְאֹיְבַי לִי הֵמָּה כָשְׁלוּ וְנָפָלוּ:

ג: אִם תַּחֲנֶה עָלַי מַחֲנֶה לֹא יִירָא לִבִּי אִם תָּקוּם עָלַי מִלְחָמָה בְּזֹאת אֲנִי בוֹטֵחַ:

ד: אַחַת שָׁאַלְתִּי מֵאֵת יְהוָה אוֹתָהּ אֲבַקֵּשׁ שִׁבְתִּי בְּבֵית יְהוָה כָּל יְמֵי חַיַּי לַחֲזוֹת בְּנֹעַם יְהוָה וּלְבַקֵּר בְּהֵיכָלוֹ:

ה: כִּי יִצְפְּנֵנִי בְּסֻכֹּה בְּיוֹם רָעָה יַסְתִּרֵנִי בְּסֵתֶר אָהֳלוֹ בְּצוּר יְרוֹמְמֵנִי:

ו: וְעַתָּה יָרוּם רֹאשִׁי עַל אֹיְבַי סְבִיבוֹתַי וְאֶזְבְּחָה בְאָהֳלוֹ זִבְחֵי תְרוּעָה אָשִׁירָה וַאֲזַמְּרָה לַיהוָה:

ז: שְׁמַע יְהוָה קוֹלִי אֶקְרָא וְחָנֵּנִי וַעֲנֵנִי:

ח: לְךָ אָמַר לִבִּי בַּקְּשׁוּ פָנָי אֶת פָּנֶיךָ יְהֹוָה אֲבַקֵּשׁ:

ט: אַל תַּסְתֵּר פָּנֶיךָ מִמֶּנִּי אַל תַּט בְּאַף עַבְדֶּךָ עֶזְרָתִי הָיִיתָ אַל תִּטְּשֵׁנִי וְאַל תַּעַזְבֵנִי אֱלֹהֵי יִשְׁעִי:

י: כִּי אָבִי וְאִמִּי עֲזָבוּנִי וַיהֹוָה יַאַסְפֵנִי:

יא: הוֹרֵנִי יְהֹוָה דַּרְכֶּךָ וּנְחֵנִי בְּאֹרַח מִישׁוֹר לְמַעַן שׁוֹרְרָי:

יב: אַל תִּתְּנֵנִי בְּנֶפֶשׁ צָרָי כִּי קָמוּ בִי עֵדֵי שֶׁקֶר וִיפֵחַ חָמָס:

יג: לוּלֵא הֶאֱמַנְתִּי לִרְאוֹת בְּטוּב יְהֹוָה בְּאֶרֶץ חַיִּים:

יד: קַוֵּה אֶל יְהֹוָה חֲזַק וְיַאֲמֵץ לִבֶּךָ וְקַוֵּה אֶל יְהֹוָה:

פרק כח

א: לְדָוִד אֵלֶיךָ יְהֹוָה אֶקְרָא צוּרִי אַל תֶּחֱרַשׁ מִמֶּנִּי פֶּן תֶּחֱשֶׁה מִמֶּנִּי וְנִמְשַׁלְתִּי עִם יוֹרְדֵי בוֹר:

ב: שְׁמַע קוֹל תַּחֲנוּנַי בְּשַׁוְּעִי אֵלֶיךָ בְּנָשְׂאִי יָדַי אֶל דְּבִיר קָדְשֶׁךָ:

ג: אַל תִּמְשְׁכֵנִי עִם רְשָׁעִים וְעִם פֹּעֲלֵי אָוֶן דֹּבְרֵי שָׁלוֹם עִם רֵעֵיהֶם וְרָעָה בִּלְבָבָם:

ד: תֶּן לָהֶם כְּפָעֳלָם וּכְרֹעַ מַעַלְלֵיהֶם כְּמַעֲשֵׂה יְדֵיהֶם תֵּן לָהֶם הָשֵׁב גְּמוּלָם לָהֶם:

ה: כִּי לֹא יָבִינוּ אֶל פְּעֻלֹּת יְהֹוָה וְאֶל מַעֲשֵׂה יָדָיו יֶהֶרְסֵם וְלֹא יִבְנֵם:

ו: בָּרוּךְ יְהֹוָה כִּי שָׁמַע קוֹל תַּחֲנוּנָי:

ז: יְהֹוָה עֻזִּי וּמָגִנִּי בּוֹ בָטַח לִבִּי וְנֶעֱזָרְתִּי וַיַּעֲלֹז לִבִּי וּמִשִּׁירִי אֲהוֹדֶנּוּ:

ח: יְהֹוָה עֹז לָמוֹ וּמָעוֹז יְשׁוּעוֹת מְשִׁיחוֹ הוּא:

ט: הוֹשִׁיעָה אֶת עַמֶּךָ וּבָרֵךְ אֶת נַחֲלָתֶךָ וּרְעֵם וְנַשְּׂאֵם עַד הָעוֹלָם:

פרק כט

א: מִזְמוֹר לְדָוִד הָבוּ לַיהֹוָה בְּנֵי אֵלִים הָבוּ לַיהֹוָה כָּבוֹד וָעֹז:

ב: הָבוּ לַיהֹוָה כְּבוֹד שְׁמוֹ הִשְׁתַּחֲווּ לַיהֹוָה בְּהַדְרַת קֹדֶשׁ:

ג: קוֹל יְהֹוָה עַל הַמָּיִם אֵל הַכָּבוֹד הִרְעִים יְהֹוָה עַל מַיִם רַבִּים:

ד: קוֹל יְהֹוָה בַּכֹּחַ קוֹל יְהֹוָה בֶּהָדָר:

ה: קוֹל יְהֹוָה שֹׁבֵר אֲרָזִים וַיְשַׁבֵּר יְהֹוָה אֶת אַרְזֵי הַלְּבָנוֹן:

ו: וַיַּרְקִידֵם כְּמוֹ עֵגֶל לְבָנוֹן וְשִׂרְיֹן כְּמוֹ בֶן רְאֵמִים:

ז: קוֹל יְהֹוָה חֹצֵב לַהֲבוֹת אֵשׁ:

ח: קוֹל יְהֹוָה יָחִיל מִדְבָּר יָחִיל יְהֹוָה מִדְבַּר קָדֵשׁ:

ט: קוֹל יְהֹוָה יְחוֹלֵל אַיָּלוֹת וַיֶּחֱשֹׂף יְעָרוֹת וּבְהֵיכָלוֹ כֻּלּוֹ אֹמֵר כָּבוֹד:

י: יְהֹוָה לַמַּבּוּל יָשָׁב וַיֵּשֶׁב יְהֹוָה מֶלֶךְ לְעוֹלָם:

יא: יְהֹוָה עֹז לְעַמּוֹ יִתֵּן יְהֹוָה יְבָרֵךְ אֶת עַמּוֹ בַשָּׁלוֹם:

פרק ל

א: מִזְמוֹר שִׁיר חֲנֻכַּת הַבַּיִת לְדָוִד:

ב: אֲרוֹמִמְךָ יְהֹוָה כִּי דִלִּיתָנִי וְלֹא שִׂמַּחְתָּ אֹיְבַי לִי:

ג: יְהֹוָה אֱלֹהָי שִׁוַּעְתִּי אֵלֶיךָ וַתִּרְפָּאֵנִי:

ד: יְהֹוָה הֶעֱלִיתָ מִן שְׁאוֹל נַפְשִׁי חִיִּיתַנִי מִיָּרְדִי בוֹר {מִיָּרְדִי בוֹר}:

ה: זַמְּרוּ לַיהֹוָה חֲסִידָיו וְהוֹדוּ לְזֵכֶר קָדְשׁוֹ:

ו: כִּי רֶגַע בְּאַפּוֹ חַיִּים בִּרְצוֹנוֹ בָּעֶרֶב יָלִין בֶּכִי וְלַבֹּקֶר רִנָּה:

ז: וַאֲנִי אָמַרְתִּי בְשַׁלְוִי בַּל אֶמּוֹט לְעוֹלָם:

ח: יְהֹוָה בִּרְצוֹנְךָ הֶעֱמַדְתָּה לְהַרְרִי עֹז הִסְתַּרְתָּ פָנֶיךָ הָיִיתִי נִבְהָל:

ט: אֵלֶיךָ יְהֹוָה אֶקְרָא וְאֶל אֲדֹנָי אֶתְחַנָּן:

י: מַה בֶּצַע בְּדָמִי בְּרִדְתִּי אֶל שָׁחַת הֲיוֹדְךָ עָפָר הֲיַגִּיד אֲמִתֶּךָ:

יא: שְׁמַע יְהֹוָה וְחָנֵּנִי יְהֹוָה הֱיֵה עֹזֵר לִי:

יב: הָפַכְתָּ מִסְפְּדִי לְמָחוֹל לִי פִּתַּחְתָּ שַׂקִּי וַתְּאַזְּרֵנִי שִׂמְחָה:

יג: לְמַעַן יְזַמֶּרְךָ כָבוֹד וְלֹא יִדֹּם יְהֹוָה אֱלֹהַי לְעוֹלָם אוֹדֶךָּ:

פרק לא

א: לַמְנַצֵּחַ מִזְמוֹר לְדָוִד:

ב: בְּךָ יְהוָה חָסִיתִי אַל אֵבוֹשָׁה לְעוֹלָם בְּצִדְקָתְךָ פַלְּטֵנִי:

ג: הַטֵּה אֵלַי אָזְנְךָ מְהֵרָה הַצִּילֵנִי הֱיֵה לִי לְצוּר מָעוֹז לְבֵית מְצוּדוֹת לְהוֹשִׁיעֵנִי:

ד: כִּי סַלְעִי וּמְצוּדָתִי אָתָּה וּלְמַעַן שִׁמְךָ תַּנְחֵנִי וּתְנַהֲלֵנִי:

ה: תּוֹצִיאֵנִי מֵרֶשֶׁת זוּ טָמְנוּ לִי כִּי אַתָּה מָעוּזִּי:

ו: בְּיָדְךָ אַפְקִיד רוּחִי פָּדִיתָה אוֹתִי יְהוָה אֵל אֱמֶת:

ז: שָׂנֵאתִי הַשֹּׁמְרִים הַבְלֵי שָׁוְא וַאֲנִי אֶל יְהוָה בָּטָחְתִּי:

ח: אָגִילָה וְאֶשְׂמְחָה בְּחַסְדֶּךָ אֲשֶׁר רָאִיתָ אֶת עָנְיִי יָדַעְתָּ בְּצָרוֹת נַפְשִׁי:

ט: וְלֹא הִסְגַּרְתַּנִי בְּיַד אוֹיֵב הֶעֱמַדְתָּ בַמֶּרְחָב רַגְלָי:

י: חָנֵּנִי יְהוָה כִּי צַר לִי עָשְׁשָׁה בְכַעַס עֵינִי נַפְשִׁי וּבִטְנִי:

יא: כִּי כָלוּ בְיָגוֹן חַיַּי וּשְׁנוֹתַי בַּאֲנָחָה כָּשַׁל בַּעֲוֹנִי כֹחִי וַעֲצָמַי עָשֵׁשׁוּ:

יב: מִכָּל צֹרְרַי הָיִיתִי חֶרְפָּה וְלִשְׁכֵנַי מְאֹד וּפַחַד לִמְיֻדָּעָי רֹאַי בַּחוּץ נָדְדוּ מִמֶּנִּי:

יג: נִשְׁכַּחְתִּי כְּמֵת מִלֵּב הָיִיתִי כִּכְלִי אֹבֵד:

יד: כִּי שָׁמַעְתִּי דִּבַּת רַבִּים מָגוֹר מִסָּבִיב בְּהִוָּסְדָם יַחַד עָלַי לָקַחַת נַפְשִׁי זָמָמוּ:

טו: וַאֲנִי עָלֶיךָ בָטַחְתִּי יְהוָה אָמַרְתִּי אֱלֹהַי אָתָּה:

טז: בְּיָדְךָ עִתֹּתָי הַצִּילֵנִי מִיַּד אוֹיְבַי וּמֵרֹדְפָי:

יז: הָאִירָה פָנֶיךָ עַל עַבְדֶּךָ הוֹשִׁיעֵנִי בְחַסְדֶּךָ:

יח: יְהוָה אַל אֵבוֹשָׁה כִּי קְרָאתִיךָ יֵבֹשׁוּ רְשָׁעִים יִדְּמוּ לִשְׁאוֹל:

יט: תֵּאָלַמְנָה שִׂפְתֵי שָׁקֶר הַדֹּבְרוֹת עַל צַדִּיק עָתָק בְּגַאֲוָה וָבוּז:

כ: מָה רַב טוּבְךָ אֲשֶׁר צָפַנְתָּ לִּירֵאֶיךָ פָּעַלְתָּ לַחֹסִים בָּךְ נֶגֶד בְּנֵי אָדָם:

כא: תַּסְתִּירֵם בְּסֵתֶר פָּנֶיךָ מֵרֻכְסֵי אִישׁ תִּצְפְּנֵם בְּסֻכָּה מֵרִיב לְשֹׁנוֹת:

כב: בָּרוּךְ יְהוָה כִּי הִפְלִיא חַסְדּוֹ לִי בְּעִיר מָצוֹר:

כג: וַאֲנִי אָמַרְתִּי בְחָפְזִי נִגְרַזְתִּי מִנֶּגֶד עֵינֶיךָ אָכֵן שָׁמַעְתָּ קוֹל תַּחֲנוּנַי בְּשַׁוְּעִי אֵלֶיךָ:

כד: אֶהֱבוּ אֶת יְהוָה כָּל חֲסִידָיו אֱמוּנִים נֹצֵר יְהוָה וּמְשַׁלֵּם עַל יֶתֶר עֹשֵׂה גַאֲוָה:

כה: חִזְקוּ וְיַאֲמֵץ לְבַבְכֶם כָּל הַמְיַחֲלִים לַיהוָה:

פרק לב

א: לְדָוִד מַשְׂכִּיל אַשְׁרֵי נְשׂוּי פֶּשַׁע כְּסוּי חֲטָאָה:

ב: אַשְׁרֵי אָדָם לֹא יַחְשֹׁב יְהוָה לוֹ עָוֹן וְאֵין בְּרוּחוֹ רְמִיָּה:

ג: כִּי הֶחֱרַשְׁתִּי בָּלוּ עֲצָמָי בְּשַׁאֲגָתִי כָּל הַיּוֹם:

ד: כִּי יוֹמָם וָלַיְלָה תִּכְבַּד עָלַי יָדֶךָ נֶהְפַּךְ לְשַׁדִּי בְּחַרְבֹנֵי קַיִץ סֶלָה:

ה: חַטָּאתִי אוֹדִיעֲךָ וַעֲוֹנִי לֹא כִסִּיתִי אָמַרְתִּי אוֹדֶה עֲלֵי פְשָׁעַי לַיהוָה וְאַתָּה נָשָׂאתָ עֲוֹן חַטָּאתִי סֶלָה:

ו: עַל זֹאת יִתְפַּלֵּל כָּל חָסִיד אֵלֶיךָ לְעֵת מְצֹא רַק לְשֵׁטֶף מַיִם רַבִּים אֵלָיו לֹא יַגִּיעוּ:

ז: אַתָּה סֵתֶר לִי מִצַּר תִּצְּרֵנִי רָנֵּי פַלֵּט תְּסוֹבְבֵנִי סֶלָה:

ח: אַשְׂכִּילְךָ וְאוֹרְךָ בְּדֶרֶךְ זוּ תֵלֵךְ אִיעֲצָה עָלֶיךָ עֵינִי:

ט: אַל תִּהְיוּ כְּסוּס כְּפֶרֶד אֵין הָבִין בְּמֶתֶג וָרֶסֶן עֶדְיוֹ לִבְלוֹם בַּל קְרֹב אֵלֶיךָ:

י: רַבִּים מַכְאוֹבִים לָרָשָׁע וְהַבּוֹטֵחַ בַּיהוָה חֶסֶד יְסוֹבְבֶנּוּ:

יא: שִׂמְחוּ בַיהוָה וְגִילוּ צַדִּיקִים וְהַרְנִינוּ כָּל יִשְׁרֵי לֵב:

פרק לג

א: רַנְּנוּ צַדִּיקִים בַּיהוָה לַיְשָׁרִים נָאוָה תְהִלָּה:

ב: הוֹדוּ לַיהוָה בְּכִנּוֹר בְּנֵבֶל עָשׂוֹר זַמְּרוּ לוֹ:

ג: שִׁירוּ לוֹ שִׁיר חָדָשׁ הֵיטִיבוּ נַגֵּן בִּתְרוּעָה:

ד: כִּי יָשָׁר דְּבַר יְהוָה וְכָל מַעֲשֵׂהוּ בֶּאֱמוּנָה:

ה: אֹהֵב צְדָקָה וּמִשְׁפָּט חֶסֶד יְהוָה מָלְאָה הָאָרֶץ:

ו: בִּדְבַר יְהוָה שָׁמַיִם נַעֲשׂוּ וּבְרוּחַ פִּיו כָּל צְבָאָם:
ז: כֹּנֵס כַּנֵּד מֵי הַיָּם נֹתֵן בְּאֹצָרוֹת תְּהוֹמוֹת:
ח: יִירְאוּ מֵיְהוָה כָּל הָאָרֶץ מִמֶּנּוּ יָגוּרוּ כָּל יֹשְׁבֵי תֵבֵל:
ט: כִּי הוּא אָמַר וַיֶּהִי הוּא צִוָּה וַיַּעֲמֹד:
י: יְהוָה הֵפִיר עֲצַת גּוֹיִם הֵנִיא מַחְשְׁבוֹת עַמִּים:
יא: עֲצַת יְהוָה לְעוֹלָם תַּעֲמֹד מַחְשְׁבוֹת לִבּוֹ לְדֹר וָדֹר:
יב: אַשְׁרֵי הַגּוֹי אֲשֶׁר יְהוָה אֱלֹהָיו הָעָם בָּחַר לְנַחֲלָה לוֹ:
יג: מִשָּׁמַיִם הִבִּיט יְהוָה רָאָה אֶת כָּל בְּנֵי הָאָדָם:
יד: מִמְּכוֹן שִׁבְתּוֹ הִשְׁגִּיחַ אֶל כָּל יֹשְׁבֵי הָאָרֶץ:
טו: הַיֹּצֵר יַחַד לִבָּם הַמֵּבִין אֶל כָּל מַעֲשֵׂיהֶם:
טז: אֵין הַמֶּלֶךְ נוֹשָׁע בְּרָב חָיִל גִּבּוֹר לֹא יִנָּצֵל בְּרָב כֹּחַ:
יז: שֶׁקֶר הַסּוּס לִתְשׁוּעָה וּבְרֹב חֵילוֹ לֹא יְמַלֵּט:
יח: הִנֵּה עֵין יְהוָה אֶל יְרֵאָיו לַמְיַחֲלִים לְחַסְדּוֹ:
יט: לְהַצִּיל מִמָּוֶת נַפְשָׁם וּלְחַיּוֹתָם בָּרָעָב:
כ: נַפְשֵׁנוּ חִכְּתָה לַיהוָה עֶזְרֵנוּ וּמָגִנֵּנוּ הוּא:
כא: כִּי בוֹ יִשְׂמַח לִבֵּנוּ כִּי בְשֵׁם קָדְשׁוֹ בָטָחְנוּ:
כב: יְהִי חַסְדְּךָ יְהוָה עָלֵינוּ כַּאֲשֶׁר יִחַלְנוּ לָךְ:

פרק לד

א: לְדָוִד בְּשַׁנּוֹתוֹ אֶת טַעְמוֹ לִפְנֵי אֲבִימֶלֶךְ וַיְגָרְשֵׁהוּ וַיֵּלַךְ:
ב: אֲבָרְכָה אֶת יְהוָה בְּכָל עֵת תָּמִיד תְּהִלָּתוֹ בְּפִי:
ג: בַּיהוָה תִּתְהַלֵּל נַפְשִׁי יִשְׁמְעוּ עֲנָוִים וְיִשְׂמָחוּ:
ד: גַּדְּלוּ לַיהוָה אִתִּי וּנְרוֹמְמָה שְׁמוֹ יַחְדָּו:
ה: דָּרַשְׁתִּי אֶת יְהוָה וְעָנָנִי וּמִכָּל מְגוּרוֹתַי הִצִּילָנִי:
ו: הִבִּיטוּ אֵלָיו וְנָהָרוּ וּפְנֵיהֶם אַל יֶחְפָּרוּ:
ז: זֶה עָנִי קָרָא וַיהוָה שָׁמֵעַ וּמִכָּל צָרוֹתָיו הוֹשִׁיעוֹ:
ח: חֹנֶה מַלְאַךְ יְהוָה סָבִיב לִירֵאָיו וַיְחַלְּצֵם:
ט: טַעֲמוּ וּרְאוּ כִּי טוֹב יְהוָה אַשְׁרֵי הַגֶּבֶר יֶחֱסֶה בּוֹ:
י: יְראוּ אֶת יְהוָה קְדֹשָׁיו כִּי אֵין מַחְסוֹר לִירֵאָיו:
יא: כְּפִירִים רָשׁוּ וְרָעֵבוּ וְדֹרְשֵׁי יְהוָה לֹא יַחְסְרוּ כָל טוֹב:
יב: לְכוּ בָנִים שִׁמְעוּ לִי יִרְאַת יְהוָה אֲלַמֶּדְכֶם:
יג: מִי הָאִישׁ הֶחָפֵץ חַיִּים אֹהֵב יָמִים לִרְאוֹת טוֹב:
יד: נְצֹר לְשׁוֹנְךָ מֵרָע וּשְׂפָתֶיךָ מִדַּבֵּר מִרְמָה:
טו: סוּר מֵרָע וַעֲשֵׂה טוֹב בַּקֵּשׁ שָׁלוֹם וְרָדְפֵהוּ:
טז: עֵינֵי יְהוָה אֶל צַדִּיקִים וְאָזְנָיו אֶל שַׁוְעָתָם:
יז: פְּנֵי יְהוָה בְּעֹשֵׂי רָע לְהַכְרִית מֵאֶרֶץ זִכְרָם:
יח: צָעֲקוּ וַיהוָה שָׁמֵעַ וּמִכָּל צָרוֹתָם הִצִּילָם:
יט: קָרוֹב יְהוָה לְנִשְׁבְּרֵי לֵב וְאֶת דַּכְּאֵי רוּחַ יוֹשִׁיעַ:
כ: רַבּוֹת רָעוֹת צַדִּיק וּמִכֻּלָּם יַצִּילֶנּוּ יְהוָה:
כא: שֹׁמֵר כָּל עַצְמוֹתָיו אַחַת מֵהֵנָּה לֹא נִשְׁבָּרָה:
כב: תְּמוֹתֵת רָשָׁע רָעָה וְשֹׂנְאֵי צַדִּיק יֶאְשָׁמוּ:
כג: פֹּדֶה יְהוָה נֶפֶשׁ עֲבָדָיו וְלֹא יֶאְשְׁמוּ כָּל הַחֹסִים בּוֹ:

פרק לה

א: לְדָוִד רִיבָה יְהוָה אֶת יְרִיבַי לְחַם אֶת לֹחֲמָי:
ב: הַחֲזֵק מָגֵן וְצִנָּה וְקוּמָה בְּעֶזְרָתִי:
ג: וְהָרֵק חֲנִית וּסְגֹר לִקְרַאת רֹדְפָי אֱמֹר לְנַפְשִׁי יְשֻׁעָתֵךְ אָנִי:

ספר תהילים

ד: יֵבֹשׁוּ וְיִכָּלְמוּ מְבַקְשֵׁי נַפְשִׁי יִסֹּגוּ אָחוֹר וְיַחְפְּרוּ חֹשְׁבֵי רָעָתִי:

ה: יִהְיוּ כְּמֹץ לִפְנֵי רוּחַ וּמַלְאַךְ יְהוָה דּוֹחֶה:

ו: יְהִי דַרְכָּם חֹשֶׁךְ וַחֲלַקְלַקּוֹת וּמַלְאַךְ יְהוָה רֹדְפָם:

ז: כִּי חִנָּם טָמְנוּ לִי שַׁחַת רִשְׁתָּם חִנָּם חָפְרוּ לְנַפְשִׁי:

ח: תְּבוֹאֵהוּ שׁוֹאָה לֹא יֵדָע וְרִשְׁתּוֹ אֲשֶׁר טָמַן תִּלְכְּדוֹ בְּשׁוֹאָה יִפָּל בָּהּ:

ט: וְנַפְשִׁי תָּגִיל בַּיהוָה תָּשִׂישׂ בִּישׁוּעָתוֹ:

י: כָּל עַצְמוֹתַי תֹּאמַרְנָה יְהוָה מִי כָמוֹךָ מַצִּיל עָנִי מֵחָזָק מִמֶּנּוּ וְעָנִי וְאֶבְיוֹן מִגֹּזְלוֹ:

יא: יְקוּמוּן עֵדֵי חָמָס אֲשֶׁר לֹא יָדַעְתִּי יִשְׁאָלוּנִי:

יב: יְשַׁלְּמוּנִי רָעָה תַּחַת טוֹבָה שְׁכוֹל לְנַפְשִׁי:

יג: וַאֲנִי בַּחֲלוֹתָם לְבוּשִׁי שָׂק עִנֵּיתִי בַצּוֹם נַפְשִׁי וּתְפִלָּתִי עַל חֵיקִי תָשׁוּב:

יד: כְּרֵעַ כְּאָח לִי הִתְהַלָּכְתִּי כַּאֲבֶל אֵם קֹדֵר שַׁחוֹתִי:

טו: וּבְצַלְעִי שָׂמְחוּ וְנֶאֱסָפוּ נֶאֶסְפוּ עָלַי נֵכִים וְלֹא יָדַעְתִּי קָרְעוּ וְלֹא דָמּוּ:

טז: בְּחַנְפֵי לַעֲגֵי מָעוֹג חָרֹק עָלַי שִׁנֵּימוֹ:

יז: אֲדֹנָי כַּמָּה תִּרְאֶה הָשִׁיבָה נַפְשִׁי מִשֹּׁאֵיהֶם מִכְּפִירִים יְחִידָתִי:

יח: אוֹדְךָ בְּקָהָל רָב בְּעַם עָצוּם אֲהַלְלֶךָּ:

יט: אַל יִשְׂמְחוּ לִי אֹיְבַי שֶׁקֶר שֹׂנְאַי חִנָּם יִקְרְצוּ עָיִן:

כ: כִּי לֹא שָׁלוֹם יְדַבֵּרוּ וְעַל רִגְעֵי אֶרֶץ דִּבְרֵי מִרְמוֹת יַחֲשֹׁבוּן:

כא: וַיַּרְחִיבוּ עָלַי פִּיהֶם אָמְרוּ הֶאָח הֶאָח רָאֲתָה עֵינֵינוּ:

כב: רָאִיתָה יְהוָה אַל תֶּחֱרַשׁ אֲדֹנָי אֲל תִּרְחַק מִמֶּנִּי:

כג: הָעִירָה וְהָקִיצָה לְמִשְׁפָּטִי אֱלֹהַי וַאדֹנָי לְרִיבִי:

כד: שָׁפְטֵנִי כְצִדְקְךָ יְהוָה אֱלֹהָי וְאַל יִשְׂמְחוּ לִי:

כה: אַל יֹאמְרוּ בְלִבָּם הֶאָח נַפְשֵׁנוּ אַל יֹאמְרוּ בִּלַּעֲנוּהוּ:

כו: יֵבֹשׁוּ וְיַחְפְּרוּ יַחְדָּו שְׂמֵחֵי רָעָתִי יִלְבְּשׁוּ בֹשֶׁת וּכְלִמָּה הַמַּגְדִּילִים עָלָי:

כז: יָרֹנּוּ וְיִשְׂמְחוּ חֲפֵצֵי צִדְקִי וְיֹאמְרוּ תָמִיד יִגְדַּל יְהוָה הֶחָפֵץ שְׁלוֹם עַבְדּוֹ:

כח: וּלְשׁוֹנִי תֶּהְגֶּה צִדְקֶךָ כָּל הַיּוֹם תְּהִלָּתֶךָ:

פרק לו

א: לַמְנַצֵּחַ לְעֶבֶד יְהוָה לְדָוִד:

ב: נְאֻם פֶּשַׁע לָרָשָׁע בְּקֶרֶב לִבִּי אֵין פַּחַד אֱלֹהִים לְנֶגֶד עֵינָיו:

ג: כִּי הֶחֱלִיק אֵלָיו בְּעֵינָיו לִמְצֹא עֲוֹנוֹ לִשְׂנֹא:

ד: דִּבְרֵי פִיו אָוֶן וּמִרְמָה חָדַל לְהַשְׂכִּיל לְהֵיטִיב:

ה: אָוֶן יַחְשֹׁב עַל מִשְׁכָּבוֹ יִתְיַצֵּב עַל דֶּרֶךְ לֹא טוֹב רָע לֹא יִמְאָס:

ו: יְהוָה בְּהַשָּׁמַיִם חַסְדֶּךָ אֱמוּנָתְךָ עַד שְׁחָקִים:

ז: צִדְקָתְךָ כְּהַרְרֵי אֵל מִשְׁפָּטֶךָ תְּהוֹם רַבָּה אָדָם וּבְהֵמָה תוֹשִׁיעַ יְהוָה:

ח: מַה יָּקָר חַסְדְּךָ אֱלֹהִים וּבְנֵי אָדָם בְּצֵל כְּנָפֶיךָ יֶחֱסָיוּן:

ט: יִרְוְיֻן מִדֶּשֶׁן בֵּיתֶךָ וְנַחַל עֲדָנֶיךָ תַשְׁקֵם:

י: כִּי עִמְּךָ מְקוֹר חַיִּים בְּאוֹרְךָ נִרְאֶה אוֹר:

יא: מְשֹׁךְ חַסְדְּךָ לְיֹדְעֶיךָ וְצִדְקָתְךָ לְיִשְׁרֵי לֵב:

יב: אַל תְּבוֹאֵנִי רֶגֶל גַּאֲוָה וְיַד רְשָׁעִים אַל תְּנִדֵנִי:

יג: שָׁם נָפְלוּ פֹּעֲלֵי אָוֶן דֹּחוּ וְלֹא יָכְלוּ קוּם:

פרק לז

א: לְדָוִד אַל תִּתְחַר בַּמְּרֵעִים אַל תְּקַנֵּא בְּעֹשֵׂי עַוְלָה:

ב: כִּי כֶחָצִיר מְהֵרָה יִמָּלוּ וּכְיֶרֶק דֶּשֶׁא יִבּוֹלוּן:

ג: בְּטַח בַּיהוָה וַעֲשֵׂה טוֹב שְׁכָן אֶרֶץ וּרְעֵה אֱמוּנָה:

ד: וְהִתְעַנַּג עַל יְהוָה וְיִתֶּן לְךָ מִשְׁאֲלֹת לִבֶּךָ:

ה: גּוֹל עַל יְהוָה דַּרְכֶּךָ וּבְטַח עָלָיו וְהוּא יַעֲשֶׂה:

ו: וְהוֹצִיא כָאוֹר צִדְקֶךָ וּמִשְׁפָּטֶךָ כַּצָּהֳרָיִם:

ז: דּוֹם לַיהוָה וְהִתְחוֹלֵל לוֹ אַל תִּתְחַר בְּמַצְלִיחַ דַּרְכּוֹ בְּאִישׁ עֹשֶׂה מְזִמּוֹת:

ח: הֶרֶף מֵאַף וַעֲזֹב חֵמָה אַל תִּתְחַר אַךְ לְהָרֵעַ:

ט: כִּי מְרֵעִים יִכָּרֵתוּן וְקֹוֵי יְהוָה הֵמָּה יִירְשׁוּ אָרֶץ:

י: וְעוֹד מְעַט וְאֵין רָשָׁע וְהִתְבּוֹנַנְתָּ עַל מְקוֹמוֹ וְאֵינֶנּוּ:

יא: וַעֲנָוִים יִירְשׁוּ אָרֶץ וְהִתְעַנְּגוּ עַל רֹב שָׁלוֹם:

יב: זֹמֵם רָשָׁע לַצַּדִּיק וְחֹרֵק עָלָיו שִׁנָּיו:

יג: אֲדֹנָי יִשְׂחַק לוֹ כִּי רָאָה כִּי יָבֹא יוֹמוֹ:

יד: חֶרֶב פָּתְחוּ רְשָׁעִים וְדָרְכוּ קַשְׁתָּם לְהַפִּיל עָנִי וְאֶבְיוֹן לִטְבוֹחַ יִשְׁרֵי דָרֶךְ:

טו: חַרְבָּם תָּבוֹא בְלִבָּם וְקַשְּׁתוֹתָם תִּשָּׁבַרְנָה:

טז: טוֹב מְעַט לַצַּדִּיק מֵהֲמוֹן רְשָׁעִים רַבִּים:

יז: כִּי זְרוֹעוֹת רְשָׁעִים תִּשָּׁבַרְנָה וְסוֹמֵךְ צַדִּיקִים יְהוָה:

יח: יוֹדֵעַ יְהוָה יְמֵי תְמִימִם וְנַחֲלָתָם לְעוֹלָם תִּהְיֶה:

יט: לֹא יֵבֹשׁוּ בְּעֵת רָעָה וּבִימֵי רְעָבוֹן יִשְׂבָּעוּ:

כ: כִּי רְשָׁעִים יֹאבֵדוּ וְאֹיְבֵי יְהוָה כִּיקַר כָּרִים כָּלוּ בֶעָשָׁן כָּלוּ:

כא: לֹוֶה רָשָׁע וְלֹא יְשַׁלֵּם וְצַדִּיק חוֹנֵן וְנוֹתֵן:

כב: כִּי מְבֹרָכָיו יִירְשׁוּ אָרֶץ וּמְקֻלָּלָיו יִכָּרֵתוּ:

כג: מֵיְהוָה מִצְעֲדֵי גֶבֶר כּוֹנָנוּ וְדַרְכּוֹ יֶחְפָּץ:

כד: כִּי יִפֹּל לֹא יוּטָל כִּי יְהוָה סוֹמֵךְ יָדוֹ:

כה: נַעַר הָיִיתִי גַּם זָקַנְתִּי וְלֹא רָאִיתִי צַדִּיק נֶעֱזָב וְזַרְעוֹ מְבַקֶּשׁ לָחֶם:

כו: כָּל הַיּוֹם חוֹנֵן וּמַלְוֶה וְזַרְעוֹ לִבְרָכָה:

כז: סוּר מֵרָע וַעֲשֵׂה טוֹב וּשְׁכֹן לְעוֹלָם:

כח: כִּי יְהוָה אֹהֵב מִשְׁפָּט וְלֹא יַעֲזֹב אֶת חֲסִידָיו לְעוֹלָם נִשְׁמָרוּ וְזֶרַע רְשָׁעִים נִכְרָת:

כט: צַדִּיקִים יִירְשׁוּ אָרֶץ וְיִשְׁכְּנוּ לָעַד עָלֶיהָ:

ל: פִּי צַדִּיק יֶהְגֶּה חָכְמָה וּלְשׁוֹנוֹ תְּדַבֵּר מִשְׁפָּט:

לא: תּוֹרַת אֱלֹהָיו בְּלִבּוֹ לֹא תִמְעַד אֲשֻׁרָיו:

לב: צוֹפֶה רָשָׁע לַצַּדִּיק וּמְבַקֵּשׁ לַהֲמִיתוֹ:

לג: יְהוָה לֹא יַעַזְבֶנּוּ בְיָדוֹ וְלֹא יַרְשִׁיעֶנּוּ בְּהִשָּׁפְטוֹ:

לד: קַוֵּה אֶל יְהוָה וּשְׁמֹר דַּרְכּוֹ וִירוֹמִמְךָ לָרֶשֶׁת אָרֶץ בְּהִכָּרֵת רְשָׁעִים תִּרְאֶה:

לה: רָאִיתִי רָשָׁע עָרִיץ וּמִתְעָרֶה כְּאֶזְרָח רַעֲנָן:

לו: וַיַּעֲבֹר וְהִנֵּה אֵינֶנּוּ וָאֲבַקְשֵׁהוּ וְלֹא נִמְצָא:

לז: שְׁמָר תָּם וּרְאֵה יָשָׁר כִּי אַחֲרִית לְאִישׁ שָׁלוֹם:

לח: וּפֹשְׁעִים נִשְׁמְדוּ יַחְדָּו אַחֲרִית רְשָׁעִים נִכְרָתָה:

לט: וּתְשׁוּעַת צַדִּיקִים מֵיְהוָה מָעוּזָּם בְּעֵת צָרָה:

מ: וַיַּעְזְרֵם יְהוָה וַיְפַלְּטֵם יְפַלְּטֵם מֵרְשָׁעִים וְיוֹשִׁיעֵם כִּי חָסוּ בוֹ:

פרק לח

א: מִזְמוֹר לְדָוִד לְהַזְכִּיר:

ב: יְהוָה אַל בְּקֶצְפְּךָ תוֹכִיחֵנִי וּבַחֲמָתְךָ תְיַסְּרֵנִי:

ג: כִּי חִצֶּיךָ נִחֲתוּ בִי וַתִּנְחַת עָלַי יָדֶךָ:

ד: אֵין מְתֹם בִּבְשָׂרִי מִפְּנֵי זַעְמֶךָ אֵין שָׁלוֹם בַּעֲצָמַי מִפְּנֵי חַטָּאתִי:

ה: כִּי עֲוֹנֹתַי עָבְרוּ רֹאשִׁי כְּמַשָּׂא כָבֵד יִכְבְּדוּ מִמֶּנִּי:

ו: הִבְאִישׁוּ נָמַקּוּ חַבּוּרֹתָי מִפְּנֵי אִוַּלְתִּי:

ז: נַעֲוֵיתִי שַׁחֹתִי עַד מְאֹד כָּל הַיּוֹם קֹדֵר הִלָּכְתִּי:

ח: כִּי כְסָלַי מָלְאוּ נִקְלֶה וְאֵין מְתֹם בִּבְשָׂרִי:

ט: נְפוּגוֹתִי וְנִדְכֵּיתִי עַד מְאֹד שָׁאַגְתִּי מִנַּהֲמַת לִבִּי:

י: אֲדֹנָי נֶגְדְּךָ כָל תַּאֲוָתִי וְאַנְחָתִי מִמְּךָ לֹא נִסְתָּרָה:

יא: לִבִּי סְחַרְחַר עֲזָבַנִי כֹחִי וְאוֹר עֵינַי גַּם הֵם אֵין אִתִּי:
יב: אֹהֲבַי וְרֵעַי מִנֶּגֶד נִגְעִי יַעֲמֹדוּ וּקְרוֹבַי מֵרָחֹק עָמָדוּ:
יג: וַיְנַקְשׁוּ מְבַקְשֵׁי נַפְשִׁי וְדֹרְשֵׁי רָעָתִי דִּבְּרוּ הַוּוֹת וּמִרְמוֹת כָּל הַיּוֹם יֶהְגּוּ:
יד: וַאֲנִי כְחֵרֵשׁ לֹא אֶשְׁמָע וּכְאִלֵּם לֹא יִפְתַּח פִּיו:
טו: וָאֱהִי כְּאִישׁ אֲשֶׁר לֹא שֹׁמֵעַ וְאֵין בְּפִיו תּוֹכָחוֹת:
טז: כִּי לְךָ יְהֹוָה הוֹחָלְתִּי אַתָּה תַעֲנֶה אֲדֹנָי אֱלֹהָי:
יז: כִּי אָמַרְתִּי פֶּן יִשְׂמְחוּ לִי בְּמוֹט רַגְלִי עָלַי הִגְדִּילוּ:
יח: כִּי אֲנִי לְצֶלַע נָכוֹן וּמַכְאוֹבִי נֶגְדִּי תָמִיד:
יט: כִּי עֲו‍ֹנִי אַגִּיד אֶדְאַג מֵחַטָּאתִי:
כ: וְאֹיְבַי חַיִּים עָצֵמוּ וְרַבּוּ שֹׂנְאַי שָׁקֶר:
כא: וּמְשַׁלְּמֵי רָעָה תַּחַת טוֹבָה יִשְׂטְנוּנִי תַּחַת רָדְפִי טוֹב {רָדְפִי טוֹב}
כב: אַל תַּעַזְבֵנִי יְהֹוָה אֱלֹהַי אַל תִּרְחַק מִמֶּנִּי:
כג: חוּשָׁה לְעֶזְרָתִי אֲדֹנָי תְּשׁוּעָתִי:

פרק לט

א: לַמְנַצֵּחַ לִידִיתוּן {לִידוּתוּן} מִזְמוֹר לְדָוִד:
ב: אָמַרְתִּי אֶשְׁמְרָה דְרָכַי מֵחֲטוֹא בִלְשׁוֹנִי אֶשְׁמְרָה לְפִי מַחְסוֹם בְּעֹד רָשָׁע לְנֶגְדִּי:
ג: נֶאֱלַמְתִּי דוּמִיָּה הֶחֱשֵׁיתִי מִטּוֹב וּכְאֵבִי נֶעְכָּר:
ד: חַם לִבִּי בְּקִרְבִּי בַּהֲגִיגִי תִבְעַר אֵשׁ דִּבַּרְתִּי בִּלְשׁוֹנִי:
ה: הוֹדִיעֵנִי יְהֹוָה קִצִּי וּמִדַּת יָמַי מַה הִיא אֵדְעָה מֶה חָדֵל אָנִי:
ו: הִנֵּה טְפָחוֹת נָתַתָּה יָמַי וְחֶלְדִּי כְאַיִן נֶגְדֶּךָ אַךְ כָּל הֶבֶל כָּל אָדָם נִצָּב סֶלָה:
ז: אַךְ בְּצֶלֶם יִתְהַלֶּךְ אִישׁ אַךְ הֶבֶל יֶהֱמָיוּן יִצְבֹּר וְלֹא יֵדַע מִי אֹסְפָם:
ח: וְעַתָּה מַה קִּוִּיתִי אֲדֹנָי תּוֹחַלְתִּי לְךָ הִיא:
ט: מִכָּל פְּשָׁעַי הַצִּילֵנִי חֶרְפַּת נָבָל אַל תְּשִׂימֵנִי:
י: נֶאֱלַמְתִּי לֹא אֶפְתַּח פִּי כִּי אַתָּה עָשִׂיתָ:
יא: הָסֵר מֵעָלַי נִגְעֶךָ מִתִּגְרַת יָדְךָ אֲנִי כָלִיתִי:
יב: בְּתוֹכָחוֹת עַל עָו‍ֹן יִסַּרְתָּ אִישׁ וַתֶּמֶס כָּעָשׁ חֲמוּדוֹ אַךְ הֶבֶל כָּל אָדָם סֶלָה:
יג: שִׁמְעָה תְפִלָּתִי יְהֹוָה וְשַׁוְעָתִי הַאֲזִינָה אֶל דִּמְעָתִי אַל תֶּחֱרַשׁ כִּי גֵר אָנֹכִי עִמָּךְ תּוֹשָׁב כְּכָל אֲבוֹתָי:
יד: הָשַׁע מִמֶּנִּי וְאַבְלִיגָה בְּטֶרֶם אֵלֵךְ וְאֵינֶנִּי:

פרק מ

א: לַמְנַצֵּחַ לְדָוִד מִזְמוֹר:
ב: קַוֹּה קִוִּיתִי יְהֹוָה וַיֵּט אֵלַי וַיִּשְׁמַע שַׁוְעָתִי:
ג: וַיַּעֲלֵנִי מִבּוֹר שָׁאוֹן מִטִּיט הַיָּוֵן וַיָּקֶם עַל סֶלַע רַגְלַי כּוֹנֵן אֲשֻׁרָי:
ד: וַיִּתֵּן בְּפִי שִׁיר חָדָשׁ תְּהִלָּה לֵאלֹהֵינוּ יִרְאוּ רַבִּים וְיִירָאוּ וְיִבְטְחוּ בַּיהֹוָה:
ה: אַשְׁרֵי הַגֶּבֶר אֲשֶׁר שָׂם יְהֹוָה מִבְטַחוֹ וְלֹא פָנָה אֶל רְהָבִים וְשָׂטֵי כָזָב:
ו: רַבּוֹת עָשִׂיתָ אַתָּה יְהֹוָה אֱלֹהַי נִפְלְאֹתֶיךָ וּמַחְשְׁבֹתֶיךָ אֵלֵינוּ אֵין עֲרֹךְ אֵלֶיךָ אַגִּידָה וַאֲדַבֵּרָה עָצְמוּ מִסַּפֵּר:
ז: זֶבַח וּמִנְחָה לֹא חָפַצְתָּ אָזְנַיִם כָּרִיתָ לִּי עוֹלָה וַחֲטָאָה לֹא שָׁאָלְתָּ:
ח: אָז אָמַרְתִּי הִנֵּה בָאתִי בִּמְגִלַּת סֵפֶר כָּתוּב עָלָי:
ט: לַעֲשׂוֹת רְצוֹנְךָ אֱלֹהַי חָפָצְתִּי וְתוֹרָתְךָ בְּתוֹךְ מֵעָי:
י: בִּשַּׂרְתִּי צֶדֶק בְּקָהָל רָב הִנֵּה שְׂפָתַי לֹא אֶכְלָא יְהֹוָה אַתָּה יָדָעְתָּ:
יא: צִדְקָתְךָ לֹא כִסִּיתִי בְּתוֹךְ לִבִּי אֱמוּנָתְךָ וּתְשׁוּעָתְךָ אָמָרְתִּי לֹא כִחַדְתִּי חַסְדְּךָ וַאֲמִתְּךָ לְקָהָל רָב:
יב: אַתָּה יְהֹוָה לֹא תִכְלָא רַחֲמֶיךָ מִמֶּנִּי חַסְדְּךָ וַאֲמִתְּךָ תָּמִיד יִצְּרוּנִי:
יג: כִּי אָפְפוּ עָלַי רָעוֹת עַד אֵין מִסְפָּר הִשִּׂיגוּנִי עֲו‍ֹנֹתַי וְלֹא יָכֹלְתִּי לִרְאוֹת עָצְמוּ מִשַּׂעֲרוֹת רֹאשִׁי

וְלִבִּי עֲזָבָנִי:

יד: רְצֵה יְהוָה לְהַצִּילֵנִי יְהוָה לְעֶזְרָתִי חוּשָׁה:

טו: יֵבֹשׁוּ וְיַחְפְּרוּ יַחַד מְבַקְשֵׁי נַפְשִׁי לִסְפּוֹתָהּ יִסֹּגוּ אָחוֹר וְיִכָּלְמוּ חֲפֵצֵי רָעָתִי:

טז: יָשֹׁמּוּ עַל עֵקֶב בָּשְׁתָּם הָאֹמְרִים לִי הֶאָח הֶאָח:

יז: יָשִׂישׂוּ וְיִשְׂמְחוּ בְּךָ כָּל מְבַקְשֶׁיךָ יֹאמְרוּ תָמִיד יִגְדַּל יְהוָה אֹהֲבֵי תְּשׁוּעָתֶךָ:

יח: וַאֲנִי עָנִי וְאֶבְיוֹן אֲדֹנָי יַחֲשָׁב לִי עֶזְרָתִי וּמְפַלְטִי אַתָּה אֱלֹהַי אַל תְּאַחַר:

פרק מא

א: לַמְנַצֵּחַ מִזְמוֹר לְדָוִד:

ב: אַשְׁרֵי מַשְׂכִּיל אֶל דָּל בְּיוֹם רָעָה יְמַלְּטֵהוּ יְהוָה:

ג: יְהוָה יִשְׁמְרֵהוּ וִיחַיֵּהוּ יֻאַשַּׁר {וְאֻשָּׁר} בָּאָרֶץ וְאַל תִּתְּנֵהוּ בְּנֶפֶשׁ אֹיְבָיו:

ד: יְהוָה יִסְעָדֶנּוּ עַל עֶרֶשׂ דְּוָי כָּל מִשְׁכָּבוֹ הָפַכְתָּ בְחָלְיוֹ:

ה: אֲנִי אָמַרְתִּי יְהוָה חָנֵּנִי רְפָאָה נַפְשִׁי כִּי חָטָאתִי לָךְ:

ו: אוֹיְבַי יֹאמְרוּ רַע לִי מָתַי יָמוּת וְאָבַד שְׁמוֹ:

ז: וְאִם בָּא לִרְאוֹת שָׁוְא יְדַבֵּר לִבּוֹ יִקְבָּץ אָוֶן לוֹ יֵצֵא לַחוּץ יְדַבֵּר:

ח: יַחַד עָלַי יִתְלַחֲשׁוּ כָּל שֹׂנְאָי עָלַי יַחְשְׁבוּ רָעָה לִי:

ט: דְּבַר בְּלִיַּעַל יָצוּק בּוֹ וַאֲשֶׁר שָׁכַב לֹא יוֹסִיף לָקוּם:

י: גַּם אִישׁ שְׁלוֹמִי אֲשֶׁר בָּטַחְתִּי בוֹ אוֹכֵל לַחְמִי הִגְדִּיל עָלַי עָקֵב:

יא: וְאַתָּה יְהוָה חָנֵּנִי וַהֲקִימֵנִי וַאֲשַׁלְּמָה לָהֶם:

יב: בְּזֹאת יָדַעְתִּי כִּי חָפַצְתָּ בִּי כִּי לֹא יָרִיעַ אֹיְבִי עָלָי:

יג: וַאֲנִי בְּתֻמִּי תָּמַכְתָּ בִּי וַתַּצִּיבֵנִי לְפָנֶיךָ לְעוֹלָם:

יד: בָּרוּךְ יְהוָה אֱלֹהֵי יִשְׂרָאֵל מֵהָעוֹלָם וְעַד הָעוֹלָם אָמֵן וְאָמֵן:

פרק מב

א: לַמְנַצֵּחַ מַשְׂכִּיל לִבְנֵי קֹרַח:

ב: כְּאַיָּל תַּעֲרֹג עַל אֲפִיקֵי מָיִם כֵּן נַפְשִׁי תַעֲרֹג אֵלֶיךָ אֱלֹהִים:

ג: צָמְאָה נַפְשִׁי לֵאלֹהִים לְאֵל חָי מָתַי אָבוֹא וְאֵרָאֶה פְּנֵי אֱלֹהִים:

ד: הָיְתָה לִּי דִמְעָתִי לֶחֶם יוֹמָם וָלָיְלָה בֶּאֱמֹר אֵלַי כָּל הַיּוֹם אַיֵּה אֱלֹהֶיךָ:

ה: אֵלֶּה אֶזְכְּרָה וְאֶשְׁפְּכָה עָלַי נַפְשִׁי כִּי אֶעֱבֹר בַּסָּךְ אֶדַּדֵּם עַד בֵּית אֱלֹהִים בְּקוֹל רִנָּה וְתוֹדָה הָמוֹן חוֹגֵג:

ו: מַה תִּשְׁתּוֹחֲחִי נַפְשִׁי וַתֶּהֱמִי עָלַי הוֹחִילִי לֵאלֹהִים כִּי עוֹד אוֹדֶנּוּ יְשׁוּעוֹת פָּנָיו:

ז: אֱלֹהַי עָלַי נַפְשִׁי תִשְׁתּוֹחָח עַל כֵּן אֶזְכָּרְךָ מֵאֶרֶץ יַרְדֵּן וְחֶרְמוֹנִים מֵהַר מִצְעָר:

ח: תְּהוֹם אֶל תְּהוֹם קוֹרֵא לְקוֹל צִנּוֹרֶיךָ כָּל מִשְׁבָּרֶיךָ וְגַלֶּיךָ עָלַי עָבָרוּ:

ט: יוֹמָם יְצַוֶּה יְהוָה חַסְדּוֹ וּבַלַּיְלָה שִׁירֹה עִמִּי תְּפִלָּה לְאֵל חַיָּי:

י: אוֹמְרָה לְאֵל סַלְעִי לָמָה שְׁכַחְתָּנִי לָמָּה קֹדֵר אֵלֵךְ בְּלַחַץ אוֹיֵב:

יא: בְּרֶצַח בְּעַצְמוֹתַי חֵרְפוּנִי צוֹרְרָי בְּאָמְרָם אֵלַי כָּל הַיּוֹם אַיֵּה אֱלֹהֶיךָ:

יב: מַה תִּשְׁתּוֹחֲחִי נַפְשִׁי וּמַה תֶּהֱמִי עָלַי הוֹחִילִי לֵאלֹהִים כִּי עוֹד אוֹדֶנּוּ יְשׁוּעֹת פָּנַי וֵאלֹהָי:

פרק מג

א: שָׁפְטֵנִי אֱלֹהִים וְרִיבָה רִיבִי מִגּוֹי לֹא חָסִיד מֵאִישׁ מִרְמָה וְעַוְלָה תְפַלְּטֵנִי:

ב: כִּי אַתָּה אֱלֹהֵי מָעוּזִּי לָמָה זְנַחְתָּנִי לָמָּה קֹדֵר אֶתְהַלֵּךְ בְּלַחַץ אוֹיֵב:

ג: שְׁלַח אוֹרְךָ וַאֲמִתְּךָ הֵמָּה יַנְחוּנִי יְבִיאוּנִי אֶל הַר קָדְשְׁךָ וְאֶל מִשְׁכְּנוֹתֶיךָ:

ד: וְאָבוֹאָה אֶל מִזְבַּח אֱלֹהִים אֶל אֵל שִׂמְחַת גִּילִי וְאוֹדְךָ בְכִנּוֹר אֱלֹהִים אֱלֹהָי:

ה: מַה תִּשְׁתּוֹחֲחִי נַפְשִׁי וּמַה תֶּהֱמִי עָלַי הוֹחִילִי לֵאלֹהִים כִּי עוֹד אוֹדֶנּוּ יְשׁוּעֹת פָּנַי וֵאלֹהָי:

פרק מד

א: לַמְנַצֵּחַ לִבְנֵי קֹרַח מַשְׂכִּיל:

ב: אֱלֹהִים בְּאָזְנֵינוּ שָׁמַעְנוּ אֲבוֹתֵינוּ סִפְּרוּ לָנוּ פֹּעַל פָּעַלְתָּ בִימֵיהֶם בִּימֵי קֶדֶם:
ג: אַתָּה יָדְךָ גּוֹיִם הוֹרַשְׁתָּ וַתִּטָּעֵם תָּרַע לְאֻמִּים וַתְּשַׁלְּחֵם:
ד: כִּי לֹא בְחַרְבָּם יָרְשׁוּ אָרֶץ וּזְרוֹעָם לֹא הוֹשִׁיעָה לָּמוֹ כִּי יְמִינְךָ וּזְרוֹעֲךָ וְאוֹר פָּנֶיךָ כִּי רְצִיתָם:
ה: אַתָּה הוּא מַלְכִּי אֱלֹהִים צַוֵּה יְשׁוּעוֹת יַעֲקֹב:
ו: בְּךָ צָרֵינוּ נְנַגֵּחַ בְּשִׁמְךָ נָבוּס קָמֵינוּ:
ז: כִּי לֹא בְקַשְׁתִּי אֶבְטָח וְחַרְבִּי לֹא תוֹשִׁיעֵנִי:
ח: כִּי הוֹשַׁעְתָּנוּ מִצָּרֵינוּ וּמְשַׂנְאֵינוּ הֱבִישׁוֹתָ:
ט: בֵּאלֹהִים הִלַּלְנוּ כָל הַיּוֹם וְשִׁמְךָ לְעוֹלָם נוֹדֶה סֶלָה:
י: אַף זָנַחְתָּ וַתַּכְלִימֵנוּ וְלֹא תֵצֵא בְּצִבְאוֹתֵינוּ:
יא: תְּשִׁיבֵנוּ אָחוֹר מִנִּי צָר וּמְשַׂנְאֵינוּ שָׁסוּ לָמוֹ:
יב: תִּתְּנֵנוּ כְּצֹאן מַאֲכָל וּבַגּוֹיִם זֵרִיתָנוּ:
יג: תִּמְכֹּר עַמְּךָ בְלֹא הוֹן וְלֹא רִבִּיתָ בִּמְחִירֵיהֶם:
יד: תְּשִׂימֵנוּ חֶרְפָּה לִשְׁכֵנֵינוּ לַעַג וָקֶלֶס לִסְבִיבוֹתֵינוּ:
טו: תְּשִׂימֵנוּ מָשָׁל בַּגּוֹיִם מְנוֹד רֹאשׁ בַּל אֻמִּים:
טז: כָּל הַיּוֹם כְּלִמָּתִי נֶגְדִּי וּבֹשֶׁת פָּנַי כִּסָּתְנִי:
יז: מִקּוֹל מְחָרֵף וּמְגַדֵּף מִפְּנֵי אוֹיֵב וּמִתְנַקֵּם:
יח: כָּל זֹאת בָּאַתְנוּ וְלֹא שְׁכַחֲנוּךָ וְלֹא שִׁקַּרְנוּ בִּבְרִיתֶךָ:
יט: לֹא נָסוֹג אָחוֹר לִבֵּנוּ וַתֵּט אֲשֻׁרֵינוּ מִנִּי אָרְחֶךָ:
כ: כִּי דִכִּיתָנוּ בִּמְקוֹם תַּנִּים וַתְּכַס עָלֵינוּ בְצַלְמָוֶת:
כא: אִם שָׁכַחְנוּ שֵׁם אֱלֹהֵינוּ וַנִּפְרֹשׂ כַּפֵּינוּ לְאֵל זָר:
כב: הֲלֹא אֱלֹהִים יַחֲקָר זֹאת כִּי הוּא יֹדֵעַ תַּעֲלֻמוֹת לֵב:
כג: כִּי עָלֶיךָ הֹרַגְנוּ כָל הַיּוֹם נֶחְשַׁבְנוּ כְּצֹאן טִבְחָה:
כד: עוּרָה לָמָּה תִישַׁן אֲדֹנָי הָקִיצָה אַל תִּזְנַח לָנֶצַח:
כה: לָמָּה פָנֶיךָ תַסְתִּיר תִּשְׁכַּח עָנְיֵנוּ וְלַחֲצֵנוּ:
כו: כִּי שָׁחָה לֶעָפָר נַפְשֵׁנוּ דָּבְקָה לָאָרֶץ בִּטְנֵנוּ:
כז: קוּמָה עֶזְרָתָה לָּנוּ וּפְדֵנוּ לְמַעַן חַסְדֶּךָ:

פרק מה

א: לַמְנַצֵּחַ עַל שֹׁשַׁנִּים לִבְנֵי קֹרַח מַשְׂכִּיל שִׁיר יְדִידֹת:
ב: רָחַשׁ לִבִּי דָּבָר טוֹב אֹמֵר אָנִי מַעֲשַׂי לְמֶלֶךְ לְשׁוֹנִי עֵט סוֹפֵר מָהִיר:
ג: יָפְיָפִיתָ מִבְּנֵי אָדָם הוּצַק חֵן בְּשִׂפְתוֹתֶיךָ עַל כֵּן בֵּרַכְךָ אֱלֹהִים לְעוֹלָם:
ד: חֲגוֹר חַרְבְּךָ עַל יָרֵךְ גִּבּוֹר הוֹדְךָ וַהֲדָרֶךָ:
ה: וַהֲדָרְךָ צְלַח רְכַב עַל דְּבַר אֱמֶת וְעַנְוָה צֶדֶק וְתוֹרְךָ נוֹרָאוֹת יְמִינֶךָ:
ו: חִצֶּיךָ שְׁנוּנִים עַמִּים תַּחְתֶּיךָ יִפְּלוּ בְּלֵב אוֹיְבֵי הַמֶּלֶךְ:
ז: כִּסְאֲךָ אֱלֹהִים עוֹלָם וָעֶד שֵׁבֶט מִישֹׁר שֵׁבֶט מַלְכוּתֶךָ:
ח: אָהַבְתָּ צֶּדֶק וַתִּשְׂנָא רֶשַׁע עַל כֵּן מְשָׁחֲךָ אֱלֹהִים אֱלֹהֶיךָ שֶׁמֶן שָׂשׂוֹן מֵחֲבֵרֶךָ:
ט: מֹר וַאֲהָלוֹת קְצִיעוֹת כָּל בִּגְדֹתֶיךָ מִן הֵיכְלֵי שֵׁן מִנִּי שִׂמְּחוּךָ:
י: בְּנוֹת מְלָכִים בְּיִקְּרוֹתֶיךָ נִצְּבָה שֵׁגַל לִימִינְךָ בְּכֶתֶם אוֹפִיר:
יא: שִׁמְעִי בַת וּרְאִי וְהַטִּי אָזְנֵךְ וְשִׁכְחִי עַמֵּךְ וּבֵית אָבִיךְ:
יב: וְיִתְאָו הַמֶּלֶךְ יָפְיֵךְ כִּי הוּא אֲדֹנַיִךְ וְהִשְׁתַּחֲוִי לוֹ:
יג: וּבַת צֹר בְּמִנְחָה פָּנַיִךְ יְחַלּוּ עֲשִׁירֵי עָם:
יד: כָּל כְּבוּדָּה בַת מֶלֶךְ פְּנִימָה מִמִּשְׁבְּצוֹת זָהָב לְבוּשָׁהּ:
טו: לִרְקָמוֹת תּוּבַל לַמֶּלֶךְ בְּתוּלוֹת אַחֲרֶיהָ רֵעוֹתֶיהָ מוּבָאוֹת לָךְ:
טז: תּוּבַלְנָה בִּשְׂמָחֹת וָגִיל תְּבֹאֶינָה בְּהֵיכַל מֶלֶךְ:
יז: תַּחַת אֲבֹתֶיךָ יִהְיוּ בָנֶיךָ תְּשִׁיתֵמוֹ לְשָׂרִים בְּכָל הָאָרֶץ:
יח: אַזְכִּירָה שִׁמְךָ בְּכָל דֹּר וָדֹר עַל כֵּן עַמִּים יְהוֹדֻךָ לְעֹלָם וָעֶד:

פרק מו

א: לַמְנַצֵּחַ לִבְנֵי קֹרַח עַל עֲלָמוֹת שִׁיר:

ב: אֱלֹהִים לָנוּ מַחֲסֶה וָעֹז עֶזְרָה בְצָרוֹת נִמְצָא מְאֹד:

ג: עַל כֵּן לֹא נִירָא בְּהָמִיר אָרֶץ וּבְמוֹט הָרִים בְּלֵב יַמִּים:

ד: יֶהֱמוּ יֶחְמְרוּ מֵימָיו יִרְעֲשׁוּ הָרִים בְּגַאֲוָתוֹ סֶלָה:

ה: נָהָר פְּלָגָיו יְשַׂמְּחוּ עִיר אֱלֹהִים קְדֹשׁ מִשְׁכְּנֵי עֶלְיוֹן:

ו: אֱלֹהִים בְּקִרְבָּהּ בַּל תִּמּוֹט יַעְזְרֶהָ אֱלֹהִים לִפְנוֹת בֹּקֶר:

ז: הָמוּ גוֹיִם מָטוּ מַמְלָכוֹת נָתַן בְּקוֹלוֹ תָּמוּג אָרֶץ:

ח: יְהֹוָה צְבָאוֹת עִמָּנוּ מִשְׂגָּב לָנוּ אֱלֹהֵי יַעֲקֹב סֶלָה:

ט: לְכוּ חֲזוּ מִפְעֲלוֹת יְהֹוָה אֲשֶׁר שָׂם שַׁמּוֹת בָּאָרֶץ:

י: מַשְׁבִּית מִלְחָמוֹת עַד קְצֵה הָאָרֶץ קֶשֶׁת יְשַׁבֵּר וְקִצֵּץ חֲנִית עֲגָלוֹת יִשְׂרֹף בָּאֵשׁ:

יא: הַרְפּוּ וּדְעוּ כִּי אָנֹכִי אֱלֹהִים אָרוּם בַּגּוֹיִם אָרוּם בָּאָרֶץ:

יב: יְהֹוָה צְבָאוֹת עִמָּנוּ מִשְׂגָּב לָנוּ אֱלֹהֵי יַעֲקֹב סֶלָה:

פרק מז

א: לַמְנַצֵּחַ לִבְנֵי קֹרַח מִזְמוֹר:

ב: כָּל הָעַמִּים תִּקְעוּ כָף הָרִיעוּ לֵאלֹהִים בְּקוֹל רִנָּה:

ג: כִּי יְהֹוָה עֶלְיוֹן נוֹרָא מֶלֶךְ גָּדוֹל עַל כָּל הָאָרֶץ:

ד: יַדְבֵּר עַמִּים תַּחְתֵּינוּ וּלְאֻמִּים תַּחַת רַגְלֵינוּ:

ה: יִבְחַר לָנוּ אֶת נַחֲלָתֵנוּ אֶת גְּאוֹן יַעֲקֹב אֲשֶׁר אָהֵב סֶלָה:

ו: עָלָה אֱלֹהִים בִּתְרוּעָה יְהֹוָה בְּקוֹל שׁוֹפָר:

ז: זַמְּרוּ אֱלֹהִים זַמֵּרוּ זַמְּרוּ לְמַלְכֵּנוּ זַמֵּרוּ:

ח: כִּי מֶלֶךְ כָּל הָאָרֶץ אֱלֹהִים זַמְּרוּ מַשְׂכִּיל:

ט: מָלַךְ אֱלֹהִים עַל גּוֹיִם אֱלֹהִים יָשַׁב עַל כִּסֵּא קָדְשׁוֹ:

י: נְדִיבֵי עַמִּים נֶאֱסָפוּ עַם אֱלֹהֵי אַבְרָהָם כִּי לֵאלֹהִים מָגִנֵּי אֶרֶץ מְאֹד נַעֲלָה:

פרק מח

א: שִׁיר מִזְמוֹר לִבְנֵי קֹרַח:

ב: גָּדוֹל יְהֹוָה וּמְהֻלָּל מְאֹד בְּעִיר אֱלֹהֵינוּ הַר קָדְשׁוֹ:

ג: יְפֵה נוֹף מְשׂוֹשׂ כָּל הָאָרֶץ הַר צִיּוֹן יַרְכְּתֵי צָפוֹן קִרְיַת מֶלֶךְ רָב:

ד: אֱלֹהִים בְּאַרְמְנוֹתֶיהָ נוֹדַע לְמִשְׂגָּב:

ה: כִּי הִנֵּה הַמְּלָכִים נוֹעֲדוּ עָבְרוּ יַחְדָּו:

ו: הֵמָּה רָאוּ כֵּן תָּמָהוּ נִבְהֲלוּ נֶחְפָּזוּ:

ז: רְעָדָה אֲחָזָתַם שָׁם חִיל כַּיּוֹלֵדָה:

ח: בְּרוּחַ קָדִים תְּשַׁבֵּר אֳנִיּוֹת תַּרְשִׁישׁ:

ט: כַּאֲשֶׁר שָׁמַעְנוּ כֵּן רָאִינוּ בְּעִיר יְהֹוָה צְבָאוֹת בְּעִיר אֱלֹהֵינוּ אֱלֹהִים יְכוֹנְנֶהָ עַד עוֹלָם סֶלָה:

י: דִּמִּינוּ אֱלֹהִים חַסְדֶּךָ בְּקֶרֶב הֵיכָלֶךָ:

יא: כְּשִׁמְךָ אֱלֹהִים כֵּן תְּהִלָּתְךָ עַל קַצְוֵי אֶרֶץ צֶדֶק מָלְאָה יְמִינֶךָ:

יב: יִשְׂמַח הַר צִיּוֹן תָּגֵלְנָה בְּנוֹת יְהוּדָה לְמַעַן מִשְׁפָּטֶיךָ:

יג: סֹבּוּ צִיּוֹן וְהַקִּיפוּהָ סִפְרוּ מִגְדָּלֶיהָ:

יד: שִׁיתוּ לִבְּכֶם לְחֵילָה פַּסְּגוּ אַרְמְנוֹתֶיהָ לְמַעַן תְּסַפְּרוּ לְדוֹר אַחֲרוֹן:

טו: כִּי זֶה אֱלֹהִים אֱלֹהֵינוּ עוֹלָם וָעֶד הוּא יְנַהֲגֵנוּ עַל מוּת:

פרק מט

א: לַמְנַצֵּחַ לִבְנֵי קֹרַח מִזְמוֹר:

ב: שִׁמְעוּ זֹאת כָּל הָעַמִּים הַאֲזִינוּ כָּל יֹשְׁבֵי חָלֶד:

ג: גַּם בְּנֵי אָדָם גַּם בְּנֵי אִישׁ יַחַד עָשִׁיר וְאֶבְיוֹן:

ד: פִּי יְדַבֵּר חָכְמוֹת וְהָגוּת לִבִּי תְבוּנוֹת:

ה: אַטֶּה לְמָשָׁל אָזְנִי אֶפְתַּח בְּכִנּוֹר חִידָתִי:

ו: לָמָּה אִירָא בִּימֵי רָע עֲוֺן עֲקֵבַי יְסוּבֵּנִי:

ז: הַבֹּטְחִים עַל חֵילָם וּבְרֹב עָשְׁרָם יִתְהַלָּלוּ:

ח: אָח לֹא פָדֹה יִפְדֶּה אִישׁ לֹא יִתֵּן לֵאלֹהִים כָּפְרוֹ:

ט: וְיֵקַר פִּדְיוֹן נַפְשָׁם וְחָדַל לְעוֹלָם:

י: וִיחִי עוֹד לָנֶצַח לֹא יִרְאֶה הַשָּׁחַת:

יא: כִּי יִרְאֶה חֲכָמִים יָמוּתוּ יַחַד כְּסִיל וָבַעַר יֹאבֵדוּ וְעָזְבוּ לַאֲחֵרִים חֵילָם:

יב: קִרְבָּם בָּתֵּימוֹ לְעוֹלָם מִשְׁכְּנֹתָם לְדוֹר וָדֹר קָרְאוּ בִשְׁמוֹתָם עֲלֵי אֲדָמוֹת:

יג: וְאָדָם בִּיקָר בַּל יָלִין נִמְשַׁל כַּבְּהֵמוֹת נִדְמוּ:

יד: זֶה דַרְכָּם כֵּסֶל לָמוֹ וְאַחֲרֵיהֶם בְּפִיהֶם יִרְצוּ סֶלָה:

טו: כַּצֹּאן לִשְׁאוֹל שַׁתּוּ מָוֶת יִרְעֵם וַיִּרְדּוּ בָם יְשָׁרִים לַבֹּקֶר וצירם {וְצוּרָם} לְבַלּוֹת שְׁאוֹל מִזְּבֻל לוֹ:

טז: אַךְ אֱלֹהִים יִפְדֶּה נַפְשִׁי מִיַּד שְׁאוֹל כִּי יִקָּחֵנִי סֶלָה:

יז: אַל תִּירָא כִּי יַעֲשִׁר אִישׁ כִּי יִרְבֶּה כְּבוֹד בֵּיתוֹ:

יח: כִּי לֹא בְמוֹתוֹ יִקַּח הַכֹּל לֹא יֵרֵד אַחֲרָיו כְּבוֹדוֹ:

יט: כִּי נַפְשׁוֹ בְּחַיָּיו יְבָרֵךְ וְיוֹדֻךָ כִּי תֵיטִיב לָךְ:

כ: תָּבוֹא עַד דּוֹר אֲבוֹתָיו עַד נֵצַח לֹא יִרְאוּ אוֹר:

כא: אָדָם בִּיקָר וְלֹא יָבִין נִמְשַׁל כַּבְּהֵמוֹת נִדְמוּ:

פרק נ

א: מִזְמוֹר לְאָסָף אֵל אֱלֹהִים יְהוָה דִּבֶּר וַיִּקְרָא אָרֶץ מִמִּזְרַח שֶׁמֶשׁ עַד מְבֹאוֹ:

ב: מִצִּיּוֹן מִכְלַל יֹפִי אֱלֹהִים הוֹפִיעַ:

ג: יָבֹא אֱלֹהֵינוּ וְאַל יֶחֱרַשׁ אֵשׁ לְפָנָיו תֹּאכֵל וּסְבִיבָיו נִשְׂעֲרָה מְאֹד:

ד: יִקְרָא אֶל הַשָּׁמַיִם מֵעָל וְאֶל הָאָרֶץ לָדִין עַמּוֹ:

ה: אִסְפוּ לִי חֲסִידָי כֹּרְתֵי בְרִיתִי עֲלֵי זָבַח:

ו: וַיַּגִּידוּ שָׁמַיִם צִדְקוֹ כִּי אֱלֹהִים שֹׁפֵט הוּא סֶלָה:

ז: שִׁמְעָה עַמִּי וַאֲדַבֵּרָה יִשְׂרָאֵל וְאָעִידָה בָּךְ אֱלֹהִים אֱלֹהֶיךָ אָנֹכִי:

ח: לֹא עַל זְבָחֶיךָ אוֹכִיחֶךָ וְעוֹלֹתֶיךָ לְנֶגְדִּי תָמִיד:

ט: לֹא אֶקַּח מִבֵּיתְךָ פָר מִמִּכְלְאֹתֶיךָ עַתּוּדִים:

י: כִּי לִי כָל חַיְתוֹ יָעַר בְּהֵמוֹת בְּהַרְרֵי אָלֶף:

יא: יָדַעְתִּי כָּל עוֹף הָרִים וְזִיז שָׂדַי עִמָּדִי:

יב: אִם אֶרְעַב לֹא אֹמַר לָךְ כִּי לִי תֵבֵל וּמְלֹאָהּ:

יג: הַאוֹכַל בְּשַׂר אַבִּירִים וְדַם עַתּוּדִים אֶשְׁתֶּה:

יד: זְבַח לֵאלֹהִים תּוֹדָה וְשַׁלֵּם לְעֶלְיוֹן נְדָרֶיךָ:

טו: וּקְרָאֵנִי בְּיוֹם צָרָה אֲחַלֶּצְךָ וּתְכַבְּדֵנִי:

טז: וְלָרָשָׁע אָמַר אֱלֹהִים מַה לְּךָ לְסַפֵּר חֻקָּי וַתִּשָּׂא בְרִיתִי עֲלֵי פִיךָ:

יז: וְאַתָּה שָׂנֵאתָ מוּסָר וַתַּשְׁלֵךְ דְּבָרַי אַחֲרֶיךָ:

יח: אִם רָאִיתָ גַנָּב וַתִּרֶץ עִמּוֹ וְעִם מְנָאֲפִים חֶלְקֶךָ:

יט: פִּיךָ שָׁלַחְתָּ בְרָעָה וּלְשׁוֹנְךָ תַּצְמִיד מִרְמָה:

כ: תֵּשֵׁב בְּאָחִיךָ תְדַבֵּר בְּבֶן אִמְּךָ תִּתֶּן דֹּפִי:

כא: אֵלֶּה עָשִׂיתָ וְהֶחֱרַשְׁתִּי דִּמִּיתָ הֱיוֹת אֶהְיֶה כָמוֹךָ אוֹכִיחֲךָ וְאֶעֶרְכָה לְעֵינֶיךָ:

כב: בִּינוּ נָא זֹאת שֹׁכְחֵי אֱלוֹהַּ פֶּן אֶטְרֹף וְאֵין מַצִּיל:

כג: זֹבֵחַ תּוֹדָה יְכַבְּדָנְנִי וְשָׂם דֶּרֶךְ אַרְאֶנּוּ בְּיֵשַׁע אֱלֹהִים:

פרק נא

א: לַמְנַצֵּחַ מִזְמוֹר לְדָוִד:

ב: בְּבוֹא אֵלָיו נָתָן הַנָּבִיא כַּאֲשֶׁר בָּא אֶל בַּת שָׁבַע:

ג: חָנֵּנִי אֱלֹהִים כְּחַסְדֶּךָ כְּרֹב רַחֲמֶיךָ מְחֵה פְשָׁעָי:

ד: הרבה {הֶרֶב} כַּבְּסֵנִי מֵעֲוֹנִי וּמֵחַטָּאתִי טַהֲרֵנִי:

ה: כִּי פְשָׁעַי אֲנִי אֵדָע וְחַטָּאתִי נֶגְדִּי תָמִיד:

ו: לְךָ לְבַדְּךָ חָטָאתִי וְהָרַע בְּעֵינֶיךָ עָשִׂיתִי לְמַעַן תִּצְדַּק בְּדָבְרֶךָ תִּזְכֶּה בְשָׁפְטֶךָ:

ז: הֵן בְּעָווֹן חוֹלָלְתִּי וּבְחֵטְא יֶחֱמַתְנִי אִמִּי:

ח: הֵן אֱמֶת חָפַצְתָּ בַטֻּחוֹת וּבְסָתֻם חָכְמָה תוֹדִיעֵנִי:

ט: תְּחַטְּאֵנִי בְאֵזוֹב וְאֶטְהָר תְּכַבְּסֵנִי וּמִשֶּׁלֶג אַלְבִּין:

י: תַּשְׁמִיעֵנִי שָׂשׂוֹן וְשִׂמְחָה תָּגֵלְנָה עֲצָמוֹת דִּכִּיתָ:

יא: הַסְתֵּר פָּנֶיךָ מֵחֲטָאָי וְכָל עֲוֹנֹתַי מְחֵה:

יב: לֵב טָהוֹר בְּרָא לִי אֱלֹהִים וְרוּחַ נָכוֹן חַדֵּשׁ בְּקִרְבִּי:

יג: אַל תַּשְׁלִיכֵנִי מִלְּפָנֶיךָ וְרוּחַ קָדְשְׁךָ אַל תִּקַּח מִמֶּנִּי:

יד: הָשִׁיבָה לִּי שְׂשׂוֹן יִשְׁעֶךָ וְרוּחַ נְדִיבָה תִסְמְכֵנִי:

טו: אֲלַמְּדָה פֹשְׁעִים דְּרָכֶיךָ וְחַטָּאִים אֵלֶיךָ יָשׁוּבוּ:

טז: הַצִּילֵנִי מִדָּמִים אֱלֹהִים אֱלֹהֵי תְּשׁוּעָתִי תְּרַנֵּן לְשׁוֹנִי צִדְקָתֶךָ:

יז: אֲדֹנָי שְׂפָתַי תִּפְתָּח וּפִי יַגִּיד תְּהִלָּתֶךָ:

יח: כִּי לֹא תַחְפֹּץ זֶבַח וְאֶתֵּנָה עוֹלָה לֹא תִרְצֶה:

יט: זִבְחֵי אֱלֹהִים רוּחַ נִשְׁבָּרָה לֵב נִשְׁבָּר וְנִדְכֶּה אֱלֹהִים לֹא תִבְזֶה:

כ: הֵיטִיבָה בִרְצוֹנְךָ אֶת צִיּוֹן תִּבְנֶה חוֹמוֹת יְרוּשָׁלָ͏ִם:

כא: אָז תַּחְפֹּץ זִבְחֵי צֶדֶק עוֹלָה וְכָלִיל אָז יַעֲלוּ עַל מִזְבַּחֲךָ פָרִים:

פרק נב

א: לַמְנַצֵּחַ מַשְׂכִּיל לְדָוִד:

ב: בְּבוֹא דּוֹאֵג הָאֲדֹמִי וַיַּגֵּד לְשָׁאוּל וַיֹּאמֶר לוֹ בָּא דָוִד אֶל בֵּית אֲחִימֶלֶךְ:

ג: מַה תִּתְהַלֵּל בְּרָעָה הַגִּבּוֹר חֶסֶד אֵל כָּל הַיּוֹם:

ד: הַוּוֹת תַּחְשֹׁב לְשׁוֹנֶךָ כְּתַעַר מְלֻטָּשׁ עֹשֵׂה רְמִיָּה:

ה: אָהַבְתָּ רָּע מִטּוֹב שֶׁקֶר מִדַּבֵּר צֶדֶק סֶלָה:

ו: אָהַבְתָּ כָל דִּבְרֵי בָלַע לְשׁוֹן מִרְמָה:

ז: גַּם אֵל יִתָּצְךָ לָנֶצַח יַחְתְּךָ וְיִסָּחֲךָ מֵאֹהֶל וְשֵׁרֶשְׁךָ מֵאֶרֶץ חַיִּים סֶלָה:

ח: וְיִרְאוּ צַדִּיקִים וְיִירָאוּ וְעָלָיו יִשְׂחָקוּ:

ט: הִנֵּה הַגֶּבֶר לֹא יָשִׂים אֱלֹהִים מָעוּזּוֹ וַיִּבְטַח בְּרֹב עָשְׁרוֹ יָעֹז בְּהַוָּתוֹ:

י: וַאֲנִי כְּזַיִת רַעֲנָן בְּבֵית אֱלֹהִים בָּטַחְתִּי בְחֶסֶד אֱלֹהִים עוֹלָם וָעֶד:

יא: אוֹדְךָ לְעוֹלָם כִּי עָשִׂיתָ וַאֲקַוֶּה שִׁמְךָ כִי טוֹב נֶגֶד חֲסִידֶיךָ:

פרק נג

א: לַמְנַצֵּחַ עַל מָחֲלַת מַשְׂכִּיל לְדָוִד:

ב: אָמַר נָבָל בְּלִבּוֹ אֵין אֱלֹהִים הִשְׁחִיתוּ וְהִתְעִיבוּ עָוֶל אֵין עֹשֵׂה טוֹב:

ג: אֱלֹהִים מִשָּׁמַיִם הִשְׁקִיף עַל בְּנֵי אָדָם לִרְאוֹת הֲיֵשׁ מַשְׂכִּיל דֹּרֵשׁ אֶת אֱלֹהִים:

ד: כֻּלּוֹ סָג יַחְדָּו נֶאֱלָחוּ אֵין עֹשֵׂה טוֹב אֵין גַּם אֶחָד:

ה: הֲלֹא יָדְעוּ פֹּעֲלֵי אָוֶן אֹכְלֵי עַמִּי אָכְלוּ לֶחֶם אֱלֹהִים לֹא קָרָאוּ:

ו: שָׁם פָּחֲדוּ פַחַד לֹא הָיָה פָחַד כִּי אֱלֹהִים פִּזַּר עַצְמוֹת חֹנָךְ הֱבִשֹׁתָה כִּי אֱלֹהִים מְאָסָם:

ז: מִי יִתֵּן מִצִּיּוֹן יְשֻׁעוֹת יִשְׂרָאֵל בְּשׁוּב אֱלֹהִים שְׁבוּת עַמּוֹ יָגֵל יַעֲקֹב יִשְׂמַח יִשְׂרָאֵל:

פרק נד

א: לַמְנַצֵּחַ בִּנְגִינֹת מַשְׂכִּיל לְדָוִד:

ב: בְּבֹא הַזִּיפִים וַיֹּאמְרוּ לְשָׁאוּל הֲלֹא דָוִד מִסְתַּתֵּר עִמָּנוּ:

ג: אֱלֹהִים בְּשִׁמְךָ הוֹשִׁיעֵנִי וּבִגְבוּרָתְךָ תְדִינֵנִי:

ד: אֱלֹהִים שְׁמַע תְּפִלָּתִי הַאֲזִינָה לְאִמְרֵי פִי:

ה: כִּי זָרִים קָמוּ עָלַי וְעָרִיצִים בִּקְשׁוּ נַפְשִׁי לֹא שָׂמוּ אֱלֹהִים לְנֶגְדָּם סֶלָה:

ו: הִנֵּה אֱלֹהִים עֹזֵר לִי אֲדֹנָי בְּסֹמְכֵי נַפְשִׁי:

ז: יָשׁוּב {יָשִׁיב} הָרַע לְשֹׁרְרָי בַּאֲמִתְּךָ הַצְמִיתֵם:

ח: בִּנְדָבָה אֶזְבְּחָה לָּךְ אוֹדֶה שִּׁמְךָ יְהוָה כִּי טוֹב:

ט: כִּי מִכָּל צָרָה הִצִּילָנִי וּבְאֹיְבַי רָאֲתָה עֵינִי:

פרק נה

א: לַמְנַצֵּחַ בִּנְגִינֹת מַשְׂכִּיל לְדָוִד:

ב: הַאֲזִינָה אֱלֹהִים תְּפִלָּתִי וְאַל תִּתְעַלַּם מִתְּחִנָּתִי:

ג: הַקְשִׁיבָה לִּי וַעֲנֵנִי אָרִיד בְּשִׂיחִי וְאָהִימָה:

ד: מִקּוֹל אוֹיֵב מִפְּנֵי עָקַת רָשָׁע כִּי יָמִיטוּ עָלַי אָוֶן וּבְאַף יִשְׂטְמוּנִי:

ה: לִבִּי יָחִיל בְּקִרְבִּי וְאֵימוֹת מָוֶת נָפְלוּ עָלָי:

ו: יִרְאָה וָרַעַד יָבֹא בִי וַתְּכַסֵּנִי פַּלָּצוּת:

ז: וָאֹמַר מִי יִתֶּן לִי אֵבֶר כַּיּוֹנָה אָעוּפָה וְאֶשְׁכֹּנָה:

ח: הִנֵּה אַרְחִיק נְדֹד אָלִין בַּמִּדְבָּר סֶלָה:

ט: אָחִישָׁה מִפְלָט לִי מֵרוּחַ סֹעָה מִסָּעַר:

י: בַּלַּע אֲדֹנָי פַּלַּג לְשׁוֹנָם כִּי רָאִיתִי חָמָס וְרִיב בָּעִיר:

יא: יוֹמָם וָלַיְלָה יְסוֹבְבֻהָ עַל חוֹמֹתֶיהָ וְאָוֶן וְעָמָל בְּקִרְבָּהּ:

יב: הַוּוֹת בְּקִרְבָּהּ וְלֹא יָמִישׁ מֵרְחֹבָהּ תֹּךְ וּמִרְמָה:

יג: כִּי לֹא אוֹיֵב יְחָרְפֵנִי וְאֶשָּׂא לֹא מְשַׂנְאִי עָלַי הִגְדִּיל וְאֶסָּתֵר מִמֶּנּוּ:

יד: וְאַתָּה אֱנוֹשׁ כְּעֶרְכִּי אַלּוּפִי וּמְיֻדָּעִי:

טו: אֲשֶׁר יַחְדָּו נַמְתִּיק סוֹד בְּבֵית אֱלֹהִים נְהַלֵּךְ בְּרָגֶשׁ:

טז: יַשִּׁימָוֶת {יַשִּׁי מָוֶת} עָלֵימוֹ יֵרְדוּ שְׁאוֹל חַיִּים כִּי רָעוֹת בִּמְגוּרָם בְּקִרְבָּם:

יז: אֲנִי אֶל אֱלֹהִים אֶקְרָא וַיהוָה יוֹשִׁיעֵנִי:

יח: עֶרֶב וָבֹקֶר וְצָהֳרַיִם אָשִׂיחָה וְאֶהֱמֶה וַיִּשְׁמַע קוֹלִי:

יט: פָּדָה בְשָׁלוֹם נַפְשִׁי מִקְּרָב לִי כִּי בְרַבִּים הָיוּ עִמָּדִי:

כ: יִשְׁמַע אֵל וְיַעֲנֵם וְיֹשֵׁב קֶדֶם סֶלָה אֲשֶׁר אֵין חֲלִיפוֹת לָמוֹ וְלֹא יָרְאוּ אֱלֹהִים:

כא: שָׁלַח יָדָיו בִּשְׁלֹמָיו חִלֵּל בְּרִיתוֹ:

כב: חָלְקוּ מַחְמָאֹת פִּיו וּקֲרָב לִבּוֹ רַכּוּ דְבָרָיו מִשֶּׁמֶן וְהֵמָּה פְתִחוֹת:

כג: הַשְׁלֵךְ עַל יְהוָה יְהָבְךָ וְהוּא יְכַלְכְּלֶךָ לֹא יִתֵּן לְעוֹלָם מוֹט לַצַּדִּיק:

כד: וְאַתָּה אֱלֹהִים תּוֹרִדֵם לִבְאֵר שַׁחַת אַנְשֵׁי דָמִים וּמִרְמָה לֹא יֶחֱצוּ יְמֵיהֶם וַאֲנִי אֶבְטַח בָּךְ:

פרק נו

א: לַמְנַצֵּחַ עַל יוֹנַת אֵלֶם רְחֹקִים לְדָוִד מִכְתָּם בֶּאֱחֹז אֹתוֹ פְלִשְׁתִּים בְּגַת:

ב: חָנֵּנִי אֱלֹהִים כִּי שְׁאָפַנִי אֱנוֹשׁ כָּל הַיּוֹם לֹחֵם יִלְחָצֵנִי:

ג: שָׁאֲפוּ שׁוֹרְרַי כָּל הַיּוֹם כִּי רַבִּים לֹחֲמִים לִי מָרוֹם:

ד: יוֹם אִירָא אֲנִי אֵלֶיךָ אֶבְטָח:

ה: בֵּאלֹהִים אֲהַלֵּל דְּבָרוֹ בֵּאלֹהִים בָּטַחְתִּי לֹא אִירָא מַה יַּעֲשֶׂה בָשָׂר לִי:

ו: כָּל הַיּוֹם דְּבָרַי יְעַצֵּבוּ עָלַי כָּל מַחְשְׁבֹתָם לָרָע:

ז: יָגוּרוּ יִצְפֹּנוּ {יִצְפּוֹנוּ} הֵמָּה עֲקֵבַי יִשְׁמֹרוּ כַּאֲשֶׁר קִוּוּ נַפְשִׁי:

ח: עַל אָוֶן פַּלֶּט לָמוֹ בְּאַף עַמִּים הוֹרֵד אֱלֹהִים:

ט: נֹדִי סָפַרְתָּה אָתָּה שִׂימָה דִמְעָתִי בְנֹאדֶךָ הֲלֹא בְּסִפְרָתֶךָ:

י: אָז יָשׁוּבוּ אוֹיְבַי אָחוֹר בְּיוֹם אֶקְרָא זֶה יָדַעְתִּי כִּי אֱלֹהִים לִי:

יא: בֵּאלֹהִים אֲהַלֵּל דָּבָר בַּיהוָה אֲהַלֵּל דָּבָר:

יב: בֵּאלֹהִים בָּטַחְתִּי לֹא אִירָא מַה יַּעֲשֶׂה אָדָם לִי:

יג: עָלַי אֱלֹהִים נְדָרֶיךָ אֲשַׁלֵּם תּוֹדֹת לָךְ:

יד: כִּי הִצַּלְתָּ נַפְשִׁי מִמָּוֶת הֲלֹא רַגְלַי מִדֶּחִי לְהִתְהַלֵּךְ לִפְנֵי אֱלֹהִים בְּאוֹר הַחַיִּים:

פרק נז

א: לַמְנַצֵּחַ אַל תַּשְׁחֵת לְדָוִד מִכְתָּם בְּבָרְחוֹ מִפְּנֵי שָׁאוּל בַּמְּעָרָה:
ב: חָנֵּנִי אֱלֹהִים חָנֵּנִי כִּי בְךָ חָסָיָה נַפְשִׁי וּבְצֵל כְּנָפֶיךָ אֶחְסֶה עַד יַעֲבֹר הַוּוֹת:
ג: אֶקְרָא לֵאלֹהִים עֶלְיוֹן לָאֵל גֹּמֵר עָלָי:
ד: יִשְׁלַח מִשָּׁמַיִם וְיוֹשִׁיעֵנִי חֵרֵף שֹׁאֲפִי סֶלָה יִשְׁלַח אֱלֹהִים חַסְדּוֹ וַאֲמִתּוֹ:
ה: נַפְשִׁי בְּתוֹךְ לְבָאִם אֶשְׁכְּבָה לֹהֲטִים בְּנֵי אָדָם שִׁנֵּיהֶם חֲנִית וְחִצִּים וּלְשׁוֹנָם חֶרֶב חַדָּה:
ו: רוּמָה עַל הַשָּׁמַיִם אֱלֹהִים עַל כָּל הָאָרֶץ כְּבוֹדֶךָ:
ז: רֶשֶׁת הֵכִינוּ לִפְעָמַי כָּפַף נַפְשִׁי כָּרוּ לְפָנַי שִׁיחָה נָפְלוּ בְתוֹכָהּ סֶלָה:
ח: נָכוֹן לִבִּי אֱלֹהִים נָכוֹן לִבִּי אָשִׁירָה וַאֲזַמֵּרָה:
ט: עוּרָה כְבוֹדִי עוּרָה הַנֵּבֶל וְכִנּוֹר אָעִירָה שָּׁחַר:
י: אוֹדְךָ בָעַמִּים אֲדֹנָי אֲזַמֶּרְךָ בַּלְאֻמִּים:
יא: כִּי גָדֹל עַד שָׁמַיִם חַסְדֶּךָ וְעַד שְׁחָקִים אֲמִתֶּךָ:
יב: רוּמָה עַל שָׁמַיִם אֱלֹהִים עַל כָּל הָאָרֶץ כְּבוֹדֶךָ:

פרק נח

א: לַמְנַצֵּחַ אַל תַּשְׁחֵת לְדָוִד מִכְתָּם:
ב: הַאֻמְנָם אֵלֶם צֶדֶק תְּדַבֵּרוּן מֵישָׁרִים תִּשְׁפְּטוּ בְּנֵי אָדָם:
ג: אַף בְּלֵב עוֹלֹת תִּפְעָלוּן בָּאָרֶץ חֲמַס יְדֵיכֶם תְּפַלֵּסוּן:
ד: זֹרוּ רְשָׁעִים מֵרָחֶם תָּעוּ מִבֶּטֶן דֹּבְרֵי כָזָב:
ה: חֲמַת לָמוֹ כִּדְמוּת חֲמַת נָחָשׁ כְּמוֹ פֶתֶן חֵרֵשׁ יַאְטֵם אָזְנוֹ:
ו: אֲשֶׁר לֹא יִשְׁמַע לְקוֹל מְלַחֲשִׁים חוֹבֵר חֲבָרִים מְחֻכָּם:
ז: אֱלֹהִים הֲרָס שִׁנֵּימוֹ בְּפִימוֹ מַלְתְּעוֹת כְּפִירִים נְתֹץ יְהֹוָה:
ח: יִמָּאֲסוּ כְמוֹ מַיִם יִתְהַלְּכוּ לָמוֹ יִדְרֹךְ חִצָּיו כְּמוֹ יִתְמֹלָלוּ:
ט: כְּמוֹ שַׁבְּלוּל תֶּמֶס יַהֲלֹךְ נֵפֶל אֵשֶׁת בַּל חָזוּ שָׁמֶשׁ:
י: בְּטֶרֶם יָבִינוּ סִּירֹתֵכֶם אָטָד כְּמוֹ חַי כְּמוֹ חָרוֹן יִשְׂעָרֶנּוּ:
יא: יִשְׂמַח צַדִּיק כִּי חָזָה נָקָם פְּעָמָיו יִרְחַץ בְּדַם הָרָשָׁע:
יב: וְיֹאמַר אָדָם אַךְ פְּרִי לַצַּדִּיק אַךְ יֵשׁ אֱלֹהִים שֹׁפְטִים בָּאָרֶץ:

פרק נט

א: לַמְנַצֵּחַ אַל תַּשְׁחֵת לְדָוִד מִכְתָּם בִּשְׁלֹחַ שָׁאוּל וַיִּשְׁמְרוּ אֶת הַבַּיִת לַהֲמִיתוֹ:
ב: הַצִּילֵנִי מֵאֹיְבַי אֱלֹהָי מִמִּתְקוֹמְמַי תְּשַׂגְּבֵנִי:
ג: הַצִּילֵנִי מִפֹּעֲלֵי אָוֶן וּמֵאַנְשֵׁי דָמִים הוֹשִׁיעֵנִי:
ד: כִּי הִנֵּה אָרְבוּ לְנַפְשִׁי יָגוּרוּ עָלַי עַזִּים לֹא פִשְׁעִי וְלֹא חַטָּאתִי יְהֹוָה:
ה: בְּלִי עָוֹן יְרֻצוּן וְיִכּוֹנָנוּ עוּרָה לִקְרָאתִי וּרְאֵה:
ו: וְאַתָּה יְהֹוָה אֱלֹהִים צְבָאוֹת אֱלֹהֵי יִשְׂרָאֵל הָקִיצָה לִפְקֹד כָּל הַגּוֹיִם אַל תָּחֹן כָּל בֹּגְדֵי אָוֶן סֶלָה:
ז: יָשׁוּבוּ לָעֶרֶב יֶהֱמוּ כַכָּלֶב וִיסוֹבְבוּ עִיר:
ח: הִנֵּה יַבִּיעוּן בְּפִיהֶם חֲרָבוֹת בְּשִׂפְתוֹתֵיהֶם כִּי מִי שֹׁמֵעַ:
ט: וְאַתָּה יְהֹוָה תִּשְׂחַק לָמוֹ תִּלְעַג לְכָל גּוֹיִם:
י: עֻזּוֹ אֵלֶיךָ אֶשְׁמֹרָה כִּי אֱלֹהִים מִשְׂגַּבִּי:
יא: אֱלֹהֵי חַסְדּוֹ {חַסְדִּי} יְקַדְּמֵנִי אֱלֹהִים יַרְאֵנִי בְשֹׁרְרָי:
יב: אַל תַּהַרְגֵם פֶּן יִשְׁכְּחוּ עַמִּי הֲנִיעֵמוֹ בְחֵילְךָ וְהוֹרִידֵמוֹ מָגִנֵּנוּ אֲדֹנָי:
יג: חַטַּאת פִּימוֹ דְּבַר שְׂפָתֵימוֹ וְיִלָּכְדוּ בִגְאוֹנָם וּמֵאָלָה וּמִכַּחַשׁ יְסַפֵּרוּ:
יד: כַּלֵּה בְחֵמָה כַּלֵּה וְאֵינֵמוֹ וְיֵדְעוּ כִּי אֱלֹהִים מֹשֵׁל בְּיַעֲקֹב לְאַפְסֵי הָאָרֶץ סֶלָה:
טו: וְיָשׁוּבוּ לָעֶרֶב יֶהֱמוּ כַכָּלֶב וִיסוֹבְבוּ עִיר:
טז: הֵמָּה יְנִיעוּן {יְנוּעוּן} לֶאֱכֹל אִם לֹא יִשְׂבְּעוּ וַיָּלִינוּ:
יז: וַאֲנִי אָשִׁיר עֻזֶּךָ וַאֲרַנֵּן לַבֹּקֶר חַסְדֶּךָ כִּי הָיִיתָ מִשְׂגָּב לִי וּמָנוֹס בְּיוֹם צַר לִי:
יח: עֻזִּי אֵלֶיךָ אֲזַמֵּרָה כִּי אֱלֹהִים מִשְׂגַּבִּי אֱלֹהֵי חַסְדִּי:

פרק ס

א לַמְנַצֵּחַ עַל שׁוּשַׁן עֵדוּת מִכְתָּם לְדָוִד לְלַמֵּד:

ב בְּהַצּוֹתוֹ אֶת אֲרַם נַהֲרַיִם וְאֶת אֲרַם צוֹבָה וַיָּשָׁב יוֹאָב וַיַּךְ אֶת אֱדוֹם בְּגֵיא מֶלַח שְׁנֵים עָשָׂר אָלֶף:

ג אֱלֹהִים זְנַחְתָּנוּ פְרַצְתָּנוּ אָנַפְתָּ תְּשׁוֹבֵב לָנוּ:

ד הִרְעַשְׁתָּה אֶרֶץ פְּצַמְתָּהּ רְפָה שְׁבָרֶיהָ כִי מָטָה:

ה הִרְאִיתָ עַמְּךָ קָשָׁה הִשְׁקִיתָנוּ יַיִן תַּרְעֵלָה:

ו נָתַתָּה לִּירֵאֶיךָ נֵּס לְהִתְנוֹסֵס מִפְּנֵי קֹשֶׁט סֶלָה:

ז לְמַעַן יֵחָלְצוּן יְדִידֶיךָ הוֹשִׁיעָה יְמִינְךָ וַעֲנֵנוּ (וַעֲנֵנִי):

ח אֱלֹהִים דִּבֶּר בְּקָדְשׁוֹ אֶעְלֹזָה אֲחַלְּקָה שְׁכֶם וְעֵמֶק סֻכּוֹת אֲמַדֵּד:

ט לִי גִלְעָד וְלִי מְנַשֶּׁה וְאֶפְרַיִם מָעוֹז רֹאשִׁי יְהוּדָה מְחֹקְקִי:

י מוֹאָב סִיר רַחְצִי עַל אֱדוֹם אַשְׁלִיךְ נַעֲלִי עָלַי פְּלֶשֶׁת הִתְרוֹעָעִי:

יא מִי יֹבִלֵנִי עִיר מָצוֹר מִי נָחַנִי עַד אֱדוֹם:

יב הֲלֹא אַתָּה אֱלֹהִים זְנַחְתָּנוּ וְלֹא תֵצֵא אֱלֹהִים בְּצִבְאוֹתֵינוּ:

יג הָבָה לָּנוּ עֶזְרָת מִצָּר וְשָׁוְא תְּשׁוּעַת אָדָם:

יד בֵּאלֹהִים נַעֲשֶׂה חָיִל וְהוּא יָבוּס צָרֵינוּ:

פרק סא

א לַמְנַצֵּחַ עַל נְגִינַת לְדָוִד:

ב שִׁמְעָה אֱלֹהִים רִנָּתִי הַקְשִׁיבָה תְּפִלָּתִי:

ג מִקְצֵה הָאָרֶץ אֵלֶיךָ אֶקְרָא בַּעֲטֹף לִבִּי בְּצוּר יָרוּם מִמֶּנִּי תַנְחֵנִי:

ד כִּי הָיִיתָ מַחְסֶה לִי מִגְדַּל עֹז מִפְּנֵי אוֹיֵב:

ה אָגוּרָה בְאָהָלְךָ עוֹלָמִים אֶחֱסֶה בְסֵתֶר כְּנָפֶיךָ סֶּלָה:

ו כִּי אַתָּה אֱלֹהִים שָׁמַעְתָּ לִנְדָרָי נָתַתָּ יְרֻשַּׁת יִרְאֵי שְׁמֶךָ:

ז יָמִים עַל יְמֵי מֶלֶךְ תּוֹסִיף שְׁנוֹתָיו כְּמוֹ דֹר וָדֹר:

ח יֵשֵׁב עוֹלָם לִפְנֵי אֱלֹהִים חֶסֶד וֶאֱמֶת מַן יִנְצְרֻהוּ:

ט כֵּן אֲזַמְּרָה שִׁמְךָ לָעַד לְשַׁלְּמִי נְדָרַי יוֹם יוֹם:

פרק סב

א לַמְנַצֵּחַ עַל יְדוּתוּן מִזְמוֹר לְדָוִד:

ב אַךְ אֶל אֱלֹהִים דּוּמִיָּה נַפְשִׁי מִמֶּנּוּ יְשׁוּעָתִי:

ג אַךְ הוּא צוּרִי וִישׁוּעָתִי מִשְׂגַּבִּי לֹא אֶמּוֹט רַבָּה:

ד עַד אָנָה תְּהוֹתְתוּ עַל אִישׁ תְּרָצְּחוּ כֻלְּכֶם כְּקִיר נָטוּי גָּדֵר הַדְּחוּיָה:

ה אַךְ מִשְּׂאֵתוֹ יָעֲצוּ לְהַדִּיחַ יִרְצוּ כָזָב בְּפִיו יְבָרֵכוּ וּבְקִרְבָּם יְקַלְלוּ סֶלָה:

ו אַךְ לֵאלֹהִים דּוֹמִּי נַפְשִׁי כִּי מִמֶּנּוּ תִּקְוָתִי:

ז אַךְ הוּא צוּרִי וִישׁוּעָתִי מִשְׂגַּבִּי לֹא אֶמּוֹט:

ח עַל אֱלֹהִים יִשְׁעִי וּכְבוֹדִי צוּר עֻזִּי מַחְסִי בֵּאלֹהִים:

ט בִּטְחוּ בוֹ בְכָל עֵת עָם שִׁפְכוּ לְפָנָיו לְבַבְכֶם אֱלֹהִים מַחֲסֶה לָּנוּ סֶלָה:

י אַךְ הֶבֶל בְּנֵי אָדָם כָּזָב בְּנֵי אִישׁ בְּמֹאזְנַיִם לַעֲלוֹת הֵמָּה מֵהֶבֶל יָחַד:

יא אַל תִּבְטְחוּ בְעֹשֶׁק וּבְגָזֵל אַל תֶּהְבָּלוּ חַיִל כִּי יָנוּב אַל תָּשִׁיתוּ לֵב:

יב אַחַת דִּבֶּר אֱלֹהִים שְׁתַּיִם זוּ שָׁמָעְתִּי כִּי עֹז לֵאלֹהִים:

יג וּלְךָ אֲדֹנָי חָסֶד כִּי אַתָּה תְשַׁלֵּם לְאִישׁ כְּמַעֲשֵׂהוּ:

פרק סג

א מִזְמוֹר לְדָוִד בִּהְיוֹתוֹ בְּמִדְבַּר יְהוּדָה:

ב אֱלֹהִים אֵלִי אַתָּה אֲשַׁחֲרֶךָּ צָמְאָה לְךָ נַפְשִׁי כָּמַהּ לְךָ בְשָׂרִי בְּאֶרֶץ צִיָּה וְעָיֵף בְּלִי מָיִם:

ג כֵּן בַּקֹּדֶשׁ חֲזִיתִךָ לִרְאוֹת עֻזְּךָ וּכְבוֹדֶךָ:

ד: כִּי טוֹב חַסְדְּךָ מֵחַיִּים שְׂפָתַי יְשַׁבְּחוּנְךָ:

ה: כֵּן אֲבָרֶכְךָ בְחַיָּי בְּשִׁמְךָ אֶשָּׂא כַפָּי:

ו: כְּמוֹ חֵלֶב וָדֶשֶׁן תִּשְׂבַּע נַפְשִׁי וְשִׂפְתֵי רְנָנוֹת יְהַלֶּל פִּי:

ז: אִם זְכַרְתִּיךָ עַל יְצוּעָי בְּאַשְׁמֻרוֹת אֶהְגֶּה בָּךְ:

ח: כִּי הָיִיתָ עֶזְרָתָה לִּי וּבְצֵל כְּנָפֶיךָ אֲרַנֵּן:

ט: דָּבְקָה נַפְשִׁי אַחֲרֶיךָ בִּי תָּמְכָה יְמִינֶךָ:

י: וְהֵמָּה לְשׁוֹאָה יְבַקְשׁוּ נַפְשִׁי יָבֹאוּ בְּתַחְתִּיּוֹת הָאָרֶץ:

יא: יַגִּירֻהוּ עַל יְדֵי חָרֶב מְנָת שֻׁעָלִים יִהְיוּ:

יב: וְהַמֶּלֶךְ יִשְׂמַח בֵּאלֹהִים יִתְהַלֵּל כָּל הַנִּשְׁבָּע בּוֹ כִּי יִסָּכֵר פִּי דוֹבְרֵי שָׁקֶר:

פרק סד

א: לַמְנַצֵּחַ מִזְמוֹר לְדָוִד:

ב: שְׁמַע אֱלֹהִים קוֹלִי בְשִׂיחִי מִפַּחַד אוֹיֵב תִּצֹּר חַיָּי:

ג: תַּסְתִּירֵנִי מִסּוֹד מְרֵעִים מֵרִגְשַׁת פֹּעֲלֵי אָוֶן:

ד: אֲשֶׁר שָׁנְנוּ כַחֶרֶב לְשׁוֹנָם דָּרְכוּ חִצָּם דָּבָר מָר:

ה: לִירֹת בַּמִּסְתָּרִים תָּם פִּתְאֹם יֹרֻהוּ וְלֹא יִירָאוּ:

ו: יְחַזְּקוּ לָמוֹ דָּבָר רָע יְסַפְּרוּ לִטְמוֹן מוֹקְשִׁים אָמְרוּ מִי יִרְאֶה לָּמוֹ:

ז: יַחְפְּשׂוּ עוֹלֹת תַּמְנוּ חֵפֶשׂ מְחֻפָּשׂ וְקֶרֶב אִישׁ וְלֵב עָמֹק:

ח: וַיֹּרֵם אֱלֹהִים חֵץ פִּתְאוֹם הָיוּ מַכּוֹתָם:

ט: וַיַּכְשִׁילוּהוּ עָלֵימוֹ לְשׁוֹנָם יִתְנֹדְדוּ כָּל רֹאֵה בָם:

י: וַיִּירְאוּ כָּל אָדָם וַיַּגִּידוּ פֹּעַל אֱלֹהִים וּמַעֲשֵׂהוּ הִשְׂכִּילוּ:

יא: יִשְׂמַח צַדִּיק בַּיהוָה וְחָסָה בוֹ וְיִתְהַלְלוּ כָּל יִשְׁרֵי לֵב:

פרק סה

א: לַמְנַצֵּחַ מִזְמוֹר לְדָוִד שִׁיר:

ב: לְךָ דֻמִיָּה תְהִלָּה אֱלֹהִים בְּצִיּוֹן וּלְךָ יְשֻׁלַּם נֶדֶר:

ג: שֹׁמֵעַ תְּפִלָּה עָדֶיךָ כָּל בָּשָׂר יָבֹאוּ:

ד: דִּבְרֵי עֲוֹנֹת גָּבְרוּ מֶנִּי פְּשָׁעֵינוּ אַתָּה תְכַפְּרֵם:

ה: אַשְׁרֵי תִּבְחַר וּתְקָרֵב יִשְׁכֹּן חֲצֵרֶיךָ נִשְׂבְּעָה בְּטוּב בֵּיתֶךָ קְדֹשׁ הֵיכָלֶךָ:

ו: נוֹרָאוֹת בְּצֶדֶק תַּעֲנֵנוּ אֱלֹהֵי יִשְׁעֵנוּ מִבְטָח כָּל קַצְוֵי אֶרֶץ וְיָם רְחֹקִים:

ז: מֵכִין הָרִים בְּכֹחוֹ נֶאְזָר בִּגְבוּרָה:

ח: מַשְׁבִּיחַ שְׁאוֹן יַמִּים שְׁאוֹן גַּלֵּיהֶם וַהֲמוֹן לְאֻמִּים:

ט: וַיִּירְאוּ יֹשְׁבֵי קְצָוֹת מֵאוֹתֹתֶיךָ מוֹצָאֵי בֹקֶר וָעֶרֶב תַּרְנִין:

י: פָּקַדְתָּ הָאָרֶץ וַתְּשֹׁקְקֶהָ רַבַּת תַּעְשְׁרֶנָּה פֶּלֶג אֱלֹהִים מָלֵא מָיִם תָּכִין דְּגָנָם כִּי כֵן תְּכִינֶהָ:

יא: תְּלָמֶיהָ רַוֵּה נַחֵת גְּדוּדֶהָ בִּרְבִיבִים תְּמֹגְגֶנָּה צִמְחָהּ תְּבָרֵךְ:

יב: עִטַּרְתָּ שְׁנַת טוֹבָתֶךָ וּמַעְגָּלֶיךָ יִרְעֲפוּן דָּשֶׁן:

יג: יִרְעֲפוּ נְאוֹת מִדְבָּר וְגִיל גְּבָעוֹת תַּחְגֹּרְנָה:

יד: לָבְשׁוּ כָרִים הַצֹּאן וַעֲמָקִים יַעַטְפוּ בָר יִתְרוֹעֲעוּ אַף יָשִׁירוּ:

פרק סו

א: לַמְנַצֵּחַ שִׁיר מִזְמוֹר הָרִיעוּ לֵאלֹהִים כָּל הָאָרֶץ:

ב: זַמְּרוּ כְבוֹד שְׁמוֹ שִׂימוּ כָבוֹד תְּהִלָּתוֹ:

ג: אִמְרוּ לֵאלֹהִים מַה נּוֹרָא מַעֲשֶׂיךָ בְּרֹב עֻזְּךָ יְכַחֲשׁוּ לְךָ אֹיְבֶיךָ:

ד: כָּל הָאָרֶץ יִשְׁתַּחֲווּ לְךָ וִיזַמְּרוּ לָךְ יְזַמְּרוּ שִׁמְךָ סֶלָה:

ה: לְכוּ וּרְאוּ מִפְעֲלוֹת אֱלֹהִים נוֹרָא עֲלִילָה עַל בְּנֵי אָדָם:

ו: הָפַךְ יָם לְיַבָּשָׁה בַּנָּהָר יַעַבְרוּ בְרָגֶל שָׁם נִשְׂמְחָה בּוֹ:

ז: מֹשֵׁל בִּגְבוּרָתוֹ עוֹלָם עֵינָיו בַּגּוֹיִם תִּצְפֶּינָה הַסּוֹרְרִים אַל יָרִימוּ {יָרוּמוּ} לָמוֹ סֶלָה:

ח: בָּרְכוּ עַמִּים אֱלֹהֵינוּ וְהַשְׁמִיעוּ קוֹל תְּהִלָּתוֹ:
ט: הַשָּׂם נַפְשֵׁנוּ בַּחַיִּים וְלֹא נָתַן לַמּוֹט רַגְלֵנוּ:
י: כִּי בְחַנְתָּנוּ אֱלֹהִים צְרַפְתָּנוּ כִּצְרָף כָּסֶף:
יא: הֲבֵאתָנוּ בַמְּצוּדָה שַׂמְתָּ מוּעָקָה בְמָתְנֵינוּ:
יב: הִרְכַּבְתָּ אֱנוֹשׁ לְרֹאשֵׁנוּ בָּאנוּ בָאֵשׁ וּבַמַּיִם וַתּוֹצִיאֵנוּ לָרְוָיָה:
יג: אָבוֹא בֵיתְךָ בְעוֹלוֹת אֲשַׁלֵּם לְךָ נְדָרָי:
יד: אֲשֶׁר פָּצוּ שְׂפָתָי וְדִבֶּר פִּי בַּצַּר לִי:
טו: עֹלוֹת מֵחִים אַעֲלֶה לָּךְ עִם קְטֹרֶת אֵילִים אֶעֱשֶׂה בָקָר עִם עַתּוּדִים סֶלָה:
טז: לְכוּ שִׁמְעוּ וַאֲסַפְּרָה כָּל יִרְאֵי אֱלֹהִים אֲשֶׁר עָשָׂה לְנַפְשִׁי:
יז: אֵלָיו פִּי קָרָאתִי וְרוֹמַם תַּחַת לְשׁוֹנִי:
יח: אָוֶן אִם רָאִיתִי בְלִבִּי לֹא יִשְׁמַע אֲדֹנָי:
יט: אָכֵן שָׁמַע אֱלֹהִים הִקְשִׁיב בְּקוֹל תְּפִלָּתִי:
כ: בָּרוּךְ אֱלֹהִים אֲשֶׁר לֹא הֵסִיר תְּפִלָּתִי וְחַסְדּוֹ מֵאִתִּי:

פרק סז

א: לַמְנַצֵּחַ בִּנְגִינֹת מִזְמוֹר שִׁיר:
ב: אֱלֹהִים יְחָנֵּנוּ וִיבָרְכֵנוּ יָאֵר פָּנָיו אִתָּנוּ סֶלָה:
ג: לָדַעַת בָּאָרֶץ דַּרְכֶּךָ בְּכָל גּוֹיִם יְשׁוּעָתֶךָ:
ד: יוֹדוּךָ עַמִּים אֱלֹהִים יוֹדוּךָ עַמִּים כֻּלָּם:
ה: יִשְׂמְחוּ וִירַנְּנוּ לְאֻמִּים כִּי תִשְׁפֹּט עַמִּים מִישֹׁר וּלְאֻמִּים בָּאָרֶץ תַּנְחֵם סֶלָה:
ו: יוֹדוּךָ עַמִּים אֱלֹהִים יוֹדוּךָ עַמִּים כֻּלָּם:
ז: אֶרֶץ נָתְנָה יְבוּלָהּ יְבָרְכֵנוּ אֱלֹהִים אֱלֹהֵינוּ:
ח: יְבָרְכֵנוּ אֱלֹהִים וְיִירְאוּ אוֹתוֹ כָּל אַפְסֵי אָרֶץ:

פרק סח

א: לַמְנַצֵּחַ לְדָוִד מִזְמוֹר שִׁיר:
ב: יָקוּם אֱלֹהִים יָפוּצוּ אוֹיְבָיו וְיָנוּסוּ מְשַׂנְאָיו מִפָּנָיו:
ג: כְּהִנְדֹּף עָשָׁן תִּנְדֹּף כְּהִמֵּס דּוֹנַג מִפְּנֵי אֵשׁ יֹאבְדוּ רְשָׁעִים מִפְּנֵי אֱלֹהִים:
ד: וְצַדִּיקִים יִשְׂמְחוּ יַעַלְצוּ לִפְנֵי אֱלֹהִים וְיָשִׂישׂוּ בְשִׂמְחָה:
ה: שִׁירוּ לֵאלֹהִים זַמְּרוּ שְׁמוֹ סֹלּוּ לָרֹכֵב בָּעֲרָבוֹת בְּיָהּ שְׁמוֹ וְעִלְזוּ לְפָנָיו:
ו: אֲבִי יְתוֹמִים וְדַיַּן אַלְמָנוֹת אֱלֹהִים בִּמְעוֹן קָדְשׁוֹ:
ז: אֱלֹהִים מוֹשִׁיב יְחִידִים בַּיְתָה מוֹצִיא אֲסִירִים בַּכּוֹשָׁרוֹת אַךְ סוֹרְרִים שָׁכְנוּ צְחִיחָה:
ח: אֱלֹהִים בְּצֵאתְךָ לִפְנֵי עַמֶּךָ בְּצַעְדְּךָ בִישִׁימוֹן סֶלָה:
ט: אֶרֶץ רָעָשָׁה אַף שָׁמַיִם נָטְפוּ מִפְּנֵי אֱלֹהִים זֶה סִינַי מִפְּנֵי אֱלֹהִים אֱלֹהֵי יִשְׂרָאֵל:
י: גֶּשֶׁם נְדָבוֹת תָּנִיף אֱלֹהִים נַחֲלָתְךָ וְנִלְאָה אַתָּה כוֹנַנְתָּהּ:
יא: חַיָּתְךָ יָשְׁבוּ בָהּ תָּכִין בְּטוֹבָתְךָ לֶעָנִי אֱלֹהִים:
יב: אֲדֹנָי יִתֶּן אֹמֶר הַמְבַשְּׂרוֹת צָבָא רָב:
יג: מַלְכֵי צְבָאוֹת יִדֹּדוּן יִדֹּדוּן וּנְוַת בַּיִת תְּחַלֵּק שָׁלָל:
יד: אִם תִּשְׁכְּבוּן בֵּין שְׁפַתָּיִם כַּנְפֵי יוֹנָה נֶחְפָּה בַכֶּסֶף וְאֶבְרוֹתֶיהָ בִּירַקְרַק חָרוּץ:
טו: בְּפָרֵשׂ שַׁדַּי מְלָכִים בָּהּ תַּשְׁלֵג בְּצַלְמוֹן:
טז: הַר אֱלֹהִים הַר בָּשָׁן הַר גַּבְנֻנִּים הַר בָּשָׁן:
יז: לָמָּה תְּרַצְּדוּן הָרִים גַּבְנֻנִּים הָהָר חָמַד אֱלֹהִים לְשִׁבְתּוֹ אַף יְהוָה יִשְׁכֹּן לָנֶצַח:
יח: רֶכֶב אֱלֹהִים רִבֹּתַיִם אַלְפֵי שִׁנְאָן אֲדֹנָי בָם סִינַי בַּקֹּדֶשׁ:
יט: עָלִיתָ לַמָּרוֹם שָׁבִיתָ שֶּׁבִי לָקַחְתָּ מַתָּנוֹת בָּאָדָם וְאַף סוֹרְרִים לִשְׁכֹּן יָהּ אֱלֹהִים:
כ: בָּרוּךְ אֲדֹנָי יוֹם יוֹם יַעֲמָס לָנוּ הָאֵל יְשׁוּעָתֵנוּ סֶלָה:
כא: הָאֵל לָנוּ אֵל לְמוֹשָׁעוֹת וְלֵיהוִה אֲדֹנָי לַמָּוֶת תּוֹצָאוֹת:
כב: אַךְ אֱלֹהִים יִמְחַץ רֹאשׁ אֹיְבָיו קָדְקֹד שֵׂעָר מִתְהַלֵּךְ בַּאֲשָׁמָיו:

כג: אָמַר אֲדֹנָי מִבָּשָׁן אָשִׁיב אָשִׁיב מִמְּצֻלוֹת יָם:
כד: לְמַעַן תִּמְחַץ רַגְלְךָ בְּדָם לְשׁוֹן כְּלָבֶיךָ מֵאֹיְבִים מִנֵּהוּ:
כה: רָאוּ הֲלִיכוֹתֶיךָ אֱלֹהִים הֲלִיכוֹת אֵלִי מַלְכִּי בַקֹּדֶשׁ:
כו: קִדְּמוּ שָׁרִים אַחַר נֹגְנִים בְּתוֹךְ עֲלָמוֹת תּוֹפֵפוֹת:
כז: בְּמַקְהֵלוֹת בָּרְכוּ אֱלֹהִים אֲדֹנָי מִמְּקוֹר יִשְׂרָאֵל:
כח: שָׁם בִּנְיָמִן צָעִיר רֹדֵם שָׂרֵי יְהוּדָה רִגְמָתָם שָׂרֵי זְבֻלוּן שָׂרֵי נַפְתָּלִי:
כט: צִוָּה אֱלֹהֶיךָ עֻזֶּךָ עוּזָּה אֱלֹהִים זוּ פָּעַלְתָּ לָּנוּ:
ל: מֵהֵיכָלֶךָ עַל יְרוּשָׁלָ͏ִם לְךָ יוֹבִילוּ מְלָכִים שָׁי:
לא: גְּעַר חַיַּת קָנֶה עֲדַת אַבִּירִים בְּעֶגְלֵי עַמִּים מִתְרַפֵּס בְּרַצֵּי כָסֶף בִּזַּר עַמִּים קְרָבוֹת יֶחְפָּצוּ:
לב: יֶאֱתָיוּ חַשְׁמַנִּים מִנִּי מִצְרָיִם כּוּשׁ תָּרִיץ יָדָיו לֵאלֹהִים:
לג: מַמְלְכוֹת הָאָרֶץ שִׁירוּ לֵאלֹהִים זַמְּרוּ אֲדֹנָי סֶלָה:
לד: לָרֹכֵב בִּשְׁמֵי שְׁמֵי קֶדֶם הֵן יִתֵּן בְּקוֹלוֹ קוֹל עֹז:
לה: תְּנוּ עֹז לֵאלֹהִים עַל יִשְׂרָאֵל גַּאֲוָתוֹ וְעֻזּוֹ בַּשְּׁחָקִים:
לו: נוֹרָא אֱלֹהִים מִמִּקְדָּשֶׁיךָ אֵל יִשְׂרָאֵל הוּא נֹתֵן עֹז וְתַעֲצֻמוֹת לָעָם בָּרוּךְ אֱלֹהִים:

פרק סט

א: לַמְנַצֵּחַ עַל שׁוֹשַׁנִּים לְדָוִד:
ב: הוֹשִׁיעֵנִי אֱלֹהִים כִּי בָאוּ מַיִם עַד נָפֶשׁ:
ג: טָבַעְתִּי בִּיוֵן מְצוּלָה וְאֵין מָעֳמָד בָּאתִי בְמַעֲמַקֵּי מַיִם וְשִׁבֹּלֶת שְׁטָפָתְנִי:
ד: יָגַעְתִּי בְקָרְאִי נִחַר גְּרוֹנִי כָּלוּ עֵינַי מְיַחֵל לֵאלֹהָי:
ה: רַבּוּ מִשַּׂעֲרוֹת רֹאשִׁי שֹׂנְאַי חִנָּם עָצְמוּ מַצְמִיתַי אֹיְבַי שֶׁקֶר אֲשֶׁר לֹא גָזַלְתִּי אָז אָשִׁיב:
ו: אֱלֹהִים אַתָּה יָדַעְתָּ לְאִוַּלְתִּי וְאַשְׁמוֹתַי מִמְּךָ לֹא נִכְחָדוּ:
ז: אַל יֵבֹשׁוּ בִי קֹוֶיךָ אֲדֹנָי יְהֹוִה צְבָאוֹת אַל יִכָּלְמוּ בִי מְבַקְשֶׁיךָ אֱלֹהֵי יִשְׂרָאֵל:
ח: כִּי עָלֶיךָ נָשָׂאתִי חֶרְפָּה כִּסְּתָה כְלִמָּה פָנָי:
ט: מוּזָר הָיִיתִי לְאֶחָי וְנָכְרִי לִבְנֵי אִמִּי:
י: כִּי קִנְאַת בֵּיתְךָ אֲכָלָתְנִי וְחֶרְפּוֹת חוֹרְפֶיךָ נָפְלוּ עָלָי:
יא: וָאֶבְכֶּה בַצּוֹם נַפְשִׁי וַתְּהִי לַחֲרָפוֹת לִי:
יב: וָאֶתְּנָה לְבוּשִׁי שָׂק וָאֱהִי לָהֶם לְמָשָׁל:
יג: יָשִׂיחוּ בִי יֹשְׁבֵי שָׁעַר וּנְגִינוֹת שׁוֹתֵי שֵׁכָר:
יד: וַאֲנִי תְפִלָּתִי לְךָ יְהֹוָה עֵת רָצוֹן אֱלֹהִים בְּרָב חַסְדֶּךָ עֲנֵנִי בֶּאֱמֶת יִשְׁעֶךָ:
טו: הַצִּילֵנִי מִטִּיט וְאַל אֶטְבָּעָה אִנָּצְלָה מִשֹּׂנְאַי וּמִמַּעֲמַקֵּי מָיִם:
טז: אַל תִּשְׁטְפֵנִי שִׁבֹּלֶת מַיִם וְאַל תִּבְלָעֵנִי מְצוּלָה וְאַל תֶּאְטַר עָלַי בְּאֵר פִּיהָ:
יז: עֲנֵנִי יְהֹוָה כִּי טוֹב חַסְדֶּךָ כְּרֹב רַחֲמֶיךָ פְּנֵה אֵלָי:
יח: וְאַל תַּסְתֵּר פָּנֶיךָ מֵעַבְדֶּךָ כִּי צַר לִי מַהֵר עֲנֵנִי:
יט: קָרְבָה אֶל נַפְשִׁי גְאָלָהּ לְמַעַן אֹיְבַי פְּדֵנִי:
כ: אַתָּה יָדַעְתָּ חֶרְפָּתִי וּבָשְׁתִּי וּכְלִמָּתִי נֶגְדְּךָ כָּל צוֹרְרָי:
כא: חֶרְפָּה שָׁבְרָה לִבִּי וָאָנוּשָׁה וָאֲקַוֶּה לָנוּד וָאַיִן וְלַמְנַחֲמִים וְלֹא מָצָאתִי:
כב: וַיִּתְּנוּ בְּבָרוּתִי רֹאשׁ וְלִצְמָאִי יַשְׁקוּנִי חֹמֶץ:
כג: יְהִי שֻׁלְחָנָם לִפְנֵיהֶם לְפָח וְלִשְׁלוֹמִים לְמוֹקֵשׁ:
כד: תֶּחְשַׁכְנָה עֵינֵיהֶם מֵרְאוֹת וּמָתְנֵיהֶם תָּמִיד הַמְעַד:
כה: שְׁפָךְ עֲלֵיהֶם זַעְמֶךָ וַחֲרוֹן אַפְּךָ יַשִּׂיגֵם:
כו: תְּהִי טִירָתָם נְשַׁמָּה בְּאָהֳלֵיהֶם אַל יְהִי יֹשֵׁב:
כז: כִּי אַתָּה אֲשֶׁר הִכִּיתָ רָדָפוּ וְאֶל מַכְאוֹב חֲלָלֶיךָ יְסַפֵּרוּ:
כח: תְּנָה עָוֹן עַל עֲוֹנָם וְאַל יָבֹאוּ בְּצִדְקָתֶךָ:
כט: יִמָּחוּ מִסֵּפֶר חַיִּים וְעִם צַדִּיקִים אַל יִכָּתֵבוּ:
ל: וַאֲנִי עָנִי וְכוֹאֵב יְשׁוּעָתְךָ אֱלֹהִים תְּשַׂגְּבֵנִי:
לא: אֲהַלְלָה שֵׁם אֱלֹהִים בְּשִׁיר וַאֲגַדְּלֶנּוּ בְתוֹדָה:

לב: וְתִיטַב לַיהֹוָה מִשּׁוֹר פָּר מַקְרִן מַפְרִיס:
לג: רָאוּ עֲנָוִים יִשְׂמָחוּ דֹּרְשֵׁי אֱלֹהִים וִיחִי לְבַבְכֶם:
לד: כִּי שֹׁמֵעַ אֶל אֶבְיוֹנִים יְהֹוָה וְאֶת אֲסִירָיו לֹא בָזָה:
לה: יְהַלְלוּהוּ שָׁמַיִם וָאָרֶץ יַמִּים וְכָל רֹמֵשׂ בָּם:
לו: כִּי אֱלֹהִים יוֹשִׁיעַ צִיּוֹן וְיִבְנֶה עָרֵי יְהוּדָה וְיָשְׁבוּ שָׁם וִירֵשׁוּהָ:
לז: וְזֶרַע עֲבָדָיו יִנְחָלוּהָ וְאֹהֲבֵי שְׁמוֹ יִשְׁכְּנוּ בָהּ:

פרק ע

א: לַמְנַצֵּחַ לְדָוִד לְהַזְכִּיר:
ב: אֱלֹהִים לְהַצִּילֵנִי יְהֹוָה לְעֶזְרָתִי חוּשָׁה:
ג: יֵבֹשׁוּ וְיַחְפְּרוּ מְבַקְשֵׁי נַפְשִׁי יִסֹּגוּ אָחוֹר וְיִכָּלְמוּ חֲפֵצֵי רָעָתִי:
ד: יָשׁוּבוּ עַל עֵקֶב בָּשְׁתָּם הָאֹמְרִים הֶאָח הֶאָח:
ה: יָשִׂישׂוּ וְיִשְׂמְחוּ בְּךָ כָּל מְבַקְשֶׁיךָ וְיֹאמְרוּ תָמִיד יִגְדַּל אֱלֹהִים אֹהֲבֵי יְשׁוּעָתֶךָ:
ו: וַאֲנִי עָנִי וְאֶבְיוֹן אֱלֹהִים חוּשָׁה לִּי עֶזְרִי וּמְפַלְטִי אַתָּה יְהֹוָה אַל תְּאַחַר:

פרק עא

א: בְּךָ יְהֹוָה חָסִיתִי אַל אֵבוֹשָׁה לְעוֹלָם:
ב: בְּצִדְקָתְךָ תַּצִּילֵנִי וּתְפַלְּטֵנִי הַטֵּה אֵלַי אָזְנְךָ וְהוֹשִׁיעֵנִי:
ג: הֱיֵה לִי לְצוּר מָעוֹן לָבוֹא תָּמִיד צִוִּיתָ לְהוֹשִׁיעֵנִי כִּי סַלְעִי וּמְצוּדָתִי אָתָּה:
ד: אֱלֹהַי פַּלְּטֵנִי מִיַּד רָשָׁע מִכַּף מְעַוֵּל וְחוֹמֵץ:
ה: כִּי אַתָּה תִקְוָתִי אֲדֹנָי יְהֹוִה מִבְטַחִי מִנְּעוּרָי:
ו: עָלֶיךָ נִסְמַכְתִּי מִבֶּטֶן מִמְּעֵי אִמִּי אַתָּה גוֹזִי בְּךָ תְהִלָּתִי תָמִיד:
ז: כְּמוֹפֵת הָיִיתִי לְרַבִּים וְאַתָּה מַחֲסִי עֹז:
ח: יִמָּלֵא פִי תְּהִלָּתֶךָ כָּל הַיּוֹם תִּפְאַרְתֶּךָ:
ט: אַל תַּשְׁלִיכֵנִי לְעֵת זִקְנָה כִּכְלוֹת כֹּחִי אַל תַּעַזְבֵנִי:
י: כִּי אָמְרוּ אוֹיְבַי לִי וְשֹׁמְרֵי נַפְשִׁי נוֹעֲצוּ יַחְדָּו:
יא: לֵאמֹר אֱלֹהִים עֲזָבוֹ רִדְפוּ וְתִפְשׂוּהוּ כִּי אֵין מַצִּיל:
יב: אֱלֹהִים אַל תִּרְחַק מִמֶּנִּי אֱלֹהַי לְעֶזְרָתִי חִישָׁה {חוּשָׁה}:
יג: יֵבֹשׁוּ יִכְלוּ שֹׂטְנֵי נַפְשִׁי יַעֲטוּ חֶרְפָּה וּכְלִמָּה מְבַקְשֵׁי רָעָתִי:
יד: וַאֲנִי תָּמִיד אֲיַחֵל וְהוֹסַפְתִּי עַל כָּל תְּהִלָּתֶךָ:
טו: פִּי יְסַפֵּר צִדְקָתֶךָ כָּל הַיּוֹם תְּשׁוּעָתֶךָ כִּי לֹא יָדַעְתִּי סְפֹרוֹת:
טז: אָבוֹא בִּגְבֻרוֹת אֲדֹנָי יְהֹוִה אַזְכִּיר צִדְקָתְךָ לְבַדֶּךָ:
יז: אֱלֹהִים לִמַּדְתַּנִי מִנְּעוּרָי וְעַד הֵנָּה אַגִּיד נִפְלְאוֹתֶיךָ:
יח: וְגַם עַד זִקְנָה וְשֵׂיבָה אֱלֹהִים אַל תַּעַזְבֵנִי עַד אַגִּיד זְרוֹעֲךָ לְדוֹר לְכָל יָבוֹא גְּבוּרָתֶךָ:
יט: וְצִדְקָתְךָ אֱלֹהִים עַד מָרוֹם אֲשֶׁר עָשִׂיתָ גְדֹלוֹת אֱלֹהִים מִי כָמוֹךָ:
כ: אֲשֶׁר הִרְאִיתַנוּ {הִרְאִיתַנִי} צָרוֹת רַבּוֹת וְרָעוֹת תָּשׁוּב תְּחַיֵּינוּ {תְּחַיֵּנִי} וּמִתְּהֹמוֹת הָאָרֶץ תָּשׁוּב תַּעֲלֵנִי:
כא: תֶּרֶב גְּדֻלָּתִי וְתִסֹּב תְּנַחֲמֵנִי:
כב: גַּם אֲנִי אוֹדְךָ בִכְלִי נֶבֶל אֲמִתְּךָ אֱלֹהָי אֲזַמְּרָה לְךָ בְכִנּוֹר קְדוֹשׁ יִשְׂרָאֵל:
כג: תְּרַנֵּנָּה שְׂפָתַי כִּי אֲזַמְּרָה לָּךְ וְנַפְשִׁי אֲשֶׁר פָּדִיתָ:
כד: גַּם לְשׁוֹנִי כָּל הַיּוֹם תֶּהְגֶּה צִדְקָתֶךָ כִּי בֹשׁוּ כִי חָפְרוּ מְבַקְשֵׁי רָעָתִי:

פרק עב

א: לִשְׁלֹמֹה אֱלֹהִים מִשְׁפָּטֶיךָ לְמֶלֶךְ תֵּן וְצִדְקָתְךָ לְבֶן מֶלֶךְ:
ב: יָדִין עַמְּךָ בְצֶדֶק וַעֲנִיֶּיךָ בְמִשְׁפָּט:
ג: יִשְׂאוּ הָרִים שָׁלוֹם לָעָם וּגְבָעוֹת בִּצְדָקָה:
ד: יִשְׁפֹּט עֲנִיֵּי עָם יוֹשִׁיעַ לִבְנֵי אֶבְיוֹן וִידַכֵּא עוֹשֵׁק:

ה: וְיִירָאוּךָ עִם שָׁמֶשׁ וְלִפְנֵי יָרֵחַ דּוֹר דּוֹרִים:
ו: יֵרֵד כְּמָטָר עַל גֵּז כִּרְבִיבִים זַרְזִיף אָרֶץ:
ז: יִפְרַח בְּיָמָיו צַדִּיק וְרֹב שָׁלוֹם עַד בְּלִי יָרֵחַ:
ח: וְיֵרְדְּ מִיָּם עַד יָם וּמִנָּהָר עַד אַפְסֵי אָרֶץ:
ט: לְפָנָיו יִכְרְעוּ צִיִּים וְאֹיְבָיו עָפָר יְלַחֵכוּ:
י: מַלְכֵי תַרְשִׁישׁ וְאִיִּים מִנְחָה יָשִׁיבוּ מַלְכֵי שְׁבָא וּסְבָא אֶשְׁכָּר יַקְרִיבוּ:
יא: וְיִשְׁתַּחֲווּ לוֹ כָל מְלָכִים כָּל גּוֹיִם יַעַבְדוּהוּ:
יב: כִּי יַצִּיל אֶבְיוֹן מְשַׁוֵּעַ וְעָנִי וְאֵין עֹזֵר לוֹ:
יג: יָחֹס עַל דַּל וְאֶבְיוֹן וְנַפְשׁוֹת אֶבְיוֹנִים יוֹשִׁיעַ:
יד: מִתּוֹךְ וּמֵחָמָס יִגְאַל נַפְשָׁם וְיֵיקַר דָּמָם בְּעֵינָיו:
טו: וִיחִי וְיִתֶּן לוֹ מִזְּהַב שְׁבָא וְיִתְפַּלֵּל בַּעֲדוֹ תָמִיד כָּל הַיּוֹם יְבָרֲכֶנְהוּ:
טז: יְהִי פִסַּת בַּר בָּאָרֶץ בְּרֹאשׁ הָרִים יִרְעַשׁ כַּלְּבָנוֹן פִּרְיוֹ וְיָצִיצוּ מֵעִיר כְּעֵשֶׂב הָאָרֶץ:
יז: יְהִי שְׁמוֹ לְעוֹלָם לִפְנֵי שֶׁמֶשׁ יָנִין {יִנּוֹן} שְׁמוֹ וְיִתְבָּרְכוּ בוֹ כָּל גּוֹיִם יְאַשְּׁרוּהוּ:
יח: בָּרוּךְ יְהֹוָה אֱלֹהִים אֱלֹהֵי יִשְׂרָאֵל עֹשֵׂה נִפְלָאוֹת לְבַדּוֹ:
יט: וּבָרוּךְ שֵׁם כְּבוֹדוֹ לְעוֹלָם וְיִמָּלֵא כְבוֹדוֹ אֶת כֹּל הָאָרֶץ אָמֵן וְאָמֵן:
כ: כָּלּוּ תְפִלּוֹת דָּוִד בֶּן יִשָׁי:

פרק עג
א: מִזְמוֹר לְאָסָף אַךְ טוֹב לְיִשְׂרָאֵל אֱלֹהִים לְבָרֵי לֵבָב:
ב: וַאֲנִי כִּמְעַט נטוּ {נָטָיוּ} רַגְלָי כְּאַיִן שֻׁפְּכָה {שֻׁפְּכוּ} אֲשֻׁרָי:
ג: כִּי קִנֵּאתִי בַּהוֹלְלִים שְׁלוֹם רְשָׁעִים אֶרְאֶה:
ד: כִּי אֵין חַרְצֻבּוֹת לְמוֹתָם וּבָרִיא אוּלָם:
ה: בַּעֲמַל אֱנוֹשׁ אֵינֵמוֹ וְעִם אָדָם לֹא יְנֻגָּעוּ:
ו: לָכֵן עֲנָקַתְמוֹ גַאֲוָה יַעֲטָף שִׁית חָמָס לָמוֹ:
ז: יָצָא מֵחֵלֶב עֵינֵמוֹ עָבְרוּ מַשְׂכִּיּוֹת לֵבָב:
ח: יָמִיקוּ וִידַבְּרוּ בְרָע עֹשֶׁק מִמָּרוֹם יְדַבֵּרוּ:
ט: שַׁתּוּ בַשָּׁמַיִם פִּיהֶם וּלְשׁוֹנָם תִּהֲלַךְ בָּאָרֶץ:
י: לָכֵן ישיב {יָשׁוּב} עַמּוֹ הֲלֹם וּמֵי מָלֵא יִמָּצוּ לָמוֹ:
יא: וְאָמְרוּ אֵיכָה יָדַע אֵל וְיֵשׁ דֵּעָה בְעֶלְיוֹן:
יב: הִנֵּה אֵלֶּה רְשָׁעִים וְשַׁלְוֵי עוֹלָם הִשְׂגּוּ חָיִל:
יג: אַךְ רִיק זִכִּיתִי לְבָבִי וָאֶרְחַץ בְּנִקָּיוֹן כַּפָּי:
יד: וָאֱהִי נָגוּעַ כָּל הַיּוֹם וְתוֹכַחְתִּי לַבְּקָרִים:
טו: אִם אָמַרְתִּי אֲסַפְּרָה כְמוֹ הִנֵּה דוֹר בָּנֶיךָ בָגָדְתִּי:
טז: וָאֲחַשְּׁבָה לָדַעַת זֹאת עָמָל היא {הוּא} בְעֵינָי:
יז: עַד אָבוֹא אֶל מִקְדְּשֵׁי אֵל אָבִינָה לְאַחֲרִיתָם:
יח: אַךְ בַּחֲלָקוֹת תָּשִׁית לָמוֹ הִפַּלְתָּם לְמַשּׁוּאוֹת:
יט: אֵיךְ הָיוּ לְשַׁמָּה כְרָגַע סָפוּ תַמּוּ מִן בַּלָּהוֹת:
כ: כַּחֲלוֹם מֵהָקִיץ אֲדֹנָי בָּעִיר צַלְמָם תִּבְזֶה:
כא: כִּי יִתְחַמֵּץ לְבָבִי וְכִלְיוֹתַי אֶשְׁתּוֹנָן:
כב: וַאֲנִי בַעַר וְלֹא אֵדָע בְּהֵמוֹת הָיִיתִי עִמָּךְ:
כג: וַאֲנִי תָמִיד עִמָּךְ אָחַזְתָּ בְּיַד יְמִינִי:
כד: בַּעֲצָתְךָ תַנְחֵנִי וְאַחַר כָּבוֹד תִּקָּחֵנִי:
כה: מִי לִי בַשָּׁמָיִם וְעִמְּךָ לֹא חָפַצְתִּי בָאָרֶץ:
כו: כָּלָה שְׁאֵרִי וּלְבָבִי צוּר לְבָבִי וְחֶלְקִי אֱלֹהִים לְעוֹלָם:
כז: כִּי הִנֵּה רְחֵקֶיךָ יֹאבֵדוּ הִצְמַתָּה כָּל זוֹנֶה מִמֶּךָּ:
כח: וַאֲנִי קִרֲבַת אֱלֹהִים לִי טוֹב שַׁתִּי בַּאדֹנָי יֱהֹוִה מַחְסִי לְסַפֵּר כָּל מַלְאֲכוֹתֶיךָ:

פרק עד

א: מַשְׂכִּיל לְאָסָף לָמָה אֱלֹהִים זָנַחְתָּ לָנֶצַח יֶעְשַׁן אַפְּךָ בְּצֹאן מַרְעִיתֶךָ:
ב: זְכֹר עֲדָתְךָ קָנִיתָ קֶּדֶם גָּאַלְתָּ שֵׁבֶט נַחֲלָתֶךָ הַר צִיּוֹן זֶה שָׁכַנְתָּ בּוֹ:
ג: הָרִימָה פְעָמֶיךָ לְמַשֻּׁאוֹת נֶצַח כָּל הֵרַע אוֹיֵב בַּקֹּדֶשׁ:
ד: שָׁאֲגוּ צֹרְרֶיךָ בְּקֶרֶב מוֹעֲדֶךָ שָׂמוּ אוֹתֹתָם אֹתוֹת:
ה: יִוָּדַע כְּמֵבִיא לְמָעְלָה בִּסְבָךְ עֵץ קַרְדֻּמּוֹת:
ו: וְעַתָּ פִּתּוּחֶיהָ יָּחַד בְּכַשִּׁיל וְכֵילַפּוֹת יַהֲלֹמוּן:
ז: שִׁלְחוּ בָאֵשׁ מִקְדָּשֶׁךָ לָאָרֶץ חִלְּלוּ מִשְׁכַּן שְׁמֶךָ:
ח: אָמְרוּ בְלִבָּם נִינָם יָּחַד שָׂרְפוּ כָל מוֹעֲדֵי אֵל בָּאָרֶץ:
ט: אוֹתֹתֵינוּ לֹא רָאִינוּ אֵין עוֹד נָבִיא וְלֹא אִתָּנוּ יֹדֵעַ עַד מָה:
י: עַד מָתַי אֱלֹהִים יְחָרֶף צָר יְנָאֵץ אוֹיֵב שִׁמְךָ לָנֶצַח:
יא: לָמָּה תָשִׁיב יָדְךָ וִימִינֶךָ מִקֶּרֶב חוקך {חֵיקְךָ} כַלֵּה:
יב: וֵאלֹהִים מַלְכִּי מִקֶּדֶם פֹּעֵל יְשׁוּעוֹת בְּקֶרֶב הָאָרֶץ:
יג: אַתָּה פוֹרַרְתָּ בְעָזְּךָ יָם שִׁבַּרְתָּ רָאשֵׁי תַנִּינִים עַל הַמָּיִם:
יד: אַתָּה רִצַּצְתָּ רָאשֵׁי לִוְיָתָן תִּתְּנֶנּוּ מַאֲכָל לְעָם לְצִיִּים:
טו: אַתָּה בָקַעְתָּ מַעְיָן וָנָחַל אַתָּה הוֹבַשְׁתָּ נַהֲרוֹת אֵיתָן:
טז: לְךָ יוֹם אַף לְךָ לָיְלָה אַתָּה הֲכִינוֹתָ מָאוֹר וָשָׁמֶשׁ:
יז: אַתָּה הִצַּבְתָּ כָּל גְּבוּלוֹת אָרֶץ קַיִץ וָחֹרֶף אַתָּה יְצַרְתָּם:
יח: זְכָר זֹאת אוֹיֵב חֵרֵף יְהוָה וְעַם נָבָל נִאֲצוּ שְׁמֶךָ:
יט: אַל תִּתֵּן לְחַיַּת נֶפֶשׁ תּוֹרֶךָ חַיַּת עֲנִיֶּיךָ אַל תִּשְׁכַּח לָנֶצַח:
כ: הַבֵּט לַבְּרִית כִּי מָלְאוּ מַחֲשַׁכֵּי אֶרֶץ נְאוֹת חָמָס:
כא: אַל יָשֹׁב דַּךְ נִכְלָם עָנִי וְאֶבְיוֹן יְהַלְלוּ שְׁמֶךָ:
כב: קוּמָה אֱלֹהִים רִיבָה רִיבֶךָ זְכֹר חֶרְפָּתְךָ מִנִּי נָבָל כָּל הַיּוֹם:
כג: אַל תִּשְׁכַּח קוֹל צֹרְרֶיךָ שְׁאוֹן קָמֶיךָ עֹלֶה תָמִיד:

פרק עה

א: לַמְנַצֵּחַ אַל תַּשְׁחֵת מִזְמוֹר לְאָסָף שִׁיר:
ב: הוֹדִינוּ לְּךָ אֱלֹהִים הוֹדִינוּ וְקָרוֹב שְׁמֶךָ סִפְּרוּ נִפְלְאוֹתֶיךָ:
ג: כִּי אֶקַּח מוֹעֵד אֲנִי מֵישָׁרִים אֶשְׁפֹּט:
ד: נְמֹגִים אֶרֶץ וְכָל יֹשְׁבֶיהָ אָנֹכִי תִכַּנְתִּי עַמּוּדֶיהָ סֶּלָה:
ה: אָמַרְתִּי לַהוֹלְלִים אַל תָּהֹלּוּ וְלָרְשָׁעִים אַל תָּרִימוּ קָרֶן:
ו: אַל תָּרִימוּ לַמָּרוֹם קַרְנְכֶם תְּדַבְּרוּ בְצַוָּאר עָתָק:
ז: כִּי לֹא מִמּוֹצָא וּמִמַּעֲרָב וְלֹא מִמִּדְבַּר הָרִים:
ח: כִּי אֱלֹהִים שֹׁפֵט זֶה יַשְׁפִּיל וְזֶה יָרִים:
ט: כִּי כוֹס בְּיַד יְהוָה וְיַיִן חָמַר מָלֵא מֶסֶךְ וַיַּגֵּר מִזֶּה אַךְ שְׁמָרֶיהָ יִמְצוּ יִשְׁתּוּ כֹּל רִשְׁעֵי אָרֶץ:
י: וַאֲנִי אַגִּיד לְעֹלָם אֲזַמְּרָה לֵאלֹהֵי יַעֲקֹב:
יא: וְכָל קַרְנֵי רְשָׁעִים אֲגַדֵּעַ תְּרוֹמַמְנָה קַרְנוֹת צַדִּיק:

פרק עו

א: לַמְנַצֵּחַ בִּנְגִינֹת מִזְמוֹר לְאָסָף שִׁיר:
ב: נוֹדָע בִּיהוּדָה אֱלֹהִים בְּיִשְׂרָאֵל גָּדוֹל שְׁמוֹ:
ג: וַיְהִי בְשָׁלֵם סוּכּוֹ וּמְעוֹנָתוֹ בְצִיּוֹן:
ד: שָׁמָּה שִׁבַּר רִשְׁפֵי קָשֶׁת מָגֵן וְחֶרֶב וּמִלְחָמָה סֶלָה:
ה: נָאוֹר אַתָּה אַדִּיר מֵהַרְרֵי טָרֶף:
ו: אֶשְׁתּוֹלְלוּ אַבִּירֵי לֵב נָמוּ שְׁנָתָם וְלֹא מָצְאוּ כָל אַנְשֵׁי חַיִל יְדֵיהֶם:
ז: מִגַּעֲרָתְךָ אֱלֹהֵי יַעֲקֹב נִרְדָּם וְרֶכֶב וָסוּס:
ח: אַתָּה נוֹרָא אַתָּה וּמִי יַעֲמֹד לְפָנֶיךָ מֵאָז אַפֶּךָ:

ט: מִשָּׁמַיִם הִשְׁמַעְתָּ דִּין אֶרֶץ יָרְאָה וְשָׁקָטָה:
י: בְּקוּם לַמִּשְׁפָּט אֱלֹהִים לְהוֹשִׁיעַ כָּל עַנְוֵי אֶרֶץ סֶלָה:
יא: כִּי חֲמַת אָדָם תּוֹדֶךָּ שְׁאֵרִית חֵמֹת תַּחְגֹּר:
יב: נִדְרוּ וְשַׁלְּמוּ לַיהֹוָה אֱלֹהֵיכֶם כָּל סְבִיבָיו יוֹבִילוּ שַׁי לַמּוֹרָא:
יג: יִבְצֹר רוּחַ נְגִידִים נוֹרָא לְמַלְכֵי אָרֶץ:

פרק עז

א: לַמְנַצֵּחַ עַל יְדִיתוּן {יְדוּתוּן} לְאָסָף מִזְמוֹר:
ב: קוֹלִי אֶל אֱלֹהִים וְאֶצְעָקָה קוֹלִי אֶל אֱלֹהִים וְהַאֲזִין אֵלָי:
ג: בְּיוֹם צָרָתִי אֲדֹנָי דָּרָשְׁתִּי יָדִי לַיְלָה נִגְּרָה וְלֹא תָפוּג מֵאֲנָה הִנָּחֵם נַפְשִׁי:
ד: אֶזְכְּרָה אֱלֹהִים וְאֶהֱמָיָה אָשִׂיחָה וְתִתְעַטֵּף רוּחִי סֶלָה:
ה: אָחַזְתָּ שְׁמֻרוֹת עֵינָי נִפְעַמְתִּי וְלֹא אֲדַבֵּר:
ו: חִשַּׁבְתִּי יָמִים מִקֶּדֶם שְׁנוֹת עוֹלָמִים:
ז: אֶזְכְּרָה נְגִינָתִי בַּלָּיְלָה עִם לְבָבִי אָשִׂיחָה וַיְחַפֵּשׂ רוּחִי:
ח: הַלְעוֹלָמִים יִזְנַח אֲדֹנָי וְלֹא יֹסִיף לִרְצוֹת עוֹד:
ט: הֶאָפֵס לָנֶצַח חַסְדּוֹ גָּמַר אֹמֶר לְדֹר וָדֹר:
י: הֲשָׁכַח חַנּוֹת אֵל אִם קָפַץ בְּאַף רַחֲמָיו סֶלָה:
יא: וָאֹמַר חַלּוֹתִי הִיא שְׁנוֹת יְמִין עֶלְיוֹן:
יב: אַזְכִּיר {אֶזְכּוֹר} מַעַלְלֵי יָהּ כִּי אֶזְכְּרָה מִקֶּדֶם פִּלְאֶךָ:
יג: וְהָגִיתִי בְכָל פָּעֳלֶךָ וּבַעֲלִילוֹתֶיךָ אָשִׂיחָה:
יד: אֱלֹהִים בַּקֹּדֶשׁ דַּרְכֶּךָ מִי אֵל גָּדוֹל כֵּאלֹהִים:
טו: אַתָּה הָאֵל עֹשֵׂה פֶלֶא הוֹדַעְתָּ בָעַמִּים עֻזֶּךָ:
טז: גָּאַלְתָּ בִּזְרוֹעַ עַמֶּךָ בְּנֵי יַעֲקֹב וְיוֹסֵף סֶלָה:
יז: רָאוּךָ מַּיִם אֱלֹהִים רָאוּךָ מַּיִם יָחִילוּ אַף יִרְגְּזוּ תְהֹמוֹת:
יח: זֹרְמוּ מַיִם עָבוֹת קוֹל נָתְנוּ שְׁחָקִים אַף חֲצָצֶיךָ יִתְהַלָּכוּ:
יט: קוֹל רַעַמְךָ בַּגַּלְגַּל הֵאִירוּ בְרָקִים תֵּבֵל רָגְזָה וַתִּרְעַשׁ הָאָרֶץ:
כ: בַּיָּם דַּרְכֶּךָ וּשְׁבִילֶיךָ {וּשְׁבִילְךָ} בְּמַיִם רַבִּים וְעִקְּבוֹתֶיךָ לֹא נֹדָעוּ:
כא: נָחִיתָ כַצֹּאן עַמֶּךָ בְּיַד מֹשֶׁה וְאַהֲרֹן:

פרק עח

א: מַשְׂכִּיל לְאָסָף הַאֲזִינָה עַמִּי תּוֹרָתִי הַטּוּ אָזְנְכֶם לְאִמְרֵי פִי:
ב: אֶפְתְּחָה בְמָשָׁל פִּי אַבִּיעָה חִידוֹת מִנִּי קֶדֶם:
ג: אֲשֶׁר שָׁמַעְנוּ וַנֵּדָעֵם וַאֲבוֹתֵינוּ סִפְּרוּ לָנוּ:
ד: לֹא נְכַחֵד מִבְּנֵיהֶם לְדוֹר אַחֲרוֹן מְסַפְּרִים תְּהִלּוֹת יְהֹוָה וֶעֱזוּזוֹ וְנִפְלְאֹתָיו אֲשֶׁר עָשָׂה:
ה: וַיָּקֶם עֵדוּת בְּיַעֲקֹב וְתוֹרָה שָׂם בְּיִשְׂרָאֵל אֲשֶׁר צִוָּה אֶת אֲבוֹתֵינוּ לְהוֹדִיעָם לִבְנֵיהֶם:
ו: לְמַעַן יֵדְעוּ דּוֹר אַחֲרוֹן בָּנִים יִוָּלֵדוּ יָקֻמוּ וִיסַפְּרוּ לִבְנֵיהֶם:
ז: וְיָשִׂימוּ בֵאלֹהִים כִּסְלָם וְלֹא יִשְׁכְּחוּ מַעַלְלֵי אֵל וּמִצְוֹתָיו יִנְצֹרוּ:
ח: וְלֹא יִהְיוּ כַּאֲבוֹתָם דּוֹר סוֹרֵר וּמֹרֶה דּוֹר לֹא הֵכִין לִבּוֹ וְלֹא נֶאֶמְנָה אֶת אֵל רוּחוֹ:
ט: בְּנֵי אֶפְרַיִם נוֹשְׁקֵי רוֹמֵי קָשֶׁת הָפְכוּ בְּיוֹם קְרָב:
י: לֹא שָׁמְרוּ בְּרִית אֱלֹהִים וּבְתוֹרָתוֹ מֵאֲנוּ לָלֶכֶת:
יא: וַיִּשְׁכְּחוּ עֲלִילוֹתָיו וְנִפְלְאוֹתָיו אֲשֶׁר הֶרְאָם:
יב: נֶגֶד אֲבוֹתָם עָשָׂה פֶלֶא בְּאֶרֶץ מִצְרַיִם שְׂדֵה צֹעַן:
יג: בָּקַע יָם וַיַּעֲבִירֵם וַיַּצֶּב מַיִם כְּמוֹ נֵד:
יד: וַיַּנְחֵם בֶּעָנָן יוֹמָם וְכָל הַלַּיְלָה בְּאוֹר אֵשׁ:
טו: יְבַקַּע צֻרִים בַּמִּדְבָּר וַיַּשְׁקְ כִּתְהֹמוֹת רַבָּה:
טז: וַיּוֹצִא נוֹזְלִים מִסָּלַע וַיּוֹרֶד כַּנְּהָרוֹת מָיִם:
יז: וַיּוֹסִיפוּ עוֹד לַחֲטֹא לוֹ לַמְרוֹת עֶלְיוֹן בַּצִּיָּה:

יח: וַיְנַסּוּ אֵל בִּלְבָבָם לִשְׁאָל אֹכֶל לְנַפְשָׁם:

יט: וַיְדַבְּרוּ בֵּאלֹהִים אָמְרוּ הֲיוּכַל אֵל לַעֲרֹךְ שֻׁלְחָן בַּמִּדְבָּר:

כ: הֵן הִכָּה צוּר וַיָּזוּבוּ מַיִם וּנְחָלִים יִשְׁטֹפוּ הֲגַם לֶחֶם יוּכַל תֵּת אִם יָכִין שְׁאֵר לְעַמּוֹ:

כא: לָכֵן שָׁמַע יְהוָה וַיִּתְעַבָּר וְאֵשׁ נִשְּׂקָה בְיַעֲקֹב וְגַם אַף עָלָה בְיִשְׂרָאֵל:

כב: כִּי לֹא הֶאֱמִינוּ בֵּאלֹהִים וְלֹא בָטְחוּ בִּישׁוּעָתוֹ:

כג: וַיְצַו שְׁחָקִים מִמָּעַל וְדַלְתֵי שָׁמַיִם פָּתָח:

כד: וַיַּמְטֵר עֲלֵיהֶם מָן לֶאֱכֹל וּדְגַן שָׁמַיִם נָתַן לָמוֹ:

כה: לֶחֶם אַבִּירִים אָכַל אִישׁ צֵידָה שָׁלַח לָהֶם לָשֹׂבַע:

כו: יַסַּע קָדִים בַּשָּׁמָיִם וַיְנַהֵג בְּעֻזּוֹ תֵימָן:

כז: וַיַּמְטֵר עֲלֵיהֶם כֶּעָפָר שְׁאֵר וּכְחוֹל יַמִּים עוֹף כָּנָף:

כח: וַיַּפֵּל בְּקֶרֶב מַחֲנֵהוּ סָבִיב לְמִשְׁכְּנֹתָיו:

כט: וַיֹּאכְלוּ וַיִּשְׂבְּעוּ מְאֹד וְתַאֲוָתָם יָבִא לָהֶם:

ל: לֹא זָרוּ מִתַּאֲוָתָם עוֹד אָכְלָם בְּפִיהֶם:

לא: וְאַף אֱלֹהִים עָלָה בָהֶם וַיַּהֲרֹג בְּמִשְׁמַנֵּיהֶם וּבַחוּרֵי יִשְׂרָאֵל הִכְרִיעַ:

לב: בְּכָל זֹאת חָטְאוּ עוֹד וְלֹא הֶאֱמִינוּ בְּנִפְלְאוֹתָיו:

לג: וַיְכַל בַּהֶבֶל יְמֵיהֶם וּשְׁנוֹתָם בַּבֶּהָלָה:

לד: אִם הֲרָגָם וּדְרָשׁוּהוּ וְשָׁבוּ וְשִׁחֲרוּ אֵל:

לה: וַיִּזְכְּרוּ כִּי אֱלֹהִים צוּרָם וְאֵל עֶלְיוֹן גֹּאֲלָם:

לו: וַיְפַתּוּהוּ בְּפִיהֶם וּבִלְשׁוֹנָם יְכַזְּבוּ לוֹ:

לז: וְלִבָּם לֹא נָכוֹן עִמּוֹ וְלֹא נֶאֶמְנוּ בִּבְרִיתוֹ:

לח: וְהוּא רַחוּם יְכַפֵּר עָוֹן וְלֹא יַשְׁחִית וְהִרְבָּה לְהָשִׁיב אַפּוֹ וְלֹא יָעִיר כָּל חֲמָתוֹ:

לט: וַיִּזְכֹּר כִּי בָשָׂר הֵמָּה רוּחַ הוֹלֵךְ וְלֹא יָשׁוּב:

מ: כַּמָּה יַמְרוּהוּ בַמִּדְבָּר יַעֲצִיבוּהוּ בִּישִׁימוֹן:

מא: וַיָּשׁוּבוּ וַיְנַסּוּ אֵל וּקְדוֹשׁ יִשְׂרָאֵל הִתְווּ:

מב: לֹא זָכְרוּ אֶת יָדוֹ יוֹם אֲשֶׁר פָּדָם מִנִּי צָר:

מג: אֲשֶׁר שָׂם בְּמִצְרַיִם אֹתוֹתָיו וּמוֹפְתָיו בִּשְׂדֵה צֹעַן:

מד: וַיַּהֲפֹךְ לְדָם יְאֹרֵיהֶם וְנֹזְלֵיהֶם בַּל יִשְׁתָּיוּן:

מה: יְשַׁלַּח בָּהֶם עָרֹב וַיֹּאכְלֵם וּצְפַרְדֵּעַ וַתַּשְׁחִיתֵם:

מו: וַיִּתֵּן לֶחָסִיל יְבוּלָם וִיגִיעָם לָאַרְבֶּה:

מז: יַהֲרֹג בַּבָּרָד גַּפְנָם וְשִׁקְמוֹתָם בַּחֲנָמַל:

מח: וַיַּסְגֵּר לַבָּרָד בְּעִירָם וּמִקְנֵיהֶם לָרְשָׁפִים:

מט: יְשַׁלַּח בָּם חֲרוֹן אַפּוֹ עֶבְרָה וָזַעַם וְצָרָה מִשְׁלַחַת מַלְאֲכֵי רָעִים:

נ: יְפַלֵּס נָתִיב לְאַפּוֹ לֹא חָשַׂךְ מִמָּוֶת נַפְשָׁם וְחַיָּתָם לַדֶּבֶר הִסְגִּיר:

נא: וַיַּךְ כָּל בְּכוֹר בְּמִצְרָיִם רֵאשִׁית אוֹנִים בְּאָהֳלֵי חָם:

נב: וַיַּסַּע כַּצֹּאן עַמּוֹ וַיְנַהֲגֵם כַּעֵדֶר בַּמִּדְבָּר:

נג: וַיַּנְחֵם לָבֶטַח וְלֹא פָחָדוּ וְאֶת אוֹיְבֵיהֶם כִּסָּה הַיָּם:

נד: וַיְבִיאֵם אֶל גְּבוּל קָדְשׁוֹ הַר זֶה קָנְתָה יְמִינוֹ:

נה: וַיְגָרֶשׁ מִפְּנֵיהֶם גּוֹיִם וַיַּפִּילֵם בְּחֶבֶל נַחֲלָה וַיַּשְׁכֵּן בְּאָהֳלֵיהֶם שִׁבְטֵי יִשְׂרָאֵל:

נו: וַיְנַסּוּ וַיַּמְרוּ אֶת אֱלֹהִים עֶלְיוֹן וְעֵדוֹתָיו לֹא שָׁמָרוּ:

נז: וַיִּסֹּגוּ וַיִּבְגְּדוּ כַּאֲבוֹתָם נֶהְפְּכוּ כְּקֶשֶׁת רְמִיָּה:

נח: וַיַּכְעִיסוּהוּ בְּבָמוֹתָם וּבִפְסִילֵיהֶם יַקְנִיאוּהוּ:

נט: שָׁמַע אֱלֹהִים וַיִּתְעַבָּר וַיִּמְאַס מְאֹד בְּיִשְׂרָאֵל:

ס: וַיִּטֹּשׁ מִשְׁכַּן שִׁלוֹ אֹהֶל שִׁכֵּן בָּאָדָם:

סא: וַיִּתֵּן לַשְּׁבִי עֻזּוֹ וְתִפְאַרְתּוֹ בְיַד צָר:

סב: וַיַּסְגֵּר לַחֶרֶב עַמּוֹ וּבְנַחֲלָתוֹ הִתְעַבָּר:

סג: בַּחוּרָיו אָכְלָה אֵשׁ וּבְתוּלֹתָיו לֹא הוּלָּלוּ:

סד: כֹּהֲנָיו בַּחֶרֶב נָפָלוּ וְאַלְמְנֹתָיו לֹא תִבְכֶּינָה:

סה: וַיִּקַץ כְּיָשֵׁן אֲדֹנָי כְּגִבּוֹר מִתְרוֹנֵן מִיָּיִן:

סו: וַיַּךְ צָרָיו אָחוֹר חֶרְפַּת עוֹלָם נָתַן לָמוֹ:

סז: וַיִּמְאַס בְּאֹהֶל יוֹסֵף וּבְשֵׁבֶט אֶפְרַיִם לֹא בָחָר:

סח: וַיִּבְחַר אֶת שֵׁבֶט יְהוּדָה אֶת הַר צִיּוֹן אֲשֶׁר אָהֵב:

סט: וַיִּבֶן כְּמוֹ רָמִים מִקְדָּשׁוֹ כְּאֶרֶץ יְסָדָהּ לְעוֹלָם:

ע: וַיִּבְחַר בְּדָוִד עַבְדּוֹ וַיִּקָּחֵהוּ מִמִּכְלְאֹת צֹאן:

עא: מֵאַחַר עָלוֹת הֱבִיאוֹ לִרְעוֹת בְּיַעֲקֹב עַמּוֹ וּבְיִשְׂרָאֵל נַחֲלָתוֹ:

עב: וַיִּרְעֵם כְּתֹם לְבָבוֹ וּבִתְבוּנוֹת כַּפָּיו יַנְחֵם:

פרק עט

א: מִזְמוֹר לְאָסָף אֱלֹהִים בָּאוּ גוֹיִם בְּנַחֲלָתֶךָ טִמְּאוּ אֶת הֵיכַל קָדְשֶׁךָ שָׂמוּ אֶת יְרוּשָׁלַ͏ִם לְעִיִּים:

ב: נָתְנוּ אֶת נִבְלַת עֲבָדֶיךָ מַאֲכָל לְעוֹף הַשָּׁמָיִם בְּשַׂר חֲסִידֶיךָ לְחַיְתוֹ אָרֶץ:

ג: שָׁפְכוּ דָמָם כַּמַּיִם סְבִיבוֹת יְרוּשָׁלַ͏ִם וְאֵין קוֹבֵר:

ד: הָיִינוּ חֶרְפָּה לִשְׁכֵנֵינוּ לַעַג וָקֶלֶס לִסְבִיבוֹתֵינוּ:

ה: עַד מָה יְהוָה תֶּאֱנַף לָנֶצַח תִּבְעַר כְּמוֹ אֵשׁ קִנְאָתֶךָ:

ו: שְׁפֹךְ חֲמָתְךָ אֶל הַגּוֹיִם אֲשֶׁר לֹא יְדָעוּךָ וְעַל מַמְלָכוֹת אֲשֶׁר בְּשִׁמְךָ לֹא קָרָאוּ:

ז: כִּי אָכַל אֶת יַעֲקֹב וְאֶת נָוֵהוּ הֵשַׁמּוּ:

ח: אַל תִּזְכָּר לָנוּ עֲוֺנֹת רִאשֹׁנִים מַהֵר יְקַדְּמוּנוּ רַחֲמֶיךָ כִּי דַלּוֹנוּ מְאֹד:

ט: עָזְרֵנוּ אֱלֹהֵי יִשְׁעֵנוּ עַל דְּבַר כְּבוֹד שְׁמֶךָ וְהַצִּילֵנוּ וְכַפֵּר עַל חַטֹּאתֵינוּ לְמַעַן שְׁמֶךָ:

י: לָמָּה יֹאמְרוּ הַגּוֹיִם אַיֵּה אֱלֹהֵיהֶם יִוָּדַע בַּגֹּיִים {בַּגּוֹיִם} לְעֵינֵינוּ נִקְמַת דַּם עֲבָדֶיךָ הַשָּׁפוּךְ:

יא: תָּבוֹא לְפָנֶיךָ אֶנְקַת אָסִיר כְּגֹדֶל זְרוֹעֲךָ הוֹתֵר בְּנֵי תְמוּתָה:

יב: וְהָשֵׁב לִשְׁכֵנֵינוּ שִׁבְעָתַיִם אֶל חֵיקָם חֶרְפָּתָם אֲשֶׁר חֵרְפוּךָ אֲדֹנָי:

יג: וַאֲנַחְנוּ עַמְּךָ וְצֹאן מַרְעִיתֶךָ נוֹדֶה לְּךָ לְעוֹלָם לְדוֹר וָדֹר נְסַפֵּר תְּהִלָּתֶךָ:

פרק פ

א: לַמְנַצֵּחַ אֶל שֹׁשַׁנִּים עֵדוּת לְאָסָף מִזְמוֹר:

ב: רֹעֵה יִשְׂרָאֵל הַאֲזִינָה נֹהֵג כַּצֹּאן יוֹסֵף יֹשֵׁב הַכְּרוּבִים הוֹפִיעָה:

ג: לִפְנֵי אֶפְרַיִם וּבִנְיָמִן וּמְנַשֶּׁה עוֹרְרָה אֶת גְּבוּרָתֶךָ וּלְכָה לִישֻׁעָתָה לָּנוּ:

ד: אֱלֹהִים הֲשִׁיבֵנוּ וְהָאֵר פָּנֶיךָ וְנִוָּשֵׁעָה:

ה: יְהוָה אֱלֹהִים צְבָאוֹת עַד מָתַי עָשַׁנְתָּ בִּתְפִלַּת עַמֶּךָ:

ו: הֶאֱכַלְתָּם לֶחֶם דִּמְעָה וַתַּשְׁקֵמוֹ בִּדְמָעוֹת שָׁלִישׁ:

ז: תְּשִׂימֵנוּ מָדוֹן לִשְׁכֵנֵינוּ וְאֹיְבֵינוּ יִלְעֲגוּ לָמוֹ:

ח: אֱלֹהִים צְבָאוֹת הֲשִׁיבֵנוּ וְהָאֵר פָּנֶיךָ וְנִוָּשֵׁעָה:

ט: גֶּפֶן מִמִּצְרַיִם תַּסִּיעַ תְּגָרֵשׁ גּוֹיִם וַתִּטָּעֶהָ:

י: פִּנִּיתָ לְפָנֶיהָ וַתַּשְׁרֵשׁ שָׁרָשֶׁיהָ וַתְּמַלֵּא אָרֶץ:

יא: כָּסּוּ הָרִים צִלָּהּ וַעֲנָפֶיהָ אַרְזֵי אֵל:

יב: תְּשַׁלַּח קְצִירֶהָ עַד יָם וְאֶל נָהָר יוֹנְקוֹתֶיהָ:

יג: לָמָּה פָּרַצְתָּ גְדֵרֶיהָ וְאָרוּהָ כָּל עֹבְרֵי דָרֶךְ:

יד: יְכַרְסְמֶנָּה חֲזִיר מִיָּעַר וְזִיז שָׂדַי יִרְעֶנָּה:

טו: אֱלֹהִים צְבָאוֹת שׁוּב נָא הַבֵּט מִשָּׁמַיִם וּרְאֵה וּפְקֹד גֶּפֶן זֹאת:

טז: וְכַנָּה אֲשֶׁר נָטְעָה יְמִינֶךָ וְעַל בֵּן אִמַּצְתָּה לָּךְ:

יז: שְׂרֻפָה בָאֵשׁ כְּסוּחָה מִגַּעֲרַת פָּנֶיךָ יֹאבֵדוּ:

יח: תְּהִי יָדְךָ עַל אִישׁ יְמִינֶךָ עַל בֶּן אָדָם אִמַּצְתָּ לָּךְ:

יט: וְלֹא נָסוֹג מִמֶּךָּ תְּחַיֵּנוּ וּבְשִׁמְךָ נִקְרָא:

כ: יְהוָה אֱלֹהִים צְבָאוֹת הֲשִׁיבֵנוּ הָאֵר פָּנֶיךָ וְנִוָּשֵׁעָה:

פרק פא

א: לַמְנַצֵּחַ עַל הַגִּתִּית לְאָסָף:

ב: הַרְנִינוּ לֵאלֹהִים עוּזֵּנוּ הָרִיעוּ לֵאלֹהֵי יַעֲקֹב:

ג: שְׂאוּ זִמְרָה וּתְנוּ תֹף כִּנּוֹר נָעִים עִם נָבֶל:

ד: תִּקְעוּ בַחֹדֶשׁ שׁוֹפָר בַּכֵּסֶה לְיוֹם חַגֵּנוּ:

ה: כִּי חֹק לְיִשְׂרָאֵל הוּא מִשְׁפָּט לֵאלֹהֵי יַעֲקֹב:

ו: עֵדוּת בִּיהוֹסֵף שָׂמוֹ בְּצֵאתוֹ עַל אֶרֶץ מִצְרָיִם שְׂפַת לֹא יָדַעְתִּי אֶשְׁמָע:

ז: הֲסִירוֹתִי מִסֵּבֶל שִׁכְמוֹ כַּפָּיו מִדּוּד תַּעֲבֹרְנָה:

ח: בַּצָּרָה קָרָאתָ וָאֲחַלְּצֶךָּ אֶעֶנְךָ בְּסֵתֶר רַעַם אֶבְחָנְךָ עַל מֵי מְרִיבָה סֶלָה:

ט: שְׁמַע עַמִּי וְאָעִידָה בָּךְ יִשְׂרָאֵל אִם תִּשְׁמַע לִי:

י: לֹא יִהְיֶה בְךָ אֵל זָר וְלֹא תִשְׁתַּחֲוֶה לְאֵל נֵכָר:

יא: אָנֹכִי יְהוָה אֱלֹהֶיךָ הַמַּעַלְךָ מֵאֶרֶץ מִצְרָיִם הַרְחֶב פִּיךָ וַאֲמַלְאֵהוּ:

יב: וְלֹא שָׁמַע עַמִּי לְקוֹלִי וְיִשְׂרָאֵל לֹא אָבָה לִי:

יג: וָאֲשַׁלְּחֵהוּ בִּשְׁרִירוּת לִבָּם יֵלְכוּ בְּמוֹעֲצוֹתֵיהֶם:

יד: לוּ עַמִּי שֹׁמֵעַ לִי יִשְׂרָאֵל בִּדְרָכַי יְהַלֵּכוּ:

טו: כִּמְעַט אוֹיְבֵיהֶם אַכְנִיעַ וְעַל צָרֵיהֶם אָשִׁיב יָדִי:

טז: מְשַׂנְאֵי יְהוָה יְכַחֲשׁוּ לוֹ וִיהִי עִתָּם לְעוֹלָם:

יז: וַיַּאֲכִילֵהוּ מֵחֵלֶב חִטָּה וּמִצּוּר דְּבַשׁ אַשְׂבִּיעֶךָ:

פרק פב

א: מִזְמוֹר לְאָסָף אֱלֹהִים נִצָּב בַּעֲדַת אֵל בְּקֶרֶב אֱלֹהִים יִשְׁפֹּט:

ב: עַד מָתַי תִּשְׁפְּטוּ עָוֶל וּפְנֵי רְשָׁעִים תִּשְׂאוּ סֶלָה:

ג: שִׁפְטוּ דַל וְיָתוֹם עָנִי וָרָשׁ הַצְדִּיקוּ:

ד: פַּלְּטוּ דַל וְאֶבְיוֹן מִיַּד רְשָׁעִים הַצִּילוּ:

ה: לֹא יָדְעוּ וְלֹא יָבִינוּ בַּחֲשֵׁכָה יִתְהַלָּכוּ יִמּוֹטוּ כָּל מוֹסְדֵי אָרֶץ:

ו: אֲנִי אָמַרְתִּי אֱלֹהִים אַתֶּם וּבְנֵי עֶלְיוֹן כֻּלְּכֶם:

ז: אָכֵן כְּאָדָם תְּמוּתוּן וּכְאַחַד הַשָּׂרִים תִּפֹּלוּ:

ח: קוּמָה אֱלֹהִים שָׁפְטָה הָאָרֶץ כִּי אַתָּה תִנְחַל בְּכָל הַגּוֹיִם:

פרק פג

א: שִׁיר מִזְמוֹר לְאָסָף:

ב: אֱלֹהִים אַל דֳּמִי לָךְ אַל תֶּחֱרַשׁ וְאַל תִּשְׁקֹט אֵל:

ג: כִּי הִנֵּה אוֹיְבֶיךָ יֶהֱמָיוּן וּמְשַׂנְאֶיךָ נָשְׂאוּ רֹאשׁ:

ד: עַל עַמְּךָ יַעֲרִימוּ סוֹד וְיִתְיָעֲצוּ עַל צְפוּנֶיךָ:

ה: אָמְרוּ לְכוּ וְנַכְחִידֵם מִגּוֹי וְלֹא יִזָּכֵר שֵׁם יִשְׂרָאֵל עוֹד:

ו: כִּי נוֹעֲצוּ לֵב יַחְדָּו עָלֶיךָ בְּרִית יִכְרֹתוּ:

ז: אָהֳלֵי אֱדוֹם וְיִשְׁמְעֵאלִים מוֹאָב וְהַגְרִים:

ח: גְּבָל וְעַמּוֹן וַעֲמָלֵק פְּלֶשֶׁת עִם יֹשְׁבֵי צוֹר:

ט: גַּם אַשּׁוּר נִלְוָה עִמָּם הָיוּ זְרוֹעַ לִבְנֵי לוֹט סֶלָה:

י: עֲשֵׂה לָהֶם כְּמִדְיָן כְּסִיסְרָא כְיָבִין בְּנַחַל קִישׁוֹן:

יא: נִשְׁמְדוּ בְעֵין דֹּאר הָיוּ דֹּמֶן לָאֲדָמָה:

יב: שִׁיתֵמוֹ נְדִיבֵימוֹ כְּעֹרֵב וְכִזְאֵב וּכְזֶבַח וּכְצַלְמֻנָּע כָּל נְסִיכֵימוֹ:

יג: אֲשֶׁר אָמְרוּ נִירְשָׁה לָּנוּ אֵת נְאוֹת אֱלֹהִים:

יד: אֱלֹהַי שִׁיתֵמוֹ כַגַּלְגַּל כְּקַשׁ לִפְנֵי רוּחַ:

טו: כְּאֵשׁ תִּבְעַר יָעַר וּכְלֶהָבָה תְּלַהֵט הָרִים:

טז: כֵּן תִּרְדְּפֵם בְּסַעֲרֶךָ וּבְסוּפָתְךָ תְבַהֲלֵם:

יז: מַלֵּא פְנֵיהֶם קָלוֹן וִיבַקְשׁוּ שִׁמְךָ יְהוָה:

יח: יֵבֹשׁוּ וְיִבָּהֲלוּ עֲדֵי עַד וְיַחְפְּרוּ וְיֹאבֵדוּ:
יט: וְיֵדְעוּ כִּי אַתָּה שִׁמְךָ יְהֹוָה לְבַדֶּךָ עֶלְיוֹן עַל כָּל הָאָרֶץ:

פרק פד

א: לַמְנַצֵּחַ עַל הַגִּתִּית לִבְנֵי קֹרַח מִזְמוֹר:
ב: מַה יְּדִידוֹת מִשְׁכְּנוֹתֶיךָ יְהֹוָה צְבָאוֹת:
ג: נִכְסְפָה וְגַם כָּלְתָה נַפְשִׁי לְחַצְרוֹת יְהֹוָה לִבִּי וּבְשָׂרִי יְרַנְּנוּ אֶל אֵל חָי:
ד: גַּם צִפּוֹר מָצְאָה בַיִת וּדְרוֹר קֵן לָהּ אֲשֶׁר שָׁתָה אֶפְרֹחֶיהָ אֶת מִזְבְּחוֹתֶיךָ יְהֹוָה צְבָאוֹת מַלְכִּי וֵאלֹהָי:
ה: אַשְׁרֵי יוֹשְׁבֵי בֵיתֶךָ עוֹד יְהַלְלוּךָ סֶּלָה:
ו: אַשְׁרֵי אָדָם עוֹז לוֹ בָךְ מְסִלּוֹת בִּלְבָבָם:
ז: עֹבְרֵי בְּעֵמֶק הַבָּכָא מַעְיָן יְשִׁיתוּהוּ גַּם בְּרָכוֹת יַעְטֶה מוֹרֶה:
ח: יֵלְכוּ מֵחַיִל אֶל חָיִל יֵרָאֶה אֶל אֱלֹהִים בְּצִיּוֹן:
ט: יְהֹוָה אֱלֹהִים צְבָאוֹת שִׁמְעָה תְפִלָּתִי הַאֲזִינָה אֱלֹהֵי יַעֲקֹב סֶלָה:
י: מָגִנֵּנוּ רְאֵה אֱלֹהִים וְהַבֵּט פְּנֵי מְשִׁיחֶךָ:
יא: כִּי טוֹב יוֹם בַּחֲצֵרֶיךָ מֵאָלֶף בָּחַרְתִּי הִסְתּוֹפֵף בְּבֵית אֱלֹהַי מִדּוּר בְּאָהֳלֵי רֶשַׁע:
יב: כִּי שֶׁמֶשׁ וּמָגֵן יְהֹוָה אֱלֹהִים חֵן וְכָבוֹד יִתֵּן יְהֹוָה לֹא יִמְנַע טוֹב לַהֹלְכִים בְּתָמִים:
יג: יְהֹוָה צְבָאוֹת אַשְׁרֵי אָדָם בֹּטֵחַ בָּךְ:

פרק פה

א: לַמְנַצֵּחַ לִבְנֵי קֹרַח מִזְמוֹר:
ב: רָצִיתָ יְהֹוָה אַרְצֶךָ שַׁבְתָּ שְׁבוּת {שְׁבִית} יַעֲקֹב:
ג: נָשָׂאתָ עֲוֹן עַמֶּךָ כִּסִּיתָ כָל חַטָּאתָם סֶלָה:
ד: אָסַפְתָּ כָל עֶבְרָתֶךָ הֱשִׁיבוֹתָ מֵחֲרוֹן אַפֶּךָ:
ה: שׁוּבֵנוּ אֱלֹהֵי יִשְׁעֵנוּ וְהָפֵר כַּעַסְךָ עִמָּנוּ:
ו: הַלְעוֹלָם תֶּאֱנַף בָּנוּ תִּמְשֹׁךְ אַפְּךָ לְדֹר וָדֹר:
ז: הֲלֹא אַתָּה תָּשׁוּב תְּחַיֵּנוּ וְעַמְּךָ יִשְׂמְחוּ בָךְ:
ח: הַרְאֵנוּ יְהֹוָה חַסְדֶּךָ וְיֶשְׁעֲךָ תִּתֶּן לָנוּ:
ט: אֶשְׁמְעָה מַה יְדַבֵּר הָאֵל יְהֹוָה כִּי יְדַבֵּר שָׁלוֹם אֶל עַמּוֹ וְאֶל חֲסִידָיו וְאַל יָשׁוּבוּ לְכִסְלָה:
י: אַךְ קָרוֹב לִירֵאָיו יִשְׁעוֹ לִשְׁכֹּן כָּבוֹד בְּאַרְצֵנוּ:
יא: חֶסֶד וֶאֱמֶת נִפְגָּשׁוּ צֶדֶק וְשָׁלוֹם נָשָׁקוּ:
יב: אֱמֶת מֵאֶרֶץ תִּצְמָח וְצֶדֶק מִשָּׁמַיִם נִשְׁקָף:
יג: גַּם יְהֹוָה יִתֵּן הַטּוֹב וְאַרְצֵנוּ תִּתֵּן יְבוּלָהּ:
יד: צֶדֶק לְפָנָיו יְהַלֵּךְ וְיָשֵׂם לְדֶרֶךְ פְּעָמָיו:

פרק פו

א: תְּפִלָּה לְדָוִד הַטֵּה יְהֹוָה אָזְנְךָ עֲנֵנִי כִּי עָנִי וְאֶבְיוֹן אָנִי:
ב: שָׁמְרָה נַפְשִׁי כִּי חָסִיד אָנִי הוֹשַׁע עַבְדְּךָ אַתָּה אֱלֹהַי הַבּוֹטֵחַ אֵלֶיךָ:
ג: חָנֵּנִי אֲדֹנָי כִּי אֵלֶיךָ אֶקְרָא כָּל הַיּוֹם:
ד: שַׂמֵּחַ נֶפֶשׁ עַבְדֶּךָ כִּי אֵלֶיךָ אֲדֹנָי נַפְשִׁי אֶשָּׂא:
ה: כִּי אַתָּה אֲדֹנָי טוֹב וְסַלָּח וְרַב חֶסֶד לְכָל קֹרְאֶיךָ:
ו: הַאֲזִינָה יְהֹוָה תְּפִלָּתִי וְהַקְשִׁיבָה בְּקוֹל תַּחֲנוּנוֹתָי:
ז: בְּיוֹם צָרָתִי אֶקְרָאֶךָּ כִּי תַעֲנֵנִי:
ח: אֵין כָּמוֹךָ בָאֱלֹהִים אֲדֹנָי וְאֵין כְּמַעֲשֶׂיךָ:
ט: כָּל גּוֹיִם אֲשֶׁר עָשִׂיתָ יָבוֹאוּ וְיִשְׁתַּחֲווּ לְפָנֶיךָ אֲדֹנָי וִיכַבְּדוּ לִשְׁמֶךָ:
י: כִּי גָדוֹל אַתָּה וְעֹשֵׂה נִפְלָאוֹת אַתָּה אֱלֹהִים לְבַדֶּךָ:
יא: הוֹרֵנִי יְהֹוָה דַּרְכֶּךָ אֲהַלֵּךְ בַּאֲמִתֶּךָ יַחֵד לְבָבִי לְיִרְאָה שְׁמֶךָ:

יב: אוֹדְךָ אֲדֹנָי אֱלֹהַי בְּכָל לְבָבִי וַאֲכַבְּדָה שִׁמְךָ לְעוֹלָם:
יג: כִּי חַסְדְּךָ גָּדוֹל עָלָי וְהִצַּלְתָּ נַפְשִׁי מִשְּׁאוֹל תַּחְתִּיָּה:
יד: אֱלֹהִים זֵדִים קָמוּ עָלַי וַעֲדַת עָרִיצִים בִּקְשׁוּ נַפְשִׁי וְלֹא שָׂמוּךָ לְנֶגְדָּם:
טו: וְאַתָּה אֲדֹנָי אֵל רַחוּם וְחַנּוּן אֶרֶךְ אַפַּיִם וְרַב חֶסֶד וֶאֱמֶת:
טז: פְּנֵה אֵלַי וְחָנֵּנִי תְּנָה עֻזְּךָ לְעַבְדֶּךָ וְהוֹשִׁיעָה לְבֶן אֲמָתֶךָ:
יז: עֲשֵׂה עִמִּי אוֹת לְטוֹבָה וְיִרְאוּ שֹׂנְאַי וְיֵבֹשׁוּ כִּי אַתָּה יְהוָה עֲזַרְתַּנִי וְנִחַמְתָּנִי:

פרק פז

א: לִבְנֵי קֹרַח מִזְמוֹר שִׁיר יְסוּדָתוֹ בְּהַרְרֵי קֹדֶשׁ:
ב: אֹהֵב יְהוָה שַׁעֲרֵי צִיּוֹן מִכֹּל מִשְׁכְּנוֹת יַעֲקֹב:
ג: נִכְבָּדוֹת מְדֻבָּר בָּךְ עִיר הָאֱלֹהִים סֶלָה:
ד: אַזְכִּיר רַהַב וּבָבֶל לְיֹדְעָי הִנֵּה פְלֶשֶׁת וְצֹר עִם כּוּשׁ זֶה יֻלַּד שָׁם:
ה: וּלְצִיּוֹן יֵאָמַר אִישׁ וְאִישׁ יֻלַּד בָּהּ וְהוּא יְכוֹנְנֶהָ עֶלְיוֹן:
ו: יְהוָה יִסְפֹּר בִּכְתוֹב עַמִּים זֶה יֻלַּד שָׁם סֶלָה:
ז: וְשָׁרִים כְּחֹלְלִים כָּל מַעְיָנַי בָּךְ:

פרק פח

א: שִׁיר מִזְמוֹר לִבְנֵי קֹרַח לַמְנַצֵּחַ עַל מָחֲלַת לְעַנּוֹת מַשְׂכִּיל לְהֵימָן הָאֶזְרָחִי:
ב: יְהוָה אֱלֹהֵי יְשׁוּעָתִי יוֹם צָעַקְתִּי בַלַּיְלָה נֶגְדֶּךָ:
ג: תָּבוֹא לְפָנֶיךָ תְּפִלָּתִי הַטֵּה אָזְנְךָ לְרִנָּתִי:
ד: כִּי שָׂבְעָה בְרָעוֹת נַפְשִׁי וְחַיַּי לִשְׁאוֹל הִגִּיעוּ:
ה: נֶחְשַׁבְתִּי עִם יוֹרְדֵי בוֹר הָיִיתִי כְּגֶבֶר אֵין אֱיָל:
ו: בַּמֵּתִים חָפְשִׁי כְּמוֹ חֲלָלִים שֹׁכְבֵי קֶבֶר אֲשֶׁר לֹא זְכַרְתָּם עוֹד וְהֵמָּה מִיָּדְךָ נִגְזָרוּ:
ז: שַׁתַּנִי בְּבוֹר תַּחְתִּיּוֹת בְּמַחֲשַׁכִּים בִּמְצֹלוֹת:
ח: עָלַי סָמְכָה חֲמָתֶךָ וְכָל מִשְׁבָּרֶיךָ עִנִּיתָ סֶּלָה:
ט: הִרְחַקְתָּ מְיֻדָּעַי מִמֶּנִּי שַׁתַּנִי תוֹעֵבוֹת לָמוֹ כָּלֻא וְלֹא אֵצֵא:
י: עֵינִי דָאֲבָה מִנִּי עֹנִי קְרָאתִיךָ יְהוָה בְּכָל יוֹם שִׁטַּחְתִּי אֵלֶיךָ כַפָּי:
יא: הֲלַמֵּתִים תַּעֲשֶׂה פֶּלֶא אִם רְפָאִים יָקוּמוּ יוֹדוּךָ סֶּלָה:
יב: הַיְסֻפַּר בַּקֶּבֶר חַסְדֶּךָ אֱמוּנָתְךָ בָּאֲבַדּוֹן:
יג: הֲיִוָּדַע בַּחֹשֶׁךְ פִּלְאֶךָ וְצִדְקָתְךָ בְּאֶרֶץ נְשִׁיָּה:
יד: וַאֲנִי אֵלֶיךָ יְהוָה שִׁוַּעְתִּי וּבַבֹּקֶר תְּפִלָּתִי תְקַדְּמֶךָּ:
טו: לָמָה יְהוָה תִּזְנַח נַפְשִׁי תַּסְתִּיר פָּנֶיךָ מִמֶּנִּי:
טז: עָנִי אֲנִי וְגֹוֵעַ מִנֹּעַר נָשָׂאתִי אֵמֶיךָ אָפוּנָה:
יז: עָלַי עָבְרוּ חֲרוֹנֶיךָ בִּעוּתֶיךָ צִמְּתוּתֻנִי:
יח: סַבּוּנִי כַמַּיִם כָּל הַיּוֹם הִקִּיפוּ עָלַי יָחַד:
יט: הִרְחַקְתָּ מִמֶּנִּי אֹהֵב וָרֵעַ מְיֻדָּעַי מַחְשָׁךְ:

פרק פט

א: מַשְׂכִּיל לְאֵיתָן הָאֶזְרָחִי:
ב: חַסְדֵי יְהוָה עוֹלָם אָשִׁירָה לְדֹר וָדֹר אוֹדִיעַ אֱמוּנָתְךָ בְּפִי:
ג: כִּי אָמַרְתִּי עוֹלָם חֶסֶד יִבָּנֶה שָׁמַיִם תָּכִן אֱמוּנָתְךָ בָהֶם:
ד: כָּרַתִּי בְרִית לִבְחִירִי נִשְׁבַּעְתִּי לְדָוִד עַבְדִּי:
ה: עַד עוֹלָם אָכִין זַרְעֶךָ וּבָנִיתִי לְדֹר וָדוֹר כִּסְאֲךָ סֶלָה:
ו: וְיוֹדוּ שָׁמַיִם פִּלְאֲךָ יְהוָה אַף אֱמוּנָתְךָ בִּקְהַל קְדֹשִׁים:
ז: כִּי מִי בַשַּׁחַק יַעֲרֹךְ לַיהוָה יִדְמֶה לַיהוָה בִּבְנֵי אֵלִים:
ח: אֵל נַעֲרָץ בְּסוֹד קְדֹשִׁים רַבָּה וְנוֹרָא עַל כָּל סְבִיבָיו:
ט: יְהוָה אֱלֹהֵי צְבָאוֹת מִי כָמוֹךָ חֲסִין יָהּ וֶאֱמוּנָתְךָ סְבִיבוֹתֶיךָ:

י: אַתָּה מוֹשֵׁל בְּגֵאוּת הַיָּם בְּשׂוֹא גַלָּיו אַתָּה תְשַׁבְּחֵם:

יא: אַתָּה דִכִּאתָ כֶחָלָל רָהַב בִּזְרוֹעַ עֻזְּךָ פִּזַּרְתָּ אוֹיְבֶיךָ:

יב: לְךָ שָׁמַיִם אַף לְךָ אָרֶץ תֵּבֵל וּמְלֹאָהּ אַתָּה יְסַדְתָּם:

יג: צָפוֹן וְיָמִין אַתָּה בְרָאתָם תָּבוֹר וְחֶרְמוֹן בְּשִׁמְךָ יְרַנֵּנוּ:

יד: לְךָ זְרוֹעַ עִם גְּבוּרָה תָּעֹז יָדְךָ תָּרוּם יְמִינֶךָ:

טו: צֶדֶק וּמִשְׁפָּט מְכוֹן כִּסְאֶךָ חֶסֶד וֶאֱמֶת יְקַדְּמוּ פָנֶיךָ:

טז: אַשְׁרֵי הָעָם יֹדְעֵי תְרוּעָה יְהוָה בְּאוֹר פָּנֶיךָ יְהַלֵּכוּן:

יז: בְּשִׁמְךָ יְגִילוּן כָּל הַיּוֹם וּבְצִדְקָתְךָ יָרוּמוּ:

יח: כִּי תִפְאֶרֶת עֻזָּמוֹ אָתָּה וּבִרְצוֹנְךָ {תָּרוּם תרים} קַרְנֵנוּ:

יט: כִּי לַיהוָה מָגִנֵּנוּ וְלִקְדוֹשׁ יִשְׂרָאֵל מַלְכֵּנוּ:

כ: אָז דִּבַּרְתָּ בְחָזוֹן לַחֲסִידֶיךָ וַתֹּאמֶר שִׁוִּיתִי עֵזֶר עַל גִּבּוֹר הֲרִימוֹתִי בָחוּר מֵעָם:

כא: מָצָאתִי דָּוִד עַבְדִּי בְּשֶׁמֶן קָדְשִׁי מְשַׁחְתִּיו:

כב: אֲשֶׁר יָדִי תִּכּוֹן עִמּוֹ אַף זְרוֹעִי תְאַמְּצֶנּוּ:

כג: לֹא יַשִּׁא אוֹיֵב בּוֹ וּבֶן עַוְלָה לֹא יְעַנֶּנּוּ:

כד: וְכַתּוֹתִי מִפָּנָיו צָרָיו וּמְשַׂנְאָיו אֶגּוֹף:

כה: וֶאֱמוּנָתִי וְחַסְדִּי עִמּוֹ וּבִשְׁמִי תָּרוּם קַרְנוֹ:

כו: וְשַׂמְתִּי בַיָּם יָדוֹ וּבַנְּהָרוֹת יְמִינוֹ:

כז: הוּא יִקְרָאֵנִי אָבִי אָתָּה אֵלִי וְצוּר יְשׁוּעָתִי:

כח: אַף אָנִי בְּכוֹר אֶתְּנֵהוּ עֶלְיוֹן לְמַלְכֵי אָרֶץ:

כט: לְעוֹלָם אֶשְׁמָר לוֹ {אֶשְׁמָר לוֹ} חַסְדִּי וּבְרִיתִי נֶאֱמֶנֶת לוֹ:

ל: וְשַׂמְתִּי לָעַד זַרְעוֹ וְכִסְאוֹ כִּימֵי שָׁמָיִם:

לא: אִם יַעַזְבוּ בָנָיו תּוֹרָתִי וּבְמִשְׁפָּטַי לֹא יֵלֵכוּן:

לב: אִם חֻקֹּתַי יְחַלֵּלוּ וּמִצְוֹתַי לֹא יִשְׁמֹרוּ:

לג: וּפָקַדְתִּי בְשֵׁבֶט פִּשְׁעָם וּבִנְגָעִים עֲוֹנָם:

לד: וְחַסְדִּי לֹא אָפִיר מֵעִמּוֹ וְלֹא אֲשַׁקֵּר בֶּאֱמוּנָתִי:

לה: לֹא אֲחַלֵּל בְּרִיתִי וּמוֹצָא שְׂפָתַי לֹא אֲשַׁנֶּה:

לו: אַחַת נִשְׁבַּעְתִּי בְקָדְשִׁי אִם לְדָוִד אֲכַזֵּב:

לז: זַרְעוֹ לְעוֹלָם יִהְיֶה וְכִסְאוֹ כַשֶּׁמֶשׁ נֶגְדִּי:

לח: כְּיָרֵחַ יִכּוֹן עוֹלָם וְעֵד בַּשַּׁחַק נֶאֱמָן סֶלָה:

לט: וְאַתָּה זָנַחְתָּ וַתִּמְאָס הִתְעַבַּרְתָּ עִם מְשִׁיחֶךָ:

מ: נֵאַרְתָּה בְּרִית עַבְדֶּךָ חִלַּלְתָּ לָאָרֶץ נִזְרוֹ:

מא: פָּרַצְתָּ כָל גְּדֵרֹתָיו שַׂמְתָּ מִבְצָרָיו מְחִתָּה:

מב: שַׁסֻּהוּ כָּל עֹבְרֵי דָרֶךְ הָיָה חֶרְפָּה לִשְׁכֵנָיו:

מג: הֲרִימוֹתָ יְמִין צָרָיו הִשְׂמַחְתָּ כָּל אוֹיְבָיו:

מד: אַף תָּשִׁיב צוּר חַרְבּוֹ וְלֹא הֲקֵמֹתוֹ בַּמִּלְחָמָה:

מה: הִשְׁבַּתָּ מִטְּהָרוֹ וְכִסְאוֹ לָאָרֶץ מִגַּרְתָּה:

מו: הִקְצַרְתָּ יְמֵי עֲלוּמָיו הֶעֱטִיתָ עָלָיו בּוּשָׁה סֶלָה:

מז: עַד מָה יְהוָה תִּסָּתֵר לָנֶצַח תִּבְעַר כְּמוֹ אֵשׁ חֲמָתֶךָ:

מח: זְכָר אֲנִי מֶה חָלֶד עַל מַה שָּׁוְא בָּרָאתָ כָל בְּנֵי אָדָם:

מט: מִי גֶבֶר יִחְיֶה וְלֹא יִרְאֶה מָּוֶת יְמַלֵּט נַפְשׁוֹ מִיַּד שְׁאוֹל סֶלָה:

נ: אַיֵּה חֲסָדֶיךָ הָרִאשֹׁנִים אֲדֹנָי נִשְׁבַּעְתָּ לְדָוִד בֶּאֱמוּנָתֶךָ:

נא: זְכֹר אֲדֹנָי חֶרְפַּת עֲבָדֶיךָ שְׂאֵתִי בְחֵיקִי כָּל רַבִּים עַמִּים:

נב: אֲשֶׁר חֵרְפוּ אוֹיְבֶיךָ יְהוָה אֲשֶׁר חֵרְפוּ עִקְּבוֹת מְשִׁיחֶךָ:

נג: בָּרוּךְ יְהוָה לְעוֹלָם אָמֵן וְאָמֵן:

פרק צ

א: תְּפִלָּה לְמֹשֶׁה אִישׁ הָאֱלֹהִים אֲדֹנָי מָעוֹן אַתָּה הָיִיתָ לָּנוּ בְּדֹר וָדֹר:

ספר תהילים

ב: בְּטֶרֶם הָרִים יֻלָּדוּ וַתְּחוֹלֵל אֶרֶץ וְתֵבֵל וּמֵעוֹלָם עַד עוֹלָם אַתָּה אֵל:

ג: תָּשֵׁב אֱנוֹשׁ עַד דַּכָּא וַתֹּאמֶר שׁוּבוּ בְנֵי אָדָם:

ד: כִּי אֶלֶף שָׁנִים בְּעֵינֶיךָ כְּיוֹם אֶתְמוֹל כִּי יַעֲבֹר וְאַשְׁמוּרָה בַלָּיְלָה:

ה: זְרַמְתָּם שֵׁנָה יִהְיוּ בַּבֹּקֶר כֶּחָצִיר יַחֲלֹף:

ו: בַּבֹּקֶר יָצִיץ וְחָלָף לָעֶרֶב יְמוֹלֵל וְיָבֵשׁ:

ז: כִּי כָלִינוּ בְאַפֶּךָ וּבַחֲמָתְךָ נִבְהָלְנוּ:

ח: שַׁתָּ עֲוֹנֹתֵינוּ לְנֶגְדֶּךָ עֲלֻמֵנוּ לִמְאוֹר פָּנֶיךָ:

ט: כִּי כָל יָמֵינוּ פָּנוּ בְעֶבְרָתֶךָ כִּלִּינוּ שָׁנֵינוּ כְמוֹ הֶגֶה:

י: יְמֵי שְׁנוֹתֵינוּ בָהֶם שִׁבְעִים שָׁנָה וְאִם בִּגְבוּרֹת שְׁמוֹנִים שָׁנָה וְרָהְבָּם עָמָל וָאָוֶן כִּי גָז חִישׁ וַנָּעֻפָה:

יא: מִי יוֹדֵעַ עֹז אַפֶּךָ וּכְיִרְאָתְךָ עֶבְרָתֶךָ:

יב: לִמְנוֹת יָמֵינוּ כֵּן הוֹדַע וְנָבִיא לְבַב חָכְמָה:

יג: שׁוּבָה יְהוָה עַד מָתָי וְהִנָּחֵם עַל עֲבָדֶיךָ:

יד: שַׂבְּעֵנוּ בַבֹּקֶר חַסְדֶּךָ וּנְרַנְּנָה וְנִשְׂמְחָה בְּכָל יָמֵינוּ:

טו: שַׂמְּחֵנוּ כִּימוֹת עִנִּיתָנוּ שְׁנוֹת רָאִינוּ רָעָה:

טז: יֵרָאֶה אֶל עֲבָדֶיךָ פָעֳלֶךָ וַהֲדָרְךָ עַל בְּנֵיהֶם:

יז: וִיהִי נֹעַם אֲדֹנָי אֱלֹהֵינוּ עָלֵינוּ וּמַעֲשֵׂה יָדֵינוּ כּוֹנְנָה עָלֵינוּ וּמַעֲשֵׂה יָדֵינוּ כּוֹנְנֵהוּ:

פרק צא

א: יֹשֵׁב בְּסֵתֶר עֶלְיוֹן בְּצֵל שַׁדַּי יִתְלוֹנָן:

ב: אֹמַר לַיהוָה מַחְסִי וּמְצוּדָתִי אֱלֹהַי אֶבְטַח בּוֹ:

ג: כִּי הוּא יַצִּילְךָ מִפַּח יָקוּשׁ מִדֶּבֶר הַוּוֹת:

ד: בְּאֶבְרָתוֹ יָסֶךְ לָךְ וְתַחַת כְּנָפָיו תֶּחְסֶה צִנָּה וְסֹחֵרָה אֲמִתּוֹ:

ה: לֹא תִירָא מִפַּחַד לָיְלָה מֵחֵץ יָעוּף יוֹמָם:

ו: מִדֶּבֶר בָּאֹפֶל יַהֲלֹךְ מִקֶּטֶב יָשׁוּד צָהֳרָיִם:

ז: יִפֹּל מִצִּדְּךָ אֶלֶף וּרְבָבָה מִימִינֶךָ אֵלֶיךָ לֹא יִגָּשׁ:

ח: רַק בְּעֵינֶיךָ תַבִּיט וְשִׁלֻּמַת רְשָׁעִים תִּרְאֶה:

ט: כִּי אַתָּה יְהוָה מַחְסִי עֶלְיוֹן שַׂמְתָּ מְעוֹנֶךָ:

י: לֹא תְאֻנֶּה אֵלֶיךָ רָעָה וְנֶגַע לֹא יִקְרַב בְּאָהֳלֶךָ:

יא: כִּי מַלְאָכָיו יְצַוֶּה לָּךְ לִשְׁמָרְךָ בְּכָל דְּרָכֶיךָ:

יב: עַל כַּפַּיִם יִשָּׂאוּנְךָ פֶּן תִּגֹּף בָּאֶבֶן רַגְלֶךָ:

יג: עַל שַׁחַל וָפֶתֶן תִּדְרֹךְ תִּרְמֹס כְּפִיר וְתַנִּין:

יד: כִּי בִי חָשַׁק וַאֲפַלְּטֵהוּ אֲשַׂגְּבֵהוּ כִּי יָדַע שְׁמִי:

טו: יִקְרָאֵנִי וְאֶעֱנֵהוּ עִמּוֹ אָנֹכִי בְצָרָה אֲחַלְּצֵהוּ וַאֲכַבְּדֵהוּ:

טז: אֹרֶךְ יָמִים אַשְׂבִּיעֵהוּ וְאַרְאֵהוּ בִּישׁוּעָתִי:

פרק צב

א: מִזְמוֹר שִׁיר לְיוֹם הַשַּׁבָּת:

ב: טוֹב לְהֹדוֹת לַיהוָה וּלְזַמֵּר לְשִׁמְךָ עֶלְיוֹן:

ג: לְהַגִּיד בַּבֹּקֶר חַסְדֶּךָ וֶאֱמוּנָתְךָ בַּלֵּילוֹת:

ד: עֲלֵי עָשׂוֹר וַעֲלֵי נָבֶל עֲלֵי הִגָּיוֹן בְּכִנּוֹר:

ה: כִּי שִׂמַּחְתַּנִי יְהוָה בְּפָעֳלֶךָ בְּמַעֲשֵׂי יָדֶיךָ אֲרַנֵּן:

ו: מַה גָּדְלוּ מַעֲשֶׂיךָ יְהוָה מְאֹד עָמְקוּ מַחְשְׁבֹתֶיךָ:

ז: אִישׁ בַּעַר לֹא יֵדָע וּכְסִיל לֹא יָבִין אֶת זֹאת:

ח: בִּפְרֹחַ רְשָׁעִים כְּמוֹ עֵשֶׂב וַיָּצִיצוּ כָּל פֹּעֲלֵי אָוֶן לְהִשָּׁמְדָם עֲדֵי עַד:

ט: וְאַתָּה מָרוֹם לְעֹלָם יְהוָה:

י: כִּי הִנֵּה אֹיְבֶיךָ יְהוָה כִּי הִנֵּה אֹיְבֶיךָ יֹאבֵדוּ יִתְפָּרְדוּ כָּל פֹּעֲלֵי אָוֶן:

יא: וַתָּרֶם כִּרְאֵים קַרְנִי בַּלֹּתִי בְּשֶׁמֶן רַעֲנָן:

יב: וַתַּבֵּט עֵינִי בְּשׁוּרָי בַּקָּמִים עָלַי מְרֵעִים תִּשְׁמַעְנָה אָזְנָי:

יג: צַדִּיק כַּתָּמָר יִפְרָח כְּאֶרֶז בַּלְּבָנוֹן יִשְׂגֶּה:

יד: שְׁתוּלִים בְּבֵית יְהוָה בְּחַצְרוֹת אֱלֹהֵינוּ יַפְרִיחוּ:

טו: עוֹד יְנוּבוּן בְּשֵׂיבָה דְּשֵׁנִים וְרַעֲנַנִּים יִהְיוּ:

טז: לְהַגִּיד כִּי יָשָׁר יְהוָה צוּרִי וְלֹא עֹלָתָה {עַוְלָתָה} בּוֹ:

פרק צג

א: יְהוָה מָלָךְ גֵּאוּת לָבֵשׁ לָבֵשׁ יְהוָה עֹז הִתְאַזָּר אַף תִּכּוֹן תֵּבֵל בַּל תִּמּוֹט:

ב: נָכוֹן כִּסְאֲךָ מֵאָז מֵעוֹלָם אָתָּה:

ג: נָשְׂאוּ נְהָרוֹת יְהוָה נָשְׂאוּ נְהָרוֹת קוֹלָם יִשְׂאוּ נְהָרוֹת דָּכְיָם:

ד: מִקֹּלוֹת מַיִם רַבִּים אַדִּירִים מִשְׁבְּרֵי יָם אַדִּיר בַּמָּרוֹם יְהוָה:

ה: עֵדֹתֶיךָ נֶאֶמְנוּ מְאֹד לְבֵיתְךָ נַאֲוָה קֹדֶשׁ יְהוָה לְאֹרֶךְ יָמִים:

פרק צד

א: אֵל נְקָמוֹת יְהוָה אֵל נְקָמוֹת הוֹפִיעַ:

ב: הִנָּשֵׂא שֹׁפֵט הָאָרֶץ הָשֵׁב גְּמוּל עַל גֵּאִים:

ג: עַד מָתַי רְשָׁעִים יְהוָה עַד מָתַי רְשָׁעִים יַעֲלֹזוּ:

ד: יַבִּיעוּ יְדַבְּרוּ עָתָק יִתְאַמְּרוּ כָּל פֹּעֲלֵי אָוֶן:

ה: עַמְּךָ יְהוָה יְדַכְּאוּ וְנַחֲלָתְךָ יְעַנּוּ:

ו: אַלְמָנָה וְגֵר יַהֲרֹגוּ וִיתוֹמִים יְרַצֵּחוּ:

ז: וַיֹּאמְרוּ לֹא יִרְאֶה יָּהּ וְלֹא יָבִין אֱלֹהֵי יַעֲקֹב:

ח: בִּינוּ בֹּעֲרִים בָּעָם וּכְסִילִים מָתַי תַּשְׂכִּילוּ:

ט: הֲנֹטַע אֹזֶן הֲלֹא יִשְׁמָע אִם יֹצֵר עַיִן הֲלֹא יַבִּיט:

י: הֲיֹסֵר גּוֹיִם הֲלֹא יוֹכִיחַ הַמְלַמֵּד אָדָם דָּעַת:

יא: יְהוָה יֹדֵעַ מַחְשְׁבוֹת אָדָם כִּי הֵמָּה הָבֶל:

יב: אַשְׁרֵי הַגֶּבֶר אֲשֶׁר תְּיַסְּרֶנּוּ יָּהּ וּמִתּוֹרָתְךָ תְלַמְּדֶנּוּ:

יג: לְהַשְׁקִיט לוֹ מִימֵי רָע עַד יִכָּרֶה לָרָשָׁע שָׁחַת:

יד: כִּי לֹא יִטֹּשׁ יְהוָה עַמּוֹ וְנַחֲלָתוֹ לֹא יַעֲזֹב:

טו: כִּי עַד צֶדֶק יָשׁוּב מִשְׁפָּט וְאַחֲרָיו כָּל יִשְׁרֵי לֵב:

טז: מִי יָקוּם לִי עִם מְרֵעִים מִי יִתְיַצֵּב לִי עִם פֹּעֲלֵי אָוֶן:

יז: לוּלֵי יְהוָה עֶזְרָתָה לִּי כִּמְעַט שָׁכְנָה דוּמָה נַפְשִׁי:

יח: אִם אָמַרְתִּי מָטָה רַגְלִי חַסְדְּךָ יְהוָה יִסְעָדֵנִי:

יט: בְּרֹב שַׂרְעַפַּי בְּקִרְבִּי תַּנְחוּמֶיךָ יְשַׁעַשְׁעוּ נַפְשִׁי:

כ: הַיְחָבְרְךָ כִּסֵּא הַוּוֹת יֹצֵר עָמָל עֲלֵי חֹק:

כא: יָגוֹדּוּ עַל נֶפֶשׁ צַדִּיק וְדָם נָקִי יַרְשִׁיעוּ:

כב: וַיְהִי יְהוָה לִי לְמִשְׂגָּב וֵאלֹהַי לְצוּר מַחְסִי:

כג: וַיָּשֶׁב עֲלֵיהֶם אֶת אוֹנָם וּבְרָעָתָם יַצְמִיתֵם יַצְמִיתֵם יְהוָה אֱלֹהֵינוּ:

פרק צה

א: לְכוּ נְרַנְּנָה לַיהוָה נָרִיעָה לְצוּר יִשְׁעֵנוּ:

ב: נְקַדְּמָה פָנָיו בְּתוֹדָה בִּזְמִרוֹת נָרִיעַ לוֹ:

ג: כִּי אֵל גָּדוֹל יְהוָה וּמֶלֶךְ גָּדוֹל עַל כָּל אֱלֹהִים:

ד: אֲשֶׁר בְּיָדוֹ מֶחְקְרֵי אָרֶץ וְתוֹעֲפֹת הָרִים לוֹ:

ה: אֲשֶׁר לוֹ הַיָּם וְהוּא עָשָׂהוּ וְיַבֶּשֶׁת יָדָיו יָצָרוּ:

ו: בֹּאוּ נִשְׁתַּחֲוֶה וְנִכְרָעָה נִבְרְכָה לִפְנֵי יְהוָה עֹשֵׂנוּ:

ז: כִּי הוּא אֱלֹהֵינוּ וַאֲנַחְנוּ עַם מַרְעִיתוֹ וְצֹאן יָדוֹ הַיּוֹם אִם בְּקֹלוֹ תִשְׁמָעוּ:

ח: אַל תַּקְשׁוּ לְבַבְכֶם כִּמְרִיבָה כְּיוֹם מַסָּה בַּמִּדְבָּר:

ט: אֲשֶׁר נִסּוּנִי אֲבוֹתֵיכֶם בְּחָנוּנִי גַּם רָאוּ פָעֳלִי:

י: אַרְבָּעִים שָׁנָה אָקוּט בְּדוֹר וָאֹמַר עַם תֹּעֵי לֵבָב הֵם וְהֵם לֹא יָדְעוּ דְרָכָי:

יא: אֲשֶׁר נִשְׁבַּעְתִּי בְאַפִּי אִם יְבֹאוּן אֶל מְנוּחָתִי:

פרק צו

א: שִׁירוּ לַיהֹוָה שִׁיר חָדָשׁ שִׁירוּ לַיהֹוָה כָּל הָאָרֶץ:

ב: שִׁירוּ לַיהֹוָה בָּרְכוּ שְׁמוֹ בַּשְּׂרוּ מִיּוֹם לְיוֹם יְשׁוּעָתוֹ:

ג: סַפְּרוּ בַגּוֹיִם כְּבוֹדוֹ בְּכָל הָעַמִּים נִפְלְאוֹתָיו:

ד: כִּי גָדוֹל יְהֹוָה וּמְהֻלָּל מְאֹד נוֹרָא הוּא עַל כָּל אֱלֹהִים:

ה: כִּי כָּל אֱלֹהֵי הָעַמִּים אֱלִילִים וַיהֹוָה שָׁמַיִם עָשָׂה:

ו: הוֹד וְהָדָר לְפָנָיו עֹז וְתִפְאֶרֶת בְּמִקְדָּשׁוֹ:

ז: הָבוּ לַיהֹוָה מִשְׁפְּחוֹת עַמִּים הָבוּ לַיהֹוָה כָּבוֹד וָעֹז:

ח: הָבוּ לַיהֹוָה כְּבוֹד שְׁמוֹ שְׂאוּ מִנְחָה וּבֹאוּ לְחַצְרוֹתָיו:

ט: הִשְׁתַּחֲווּ לַיהֹוָה בְּהַדְרַת קֹדֶשׁ חִילוּ מִפָּנָיו כָּל הָאָרֶץ:

י: אִמְרוּ בַגּוֹיִם יְהֹוָה מָלָךְ אַף תִּכּוֹן תֵּבֵל בַּל תִּמּוֹט יָדִין עַמִּים בְּמֵישָׁרִים:

יא: יִשְׂמְחוּ הַשָּׁמַיִם וְתָגֵל הָאָרֶץ יִרְעַם הַיָּם וּמְלֹאוֹ:

יב: יַעֲלֹז שָׂדַי וְכָל אֲשֶׁר בּוֹ אָז יְרַנְּנוּ כָּל עֲצֵי יָעַר:

יג: לִפְנֵי יְהֹוָה כִּי בָא כִּי בָא לִשְׁפֹּט הָאָרֶץ יִשְׁפֹּט תֵּבֵל בְּצֶדֶק וְעַמִּים בֶּאֱמוּנָתוֹ:

פרק צז

א: יְהֹוָה מָלָךְ תָּגֵל הָאָרֶץ יִשְׂמְחוּ אִיִּים רַבִּים:

ב: עָנָן וַעֲרָפֶל סְבִיבָיו צֶדֶק וּמִשְׁפָּט מְכוֹן כִּסְאוֹ:

ג: אֵשׁ לְפָנָיו תֵּלֵךְ וּתְלַהֵט סָבִיב צָרָיו:

ד: הֵאִירוּ בְרָקָיו תֵּבֵל רָאֲתָה וַתָּחֵל הָאָרֶץ:

ה: הָרִים כַּדּוֹנַג נָמַסּוּ מִלִּפְנֵי יְהֹוָה מִלִּפְנֵי אֲדוֹן כָּל הָאָרֶץ:

ו: הִגִּידוּ הַשָּׁמַיִם צִדְקוֹ וְרָאוּ כָל הָעַמִּים כְּבוֹדוֹ:

ז: יֵבֹשׁוּ כָּל עֹבְדֵי פֶסֶל הַמִּתְהַלְלִים בָּאֱלִילִים הִשְׁתַּחֲווּ לוֹ כָּל אֱלֹהִים:

ח: שָׁמְעָה וַתִּשְׂמַח צִיּוֹן וַתָּגֵלְנָה בְּנוֹת יְהוּדָה לְמַעַן מִשְׁפָּטֶיךָ יְהֹוָה:

ט: כִּי אַתָּה יְהֹוָה עֶלְיוֹן עַל כָּל הָאָרֶץ מְאֹד נַעֲלֵיתָ עַל כָּל אֱלֹהִים:

י: אֹהֲבֵי יְהֹוָה שִׂנְאוּ רָע שֹׁמֵר נַפְשׁוֹת חֲסִידָיו מִיַּד רְשָׁעִים יַצִּילֵם:

יא: אוֹר זָרֻעַ לַצַּדִּיק וּלְיִשְׁרֵי לֵב שִׂמְחָה:

יב: שִׂמְחוּ צַדִּיקִים בַּיהֹוָה וְהוֹדוּ לְזֵכֶר קָדְשׁוֹ:

·

פרק צח

א: מִזְמוֹר שִׁירוּ לַיהֹוָה שִׁיר חָדָשׁ כִּי נִפְלָאוֹת עָשָׂה הוֹשִׁיעָה לּוֹ יְמִינוֹ וּזְרוֹעַ קָדְשׁוֹ:

ב: הוֹדִיעַ יְהֹוָה יְשׁוּעָתוֹ לְעֵינֵי הַגּוֹיִם גִּלָּה צִדְקָתוֹ:

ג: זָכַר חַסְדּוֹ וֶאֱמוּנָתוֹ לְבֵית יִשְׂרָאֵל רָאוּ כָל אַפְסֵי אָרֶץ אֵת יְשׁוּעַת אֱלֹהֵינוּ:

ד: הָרִיעוּ לַיהֹוָה כָּל הָאָרֶץ פִּצְחוּ וְרַנְּנוּ וְזַמֵּרוּ:

ה: זַמְּרוּ לַיהֹוָה בְּכִנּוֹר בְּכִנּוֹר וְקוֹל זִמְרָה:

ו: בַּחֲצֹצְרוֹת וְקוֹל שׁוֹפָר הָרִיעוּ לִפְנֵי הַמֶּלֶךְ יְהֹוָה:

ז: יִרְעַם הַיָּם וּמְלֹאוֹ תֵּבֵל וְיֹשְׁבֵי בָהּ:

ח: נְהָרוֹת יִמְחֲאוּ כָף יַחַד הָרִים יְרַנֵּנוּ:

ט: לִפְנֵי יְהֹוָה כִּי בָא לִשְׁפֹּט הָאָרֶץ יִשְׁפֹּט תֵּבֵל בְּצֶדֶק וְעַמִּים בְּמֵישָׁרִים:

פרק צט

א: יְהֹוָה מָלָךְ יִרְגְּזוּ עַמִּים יֹשֵׁב כְּרוּבִים תָּנוּט הָאָרֶץ:

ב: יְהוָה בְּצִיּוֹן גָּדוֹל וְרָם הוּא עַל כָּל הָעַמִּים:

ג: יוֹדוּ שִׁמְךָ גָּדוֹל וְנוֹרָא קָדוֹשׁ הוּא:

ד: וְעֹז מֶלֶךְ מִשְׁפָּט אָהֵב אַתָּה כּוֹנַנְתָּ מֵישָׁרִים מִשְׁפָּט וּצְדָקָה בְּיַעֲקֹב אַתָּה עָשִׂיתָ:

ה: רוֹמְמוּ יְהוָה אֱלֹהֵינוּ וְהִשְׁתַּחֲווּ לַהֲדֹם רַגְלָיו קָדוֹשׁ הוּא:

ו: מֹשֶׁה וְאַהֲרֹן בְּכֹהֲנָיו וּשְׁמוּאֵל בְּקֹרְאֵי שְׁמוֹ קֹרִאים אֶל יְהוָה וְהוּא יַעֲנֵם:

ז: בְּעַמּוּד עָנָן יְדַבֵּר אֲלֵיהֶם שָׁמְרוּ עֵדֹתָיו וְחֹק נָתַן לָמוֹ:

ח: יְהוָה אֱלֹהֵינוּ אַתָּה עֲנִיתָם אֵל נֹשֵׂא הָיִיתָ לָהֶם וְנֹקֵם עַל עֲלִילוֹתָם:

ט: רוֹמְמוּ יְהוָה אֱלֹהֵינוּ וְהִשְׁתַּחֲווּ לְהַר קָדְשׁוֹ כִּי קָדוֹשׁ יְהוָה אֱלֹהֵינוּ:

פרק ק

א: מִזְמוֹר לְתוֹדָה הָרִיעוּ לַיהוָה כָּל הָאָרֶץ:

ב: עִבְדוּ אֶת יְהוָה בְּשִׂמְחָה בֹּאוּ לְפָנָיו בִּרְנָנָה:

ג: דְּעוּ כִּי יְהוָה הוּא אֱלֹהִים הוּא עָשָׂנוּ וְלוֹ {וְלֹא} אֲנַחְנוּ עַמּוֹ וְצֹאן מַרְעִיתוֹ:

ד: בֹּאוּ שְׁעָרָיו בְּתוֹדָה חֲצֵרֹתָיו בִּתְהִלָּה הוֹדוּ לוֹ בָּרְכוּ שְׁמוֹ:

ה: כִּי טוֹב יְהוָה לְעוֹלָם חַסְדּוֹ וְעַד דֹּר וָדֹר אֱמוּנָתוֹ:

פרק קא

א: לְדָוִד מִזְמוֹר חֶסֶד וּמִשְׁפָּט אָשִׁירָה לְךָ יְהוָה אֲזַמֵּרָה:

ב: אַשְׂכִּילָה בְּדֶרֶךְ תָּמִים מָתַי תָּבוֹא אֵלָי אֶתְהַלֵּךְ בְּתָם לְבָבִי בְּקֶרֶב בֵּיתִי:

ג: לֹא אָשִׁית לְנֶגֶד עֵינַי דְּבַר בְּלִיָּעַל עֲשֹׂה סֵטִים שָׂנֵאתִי לֹא יִדְבַּק בִּי:

ד: לֵבָב עִקֵּשׁ יָסוּר מִמֶּנִּי רָע לֹא אֵדָע:

ה: מְלָשְׁנִי {מְלָשְׁנִי} בַסֵּתֶר רֵעֵהוּ אוֹתוֹ אַצְמִית גְּבַהּ עֵינַיִם וּרְחַב לֵבָב אֹתוֹ לֹא אוּכָל:

ו: עֵינַי בְּנֶאֶמְנֵי אֶרֶץ לָשֶׁבֶת עִמָּדִי הֹלֵךְ בְּדֶרֶךְ תָּמִים הוּא יְשָׁרְתֵנִי:

ז: לֹא יֵשֵׁב בְּקֶרֶב בֵּיתִי עֹשֵׂה רְמִיָּה דֹּבֵר שְׁקָרִים לֹא יִכּוֹן לְנֶגֶד עֵינָי:

ח: לַבְּקָרִים אַצְמִית כָּל רִשְׁעֵי אָרֶץ לְהַכְרִית מֵעִיר יְהוָה כָּל פֹּעֲלֵי אָוֶן:

פרק קב

א: תְּפִלָּה לְעָנִי כִי יַעֲטֹף וְלִפְנֵי יְהוָה יִשְׁפֹּךְ שִׂיחוֹ:

ב: יְהוָה שִׁמְעָה תְפִלָּתִי וְשַׁוְעָתִי אֵלֶיךָ תָבוֹא:

ג: אַל תַּסְתֵּר פָּנֶיךָ מִמֶּנִּי בְּיוֹם צַר לִי הַטֵּה אֵלַי אָזְנֶךָ בְּיוֹם אֶקְרָא מַהֵר עֲנֵנִי:

ד: כִּי כָלוּ בְעָשָׁן יָמָי וְעַצְמוֹתַי כְּמוֹקֵד נִחָרוּ:

ה: הוּכָּה כָעֵשֶׂב וַיִּבַשׁ לִבִּי כִּי שָׁכַחְתִּי מֵאֲכֹל לַחְמִי:

ו: מִקּוֹל אַנְחָתִי דָּבְקָה עַצְמִי לִבְשָׂרִי:

ז: דָּמִיתִי לִקְאַת מִדְבָּר הָיִיתִי כְּכוֹס חֳרָבוֹת:

ח: שָׁקַדְתִּי וָאֶהְיֶה כְּצִפּוֹר בּוֹדֵד עַל גָּג:

ט: כָּל הַיּוֹם חֵרְפוּנִי אוֹיְבָי מְהוֹלָלַי בִּי נִשְׁבָּעוּ:

י: כִּי אֵפֶר כַּלֶּחֶם אָכָלְתִּי וְשִׁקֻּוַי בִּבְכִי מָסָכְתִּי:

יא: מִפְּנֵי זַעַמְךָ וְקִצְפֶּךָ כִּי נְשָׂאתַנִי וַתַּשְׁלִיכֵנִי:

יב: יָמַי כְּצֵל נָטוּי וַאֲנִי כָּעֵשֶׂב אִיבָשׁ:

יג: וְאַתָּה יְהוָה לְעוֹלָם תֵּשֵׁב וְזִכְרְךָ לְדֹר וָדֹר:

יד: אַתָּה תָקוּם תְּרַחֵם צִיּוֹן כִּי עֵת לְחֶנְנָהּ כִּי בָא מוֹעֵד:

טו: כִּי רָצוּ עֲבָדֶיךָ אֶת אֲבָנֶיהָ וְאֶת עֲפָרָהּ יְחֹנֵנוּ:

טז: וְיִירְאוּ גוֹיִם אֶת שֵׁם יְהוָה וְכָל מַלְכֵי הָאָרֶץ אֶת כְּבוֹדֶךָ:

יז: כִּי בָנָה יְהוָה צִיּוֹן נִרְאָה בִּכְבוֹדוֹ:

יח: פָּנָה אֶל תְּפִלַּת הָעַרְעָר וְלֹא בָזָה אֶת תְּפִלָּתָם:

יט: תִּכָּתֶב זֹאת לְדוֹר אַחֲרוֹן וְעַם נִבְרָא יְהַלֶּל יָהּ:

כ: כִּי הִשְׁקִיף מִמְּרוֹם קָדְשׁוֹ יְהוָה מִשָּׁמַיִם אֶל אֶרֶץ הִבִּיט:

כא: לִשְׁמֹעַ אֶנְקַת אָסִיר לְפַתֵּחַ בְּנֵי תְמוּתָה:
כב: לְסַפֵּר בְּצִיּוֹן שֵׁם יְהוָה וּתְהִלָּתוֹ בִּירוּשָׁלָ͏ִם:
כג: בְּהִקָּבֵץ עַמִּים יַחְדָּו וּמַמְלָכוֹת לַעֲבֹד אֶת יְהוָה:
כד: עִנָּה בַדֶּרֶךְ כֹּחוֹ {כֹּחִי} קִצַּר יָמָי:
כה: אֹמַר אֵלִי אַל תַּעֲלֵנִי בַּחֲצִי יָמָי בְּדוֹר דּוֹרִים שְׁנוֹתֶיךָ:
כו: לְפָנִים הָאָרֶץ יָסַדְתָּ וּמַעֲשֵׂה יָדֶיךָ שָׁמָיִם:
כז: הֵמָּה יֹאבֵדוּ וְאַתָּה תַעֲמֹד וְכֻלָּם כַּבֶּגֶד יִבְלוּ כַּלְּבוּשׁ תַּחֲלִיפֵם וְיַחֲלֹפוּ:
כח: וְאַתָּה הוּא וּשְׁנוֹתֶיךָ לֹא יִתָּמּוּ:
כט: בְּנֵי עֲבָדֶיךָ יִשְׁכּוֹנוּ וְזַרְעָם לְפָנֶיךָ יִכּוֹן:

פרק קג

א: לְדָוִד בָּרְכִי נַפְשִׁי אֶת יְהוָה וְכָל קְרָבַי אֶת שֵׁם קָדְשׁוֹ:
ב: בָּרְכִי נַפְשִׁי אֶת יְהוָה וְאַל תִּשְׁכְּחִי כָּל גְּמוּלָיו:
ג: הַסֹּלֵחַ לְכָל עֲוֺנֵכִי הָרֹפֵא לְכָל תַּחֲלֻאָיְכִי:
ד: הַגּוֹאֵל מִשַּׁחַת חַיָּיְכִי הַמְעַטְּרֵכִי חֶסֶד וְרַחֲמִים:
ה: הַמַּשְׂבִּיעַ בַּטּוֹב עֶדְיֵךְ תִּתְחַדֵּשׁ כַּנֶּשֶׁר נְעוּרָיְכִי:
ו: עֹשֵׂה צְדָקוֹת יְהוָה וּמִשְׁפָּטִים לְכָל עֲשׁוּקִים:
ז: יוֹדִיעַ דְּרָכָיו לְמֹשֶׁה לִבְנֵי יִשְׂרָאֵל עֲלִילוֹתָיו:
ח: רַחוּם וְחַנּוּן יְהוָה אֶרֶךְ אַפַּיִם וְרַב חָסֶד:
ט: לֹא לָנֶצַח יָרִיב וְלֹא לְעוֹלָם יִטּוֹר:
י: לֹא כַחֲטָאֵינוּ עָשָׂה לָנוּ וְלֹא כַעֲוֺנֹתֵינוּ גָּמַל עָלֵינוּ:
יא: כִּי כִגְבֹהַּ שָׁמַיִם עַל הָאָרֶץ גָּבַר חַסְדּוֹ עַל יְרֵאָיו:
יב: כִּרְחֹק מִזְרָח מִמַּעֲרָב הִרְחִיק מִמֶּנּוּ אֶת פְּשָׁעֵינוּ:
יג: כְּרַחֵם אָב עַל בָּנִים רִחַם יְהוָה עַל יְרֵאָיו:
יד: כִּי הוּא יָדַע יִצְרֵנוּ זָכוּר כִּי עָפָר אֲנָחְנוּ:
טו: אֱנוֹשׁ כֶּחָצִיר יָמָיו כְּצִיץ הַשָּׂדֶה כֵּן יָצִיץ:
טז: כִּי רוּחַ עָבְרָה בּוֹ וְאֵינֶנּוּ וְלֹא יַכִּירֶנּוּ עוֹד מְקוֹמוֹ:
יז: וְחֶסֶד יְהוָה מֵעוֹלָם וְעַד עוֹלָם עַל יְרֵאָיו וְצִדְקָתוֹ לִבְנֵי בָנִים:
יח: לְשֹׁמְרֵי בְרִיתוֹ וּלְזֹכְרֵי פִקֻּדָיו לַעֲשׂוֹתָם:
יט: יְהוָה בַּשָּׁמַיִם הֵכִין כִּסְאוֹ וּמַלְכוּתוֹ בַּכֹּל מָשָׁלָה:
כ: בָּרְכוּ יְהוָה מַלְאָכָיו גִּבֹּרֵי כֹחַ עֹשֵׂי דְבָרוֹ לִשְׁמֹעַ בְּקוֹל דְּבָרוֹ:
כא: בָּרְכוּ יְהוָה כָּל צְבָאָיו מְשָׁרְתָיו עֹשֵׂי רְצוֹנוֹ:
כב: בָּרְכוּ יְהוָה כָּל מַעֲשָׂיו בְּכָל מְקֹמוֹת מֶמְשַׁלְתּוֹ בָּרְכִי נַפְשִׁי אֶת יְהוָה:

פרק קד

א: בָּרְכִי נַפְשִׁי אֶת יְהוָה יְהוָה אֱלֹהַי גָּדַלְתָּ מְּאֹד הוֹד וְהָדָר לָבָשְׁתָּ:
ב: עֹטֶה אוֹר כַּשַּׂלְמָה נוֹטֶה שָׁמַיִם כַּיְרִיעָה:
ג: הַמְקָרֶה בַמַּיִם עֲלִיּוֹתָיו הַשָּׂם עָבִים רְכוּבוֹ הַמְהַלֵּךְ עַל כַּנְפֵי רוּחַ:
ד: עֹשֶׂה מַלְאָכָיו רוּחוֹת מְשָׁרְתָיו אֵשׁ לֹהֵט:
ה: יָסַד אֶרֶץ עַל מְכוֹנֶיהָ בַּל תִּמּוֹט עוֹלָם וָעֶד:
ו: תְּהוֹם כַּלְּבוּשׁ כִּסִּיתוֹ עַל הָרִים יַעַמְדוּ מָיִם:
ז: מִן גַּעֲרָתְךָ יְנוּסוּן מִן קוֹל רַעַמְךָ יֵחָפֵזוּן:
ח: יַעֲלוּ הָרִים יֵרְדוּ בְקָעוֹת אֶל מְקוֹם זֶה יָסַדְתָּ לָהֶם:
ט: גְּבוּל שַׂמְתָּ בַּל יַעֲבֹרוּן בַּל יְשׁוּבוּן לְכַסּוֹת הָאָרֶץ:
י: הַמְשַׁלֵּחַ מַעְיָנִים בַּנְּחָלִים בֵּין הָרִים יְהַלֵּכוּן:
יא: יַשְׁקוּ כָּל חַיְתוֹ שָׂדָי יִשְׁבְּרוּ פְרָאִים צְמָאָם:
יב: עֲלֵיהֶם עוֹף הַשָּׁמַיִם יִשְׁכּוֹן מִבֵּין עֳפָאיִם יִתְּנוּ קוֹל:

יג: מַשְׁקֶה הָרִים מֵעֲלִיּוֹתָיו מִפְּרִי מַעֲשֶׂיךָ תִּשְׂבַּע הָאָרֶץ:

יד: מַצְמִיחַ חָצִיר לַבְּהֵמָה וְעֵשֶׂב לַעֲבֹדַת הָאָדָם לְהוֹצִיא לֶחֶם מִן הָאָרֶץ:

טו: וְיַיִן יְשַׂמַּח לְבַב אֱנוֹשׁ לְהַצְהִיל פָּנִים מִשָּׁמֶן וְלֶחֶם לְבַב אֱנוֹשׁ יִסְעָד:

טז: יִשְׂבְּעוּ עֲצֵי יְהוָה אַרְזֵי לְבָנוֹן אֲשֶׁר נָטָע:

יז: אֲשֶׁר שָׁם צִפֳּרִים יְקַנֵּנוּ חֲסִידָה בְּרוֹשִׁים בֵּיתָהּ:

יח: הָרִים הַגְּבֹהִים לַיְּעֵלִים סְלָעִים מַחְסֶה לַשְׁפַנִּים:

יט: עָשָׂה יָרֵחַ לְמוֹעֲדִים שֶׁמֶשׁ יָדַע מְבוֹאוֹ:

כ: תָּשֶׁת חֹשֶׁךְ וִיהִי לָיְלָה בּוֹ תִרְמֹשׂ כָּל חַיְתוֹ יָעַר:

כא: הַכְּפִירִים שֹׁאֲגִים לַטָּרֶף וּלְבַקֵּשׁ מֵאֵל אָכְלָם:

כב: תִּזְרַח הַשֶּׁמֶשׁ יֵאָסֵפוּן וְאֶל מְעוֹנֹתָם יִרְבָּצוּן:

כג: יֵצֵא אָדָם לְפָעֳלוֹ וְלַעֲבֹדָתוֹ עֲדֵי עָרֶב:

כד: מָה רַבּוּ מַעֲשֶׂיךָ יְהוָה כֻּלָּם בְּחָכְמָה עָשִׂיתָ מָלְאָה הָאָרֶץ קִנְיָנֶךָ:

כה: זֶה הַיָּם גָּדוֹל וּרְחַב יָדָיִם שָׁם רֶמֶשׂ וְאֵין מִסְפָּר חַיּוֹת קְטַנּוֹת עִם גְּדֹלוֹת:

כו: שָׁם אֳנִיּוֹת יְהַלֵּכוּן לִוְיָתָן זֶה יָצַרְתָּ לְשַׂחֶק בּוֹ:

כז: כֻּלָּם אֵלֶיךָ יְשַׂבֵּרוּן לָתֵת אָכְלָם בְּעִתּוֹ:

כח: תִּתֵּן לָהֶם יִלְקֹטוּן תִּפְתַּח יָדְךָ יִשְׂבְּעוּן טוֹב:

כט: תַּסְתִּיר פָּנֶיךָ יִבָּהֵלוּן תֹּסֵף רוּחָם יִגְוָעוּן וְאֶל עֲפָרָם יְשׁוּבוּן:

ל: תְּשַׁלַּח רוּחֲךָ יִבָּרֵאוּן וּתְחַדֵּשׁ פְּנֵי אֲדָמָה:

לא: יְהִי כְבוֹד יְהוָה לְעוֹלָם יִשְׂמַח יְהוָה בְּמַעֲשָׂיו:

לב: הַמַּבִּיט לָאָרֶץ וַתִּרְעָד יִגַּע בֶּהָרִים וְיֶעֱשָׁנוּ:

לג: אָשִׁירָה לַיהוָה בְּחַיָּי אֲזַמְּרָה לֵאלֹהַי בְּעוֹדִי:

לד: יֶעֱרַב עָלָיו שִׂיחִי אָנֹכִי אֶשְׂמַח בַּיהוָה:

לה: יִתַּמּוּ חַטָּאִים מִן הָאָרֶץ וּרְשָׁעִים עוֹד אֵינָם בָּרְכִי נַפְשִׁי אֶת יְהוָה הַלְלוּיָהּ:

פרק קה

א: הוֹדוּ לַיהוָה קִרְאוּ בִשְׁמוֹ הוֹדִיעוּ בָעַמִּים עֲלִילוֹתָיו:

ב: שִׁירוּ לוֹ זַמְּרוּ לוֹ שִׂיחוּ בְּכָל נִפְלְאוֹתָיו:

ג: הִתְהַלְלוּ בְּשֵׁם קָדְשׁוֹ יִשְׂמַח לֵב מְבַקְשֵׁי יְהוָה:

ד: דִּרְשׁוּ יְהוָה וְעֻזּוֹ בַּקְּשׁוּ פָנָיו תָּמִיד:

ה: זִכְרוּ נִפְלְאוֹתָיו אֲשֶׁר עָשָׂה מֹפְתָיו וּמִשְׁפְּטֵי פִיו:

ו: זֶרַע אַבְרָהָם עַבְדּוֹ בְּנֵי יַעֲקֹב בְּחִירָיו:

ז: הוּא יְהוָה אֱלֹהֵינוּ בְּכָל הָאָרֶץ מִשְׁפָּטָיו:

ח: זָכַר לְעוֹלָם בְּרִיתוֹ דָּבָר צִוָּה לְאֶלֶף דּוֹר:

ט: אֲשֶׁר כָּרַת אֶת אַבְרָהָם וּשְׁבוּעָתוֹ לְיִשְׂחָק:

י: וַיַּעֲמִידֶהָ לְיַעֲקֹב לְחֹק לְיִשְׂרָאֵל בְּרִית עוֹלָם:

יא: לֵאמֹר לְךָ אֶתֵּן אֶת אֶרֶץ כְּנָעַן חֶבֶל נַחֲלַתְכֶם:

יב: בִּהְיוֹתָם מְתֵי מִסְפָּר כִּמְעַט וְגָרִים בָּהּ:

יג: וַיִּתְהַלְּכוּ מִגּוֹי אֶל גּוֹי מִמַּמְלָכָה אֶל עַם אַחֵר:

יד: לֹא הִנִּיחַ אָדָם לְעָשְׁקָם וַיּוֹכַח עֲלֵיהֶם מְלָכִים:

טו: אַל תִּגְּעוּ בִמְשִׁיחָי וְלִנְבִיאַי אַל תָּרֵעוּ:

טז: וַיִּקְרָא רָעָב עַל הָאָרֶץ כָּל מַטֵּה לֶחֶם שָׁבָר:

יז: שָׁלַח לִפְנֵיהֶם אִישׁ לְעֶבֶד נִמְכַּר יוֹסֵף:

יח: עִנּוּ בַכֶּבֶל רַגְלָיו {רַגְלוֹ} בַּרְזֶל בָּאָה נַפְשׁוֹ:

יט: עַד עֵת בֹּא דְבָרוֹ אִמְרַת יְהוָה צְרָפָתְהוּ:

כ: שָׁלַח מֶלֶךְ וַיַּתִּירֵהוּ מֹשֵׁל עַמִּים וַיְפַתְּחֵהוּ:

כא: שָׂמוֹ אָדוֹן לְבֵיתוֹ וּמֹשֵׁל בְּכָל קִנְיָנוֹ:

כב: לֶאְסֹר שָׂרָיו בְּנַפְשׁוֹ וּזְקֵנָיו יְחַכֵּם:

ספר תהילים

כג. וַיָּבֹא יִשְׂרָאֵל מִצְרָיִם וְיַעֲקֹב גָּר בְּאֶרֶץ חָם:
כד. וַיֶּפֶר אֶת עַמּוֹ מְאֹד וַיַּעֲצִמֵהוּ מִצָּרָיו:
כה. הָפַךְ לִבָּם לִשְׂנֹא עַמּוֹ לְהִתְנַכֵּל בַּעֲבָדָיו:
כו. שָׁלַח מֹשֶׁה עַבְדּוֹ אַהֲרֹן אֲשֶׁר בָּחַר בּוֹ:
כז. שָׂמוּ בָם דִּבְרֵי אֹתוֹתָיו וּמֹפְתִים בְּאֶרֶץ חָם:
כח. שָׁלַח חֹשֶׁךְ וַיַּחְשִׁךְ וְלֹא מָרוּ אֶת דברי {דְּבָרוֹ}:
כט. הָפַךְ אֶת מֵימֵיהֶם לְדָם וַיָּמֶת אֶת דְּגָתָם:
ל. שָׁרַץ אַרְצָם צְפַרְדְּעִים בְּחַדְרֵי מַלְכֵיהֶם:
לא. אָמַר וַיָּבֹא עָרֹב כִּנִּים בְּכָל גְּבוּלָם:
לב. נָתַן גִּשְׁמֵיהֶם בָּרָד אֵשׁ לֶהָבוֹת בְּאַרְצָם:
לג. וַיַּךְ גַּפְנָם וּתְאֵנָתָם וַיְשַׁבֵּר עֵץ גְּבוּלָם:
לד. אָמַר וַיָּבֹא אַרְבֶּה וְיֶלֶק וְאֵין מִסְפָּר:
לה. וַיֹּאכַל כָּל עֵשֶׂב בְּאַרְצָם וַיֹּאכַל פְּרִי אַדְמָתָם:
לו. וַיַּךְ כָּל בְּכוֹר בְּאַרְצָם רֵאשִׁית לְכָל אוֹנָם:
לז. וַיּוֹצִיאֵם בְּכֶסֶף וְזָהָב וְאֵין בִּשְׁבָטָיו כּוֹשֵׁל:
לח. שָׂמַח מִצְרַיִם בְּצֵאתָם כִּי נָפַל פַּחְדָּם עֲלֵיהֶם:
לט. פָּרַשׂ עָנָן לְמָסָךְ וְאֵשׁ לְהָאִיר לָיְלָה:
מ. שָׁאַל וַיָּבֵא שְׂלָו וְלֶחֶם שָׁמַיִם יַשְׂבִּיעֵם:
מא. פָּתַח צוּר וַיָּזוּבוּ מָיִם הָלְכוּ בַּצִּיּוֹת נָהָר:
מב. כִּי זָכַר אֶת דְּבַר קָדְשׁוֹ אֶת אַבְרָהָם עַבְדּוֹ:
מג. וַיּוֹצִא עַמּוֹ בְשָׂשׂוֹן בְּרִנָּה אֶת בְּחִירָיו:
מד. וַיִּתֵּן לָהֶם אַרְצוֹת גּוֹיִם וַעֲמַל לְאֻמִּים יִירָשׁוּ:
מה. בַּעֲבוּר יִשְׁמְרוּ חֻקָּיו וְתוֹרֹתָיו יִנְצֹרוּ הַלְלוּ יָהּ:

פרק קו

א. הַלְלוּ יָהּ הוֹדוּ לַיהֹוָה כִּי טוֹב כִּי לְעוֹלָם חַסְדּוֹ:
ב. מִי יְמַלֵּל גְּבוּרוֹת יְהֹוָה יַשְׁמִיעַ כָּל תְּהִלָּתוֹ:
ג. אַשְׁרֵי שֹׁמְרֵי מִשְׁפָּט עֹשֵׂה צְדָקָה בְכָל עֵת:
ד. זָכְרֵנִי יְהֹוָה בִּרְצוֹן עַמֶּךָ פָּקְדֵנִי בִּישׁוּעָתֶךָ:
ה. לִרְאוֹת בְּטוֹבַת בְּחִירֶיךָ לִשְׂמֹחַ בְּשִׂמְחַת גּוֹיֶךָ לְהִתְהַלֵּל עִם נַחֲלָתֶךָ:
ו. חָטָאנוּ עִם אֲבוֹתֵינוּ הֶעֱוִינוּ הִרְשָׁעְנוּ:
ז. אֲבוֹתֵינוּ בְמִצְרַיִם לֹא הִשְׂכִּילוּ נִפְלְאוֹתֶיךָ לֹא זָכְרוּ אֶת רֹב חֲסָדֶיךָ וַיַּמְרוּ עַל יָם בְּיַם סוּף:
ח. וַיּוֹשִׁיעֵם לְמַעַן שְׁמוֹ לְהוֹדִיעַ אֶת גְּבוּרָתוֹ:
ט. וַיִּגְעַר בְּיַם סוּף וַיֶּחֱרָב וַיּוֹלִיכֵם בַּתְּהֹמוֹת כַּמִּדְבָּר:
י. וַיּוֹשִׁיעֵם מִיַּד שׂוֹנֵא וַיִּגְאָלֵם מִיַּד אוֹיֵב:
יא. וַיְכַסּוּ מַיִם צָרֵיהֶם אֶחָד מֵהֶם לֹא נוֹתָר:
יב. וַיַּאֲמִינוּ בִדְבָרָיו יָשִׁירוּ תְּהִלָּתוֹ:
יג. מִהֲרוּ שָׁכְחוּ מַעֲשָׂיו לֹא חִכּוּ לַעֲצָתוֹ:
יד. וַיִּתְאַוּוּ תַאֲוָה בַּמִּדְבָּר וַיְנַסּוּ אֵל בִּישִׁימוֹן:
טו. וַיִּתֵּן לָהֶם שֶׁאֱלָתָם וַיְשַׁלַּח רָזוֹן בְּנַפְשָׁם:
טז. וַיְקַנְאוּ לְמֹשֶׁה בַּמַּחֲנֶה לְאַהֲרֹן קְדוֹשׁ יְהֹוָה:
יז. תִּפְתַּח אֶרֶץ וַתִּבְלַע דָּתָן וַתְּכַס עַל עֲדַת אֲבִירָם:
יח. וַתִּבְעַר אֵשׁ בַּעֲדָתָם לֶהָבָה תְּלַהֵט רְשָׁעִים:
יט. יַעֲשׂוּ עֵגֶל בְּחֹרֵב וַיִּשְׁתַּחֲווּ לְמַסֵּכָה:
כ. וַיָּמִירוּ אֶת כְּבוֹדָם בְּתַבְנִית שׁוֹר אֹכֵל עֵשֶׂב:
כא. שָׁכְחוּ אֵל מוֹשִׁיעָם עֹשֶׂה גְדֹלוֹת בְּמִצְרָיִם:
כב. נִפְלָאוֹת בְּאֶרֶץ חָם נוֹרָאוֹת עַל יַם סוּף:

כג: וַיֹּאמֶר לְהַשְׁמִידָם לוּלֵי מֹשֶׁה בְחִירוֹ עָמַד בַּפֶּרֶץ לְפָנָיו לְהָשִׁיב חֲמָתוֹ מֵהַשְׁחִית:
כד: וַיִּמְאֲסוּ בְּאֶרֶץ חֶמְדָּה לֹא הֶאֱמִינוּ לִדְבָרוֹ:
כה: וַיֵּרָגְנוּ בְאָהֳלֵיהֶם לֹא שָׁמְעוּ בְּקוֹל יְהוָה:
כו: וַיִּשָּׂא יָדוֹ לָהֶם לְהַפִּיל אוֹתָם בַּמִּדְבָּר:
כז: וּלְהַפִּיל זַרְעָם בַּגּוֹיִם וּלְזָרוֹתָם בָּאֲרָצוֹת:
כח: וַיִּצָּמְדוּ לְבַעַל פְּעוֹר וַיֹּאכְלוּ זִבְחֵי מֵתִים:
כט: וַיַּכְעִיסוּ בְּמַעַלְלֵיהֶם וַתִּפְרָץ בָּם מַגֵּפָה:
ל: וַיַּעֲמֹד פִּינְחָס וַיְפַלֵּל וַתֵּעָצַר הַמַּגֵּפָה:
לא: וַתֵּחָשֶׁב לוֹ לִצְדָקָה לְדֹר וָדֹר עַד עוֹלָם:
לב: וַיַּקְצִיפוּ עַל מֵי מְרִיבָה וַיֵּרַע לְמֹשֶׁה בַּעֲבוּרָם:
לג: כִּי הִמְרוּ אֶת רוּחוֹ וַיְבַטֵּא בִּשְׂפָתָיו:
לד: לֹא הִשְׁמִידוּ אֶת הָעַמִּים אֲשֶׁר אָמַר יְהוָה לָהֶם:
לה: וַיִּתְעָרְבוּ בַגּוֹיִם וַיִּלְמְדוּ מַעֲשֵׂיהֶם:
לו: וַיַּעַבְדוּ אֶת עֲצַבֵּיהֶם וַיִּהְיוּ לָהֶם לְמוֹקֵשׁ:
לז: וַיִּזְבְּחוּ אֶת בְּנֵיהֶם וְאֶת בְּנוֹתֵיהֶם לַשֵּׁדִים:
לח: וַיִּשְׁפְּכוּ דָם נָקִי דַּם בְּנֵיהֶם וּבְנוֹתֵיהֶם אֲשֶׁר זִבְּחוּ לַעֲצַבֵּי כְנָעַן וַתֶּחֱנַף הָאָרֶץ בַּדָּמִים:
לט: וַיִּטְמְאוּ בְמַעֲשֵׂיהֶם וַיִּזְנוּ בְּמַעַלְלֵיהֶם:
מ: וַיִּחַר אַף יְהוָה בְּעַמּוֹ וַיְתָעֵב אֶת נַחֲלָתוֹ:
מא: וַיִּתְּנֵם בְּיַד גּוֹיִם וַיִּמְשְׁלוּ בָהֶם שֹׂנְאֵיהֶם:
מב: וַיִּלְחָצוּם אוֹיְבֵיהֶם וַיִּכָּנְעוּ תַּחַת יָדָם:
מג: פְּעָמִים רַבּוֹת יַצִּילֵם וְהֵמָּה יַמְרוּ בַעֲצָתָם וַיָּמֹכּוּ בַּעֲוֹנָם:
מד: וַיַּרְא בַּצַּר לָהֶם בְּשָׁמְעוֹ אֶת רִנָּתָם:
מה: וַיִּזְכֹּר לָהֶם בְּרִיתוֹ וַיִּנָּחֵם כְּרֹב חֲסָדָיו:
מו: וַיִּתֵּן אוֹתָם לְרַחֲמִים לִפְנֵי כָּל שׁוֹבֵיהֶם:
מז: הוֹשִׁיעֵנוּ יְהוָה אֱלֹהֵינוּ וְקַבְּצֵנוּ מִן הַגּוֹיִם לְהֹדוֹת לְשֵׁם קָדְשֶׁךָ לְהִשְׁתַּבֵּחַ בִּתְהִלָּתֶךָ:
מח: בָּרוּךְ יְהוָה אֱלֹהֵי יִשְׂרָאֵל מִן הָעוֹלָם וְעַד הָעוֹלָם וְאָמַר כָּל הָעָם אָמֵן הַלְלוּיָהּ:

פרק קז

א: הֹדוּ לַיהוָה כִּי טוֹב כִּי לְעוֹלָם חַסְדּוֹ:
ב: יֹאמְרוּ גְּאוּלֵי יְהוָה אֲשֶׁר גְּאָלָם מִיַּד צָר:
ג: וּמֵאֲרָצוֹת קִבְּצָם מִמִּזְרָח וּמִמַּעֲרָב מִצָּפוֹן וּמִיָּם:
ד: תָּעוּ בַמִּדְבָּר בִּישִׁימוֹן דָּרֶךְ עִיר מוֹשָׁב לֹא מָצָאוּ:
ה: רְעֵבִים גַּם צְמֵאִים נַפְשָׁם בָּהֶם תִּתְעַטָּף:
ו: וַיִּצְעֲקוּ אֶל יְהוָה בַּצַּר לָהֶם מִמְּצוּקוֹתֵיהֶם יַצִּילֵם:
ז: וַיַּדְרִיכֵם בְּדֶרֶךְ יְשָׁרָה לָלֶכֶת אֶל עִיר מוֹשָׁב:
ח: יוֹדוּ לַיהוָה חַסְדּוֹ וְנִפְלְאוֹתָיו לִבְנֵי אָדָם:
ט: כִּי הִשְׂבִּיעַ נֶפֶשׁ שֹׁקֵקָה וְנֶפֶשׁ רְעֵבָה מִלֵּא טוֹב:
י: יֹשְׁבֵי חֹשֶׁךְ וְצַלְמָוֶת אֲסִירֵי עֳנִי וּבַרְזֶל:
יא: כִּי הִמְרוּ אִמְרֵי אֵל וַעֲצַת עֶלְיוֹן נָאָצוּ:
יב: וַיַּכְנַע בֶּעָמָל לִבָּם כָּשְׁלוּ וְאֵין עֹזֵר:
יג: וַיִּזְעֲקוּ אֶל יְהוָה בַּצַּר לָהֶם מִמְּצֻקוֹתֵיהֶם יוֹשִׁיעֵם:
יד: יוֹצִיאֵם מֵחֹשֶׁךְ וְצַלְמָוֶת וּמוֹסְרוֹתֵיהֶם יְנַתֵּק:
טו: יוֹדוּ לַיהוָה חַסְדּוֹ וְנִפְלְאוֹתָיו לִבְנֵי אָדָם:
טז: כִּי שִׁבַּר דַּלְתוֹת נְחֹשֶׁת וּבְרִיחֵי בַרְזֶל גִּדֵּעַ:
יז: אֱוִלִים מִדֶּרֶךְ פִּשְׁעָם וּמֵעֲוֹנֹתֵיהֶם יִתְעַנּוּ:
יח: כָּל אֹכֶל תְּתַעֵב נַפְשָׁם וַיַּגִּיעוּ עַד שַׁעֲרֵי מָוֶת:
יט: וַיִּזְעֲקוּ אֶל יְהוָה בַּצַּר לָהֶם מִמְּצֻקוֹתֵיהֶם יוֹשִׁיעֵם:

כ: יִשְׁלַח דְּבָרוֹ וְיִרְפָּאֵם וִימַלֵּט מִשְּׁחִיתוֹתָם:
כא: יוֹדוּ לַיהוָה חַסְדּוֹ וְנִפְלְאוֹתָיו לִבְנֵי אָדָם:
כב: וְיִזְבְּחוּ זִבְחֵי תוֹדָה וִיסַפְּרוּ מַעֲשָׂיו בְּרִנָּה:
כג: יוֹרְדֵי הַיָּם בָּאֳנִיּוֹת עֹשֵׂי מְלָאכָה בְּמַיִם רַבִּים:
כד: הֵמָּה רָאוּ מַעֲשֵׂי יְהוָה וְנִפְלְאוֹתָיו בִּמְצוּלָה:
כה: וַיֹּאמֶר וַיַּעֲמֵד רוּחַ סְעָרָה וַתְּרוֹמֵם גַּלָּיו:
כו: יַעֲלוּ שָׁמַיִם יֵרְדוּ תְהוֹמוֹת נַפְשָׁם בְּרָעָה תִתְמוֹגָג:
כז: יָחוֹגּוּ וְיָנוּעוּ כַּשִּׁכּוֹר וְכָל חָכְמָתָם תִּתְבַּלָּע:
כח: וַיִּצְעֲקוּ אֶל יְהוָה בַּצַּר לָהֶם וּמִמְּצוּקֹתֵיהֶם יוֹצִיאֵם:
כט: יָקֵם סְעָרָה לִדְמָמָה וַיֶּחֱשׁוּ גַּלֵּיהֶם:
ל: וַיִּשְׂמְחוּ כִי יִשְׁתֹּקוּ וַיַּנְחֵם אֶל מְחוֹז חֶפְצָם:
לא: יוֹדוּ לַיהוָה חַסְדּוֹ וְנִפְלְאוֹתָיו לִבְנֵי אָדָם:
לב: וִירוֹמְמוּהוּ בִּקְהַל עָם וּבְמוֹשַׁב זְקֵנִים יְהַלְלוּהוּ:
לג: יָשֵׂם נְהָרוֹת לְמִדְבָּר וּמֹצָאֵי מַיִם לְצִמָּאוֹן:
לד: אֶרֶץ פְּרִי לִמְלֵחָה מֵרָעַת יֹשְׁבֵי בָהּ:
לה: יָשֵׂם מִדְבָּר לַאֲגַם מַיִם וְאֶרֶץ צִיָּה לְמֹצָאֵי מָיִם:
לו: וַיּוֹשֶׁב שָׁם רְעֵבִים וַיְכוֹנְנוּ עִיר מוֹשָׁב:
לז: וַיִּזְרְעוּ שָׂדוֹת וַיִּטְּעוּ כְרָמִים וַיַּעֲשׂוּ פְּרִי תְבוּאָה:
לח: וַיְבָרֲכֵם וַיִּרְבּוּ מְאֹד וּבְהֶמְתָּם לֹא יַמְעִיט:
לט: וַיִּמְעֲטוּ וַיָּשֹׁחוּ מֵעֹצֶר רָעָה וְיָגוֹן:
מ: שֹׁפֵךְ בּוּז עַל נְדִיבִים וַיַּתְעֵם בְּתֹהוּ לֹא דָרֶךְ:
מא: וַיְשַׂגֵּב אֶבְיוֹן מֵעוֹנִי וַיָּשֶׂם כַּצֹּאן מִשְׁפָּחוֹת:
מב: יִרְאוּ יְשָׁרִים וְיִשְׂמָחוּ וְכָל עַוְלָה קָפְצָה פִּיהָ:
מג: מִי חָכָם וְיִשְׁמָר אֵלֶּה וְיִתְבּוֹנְנוּ חַסְדֵי יְהוָה:

פרק קח

א: שִׁיר מִזְמוֹר לְדָוִד:
ב: נָכוֹן לִבִּי אֱלֹהִים אָשִׁירָה וַאֲזַמְּרָה אַף כְּבוֹדִי:
ג: עוּרָה הַנֵּבֶל וְכִנּוֹר אָעִירָה שָּׁחַר:
ד: אוֹדְךָ בָעַמִּים יְהוָה וַאֲזַמֶּרְךָ בַּלְאֻמִּים:
ה: כִּי גָדוֹל מֵעַל שָׁמַיִם חַסְדֶּךָ וְעַד שְׁחָקִים אֲמִתֶּךָ:
ו: רוּמָה עַל שָׁמַיִם אֱלֹהִים וְעַל כָּל הָאָרֶץ כְּבוֹדֶךָ:
ז: לְמַעַן יֵחָלְצוּן יְדִידֶיךָ הוֹשִׁיעָה יְמִינְךָ וַעֲנֵנִי:
ח: אֱלֹהִים דִּבֶּר בְּקָדְשׁוֹ אֶעְלֹזָה אֲחַלְּקָה שְׁכֶם וְעֵמֶק סֻכּוֹת אֲמַדֵּד:
ט: לִי גִלְעָד לִי מְנַשֶּׁה וְאֶפְרַיִם מָעוֹז רֹאשִׁי יְהוּדָה מְחֹקְקִי:
י: מוֹאָב סִיר רַחְצִי עַל אֱדוֹם אַשְׁלִיךְ נַעֲלִי עֲלֵי פְלֶשֶׁת אֶתְרוֹעָע:
יא: מִי יֹבִלֵנִי עִיר מִבְצָר מִי נָחַנִי עַד אֱדוֹם:
יב: הֲלֹא אֱלֹהִים זְנַחְתָּנוּ וְלֹא תֵצֵא אֱלֹהִים בְּצִבְאֹתֵינוּ:
יג: הָבָה לָּנוּ עֶזְרָת מִצָּר וְשָׁוְא תְּשׁוּעַת אָדָם:
יד: בֵּאלֹהִים נַעֲשֶׂה חָיִל וְהוּא יָבוּס צָרֵינוּ:

פרק קט

א: לַמְנַצֵּחַ לְדָוִד מִזְמוֹר אֱלֹהֵי תְהִלָּתִי אַל תֶּחֱרַשׁ:
ב: כִּי פִי רָשָׁע וּפִי מִרְמָה עָלַי פָּתָחוּ דִּבְּרוּ אִתִּי לְשׁוֹן שָׁקֶר:
ג: וְדִבְרֵי שִׂנְאָה סְבָבוּנִי וַיִּלָּחֲמוּנִי חִנָּם:
ד: תַּחַת אַהֲבָתִי יִשְׂטְנוּנִי וַאֲנִי תְפִלָּה:
ה: וַיָּשִׂימוּ עָלַי רָעָה תַּחַת טוֹבָה וְשִׂנְאָה תַּחַת אַהֲבָתִי:

ו: הַפְקֵד עָלָיו רָשָׁע וְשָׂטָן יַעֲמֹד עַל יְמִינוֹ:

ז: בְּהִשָּׁפְטוֹ יֵצֵא רָשָׁע וּתְפִלָּתוֹ תִּהְיֶה לַחֲטָאָה:

ח: יִהְיוּ יָמָיו מְעַטִּים פְּקֻדָּתוֹ יִקַּח אַחֵר:

ט: יִהְיוּ בָנָיו יְתוֹמִים וְאִשְׁתּוֹ אַלְמָנָה:

י: וְנוֹעַ יָנוּעוּ בָנָיו וְשִׁאֵלוּ וְדָרְשׁוּ מֵחָרְבוֹתֵיהֶם:

יא: יְנַקֵּשׁ נוֹשֶׁה לְכָל אֲשֶׁר לוֹ וְיָבֹזּוּ זָרִים יְגִיעוֹ:

יב: אַל יְהִי לוֹ מֹשֵׁךְ חָסֶד וְאַל יְהִי חוֹנֵן לִיתוֹמָיו:

יג: יְהִי אַחֲרִיתוֹ לְהַכְרִית בְּדוֹר אַחֵר יִמַּח שְׁמָם:

יד: יִזָּכֵר עֲוֹן אֲבֹתָיו אֶל יְהוָה וְחַטַּאת אִמּוֹ אַל תִּמָּח:

טו: יִהְיוּ נֶגֶד יְהוָה תָּמִיד וְיַכְרֵת מֵאֶרֶץ זִכְרָם:

טז: יַעַן אֲשֶׁר לֹא זָכַר עֲשׂוֹת חָסֶד וַיִּרְדֹּף אִישׁ עָנִי וְאֶבְיוֹן וְנִכְאֵה לֵבָב לְמוֹתֵת:

יז: וַיֶּאֱהַב קְלָלָה וַתְּבוֹאֵהוּ וְלֹא חָפֵץ בִּבְרָכָה וַתִּרְחַק מִמֶּנּוּ:

יח: וַיִּלְבַּשׁ קְלָלָה כְּמַדּוֹ וַתָּבֹא כַמַּיִם בְּקִרְבּוֹ וְכַשֶּׁמֶן בְּעַצְמוֹתָיו:

יט: תְּהִי לוֹ כְּבֶגֶד יַעְטֶה וּלְמֵזַח תָּמִיד יַחְגְּרֶהָ:

כ: זֹאת פְּעֻלַּת שֹׂטְנַי מֵאֵת יְהוָה וְהַדֹּבְרִים רָע עַל נַפְשִׁי:

כא: וְאַתָּה יְהוִה אֲדֹנָי עֲשֵׂה אִתִּי לְמַעַן שְׁמֶךָ כִּי טוֹב חַסְדְּךָ הַצִּילֵנִי:

כב: כִּי עָנִי וְאֶבְיוֹן אָנֹכִי וְלִבִּי חָלַל בְּקִרְבִּי:

כג: כְּצֵל כִּנְטוֹתוֹ נֶהֱלָכְתִּי נִנְעַרְתִּי כָּאַרְבֶּה:

כד: בִּרְכַּי כָּשְׁלוּ מִצּוֹם וּבְשָׂרִי כָּחַשׁ מִשָּׁמֶן:

כה: וַאֲנִי הָיִיתִי חֶרְפָּה לָהֶם יִרְאוּנִי יְנִיעוּן רֹאשָׁם:

כו: עָזְרֵנִי יְהוָה אֱלֹהָי הוֹשִׁיעֵנִי כְחַסְדֶּךָ:

כז: וְיֵדְעוּ כִּי יָדְךָ זֹּאת אַתָּה יְהוָה עֲשִׂיתָהּ:

כח: יְקַלְלוּ הֵמָּה וְאַתָּה תְבָרֵךְ קָמוּ וַיֵּבֹשׁוּ וְעַבְדְּךָ יִשְׂמָח:

כט: יִלְבְּשׁוּ שׂוֹטְנַי כְּלִמָּה וְיַעֲטוּ כַמְעִיל בָּשְׁתָּם:

ל: אוֹדֶה יְהוָה מְאֹד בְּפִי וּבְתוֹךְ רַבִּים אֲהַלְלֶנּוּ:

לא: כִּי יַעֲמֹד לִימִין אֶבְיוֹן לְהוֹשִׁיעַ מִשֹּׁפְטֵי נַפְשׁוֹ:

פרק קי

א: לְדָוִד מִזְמוֹר נְאֻם יְהוָה לַאדֹנִי שֵׁב לִימִינִי עַד אָשִׁית אֹיְבֶיךָ הֲדֹם לְרַגְלֶיךָ:

ב: מַטֵּה עֻזְּךָ יִשְׁלַח יְהוָה מִצִּיּוֹן רְדֵה בְּקֶרֶב אֹיְבֶיךָ:

ג: עַמְּךָ נְדָבֹת בְּיוֹם חֵילֶךָ בְּהַדְרֵי קֹדֶשׁ מֵרֶחֶם מִשְׁחָר לְךָ טַל יַלְדֻתֶיךָ:

ד: נִשְׁבַּע יְהוָה וְלֹא יִנָּחֵם אַתָּה כֹהֵן לְעוֹלָם עַל דִּבְרָתִי מַלְכִּי צֶדֶק:

ה: אֲדֹנָי עַל יְמִינְךָ מָחַץ בְּיוֹם אַפּוֹ מְלָכִים:

ו: יָדִין בַּגּוֹיִם מָלֵא גְוִיּוֹת מָחַץ רֹאשׁ עַל אֶרֶץ רַבָּה:

ז: מִנַּחַל בַּדֶּרֶךְ יִשְׁתֶּה עַל כֵּן יָרִים רֹאשׁ:

פרק קיא

א: הַלְלוּיָהּ אוֹדֶה יְהוָה בְּכָל לֵבָב בְּסוֹד יְשָׁרִים וְעֵדָה:

ב: גְּדֹלִים מַעֲשֵׂי יְהוָה דְּרוּשִׁים לְכָל חֶפְצֵיהֶם:

ג: הוֹד וְהָדָר פָּעֳלוֹ וְצִדְקָתוֹ עֹמֶדֶת לָעַד:

ד: זֵכֶר עָשָׂה לְנִפְלְאוֹתָיו חַנּוּן וְרַחוּם יְהוָה:

ה: טֶרֶף נָתַן לִירֵאָיו יִזְכֹּר לְעוֹלָם בְּרִיתוֹ:

ו: כֹּחַ מַעֲשָׂיו הִגִּיד לְעַמּוֹ לָתֵת לָהֶם נַחֲלַת גּוֹיִם:

ז: מַעֲשֵׂי יָדָיו אֱמֶת וּמִשְׁפָּט נֶאֱמָנִים כָּל פִּקּוּדָיו:

ח: סְמוּכִים לָעַד לְעוֹלָם עֲשׂוּיִם בֶּאֱמֶת וְיָשָׁר:

ט: פְּדוּת שָׁלַח לְעַמּוֹ צִוָּה לְעוֹלָם בְּרִיתוֹ קָדוֹשׁ וְנוֹרָא שְׁמוֹ:

י: רֵאשִׁית חָכְמָה יִרְאַת יְהוָה שֵׂכֶל טוֹב לְכָל עֹשֵׂיהֶם תְּהִלָּתוֹ עֹמֶדֶת לָעַד:

פרק קיב

א: הַלְלוּיָהּ אַשְׁרֵי אִישׁ יָרֵא אֶת יְהֹוָה בְּמִצְוֹתָיו חָפֵץ מְאֹד:
ב: גִּבּוֹר בָּאָרֶץ יִהְיֶה זַרְעוֹ דּוֹר יְשָׁרִים יְבֹרָךְ:
ג: הוֹן וָעֹשֶׁר בְּבֵיתוֹ וְצִדְקָתוֹ עֹמֶדֶת לָעַד:
ד: זָרַח בַּחֹשֶׁךְ אוֹר לַיְשָׁרִים חַנּוּן וְרַחוּם וְצַדִּיק:
ה: טוֹב אִישׁ חוֹנֵן וּמַלְוֶה יְכַלְכֵּל דְּבָרָיו בְּמִשְׁפָּט:
ו: כִּי לְעוֹלָם לֹא יִמּוֹט לְזֵכֶר עוֹלָם יִהְיֶה צַדִּיק:
ז: מִשְּׁמוּעָה רָעָה לֹא יִירָא נָכוֹן לִבּוֹ בָּטֻחַ בַּיהֹוָה:
ח: סָמוּךְ לִבּוֹ לֹא יִירָא עַד אֲשֶׁר יִרְאֶה בְצָרָיו:
ט: פִּזַּר נָתַן לָאֶבְיוֹנִים צִדְקָתוֹ עֹמֶדֶת לָעַד קַרְנוֹ תָּרוּם בְּכָבוֹד:
י: רָשָׁע יִרְאֶה וְכָעָס שִׁנָּיו יַחֲרֹק וְנָמָס תַּאֲוַת רְשָׁעִים תֹּאבֵד:

פרק קיג

א: הַלְלוּיָהּ הַלְלוּ עַבְדֵי יְהֹוָה הַלְלוּ אֶת שֵׁם יְהֹוָה:
ב: יְהִי שֵׁם יְהֹוָה מְבֹרָךְ מֵעַתָּה וְעַד עוֹלָם:
ג: מִמִּזְרַח שֶׁמֶשׁ עַד מְבוֹאוֹ מְהֻלָּל שֵׁם יְהֹוָה:
ד: רָם עַל כָּל גּוֹיִם יְהֹוָה עַל הַשָּׁמַיִם כְּבוֹדוֹ:
ה: מִי כַּיהֹוָה אֱלֹהֵינוּ הַמַּגְבִּיהִי לָשָׁבֶת:
ו: הַמַּשְׁפִּילִי לִרְאוֹת בַּשָּׁמַיִם וּבָאָרֶץ:
ז: מְקִימִי מֵעָפָר דָּל מֵאַשְׁפֹּת יָרִים אֶבְיוֹן:
ח: לְהוֹשִׁיבִי עִם נְדִיבִים עִם נְדִיבֵי עַמּוֹ:
ט: מוֹשִׁיבִי עֲקֶרֶת הַבַּיִת אֵם הַבָּנִים שְׂמֵחָה הַלְלוּיָהּ:

פרק קיד

א: בְּצֵאת יִשְׂרָאֵל מִמִּצְרָיִם בֵּית יַעֲקֹב מֵעַם לֹעֵז:
ב: הָיְתָה יְהוּדָה לְקָדְשׁוֹ יִשְׂרָאֵל מַמְשְׁלוֹתָיו:
ג: הַיָּם רָאָה וַיָּנֹס הַיַּרְדֵּן יִסֹּב לְאָחוֹר:
ד: הֶהָרִים רָקְדוּ כְאֵילִים גְּבָעוֹת כִּבְנֵי צֹאן:
ה: מַה לְּךָ הַיָּם כִּי תָנוּס הַיַּרְדֵּן תִּסֹּב לְאָחוֹר:
ו: הֶהָרִים תִּרְקְדוּ כְאֵילִים גְּבָעוֹת כִּבְנֵי צֹאן:
ז: מִלִּפְנֵי אָדוֹן חוּלִי אָרֶץ מִלִּפְנֵי אֱלוֹהַּ יַעֲקֹב:
ח: הַהֹפְכִי הַצּוּר אֲגַם מָיִם חַלָּמִישׁ לְמַעְיְנוֹ מָיִם:

פרק קטו

א: לֹא לָנוּ יְהֹוָה לֹא לָנוּ כִּי לְשִׁמְךָ תֵּן כָּבוֹד עַל חַסְדְּךָ עַל אֲמִתֶּךָ:
ב: לָמָּה יֹאמְרוּ הַגּוֹיִם אַיֵּה נָא אֱלֹהֵיהֶם:
ג: וֵאלֹהֵינוּ בַשָּׁמָיִם כֹּל אֲשֶׁר חָפֵץ עָשָׂה:
ד: עֲצַבֵּיהֶם כֶּסֶף וְזָהָב מַעֲשֵׂה יְדֵי אָדָם:
ה: פֶּה לָהֶם וְלֹא יְדַבֵּרוּ עֵינַיִם לָהֶם וְלֹא יִרְאוּ:
ו: אָזְנַיִם לָהֶם וְלֹא יִשְׁמָעוּ אַף לָהֶם וְלֹא יְרִיחוּן:
ז: יְדֵיהֶם וְלֹא יְמִישׁוּן רַגְלֵיהֶם וְלֹא יְהַלֵּכוּ לֹא יֶהְגּוּ בִּגְרוֹנָם:
ח: כְּמוֹהֶם יִהְיוּ עֹשֵׂיהֶם כֹּל אֲשֶׁר בֹּטֵחַ בָּהֶם:
ט: יִשְׂרָאֵל בְּטַח בַּיהֹוָה עֶזְרָם וּמָגִנָּם הוּא:
י: בֵּית אַהֲרֹן בִּטְחוּ בַיהֹוָה עֶזְרָם וּמָגִנָּם הוּא:
יא: יִרְאֵי יְהֹוָה בִּטְחוּ בַיהֹוָה עֶזְרָם וּמָגִנָּם הוּא:
יב: יְהֹוָה זְכָרָנוּ יְבָרֵךְ יְבָרֵךְ אֶת בֵּית יִשְׂרָאֵל יְבָרֵךְ אֶת בֵּית אַהֲרֹן:
יג: יְבָרֵךְ יִרְאֵי יְהֹוָה הַקְּטַנִּים עִם הַגְּדֹלִים:

יד: יֹסֵף יְהוָה עֲלֵיכֶם עֲלֵיכֶם וְעַל בְּנֵיכֶם:
טו: בְּרוּכִים אַתֶּם לַיהוָה עֹשֵׂה שָׁמַיִם וָאָרֶץ:
טז: הַשָּׁמַיִם שָׁמַיִם לַיהוָה וְהָאָרֶץ נָתַן לִבְנֵי אָדָם:
יז: לֹא הַמֵּתִים יְהַלְלוּ יָהּ וְלֹא כָּל יֹרְדֵי דוּמָה:
יח: וַאֲנַחְנוּ נְבָרֵךְ יָהּ מֵעַתָּה וְעַד עוֹלָם הַלְלוּ יָהּ:

פרק קטז

א: אָהַבְתִּי כִּי יִשְׁמַע יְהוָה אֶת קוֹלִי תַּחֲנוּנָי:
ב: כִּי הִטָּה אָזְנוֹ לִי וּבְיָמַי אֶקְרָא:
ג: אֲפָפוּנִי חֶבְלֵי מָוֶת וּמְצָרֵי שְׁאוֹל מְצָאוּנִי צָרָה וְיָגוֹן אֶמְצָא:
ד: וּבְשֵׁם יְהוָה אֶקְרָא אָנָּה יְהוָה מַלְּטָה נַפְשִׁי:
ה: חַנּוּן יְהוָה וְצַדִּיק וֵאלֹהֵינוּ מְרַחֵם:
ו: שֹׁמֵר פְּתָאיִם יְהוָה דַּלּוֹתִי וְלִי יְהוֹשִׁיעַ:
ז: שׁוּבִי נַפְשִׁי לִמְנוּחָיְכִי כִּי יְהוָה גָּמַל עָלָיְכִי:
ח: כִּי חִלַּצְתָּ נַפְשִׁי מִמָּוֶת אֶת עֵינִי מִן דִּמְעָה אֶת רַגְלִי מִדֶּחִי:
ט: אֶתְהַלֵּךְ לִפְנֵי יְהוָה בְּאַרְצוֹת הַחַיִּים:
י: הֶאֱמַנְתִּי כִּי אֲדַבֵּר אֲנִי עָנִיתִי מְאֹד:
יא: אֲנִי אָמַרְתִּי בְחָפְזִי כָּל הָאָדָם כֹּזֵב:
יב: מָה אָשִׁיב לַיהוָה כָּל תַּגְמוּלוֹהִי עָלָי:
יג: כּוֹס יְשׁוּעוֹת אֶשָּׂא וּבְשֵׁם יְהוָה אֶקְרָא:
יד: נְדָרַי לַיהוָה אֲשַׁלֵּם נֶגְדָה נָּא לְכָל עַמּוֹ:
טו: יָקָר בְּעֵינֵי יְהוָה הַמָּוְתָה לַחֲסִידָיו:
טז: אָנָּה יְהוָה כִּי אֲנִי עַבְדֶּךָ אֲנִי עַבְדְּךָ בֶּן אֲמָתֶךָ פִּתַּחְתָּ לְמוֹסֵרָי:
יז: לְךָ אֶזְבַּח זֶבַח תּוֹדָה וּבְשֵׁם יְהוָה אֶקְרָא:
יח: נְדָרַי לַיהוָה אֲשַׁלֵּם נֶגְדָה נָּא לְכָל עַמּוֹ:
יט: בְּחַצְרוֹת בֵּית יְהוָה בְּתוֹכֵכִי יְרוּשָׁלִָם הַלְלוּ יָהּ:

פרק קיז

א: הַלְלוּ אֶת יְהוָה כָּל גּוֹיִם שַׁבְּחוּהוּ כָּל הָאֻמִּים:
ב: כִּי גָבַר עָלֵינוּ חַסְדּוֹ וֶאֱמֶת יְהוָה לְעוֹלָם הַלְלוּיָהּ:

פרק קיח

א: הוֹדוּ לַיהוָה כִּי טוֹב כִּי לְעוֹלָם חַסְדּוֹ:
ב: יֹאמַר נָא יִשְׂרָאֵל כִּי לְעוֹלָם חַסְדּוֹ:
ג: יֹאמְרוּ נָא בֵית אַהֲרֹן כִּי לְעוֹלָם חַסְדּוֹ:
ד: יֹאמְרוּ נָא יִרְאֵי יְהוָה כִּי לְעוֹלָם חַסְדּוֹ:
ה: מִן הַמֵּצַר קָרָאתִי יָּהּ עָנָנִי בַמֶּרְחָב יָהּ:
ו: יְהוָה לִי לֹא אִירָא מַה יַּעֲשֶׂה לִי אָדָם:
ז: יְהוָה לִי בְּעֹזְרָי וַאֲנִי אֶרְאֶה בְשֹׂנְאָי:
ח: טוֹב לַחֲסוֹת בַּיהוָה מִבְּטֹחַ בָּאָדָם:
ט: טוֹב לַחֲסוֹת בַּיהוָה מִבְּטֹחַ בִּנְדִיבִים:
י: כָּל גּוֹיִם סְבָבוּנִי בְּשֵׁם יְהוָה כִּי אֲמִילַם:
יא: סַבּוּנִי גַם סְבָבוּנִי בְּשֵׁם יְהוָה כִּי אֲמִילַם:
יב: סַבּוּנִי כִדְבוֹרִים דֹּעֲכוּ כְּאֵשׁ קוֹצִים בְּשֵׁם יְהוָה כִּי אֲמִילַם:
יג: דָּחֹה דְחִיתַנִי לִנְפֹּל וַיהוָה עֲזָרָנִי:
יד: עָזִּי וְזִמְרָת יָהּ וַיְהִי לִי לִישׁוּעָה:
טו: קוֹל רִנָּה וִישׁוּעָה בְּאָהֳלֵי צַדִּיקִים יְמִין יְהוָה עֹשָׂה חָיִל:

טז: יְמִין יְהֹוָה רוֹמֵמָה יְמִין יְהֹוָה עֹשָׂה חָיִל:
יז: לֹא אָמוּת כִּי אֶחְיֶה וַאֲסַפֵּר מַעֲשֵׂי יָהּ:
יח: יַסֹּר יִסְּרַנִּי יָּהּ וְלַמָּוֶת לֹא נְתָנָנִי:
יט: פִּתְחוּ לִי שַׁעֲרֵי צֶדֶק אָבֹא בָם אוֹדֶה יָהּ:
כ: זֶה הַשַּׁעַר לַיהֹוָה צַדִּיקִים יָבֹאוּ בוֹ:
כא: אוֹדְךָ כִּי עֲנִיתָנִי וַתְּהִי לִי לִישׁוּעָה:
כב: אֶבֶן מָאֲסוּ הַבּוֹנִים הָיְתָה לְרֹאשׁ פִּנָּה:
כג: מֵאֵת יְהֹוָה הָיְתָה זֹּאת הִיא נִפְלָאת בְּעֵינֵינוּ:
כד: זֶה הַיּוֹם עָשָׂה יְהֹוָה נָגִילָה וְנִשְׂמְחָה בוֹ:
כה: אָנָּא יְהֹוָה הוֹשִׁיעָה נָּא אָנָּא יְהֹוָה הַצְלִיחָה נָּא:
כו: בָּרוּךְ הַבָּא בְּשֵׁם יְהֹוָה בֵּרַכְנוּכֶם מִבֵּית יְהֹוָה:
כז: אֵל יְהֹוָה וַיָּאֶר לָנוּ אִסְרוּ חַג בַּעֲבֹתִים עַד קַרְנוֹת הַמִּזְבֵּחַ:
כח: אֵלִי אַתָּה וְאוֹדֶךָּ אֱלֹהַי אֲרוֹמְמֶךָּ:
כט: הוֹדוּ לַיהֹוָה כִּי טוֹב כִּי לְעוֹלָם חַסְדּוֹ:

פרק קיט

א: אַשְׁרֵי תְמִימֵי דָרֶךְ הַהֹלְכִים בְּתוֹרַת יְהֹוָה:
ב: אַשְׁרֵי נֹצְרֵי עֵדֹתָיו בְּכָל לֵב יִדְרְשׁוּהוּ:
ג: אַף לֹא פָעֲלוּ עַוְלָה בִּדְרָכָיו הָלָכוּ:
ד: אַתָּה צִוִּיתָה פִקֻּדֶיךָ לִשְׁמֹר מְאֹד:
ה: אַחֲלַי יִכֹּנוּ דְרָכָי לִשְׁמֹר חֻקֶּיךָ:
ו: אָז לֹא אֵבוֹשׁ בְּהַבִּיטִי אֶל כָּל מִצְוֹתֶיךָ:
ז: אוֹדְךָ בְּיֹשֶׁר לֵבָב בְּלָמְדִי מִשְׁפְּטֵי צִדְקֶךָ:
ח: אֶת חֻקֶּיךָ אֶשְׁמֹר אַל תַּעַזְבֵנִי עַד מְאֹד:
ט: בַּמֶּה יְזַכֶּה נַּעַר אֶת אָרְחוֹ לִשְׁמֹר כִּדְבָרֶךָ:
י: בְּכָל לִבִּי דְרַשְׁתִּיךָ אַל תַּשְׁגֵּנִי מִמִּצְוֹתֶיךָ:
יא: בְּלִבִּי צָפַנְתִּי אִמְרָתֶךָ לְמַעַן לֹא אֶחֱטָא לָךְ:
יב: בָּרוּךְ אַתָּה יְהֹוָה לַמְּדֵנִי חֻקֶּיךָ:
יג: בִּשְׂפָתַי סִפַּרְתִּי כֹּל מִשְׁפְּטֵי פִיךָ:
יד: בְּדֶרֶךְ עֵדְוֹתֶיךָ שַׂשְׂתִּי כְּעַל כָּל הוֹן:
טו: בְּפִקֻּדֶיךָ אָשִׂיחָה וְאַבִּיטָה אֹרְחֹתֶיךָ:
טז: בְּחֻקֹּתֶיךָ אֶשְׁתַּעֲשָׁע לֹא אֶשְׁכַּח דְּבָרֶךָ:
יז: גְּמֹל עַל עַבְדְּךָ אֶחְיֶה וְאֶשְׁמְרָה דְבָרֶךָ:
יח: גַּל עֵינַי וְאַבִּיטָה נִפְלָאוֹת מִתּוֹרָתֶךָ:
יט: גֵּר אָנֹכִי בָאָרֶץ אַל תַּסְתֵּר מִמֶּנִּי מִצְוֹתֶיךָ:
כ: גָּרְסָה נַפְשִׁי לְתַאֲבָה אֶל מִשְׁפָּטֶיךָ בְכָל עֵת:
כא: גָּעַרְתָּ זֵדִים אֲרוּרִים הַשֹּׁגִים מִמִּצְוֹתֶיךָ:
כב: גַּל מֵעָלַי חֶרְפָּה וָבוּז כִּי עֵדֹתֶיךָ נָצָרְתִּי:
כג: גַּם יָשְׁבוּ שָׂרִים בִּי נִדְבָּרוּ עַבְדְּךָ יָשִׂיחַ בְּחֻקֶּיךָ:
כד: גַּם עֵדֹתֶיךָ שַׁעֲשֻׁעָי אַנְשֵׁי עֲצָתִי:
כה: דָּבְקָה לֶעָפָר נַפְשִׁי חַיֵּנִי כִּדְבָרֶךָ:
כו: דְּרָכַי סִפַּרְתִּי וַתַּעֲנֵנִי לַמְּדֵנִי חֻקֶּיךָ:
כז: דֶּרֶךְ פִּקּוּדֶיךָ הֲבִינֵנִי וְאָשִׂיחָה בְּנִפְלְאוֹתֶיךָ:
כח: דָּלְפָה נַפְשִׁי מִתּוּגָה קַיְּמֵנִי כִּדְבָרֶךָ:
כט: דֶּרֶךְ שֶׁקֶר הָסֵר מִמֶּנִּי וְתוֹרָתְךָ חָנֵּנִי:
ל: דֶּרֶךְ אֱמוּנָה בָחָרְתִּי מִשְׁפָּטֶיךָ שִׁוִּיתִי:
לא: דָּבַקְתִּי בְעֵדְוֹתֶיךָ יְהֹוָה אַל תְּבִישֵׁנִי:

לב: דֶּרֶךְ מִצְוֺתֶיךָ אָרוּץ כִּי תַרְחִיב לִבִּי:
לג: הוֹרֵנִי יְהוָה דֶּרֶךְ חֻקֶּיךָ וְאֶצְּרֶנָּה עֵקֶב:
לד: הֲבִינֵנִי וְאֶצְּרָה תוֹרָתֶךָ וְאֶשְׁמְרֶנָּה בְכָל לֵב:
לה: הַדְרִיכֵנִי בִּנְתִיב מִצְוֺתֶיךָ כִּי בוֹ חָפָצְתִּי:
לו: הַט לִבִּי אֶל עֵדְוֺתֶיךָ וְאַל אֶל בָּצַע:
לז: הַעֲבֵר עֵינַי מֵרְאוֹת שָׁוְא בִּדְרָכֶךָ חַיֵּנִי:
לח: הָקֵם לְעַבְדְּךָ אִמְרָתֶךָ אֲשֶׁר לְיִרְאָתֶךָ:
לט: הַעֲבֵר חֶרְפָּתִי אֲשֶׁר יָגֹרְתִּי כִּי מִשְׁפָּטֶיךָ טוֹבִים:
מ: הִנֵּה תָּאַבְתִּי לְפִקֻּדֶיךָ בְּצִדְקָתְךָ חַיֵּנִי:
מא: וִיבֹאֻנִי חֲסָדֶךָ יְהוָה תְּשׁוּעָתְךָ כְּאִמְרָתֶךָ:
מב: וְאֶעֱנֶה חֹרְפִי דָבָר כִּי בָטַחְתִּי בִּדְבָרֶךָ:
מג: וְאַל תַּצֵּל מִפִּי דְבַר אֱמֶת עַד מְאֹד כִּי לְמִשְׁפָּטֶךָ יִחָלְתִּי:
מד: וְאֶשְׁמְרָה תוֹרָתְךָ תָמִיד לְעוֹלָם וָעֶד:
מה: וְאֶתְהַלְּכָה בָרְחָבָה כִּי פִקֻּדֶיךָ דָרָשְׁתִּי:
מו: וַאֲדַבְּרָה בְעֵדֹתֶיךָ נֶגֶד מְלָכִים וְלֹא אֵבוֹשׁ:
מז: וְאֶשְׁתַּעֲשַׁע בְּמִצְוֺתֶיךָ אֲשֶׁר אָהָבְתִּי:
מח: וְאֶשָּׂא כַפַּי אֶל מִצְוֺתֶיךָ אֲשֶׁר אָהָבְתִּי וְאָשִׂיחָה בְחֻקֶּיךָ:
מט: זְכֹר דָּבָר לְעַבְדֶּךָ עַל אֲשֶׁר יִחַלְתָּנִי:
נ: זֹאת נֶחָמָתִי בְעָנְיִי כִּי אִמְרָתְךָ חִיָּתְנִי:
נא: זֵדִים הֱלִיצֻנִי עַד מְאֹד מִתּוֹרָתְךָ לֹא נָטִיתִי:
נב: זָכַרְתִּי מִשְׁפָּטֶיךָ מֵעוֹלָם יְהוָה וָאֶתְנֶחָם:
נג: זַלְעָפָה אֲחָזַתְנִי מֵרְשָׁעִים עֹזְבֵי תוֹרָתֶךָ:
נד: זְמִרוֹת הָיוּ לִי חֻקֶּיךָ בְּבֵית מְגוּרָי:
נה: זָכַרְתִּי בַלַּיְלָה שִׁמְךָ יְהוָה וָאֶשְׁמְרָה תוֹרָתֶךָ:
נו: זֹאת הָיְתָה לִּי כִּי פִקֻּדֶיךָ נָצָרְתִּי:
נז: חֶלְקִי יְהוָה אָמַרְתִּי לִשְׁמֹר דְּבָרֶיךָ:
נח: חִלִּיתִי פָנֶיךָ בְכָל לֵב חָנֵּנִי כְּאִמְרָתֶךָ:
נט: חִשַּׁבְתִּי דְרָכָי וָאָשִׁיבָה רַגְלַי אֶל עֵדֹתֶיךָ:
ס: חַשְׁתִּי וְלֹא הִתְמַהְמָהְתִּי לִשְׁמֹר מִצְוֺתֶיךָ:
סא: חֶבְלֵי רְשָׁעִים עִוְּדֻנִי תוֹרָתְךָ לֹא שָׁכָחְתִּי:
סב: חֲצוֹת לַיְלָה אָקוּם לְהוֹדוֹת לָךְ עַל מִשְׁפְּטֵי צִדְקֶךָ:
סג: חָבֵר אָנִי לְכָל אֲשֶׁר יְרֵאוּךָ וּלְשֹׁמְרֵי פִּקּוּדֶיךָ:
סד: חַסְדְּךָ יְהוָה מָלְאָה הָאָרֶץ חֻקֶּיךָ לַמְּדֵנִי:
סה: טוֹב עָשִׂיתָ עִם עַבְדְּךָ יְהוָה כִּדְבָרֶךָ:
סו: טוּב טַעַם וָדַעַת לַמְּדֵנִי כִּי בְמִצְוֺתֶיךָ הֶאֱמָנְתִּי:
סז: טֶרֶם אֶעֱנֶה אֲנִי שֹׁגֵג וְעַתָּה אִמְרָתְךָ שָׁמָרְתִּי:
סח: טוֹב אַתָּה וּמֵטִיב לַמְּדֵנִי חֻקֶּיךָ:
סט: טָפְלוּ עָלַי שֶׁקֶר זֵדִים אֲנִי בְּכָל לֵב אֶצֹּר פִּקּוּדֶיךָ:
ע: טָפַשׁ כַּחֵלֶב לִבָּם אֲנִי תּוֹרָתְךָ שִׁעֲשָׁעְתִּי:
עא: טוֹב לִי כִי עֻנֵּיתִי לְמַעַן אֶלְמַד חֻקֶּיךָ:
עב: טוֹב לִי תוֹרַת פִּיךָ מֵאַלְפֵי זָהָב וָכָסֶף:
עג: יָדֶיךָ עָשׂוּנִי וַיְכוֹנְנוּנִי הֲבִינֵנִי וְאֶלְמְדָה מִצְוֺתֶיךָ:
עד: יְרֵאֶיךָ יִרְאוּנִי וְיִשְׂמָחוּ כִּי לִדְבָרְךָ יִחָלְתִּי:
עה: יָדַעְתִּי יְהוָה כִּי צֶדֶק מִשְׁפָּטֶיךָ וֶאֱמוּנָה עִנִּיתָנִי:
עו: יְהִי נָא חַסְדְּךָ לְנַחֲמֵנִי כְּאִמְרָתְךָ לְעַבְדֶּךָ:
עז: יְבֹשׁוּ זֵדִים כִּי שֶׁקֶר עִוְּתוּנִי אֲנִי אָשִׂיחַ בְּפִקּוּדֶיךָ:
עט: יָשׁוּבוּ לִי יְרֵאֶיךָ וידעו {וְיֹדְעֵי} עֵדֹתֶיךָ:

ספר תהילים

פ: יְהִי לִבִּי תָמִים בְּחֻקֶּיךָ לְמַעַן לֹא אֵבוֹשׁ:

פא: כָּלְתָה לִתְשׁוּעָתְךָ נַפְשִׁי לִדְבָרְךָ יִחָלְתִּי:

פב: כָּלוּ עֵינַי לְאִמְרָתֶךָ לֵאמֹר מָתַי תְּנַחֲמֵנִי:

פג: כִּי הָיִיתִי כְּנֹאד בְּקִיטוֹר חֻקֶּיךָ לֹא שָׁכָחְתִּי:

פד: כַּמָּה יְמֵי עַבְדֶּךָ מָתַי תַּעֲשֶׂה בְרֹדְפַי מִשְׁפָּט:

פה: כָּרוּ לִי זֵדִים שִׁיחוֹת אֲשֶׁר לֹא כְתוֹרָתֶךָ:

פו: כָּל מִצְוֹתֶיךָ אֱמוּנָה שֶׁקֶר רְדָפוּנִי עָזְרֵנִי:

פז: כִּמְעַט כִּלּוּנִי בָאָרֶץ וַאֲנִי לֹא עָזַבְתִּי פִקּוּדֶיךָ:

פח: כְּחַסְדְּךָ חַיֵּנִי וְאֶשְׁמְרָה עֵדוּת פִּיךָ:

פט: לְעוֹלָם יְהוָה דְּבָרְךָ נִצָּב בַּשָּׁמָיִם:

צ: לְדֹר וָדֹר אֱמוּנָתֶךָ כּוֹנַנְתָּ אֶרֶץ וַתַּעֲמֹד:

צא: לְמִשְׁפָּטֶיךָ עָמְדוּ הַיּוֹם כִּי הַכֹּל עֲבָדֶיךָ:

צב: לוּלֵי תוֹרָתְךָ שַׁעֲשֻׁעָי אָז אָבַדְתִּי בְעָנְיִי:

צג: לְעוֹלָם לֹא אֶשְׁכַּח פִּקּוּדֶיךָ כִּי בָם חִיִּיתָנִי:

צד: לְךָ אֲנִי הוֹשִׁיעֵנִי כִּי פִקּוּדֶיךָ דָרָשְׁתִּי:

צה: לִי קִוּוּ רְשָׁעִים לְאַבְּדֵנִי עֵדֹתֶיךָ אֶתְבּוֹנָן:

צו: לְכָל תִּכְלָה רָאִיתִי קֵץ רְחָבָה מִצְוָתְךָ מְאֹד:

צז: מָה אָהַבְתִּי תוֹרָתֶךָ כָּל הַיּוֹם הִיא שִׂיחָתִי:

צח: מֵאֹיְבַי תְּחַכְּמֵנִי מִצְוֹתֶךָ כִּי לְעוֹלָם הִיא לִי:

צט: מִכָּל מְלַמְּדַי הִשְׂכַּלְתִּי כִּי עֵדְוֹתֶיךָ שִׂיחָה לִי:

ק: מִזְּקֵנִים אֶתְבּוֹנָן כִּי פִקּוּדֶיךָ נָצָרְתִּי:

קא: מִכָּל אֹרַח רָע כָּלִאתִי רַגְלָי לְמַעַן אֶשְׁמֹר דְּבָרֶךָ:

קב: מִמִּשְׁפָּטֶיךָ לֹא סָרְתִּי כִּי אַתָּה הוֹרֵתָנִי:

קג: מַה נִּמְלְצוּ לְחִכִּי אִמְרָתֶךָ מִדְּבַשׁ לְפִי:

קד: מִפִּקּוּדֶיךָ אֶתְבּוֹנָן עַל כֵּן שָׂנֵאתִי כָּל אֹרַח שָׁקֶר:

קה: נֵר לְרַגְלִי דְבָרֶךָ וְאוֹר לִנְתִיבָתִי:

קו: נִשְׁבַּעְתִּי וָאֲקַיֵּמָה לִשְׁמֹר מִשְׁפְּטֵי צִדְקֶךָ:

קז: נַעֲנֵיתִי עַד מְאֹד יְהוָה חַיֵּנִי כִדְבָרֶךָ:

קח: נִדְבוֹת פִּי רְצֵה נָא יְהוָה וּמִשְׁפָּטֶיךָ לַמְּדֵנִי:

קט: נַפְשִׁי בְכַפִּי תָמִיד וְתוֹרָתְךָ לֹא שָׁכָחְתִּי:

קי: נָתְנוּ רְשָׁעִים פַּח לִי וּמִפִּקּוּדֶיךָ לֹא תָעִיתִי:

קיא: נָחַלְתִּי עֵדְוֹתֶיךָ לְעוֹלָם כִּי שְׂשׂוֹן לִבִּי הֵמָּה:

קיב: נָטִיתִי לִבִּי לַעֲשׂוֹת חֻקֶּיךָ לְעוֹלָם עֵקֶב:

קיג: סֵעֲפִים שָׂנֵאתִי וְתוֹרָתְךָ אָהָבְתִּי:

קיד: סִתְרִי וּמָגִנִּי אָתָּה לִדְבָרְךָ יִחָלְתִּי:

קטו: סוּרוּ מִמֶּנִּי מְרֵעִים וְאֶצְּרָה מִצְוֹת אֱלֹהָי:

קטז: סָמְכֵנִי כְאִמְרָתְךָ וְאֶחְיֶה וְאַל תְּבִישֵׁנִי מִשִּׂבְרִי:

קיז: סְעָדֵנִי וְאִוָּשֵׁעָה וְאֶשְׁעָה בְחֻקֶּיךָ תָמִיד:

קיח: סָלִיתָ כָּל שׁוֹגִים מֵחֻקֶּיךָ כִּי שֶׁקֶר תַּרְמִיתָם:

קיט: סִגִים הִשְׁבַּתָּ כָל רִשְׁעֵי אָרֶץ לָכֵן אָהַבְתִּי עֵדֹתֶיךָ:

קכ: סָמַר מִפַּחְדְּךָ בְשָׂרִי וּמִמִּשְׁפָּטֶיךָ יָרֵאתִי:

קכא: עָשִׂיתִי מִשְׁפָּט וָצֶדֶק בַּל תַּנִּיחֵנִי לְעֹשְׁקָי:

קכב: עֲרֹב עַבְדְּךָ לְטוֹב אַל יַעַשְׁקֻנִי זֵדִים:

קכג: עֵינַי כָּלוּ לִישׁוּעָתֶךָ וּלְאִמְרַת צִדְקֶךָ:

קכד: עֲשֵׂה עִם עַבְדְּךָ כְחַסְדֶּךָ וְחֻקֶּיךָ לַמְּדֵנִי:

קכה: עַבְדְּךָ אָנִי הֲבִינֵנִי וְאֵדְעָה עֵדֹתֶיךָ:

קכו: עֵת לַעֲשׂוֹת לַיהוָה הֵפֵרוּ תּוֹרָתֶךָ:

קכז: עַל כֵּן אָהַבְתִּי מִצְוֹתֶיךָ מִזָּהָב וּמִפָּז:
קכח: עַל כֵּן כָּל פִּקּוּדֵי כֹל יִשָּׁרְתִּי כָּל אֹרַח שֶׁקֶר שָׂנֵאתִי:
קכט: פְּלָאוֹת עֵדְוֹתֶיךָ עַל כֵּן נְצָרָתַם נַפְשִׁי:
קל: פֵּתַח דְּבָרֶיךָ יָאִיר מֵבִין פְּתָיִים:
קלא: פִּי פָעַרְתִּי וָאֶשְׁאָפָה כִּי לְמִצְוֹתֶיךָ יָאָבְתִּי:
קלב: פְּנֵה אֵלַי וְחָנֵּנִי כְּמִשְׁפָּט לְאֹהֲבֵי שְׁמֶךָ:
קלג: פְּעָמַי הָכֵן בְּאִמְרָתֶךָ וְאַל תַּשְׁלֶט בִּי כָל אָוֶן:
קלד: פְּדֵנִי מֵעֹשֶׁק אָדָם וְאֶשְׁמְרָה פִּקּוּדֶיךָ:
קלה: פָּנֶיךָ הָאֵר בְּעַבְדֶּךָ וְלַמְּדֵנִי אֶת חֻקֶּיךָ:
קלו: פַּלְגֵי מַיִם יָרְדוּ עֵינָי עַל לֹא שָׁמְרוּ תוֹרָתֶךָ:
קלז: צַדִּיק אַתָּה יְהוָה וְיָשָׁר מִשְׁפָּטֶיךָ:
קלח: צִוִּיתָ צֶדֶק עֵדֹתֶיךָ וֶאֱמוּנָה מְאֹד:
קלט: צִמְּתַתְנִי קִנְאָתִי כִּי שָׁכְחוּ דְבָרֶיךָ צָרָי:
קמ: צְרוּפָה אִמְרָתְךָ מְאֹד וְעַבְדְּךָ אֲהֵבָהּ:
קמא: צָעִיר אָנֹכִי וְנִבְזֶה פִּקֻּדֶיךָ לֹא שָׁכָחְתִּי:
קמב: צִדְקָתְךָ צֶדֶק לְעוֹלָם וְתוֹרָתְךָ אֱמֶת:
קמג: צַר וּמָצוֹק מְצָאוּנִי מִצְוֹתֶיךָ שַׁעֲשֻׁעָי:
קמד: צֶדֶק עֵדְוֹתֶיךָ לְעוֹלָם הֲבִינֵנִי וְאֶחְיֶה:
קמה: קָרָאתִי בְכָל לֵב עֲנֵנִי יְהוָה חֻקֶּיךָ אֶצֹּרָה:
קמו: קְרָאתִיךָ הוֹשִׁיעֵנִי וְאֶשְׁמְרָה עֵדֹתֶיךָ:
קמז: קִדַּמְתִּי בַנֶּשֶׁף וָאֲשַׁוֵּעָה לדבריך {לִדְבָרְךָ} יִחָלְתִּי:
קמח: קִדְּמוּ עֵינַי אַשְׁמֻרוֹת לָשִׂיחַ בְּאִמְרָתֶךָ:
קמט: קוֹלִי שִׁמְעָה כְחַסְדֶּךָ יְהוָה כְּמִשְׁפָּטֶךָ חַיֵּנִי:
קנ: קָרְבוּ רֹדְפֵי זִמָּה מִתּוֹרָתְךָ רָחָקוּ:
קנא: קָרוֹב אַתָּה יְהוָה וְכָל מִצְוֹתֶיךָ אֱמֶת:
קנב: קֶדֶם יָדַעְתִּי מֵעֵדֹתֶיךָ כִּי לְעוֹלָם יְסַדְתָּם:
קנג: רְאֵה עָנְיִי וְחַלְּצֵנִי כִּי תוֹרָתְךָ לֹא שָׁכָחְתִּי:
קנד: רִיבָה רִיבִי וּגְאָלֵנִי לְאִמְרָתְךָ חַיֵּנִי:
קנה: רָחוֹק מֵרְשָׁעִים יְשׁוּעָה כִּי חֻקֶּיךָ לֹא דָרָשׁוּ:
קנו: רַחֲמֶיךָ רַבִּים יְהוָה כְּמִשְׁפָּטֶיךָ חַיֵּנִי:
קנז: רַבִּים רֹדְפַי וְצָרָי מֵעֵדְוֹתֶיךָ לֹא נָטִיתִי:
קנח: רָאִיתִי בֹגְדִים וָאֶתְקוֹטָטָה אֲשֶׁר אִמְרָתְךָ לֹא שָׁמָרוּ:
קנט: רְאֵה כִּי פִקּוּדֶיךָ אָהָבְתִּי יְהוָה כְּחַסְדְּךָ חַיֵּנִי:
קס: רֹאשׁ דְּבָרְךָ אֱמֶת וּלְעוֹלָם כָּל מִשְׁפַּט צִדְקֶךָ:
קסא: שָׂרִים רְדָפוּנִי חִנָּם ומדבריך {וּמִדְּבָרְךָ} פָּחַד לִבִּי:
קסב: שָׂשׂ אָנֹכִי עַל אִמְרָתֶךָ כְּמוֹצֵא שָׁלָל רָב:
קסג: שֶׁקֶר שָׂנֵאתִי וַאֲתַעֵבָה תּוֹרָתְךָ אָהָבְתִּי:
קסד: שֶׁבַע בַּיּוֹם הִלַּלְתִּיךָ עַל מִשְׁפְּטֵי צִדְקֶךָ:
קסה: שָׁלוֹם רָב לְאֹהֲבֵי תוֹרָתֶךָ וְאֵין לָמוֹ מִכְשׁוֹל:
קסו: שִׂבַּרְתִּי לִישׁוּעָתְךָ יְהוָה וּמִצְוֹתֶיךָ עָשִׂיתִי:
קסז: שָׁמְרָה נַפְשִׁי עֵדֹתֶיךָ וָאֹהֲבֵם מְאֹד:
קסח: שָׁמַרְתִּי פִקּוּדֶיךָ וְעֵדֹתֶיךָ כִּי כָל דְּרָכַי נֶגְדֶּךָ:
קסט: תִּקְרַב רִנָּתִי לְפָנֶיךָ יְהוָה כִּדְבָרְךָ הֲבִינֵנִי:
קע: תָּבוֹא תְחִנָּתִי לְפָנֶיךָ כְּאִמְרָתְךָ הַצִּילֵנִי:
קעא: תַּבַּעְנָה שְׂפָתַי תְּהִלָּה כִּי תְלַמְּדֵנִי חֻקֶּיךָ:
קעב: תַּעַן לְשׁוֹנִי אִמְרָתֶךָ כִּי כָל מִצְוֹתֶיךָ צֶּדֶק:
קעג: תְּהִי יָדְךָ לְעָזְרֵנִי כִּי פִקּוּדֶיךָ בָחָרְתִּי:

קעד: תָּאַבְתִּי לִישׁוּעָתְךָ יְהוָה וְתוֹרָתְךָ שַׁעֲשֻׁעָי:
קעה: תְּחִי נַפְשִׁי וּתְהַלְלֶךָּ וּמִשְׁפָּטֶךָ יַעֲזְרֻנִי:
קעו: תָּעִיתִי כְּשֶׂה אֹבֵד בַּקֵּשׁ עַבְדֶּךָ כִּי מִצְוֹתֶיךָ לֹא שָׁכָחְתִּי:

פרק קכ

א: שִׁיר הַמַּעֲלוֹת אֶל יְהוָה בַּצָּרָתָה לִּי קָרָאתִי וַיַּעֲנֵנִי:
ב: יְהוָה הַצִּילָה נַפְשִׁי מִשְּׂפַת שֶׁקֶר מִלָּשׁוֹן רְמִיָּה:
ג: מַה יִּתֵּן לְךָ וּמַה יֹּסִיף לָךְ לָשׁוֹן רְמִיָּה:
ד: חִצֵּי גִבּוֹר שְׁנוּנִים עִם גַּחֲלֵי רְתָמִים:
ה: אוֹיָה לִי כִּי גַרְתִּי מֶשֶׁךְ שָׁכַנְתִּי עִם אָהֳלֵי קֵדָר:
ו: רַבַּת שָׁכְנָה לָּהּ נַפְשִׁי עִם שׂוֹנֵא שָׁלוֹם:
ז: אֲנִי שָׁלוֹם וְכִי אֲדַבֵּר הֵמָּה לַמִּלְחָמָה:

פרק קכא

א: שִׁיר לַמַּעֲלוֹת אֶשָּׂא עֵינַי אֶל הֶהָרִים מֵאַיִן יָבֹא עֶזְרִי:
ב: עֶזְרִי מֵעִם יְהוָה עֹשֵׂה שָׁמַיִם וָאָרֶץ:
ג: אַל יִתֵּן לַמּוֹט רַגְלֶךָ אַל יָנוּם שֹׁמְרֶךָ:
ד: הִנֵּה לֹא יָנוּם וְלֹא יִישָׁן שׁוֹמֵר יִשְׂרָאֵל:
ה: יְהוָה שֹׁמְרֶךָ יְהוָה צִלְּךָ עַל יַד יְמִינֶךָ:
ו: יוֹמָם הַשֶּׁמֶשׁ לֹא יַכֶּכָּה וְיָרֵחַ בַּלָּיְלָה:
ז: יְהוָה יִשְׁמָרְךָ מִכָּל רָע יִשְׁמֹר אֶת נַפְשֶׁךָ:
ח: יְהוָה יִשְׁמָר צֵאתְךָ וּבוֹאֶךָ מֵעַתָּה וְעַד עוֹלָם:

פרק קכב

א: שִׁיר הַמַּעֲלוֹת לְדָוִד שָׂמַחְתִּי בְּאֹמְרִים לִי בֵּית יְהוָה נֵלֵךְ:
ב: עֹמְדוֹת הָיוּ רַגְלֵינוּ בִּשְׁעָרַיִךְ יְרוּשָׁלָ͏ִם:
ג: יְרוּשָׁלַ͏ִם הַבְּנוּיָה כְּעִיר שֶׁחֻבְּרָה לָּהּ יַחְדָּו:
ד: שֶׁשָּׁם עָלוּ שְׁבָטִים שִׁבְטֵי יָהּ עֵדוּת לְיִשְׂרָאֵל לְהֹדוֹת לְשֵׁם יְהוָה:
ה: כִּי שָׁמָּה יָשְׁבוּ כִסְאוֹת לְמִשְׁפָּט כִּסְאוֹת לְבֵית דָּוִד:
ו: שַׁאֲלוּ שְׁלוֹם יְרוּשָׁלָ͏ִם יִשְׁלָיוּ אֹהֲבָיִךְ:
ז: יְהִי שָׁלוֹם בְּחֵילֵךְ שַׁלְוָה בְּאַרְמְנוֹתָיִךְ:
ח: לְמַעַן אַחַי וְרֵעָי אֲדַבְּרָה נָּא שָׁלוֹם בָּךְ:
ט: לְמַעַן בֵּית יְהוָה אֱלֹהֵינוּ אֲבַקְשָׁה טוֹב לָךְ:

פרק קכג

א: שִׁיר הַמַּעֲלוֹת אֵלֶיךָ נָשָׂאתִי אֶת עֵינַי הַיֹּשְׁבִי בַּשָּׁמָיִם:
ב: הִנֵּה כְעֵינֵי עֲבָדִים אֶל יַד אֲדוֹנֵיהֶם כְּעֵינֵי שִׁפְחָה אֶל יַד גְּבִרְתָּהּ כֵּן עֵינֵינוּ אֶל יְהוָה אֱלֹהֵינוּ עַד שֶׁיְּחָנֵּנוּ:
ג: חָנֵּנוּ יְהוָה חָנֵּנוּ כִּי רַב שָׂבַעְנוּ בוּז:
ד: רַבַּת שָׂבְעָה לָּהּ נַפְשֵׁנוּ הַלַּעַג הַשַּׁאֲנַנִּים הַבּוּז לִגְאֵיוֹנִים {לִגְאֵי} יוֹנִים:

פרק קכד

א: שִׁיר הַמַּעֲלוֹת לְדָוִד לוּלֵי יְהוָה שֶׁהָיָה לָנוּ יֹאמַר נָא יִשְׂרָאֵל:
ב: לוּלֵי יְהוָה שֶׁהָיָה לָנוּ בְּקוּם עָלֵינוּ אָדָם:
ג: אֲזַי חַיִּים בְּלָעוּנוּ בַּחֲרוֹת אַפָּם בָּנוּ:
ד: אֲזַי הַמַּיִם שְׁטָפוּנוּ נַחְלָה עָבַר עַל נַפְשֵׁנוּ:
ה: אֲזַי עָבַר עַל נַפְשֵׁנוּ הַמַּיִם הַזֵּידוֹנִים:

ו: בָּרוּךְ יְהֹוָה שֶׁלֹּא נְתָנָנוּ טֶרֶף לְשִׁנֵּיהֶם:
ז: נַפְשֵׁנוּ כְּצִפּוֹר נִמְלְטָה מִפַּח יוֹקְשִׁים הַפַּח נִשְׁבָּר וַאֲנַחְנוּ נִמְלָטְנוּ:
ח: עֶזְרֵנוּ בְּשֵׁם יְהֹוָה עֹשֵׂה שָׁמַיִם וָאָרֶץ:

פרק קכה

א: שִׁיר הַמַּעֲלוֹת הַבֹּטְחִים בַּיהֹוָה כְּהַר צִיּוֹן לֹא יִמּוֹט לְעוֹלָם יֵשֵׁב:
ב: יְרוּשָׁלַם הָרִים סָבִיב לָהּ וַיהֹוָה סָבִיב לְעַמּוֹ מֵעַתָּה וְעַד עוֹלָם:
ג: כִּי לֹא יָנוּחַ שֵׁבֶט הָרֶשַׁע עַל גּוֹרַל הַצַּדִּיקִים לְמַעַן לֹא יִשְׁלְחוּ הַצַּדִּיקִים בְּעַוְלָתָה יְדֵיהֶם:
ד: הֵיטִיבָה יְהֹוָה לַטּוֹבִים וְלִישָׁרִים בְּלִבּוֹתָם:
ה: וְהַמַּטִּים עֲקַלְקַלּוֹתָם יוֹלִיכֵם יְהֹוָה אֶת פֹּעֲלֵי הָאָוֶן שָׁלוֹם עַל יִשְׂרָאֵל:

פרק קכו

א: שִׁיר הַמַּעֲלוֹת בְּשׁוּב יְהֹוָה אֶת שִׁיבַת צִיּוֹן הָיִינוּ כְּחֹלְמִים:
ב: אָז יִמָּלֵא שְׂחוֹק פִּינוּ וּלְשׁוֹנֵנוּ רִנָּה אָז יֹאמְרוּ בַגּוֹיִם הִגְדִּיל יְהֹוָה לַעֲשׂוֹת עִם אֵלֶּה:
ג: הִגְדִּיל יְהֹוָה לַעֲשׂוֹת עִמָּנוּ הָיִינוּ שְׂמֵחִים:
ד: שׁוּבָה יְהֹוָה אֶת שבותנו {שְׁבִיתֵנוּ} כַּאֲפִיקִים בַּנֶּגֶב:
ה: הַזֹּרְעִים בְּדִמְעָה בְּרִנָּה יִקְצֹרוּ:
ו: הָלוֹךְ יֵלֵךְ וּבָכֹה נֹשֵׂא מֶשֶׁךְ הַזָּרַע בֹּא יָבֹא בְרִנָּה נֹשֵׂא אֲלֻמֹּתָיו:

פרק קכז

א: שִׁיר הַמַּעֲלוֹת לִשְׁלֹמֹה אִם יְהֹוָה לֹא יִבְנֶה בַיִת שָׁוְא עָמְלוּ בוֹנָיו בּוֹ אִם יְהֹוָה לֹא יִשְׁמָר עִיר שָׁוְא שָׁקַד שׁוֹמֵר:
ב: שָׁוְא לָכֶם מַשְׁכִּימֵי קוּם מְאַחֲרֵי שֶׁבֶת אֹכְלֵי לֶחֶם הָעֲצָבִים כֵּן יִתֵּן לִידִידוֹ שֵׁנָא:
ג: הִנֵּה נַחֲלַת יְהֹוָה בָּנִים שָׂכָר פְּרִי הַבָּטֶן:
ד: כְּחִצִּים בְּיַד גִּבּוֹר כֵּן בְּנֵי הַנְּעוּרִים:
ה: אַשְׁרֵי הַגֶּבֶר אֲשֶׁר מִלֵּא אֶת אַשְׁפָּתוֹ מֵהֶם לֹא יֵבֹשׁוּ כִּי יְדַבְּרוּ אֶת אוֹיְבִים בַּשָּׁעַר:

פרק קכח

א: שִׁיר הַמַּעֲלוֹת אַשְׁרֵי כָּל יְרֵא יְהֹוָה הַהֹלֵךְ בִּדְרָכָיו:
ב: יְגִיעַ כַּפֶּיךָ כִּי תֹאכֵל אַשְׁרֶיךָ וְטוֹב לָךְ:
ג: אֶשְׁתְּךָ כְּגֶפֶן פֹּרִיָּה בְּיַרְכְּתֵי בֵיתֶךָ בָּנֶיךָ כִּשְׁתִלֵי זֵיתִים סָבִיב לְשֻׁלְחָנֶךָ:
ד: הִנֵּה כִי כֵן יְבֹרַךְ גָּבֶר יְרֵא יְהֹוָה:
ה: יְבָרֶכְךָ יְהֹוָה מִצִּיּוֹן וּרְאֵה בְּטוּב יְרוּשָׁלָם כֹּל יְמֵי חַיֶּיךָ:
ו: וּרְאֵה בָנִים לְבָנֶיךָ שָׁלוֹם עַל יִשְׂרָאֵל:

פרק קכט

א: שִׁיר הַמַּעֲלוֹת רַבַּת צְרָרוּנִי מִנְּעוּרַי יֹאמַר נָא יִשְׂרָאֵל:
ב: רַבַּת צְרָרוּנִי מִנְּעוּרָי גַּם לֹא יָכְלוּ לִי:
ג: עַל גַּבִּי חָרְשׁוּ חֹרְשִׁים הֶאֱרִיכוּ למענותם {לְמַעֲנִיתָם}:
ד: יְהֹוָה צַדִּיק קִצֵּץ עֲבוֹת רְשָׁעִים:
ה: יֵבֹשׁוּ וְיִסֹּגוּ אָחוֹר כֹּל שֹׂנְאֵי צִיּוֹן:
ו: יִהְיוּ כַּחֲצִיר גַּגּוֹת שֶׁקַּדְמַת שָׁלַף יָבֵשׁ:
ז: שֶׁלֹּא מִלֵּא כַפּוֹ קוֹצֵר וְחִצְנוֹ מְעַמֵּר:
ח: וְלֹא אָמְרוּ הָעֹבְרִים בִּרְכַּת יְהֹוָה אֲלֵיכֶם בֵּרַכְנוּ אֶתְכֶם בְּשֵׁם יְהֹוָה:

פרק קל

א: שִׁיר הַמַּעֲלוֹת מִמַּעֲמַקִּים קְרָאתִיךָ יְהֹוָה:

ספר תהילים

ב: אֲדֹנָי שִׁמְעָה בְקוֹלִי תִּהְיֶינָה אָזְנֶיךָ קַשֻּׁבוֹת לְקוֹל תַּחֲנוּנָי:

ג: אִם עֲוֹנוֹת תִּשְׁמָר יָהּ אֲדֹנָי מִי יַעֲמֹד:

ד: כִּי עִמְּךָ הַסְּלִיחָה לְמַעַן תִּוָּרֵא:

ה: קִוִּיתִי יְהֹוָה קִוְּתָה נַפְשִׁי וְלִדְבָרוֹ הוֹחָלְתִּי:

ו: נַפְשִׁי לַאדֹנָי מִשֹּׁמְרִים לַבֹּקֶר שֹׁמְרִים לַבֹּקֶר:

ז: יַחֵל יִשְׂרָאֵל אֶל יְהֹוָה כִּי עִם יְהֹוָה הַחֶסֶד וְהַרְבֵּה עִמּוֹ פְדוּת:

ח: וְהוּא יִפְדֶּה אֶת יִשְׂרָאֵל מִכֹּל עֲוֹנֹתָיו:

פרק קלא

א: שִׁיר הַמַּעֲלוֹת לְדָוִד יְהֹוָה לֹא גָבַהּ לִבִּי וְלֹא רָמוּ עֵינַי וְלֹא הִלַּכְתִּי בִּגְדֹלוֹת וּבְנִפְלָאוֹת מִמֶּנִּי:

ב: אִם לֹא שִׁוִּיתִי וְדוֹמַמְתִּי נַפְשִׁי כְּגָמֻל עֲלֵי אִמּוֹ כַּגָּמֻל עָלַי נַפְשִׁי:

ג: יַחֵל יִשְׂרָאֵל אֶל יְהֹוָה מֵעַתָּה וְעַד עוֹלָם:

פרק קלב

א: שִׁיר הַמַּעֲלוֹת זְכוֹר יְהֹוָה לְדָוִד אֵת כָּל עֻנּוֹתוֹ:

ב: אֲשֶׁר נִשְׁבַּע לַיהֹוָה נָדַר לַאֲבִיר יַעֲקֹב:

ג: אִם אָבֹא בְּאֹהֶל בֵּיתִי אִם אֶעֱלֶה עַל עֶרֶשׂ יְצוּעָי:

ד: אִם אֶתֵּן שְׁנַת לְעֵינָי לְעַפְעַפַּי תְּנוּמָה:

ה: עַד אֶמְצָא מָקוֹם לַיהֹוָה מִשְׁכָּנוֹת לַאֲבִיר יַעֲקֹב:

ו: הִנֵּה שְׁמַעֲנוּהָ בְאֶפְרָתָה מְצָאנוּהָ בִּשְׂדֵי יָעַר:

ז: נָבוֹאָה לְמִשְׁכְּנוֹתָיו נִשְׁתַּחֲוֶה לַהֲדֹם רַגְלָיו:

ח: קוּמָה יְהֹוָה לִמְנוּחָתֶךָ אַתָּה וַאֲרוֹן עֻזֶּךָ:

ט: כֹּהֲנֶיךָ יִלְבְּשׁוּ צֶדֶק וַחֲסִידֶיךָ יְרַנֵּנוּ:

י: בַּעֲבוּר דָּוִד עַבְדֶּךָ אַל תָּשֵׁב פְּנֵי מְשִׁיחֶךָ:

יא: נִשְׁבַּע יְהֹוָה לְדָוִד אֱמֶת לֹא יָשׁוּב מִמֶּנָּה מִפְּרִי בִטְנְךָ אָשִׁית לְכִסֵּא לָךְ:

יב: אִם יִשְׁמְרוּ בָנֶיךָ בְּרִיתִי וְעֵדֹתִי זוֹ אֲלַמְּדֵם גַּם בְּנֵיהֶם עֲדֵי עַד יֵשְׁבוּ לְכִסֵּא לָךְ:

יג: כִּי בָחַר יְהֹוָה בְּצִיּוֹן אִוָּהּ לְמוֹשָׁב לוֹ:

יד: זֹאת מְנוּחָתִי עֲדֵי עַד פֹּה אֵשֵׁב כִּי אִוִּתִיהָ:

טו: צֵידָהּ בָּרֵךְ אֲבָרֵךְ אֶבְיוֹנֶיהָ אַשְׂבִּיעַ לָחֶם:

טז: וְכֹהֲנֶיהָ אַלְבִּישׁ יֶשַׁע וַחֲסִידֶיהָ רַנֵּן יְרַנֵּנוּ:

יז: שָׁם אַצְמִיחַ קֶרֶן לְדָוִד עָרַכְתִּי נֵר לִמְשִׁיחִי:

יח: אוֹיְבָיו אַלְבִּישׁ בֹּשֶׁת וְעָלָיו יָצִיץ נִזְרוֹ:

פרק קלג

א: שִׁיר הַמַּעֲלוֹת לְדָוִד הִנֵּה מַה טּוֹב וּמַה נָּעִים שֶׁבֶת אַחִים גַּם יָחַד:

ב: כַּשֶּׁמֶן הַטּוֹב עַל הָרֹאשׁ יֹרֵד עַל הַזָּקָן זְקַן אַהֲרֹן שֶׁיֹּרֵד עַל פִּי מִדּוֹתָיו:

ג: כְּטַל חֶרְמוֹן שֶׁיֹּרֵד עַל הַרְרֵי צִיּוֹן כִּי שָׁם צִוָּה יְהֹוָה אֶת הַבְּרָכָה חַיִּים עַד הָעוֹלָם:

פרק קלד

א: שִׁיר הַמַּעֲלוֹת הִנֵּה בָּרְכוּ אֶת יְהֹוָה כָּל עַבְדֵי יְהֹוָה הָעֹמְדִים בְּבֵית יְהֹוָה בַּלֵּילוֹת:

ב: שְׂאוּ יְדֵכֶם קֹדֶשׁ וּבָרְכוּ אֶת יְהֹוָה:

ג: יְבָרֶכְךָ יְהֹוָה מִצִּיּוֹן עֹשֵׂה שָׁמַיִם וָאָרֶץ:

פרק קלה

א: הַלְלוּיָהּ הַלְלוּ אֶת שֵׁם יְהֹוָה הַלְלוּ עַבְדֵי יְהֹוָה:

ב: שֶׁעֹמְדִים בְּבֵית יְהֹוָה בְּחַצְרוֹת בֵּית אֱלֹהֵינוּ:

ג: הַלְלוּיָהּ כִּי טוֹב יְהֹוָה זַמְּרוּ לִשְׁמוֹ כִּי נָעִים:

ד: כִּי יַעֲקֹב בָּחַר לוֹ יָהּ יִשְׂרָאֵל לִסְגֻלָּתוֹ:
ה: כִּי אֲנִי יָדַעְתִּי כִּי גָדוֹל יְהוָה וַאֲדֹנֵינוּ מִכָּל אֱלֹהִים:
ו: כֹּל אֲשֶׁר חָפֵץ יְהוָה עָשָׂה בַּשָּׁמַיִם וּבָאָרֶץ בַּיַּמִּים וְכָל תְּהֹמוֹת:
ז: מַעֲלֶה נְשִׂאִים מִקְצֵה הָאָרֶץ בְּרָקִים לַמָּטָר עָשָׂה מוֹצֵא רוּחַ מֵאוֹצְרוֹתָיו:
ח: שֶׁהִכָּה בְּכוֹרֵי מִצְרָיִם מֵאָדָם עַד בְּהֵמָה:
ט: שָׁלַח אוֹתֹת וּמֹפְתִים בְּתוֹכֵכִי מִצְרָיִם בְּפַרְעֹה וּבְכָל עֲבָדָיו:
י: שֶׁהִכָּה גּוֹיִם רַבִּים וְהָרַג מְלָכִים עֲצוּמִים:
יא: לְסִיחוֹן מֶלֶךְ הָאֱמֹרִי וּלְעוֹג מֶלֶךְ הַבָּשָׁן וּלְכֹל מַמְלְכוֹת כְּנָעַן:
יב: וְנָתַן אַרְצָם נַחֲלָה נַחֲלָה לְיִשְׂרָאֵל עַמּוֹ:
יג: יְהוָה שִׁמְךָ לְעוֹלָם יְהוָה זִכְרְךָ לְדֹר וָדֹר:
יד: כִּי יָדִין יְהוָה עַמּוֹ וְעַל עֲבָדָיו יִתְנֶחָם:
טו: עֲצַבֵּי הַגּוֹיִם כֶּסֶף וְזָהָב מַעֲשֵׂה יְדֵי אָדָם:
טז: פֶּה לָהֶם וְלֹא יְדַבֵּרוּ עֵינַיִם לָהֶם וְלֹא יִרְאוּ:
יז: אָזְנַיִם לָהֶם וְלֹא יַאֲזִינוּ אַף אֵין יֶשׁ רוּחַ בְּפִיהֶם:
יח: כְּמוֹהֶם יִהְיוּ עֹשֵׂיהֶם כֹּל אֲשֶׁר בֹּטֵחַ בָּהֶם:
יט: בֵּית יִשְׂרָאֵל בָּרְכוּ אֶת יְהוָה בֵּית אַהֲרֹן בָּרְכוּ אֶת יְהוָה:
כ: בֵּית הַלֵּוִי בָּרְכוּ אֶת יְהוָה יִרְאֵי יְהוָה בָּרְכוּ אֶת יְהוָה:
כא: בָּרוּךְ יְהוָה מִצִּיּוֹן שֹׁכֵן יְרוּשָׁלִָם הַלְלוּיָהּ:

פרק קלו

א: הוֹדוּ לַיהוָה כִּי טוֹב כִּי לְעוֹלָם חַסְדּוֹ:
ב: הוֹדוּ לֵאלֹהֵי הָאֱלֹהִים כִּי לְעוֹלָם חַסְדּוֹ:
ג: הוֹדוּ לַאֲדֹנֵי הָאֲדֹנִים כִּי לְעוֹלָם חַסְדּוֹ:
ד: לְעֹשֵׂה נִפְלָאוֹת גְּדֹלוֹת לְבַדּוֹ כִּי לְעוֹלָם חַסְדּוֹ:
ה: לְעֹשֵׂה הַשָּׁמַיִם בִּתְבוּנָה כִּי לְעוֹלָם חַסְדּוֹ:
ו: לְרֹקַע הָאָרֶץ עַל הַמָּיִם כִּי לְעוֹלָם חַסְדּוֹ:
ז: לְעֹשֵׂה אוֹרִים גְּדֹלִים כִּי לְעוֹלָם חַסְדּוֹ:
ח: אֶת הַשֶּׁמֶשׁ לְמֶמְשֶׁלֶת בַּיּוֹם כִּי לְעוֹלָם חַסְדּוֹ:
ט: אֶת הַיָּרֵחַ וְכוֹכָבִים לְמֶמְשְׁלוֹת בַּלָּיְלָה כִּי לְעוֹלָם חַסְדּוֹ:
י: לְמַכֵּה מִצְרַיִם בִּבְכוֹרֵיהֶם כִּי לְעוֹלָם חַסְדּוֹ:
יא: וַיּוֹצֵא יִשְׂרָאֵל מִתּוֹכָם כִּי לְעוֹלָם חַסְדּוֹ:
יב: בְּיָד חֲזָקָה וּבִזְרוֹעַ נְטוּיָה כִּי לְעוֹלָם חַסְדּוֹ:
יג: לְגֹזֵר יַם סוּף לִגְזָרִים כִּי לְעוֹלָם חַסְדּוֹ:
יד: וְהֶעֱבִיר יִשְׂרָאֵל בְּתוֹכוֹ כִּי לְעוֹלָם חַסְדּוֹ:
טו: וְנִעֵר פַּרְעֹה וְחֵילוֹ בְיַם סוּף כִּי לְעוֹלָם חַסְדּוֹ:
טז: לְמוֹלִיךְ עַמּוֹ בַּמִּדְבָּר כִּי לְעוֹלָם חַסְדּוֹ:
יז: לְמַכֵּה מְלָכִים גְּדֹלִים כִּי לְעוֹלָם חַסְדּוֹ:
יח: וַיַּהֲרֹג מְלָכִים אַדִּירִים כִּי לְעוֹלָם חַסְדּוֹ:
יט: לְסִיחוֹן מֶלֶךְ הָאֱמֹרִי כִּי לְעוֹלָם חַסְדּוֹ:
כ: וּלְעוֹג מֶלֶךְ הַבָּשָׁן כִּי לְעוֹלָם חַסְדּוֹ:
כא: וְנָתַן אַרְצָם לְנַחֲלָה כִּי לְעוֹלָם חַסְדּוֹ:
כב: נַחֲלָה לְיִשְׂרָאֵל עַבְדּוֹ כִּי לְעוֹלָם חַסְדּוֹ:
כג: שֶׁבְּשִׁפְלֵנוּ זָכַר לָנוּ כִּי לְעוֹלָם חַסְדּוֹ:
כד: וַיִּפְרְקֵנוּ מִצָּרֵינוּ כִּי לְעוֹלָם חַסְדּוֹ:
כה: נֹתֵן לֶחֶם לְכָל בָּשָׂר כִּי לְעוֹלָם חַסְדּוֹ:
כו: הוֹדוּ לְאֵל הַשָּׁמָיִם כִּי לְעוֹלָם חַסְדּוֹ:

פרק קלז

א: עַל נַהֲרוֹת בָּבֶל שָׁם יָשַׁבְנוּ גַּם בָּכִינוּ בְּזָכְרֵנוּ אֶת צִיּוֹן:

ב: עַל עֲרָבִים בְּתוֹכָהּ תָּלִינוּ כִּנֹּרוֹתֵינוּ:

ג: כִּי שָׁם שְׁאֵלוּנוּ שׁוֹבֵינוּ דִּבְרֵי שִׁיר וְתוֹלָלֵינוּ שִׂמְחָה שִׁירוּ לָנוּ מִשִּׁיר צִיּוֹן:

ד: אֵיךְ נָשִׁיר אֶת שִׁיר יְהוָה עַל אַדְמַת נֵכָר:

ה: אִם אֶשְׁכָּחֵךְ יְרוּשָׁלָ‍ִם תִּשְׁכַּח יְמִינִי:

ו: תִּדְבַּק לְשׁוֹנִי לְחִכִּי אִם לֹא אֶזְכְּרֵכִי אִם לֹא אַעֲלֶה אֶת יְרוּשָׁלַ‍ִם עַל רֹאשׁ שִׂמְחָתִי:

ז: זְכֹר יְהוָה לִבְנֵי אֱדוֹם אֵת יוֹם יְרוּשָׁלָ‍ִם הָאֹמְרִים עָרוּ עָרוּ עַד הַיְסוֹד בָּהּ:

ח: בַּת בָּבֶל הַשְּׁדוּדָה אַשְׁרֵי שֶׁיְשַׁלֶּם לָךְ אֶת גְּמוּלֵךְ שֶׁגָּמַלְתְּ לָנוּ:

ט: אַשְׁרֵי שֶׁיֹּאחֵז וְנִפֵּץ אֶת עֹלָלַיִךְ אֶל הַסָּלַע:

פרק קלח

א: לְדָוִד אוֹדְךָ בְכָל לִבִּי נֶגֶד אֱלֹהִים אֲזַמְּרֶךָּ:

ב: אֶשְׁתַּחֲוֶה אֶל הֵיכַל קָדְשְׁךָ וְאוֹדֶה אֶת שְׁמֶךָ עַל חַסְדְּךָ וְעַל אֲמִתֶּךָ כִּי הִגְדַּלְתָּ עַל כָּל שִׁמְךָ אִמְרָתֶךָ:

ג: בְּיוֹם קָרָאתִי וַתַּעֲנֵנִי תַּרְהִבֵנִי בְנַפְשִׁי עֹז:

ד: יוֹדוּךָ יְהוָה כָּל מַלְכֵי אָרֶץ כִּי שָׁמְעוּ אִמְרֵי פִיךָ:

ה: וְיָשִׁירוּ בְּדַרְכֵי יְהוָה כִּי גָדוֹל כְּבוֹד יְהוָה:

ו: כִּי רָם יְהוָה וְשָׁפָל יִרְאֶה וְגָבֹהַּ מִמֶּרְחָק יְיֵדָע:

ז: אִם אֵלֵךְ בְּקֶרֶב צָרָה תְּחַיֵּנִי עַל אַף אֹיְבַי תִּשְׁלַח יָדֶךָ וְתוֹשִׁיעֵנִי יְמִינֶךָ:

ח: יְהוָה יִגְמֹר בַּעֲדִי יְהוָה חַסְדְּךָ לְעוֹלָם מַעֲשֵׂי יָדֶיךָ אַל תֶּרֶף:

פרק קלט

א: לַמְנַצֵּחַ לְדָוִד מִזְמוֹר יְהוָה חֲקַרְתַּנִי וַתֵּדָע:

ב: אַתָּה יָדַעְתָּ שִׁבְתִּי וְקוּמִי בַּנְתָּה לְרֵעִי מֵרָחוֹק:

ג: אָרְחִי וְרִבְעִי זֵרִיתָ וְכָל דְּרָכַי הִסְכַּנְתָּה:

ד: כִּי אֵין מִלָּה בִּלְשׁוֹנִי הֵן יְהוָה יָדַעְתָּ כֻלָּהּ:

ה: אָחוֹר וָקֶדֶם צַרְתָּנִי וַתָּשֶׁת עָלַי כַּפֶּכָה:

ו: פְּלִיאָה {פְּלִאיָה} דַעַת מִמֶּנִּי נִשְׂגְּבָה לֹא אוּכַל לָהּ:

ז: אָנָה אֵלֵךְ מֵרוּחֶךָ וְאָנָה מִפָּנֶיךָ אֶבְרָח:

ח: אִם אֶסַּק שָׁמַיִם שָׁם אָתָּה וְאַצִּיעָה שְּׁאוֹל הִנֶּךָּ:

ט: אֶשָּׂא כַנְפֵי שָׁחַר אֶשְׁכְּנָה בְּאַחֲרִית יָם:

י: גַּם שָׁם יָדְךָ תַנְחֵנִי וְתֹאחֲזֵנִי יְמִינֶךָ:

יא: וָאֹמַר אַךְ חֹשֶׁךְ יְשׁוּפֵנִי וְלַיְלָה אוֹר בַּעֲדֵנִי:

יב: גַּם חֹשֶׁךְ לֹא יַחְשִׁיךְ מִמֶּךָּ וְלַיְלָה כַּיּוֹם יָאִיר כַּחֲשֵׁיכָה כָּאוֹרָה:

יג: כִּי אַתָּה קָנִיתָ כִלְיֹתָי תְּסֻכֵּנִי בְּבֶטֶן אִמִּי:

יד: אוֹדְךָ עַל כִּי נוֹרָאוֹת נִפְלֵיתִי נִפְלָאִים מַעֲשֶׂיךָ וְנַפְשִׁי יֹדַעַת מְאֹד:

טו: לֹא נִכְחַד עָצְמִי מִמֶּךָּ אֲשֶׁר עֻשֵּׂיתִי בַסֵּתֶר רֻקַּמְתִּי בְּתַחְתִּיּוֹת אָרֶץ:

טז: גָּלְמִי רָאוּ עֵינֶיךָ וְעַל סִפְרְךָ כֻּלָּם יִכָּתֵבוּ יָמִים יֻצָּרוּ וְלוֹ {וְלֹא} אֶחָד בָּהֶם:

יז: וְלִי מַה יָּקְרוּ רֵעֶיךָ אֵל מֶה עָצְמוּ רָאשֵׁיהֶם:

יח: אֶסְפְּרֵם מֵחוֹל יִרְבּוּן הֱקִיצֹתִי וְעוֹדִי עִמָּךְ:

יט: אִם תִּקְטֹל אֱלוֹהַּ רָשָׁע וְאַנְשֵׁי דָמִים סוּרוּ מֶנִּי:

כ: אֲשֶׁר יֹמְרוּךָ לִמְזִמָּה נָשׂוּא לַשָּׁוְא עָרֶיךָ:

כא: הֲלוֹא מְשַׂנְאֶיךָ יְהוָה אֶשְׂנָא וּבִתְקוֹמְמֶיךָ אֶתְקוֹטָט:

כב: תַּכְלִית שִׂנְאָה שְׂנֵאתִים לְאוֹיְבִים הָיוּ לִי:

כג: חָקְרֵנִי אֵל וְדַע לְבָבִי בְּחָנֵנִי וְדַע שַׂרְעַפָּי:

כד: וּרְאֵה אִם דֶּרֶךְ עֹצֶב בִּי וּנְחֵנִי בְּדֶרֶךְ עוֹלָם:

פרק קמ

א: לַמְנַצֵּחַ מִזְמוֹר לְדָוִד:
ב: חַלְּצֵנִי יְהוָה מֵאָדָם רָע מֵאִישׁ חֲמָסִים תִּנְצְרֵנִי:
ג: אֲשֶׁר חָשְׁבוּ רָעוֹת בְּלֵב כָּל יוֹם יָגוּרוּ מִלְחָמוֹת:
ד: שָׁנֲנוּ לְשׁוֹנָם כְּמוֹ נָחָשׁ חֲמַת עַכְשׁוּב תַּחַת שְׂפָתֵימוֹ סֶלָה:
ה: שָׁמְרֵנִי יְהוָה מִידֵי רָשָׁע מֵאִישׁ חֲמָסִים תִּנְצְרֵנִי אֲשֶׁר חָשְׁבוּ לִדְחוֹת פְּעָמָי:
ו: טָמְנוּ גֵאִים פַּח לִי וַחֲבָלִים פָּרְשׂוּ רֶשֶׁת לְיַד מַעְגָּל מֹקְשִׁים שָׁתוּ לִי סֶלָה:
ז: אָמַרְתִּי לַיהוָה אֵלִי אָתָּה הַאֲזִינָה יְהוָה קוֹל תַּחֲנוּנָי:
ח: יְהוִה אֲדֹנָי עֹז יְשׁוּעָתִי סַכֹּתָה לְרֹאשִׁי בְּיוֹם נָשֶׁק:
ט: אַל תִּתֵּן יְהוָה מַאֲוַיֵּי רָשָׁע זְמָמוֹ אַל תָּפֵק יָרוּמוּ סֶלָה:
י: רֹאשׁ מְסִבָּי עֲמַל שְׂפָתֵימוֹ יְכַסּוּמוֹ {יְכַסֵּמוֹ}:
יא: יִמּוֹטוּ {יָמוּשׁוּ} עֲלֵיהֶם גֶּחָלִים בָּאֵשׁ יַפִּלֵם בְּמַהֲמֹרוֹת בַּל יָקוּמוּ:
יב: אִישׁ לָשׁוֹן בַּל יִכּוֹן בָּאָרֶץ אִישׁ חָמָס רָע יְצוּדֶנּוּ לְמַדְחֵפֹת:
יג: ידעת {יָדַעְתִּי} כִּי יַעֲשֶׂה יְהוָה דִּין עָנִי מִשְׁפַּט אֶבְיֹנִים:
יד: אַךְ צַדִּיקִים יוֹדוּ לִשְׁמֶךָ יֵשְׁבוּ יְשָׁרִים אֶת פָּנֶיךָ:

פרק קמא

א: מִזְמוֹר לְדָוִד יְהוָה קְרָאתִיךָ חוּשָׁה לִי הַאֲזִינָה קוֹלִי בְּקָרְאִי לָךְ:
ב: תִּכּוֹן תְּפִלָּתִי קְטֹרֶת לְפָנֶיךָ מַשְׂאַת כַּפַּי מִנְחַת עָרֶב:
ג: שִׁיתָה יְהוָה שָׁמְרָה לְפִי נִצְּרָה עַל דַּל שְׂפָתָי:
ד: אַל תַּט לִבִּי לְדָבָר רָע לְהִתְעוֹלֵל עֲלִלוֹת בְּרֶשַׁע אֶת אִישִׁים פֹּעֲלֵי אָוֶן וּבַל אֶלְחַם בְּמַנְעַמֵּיהֶם:
ה: יֶהֶלְמֵנִי צַדִּיק חֶסֶד וְיוֹכִיחֵנִי שֶׁמֶן רֹאשׁ אַל יָנִי רֹאשִׁי כִּי עוֹד וּתְפִלָּתִי בְּרָעוֹתֵיהֶם:
ו: נִשְׁמְטוּ בִידֵי סֶלַע שֹׁפְטֵיהֶם וְשָׁמְעוּ אֲמָרַי כִּי נָעֵמוּ:
ז: כְּמוֹ פֹלֵחַ וּבֹקֵעַ בָּאָרֶץ נִפְזְרוּ עֲצָמֵינוּ לְפִי שְׁאוֹל:
ח: כִּי אֵלֶיךָ יְהוִה אֲדֹנָי עֵינָי בְּכָה חָסִיתִי אַל תְּעַר נַפְשִׁי:
ט: שָׁמְרֵנִי מִידֵי פַח יָקְשׁוּ לִי וּמֹקְשׁוֹת פֹּעֲלֵי אָוֶן:
י: יִפְּלוּ בְמַכְמֹרָיו רְשָׁעִים יַחַד אָנֹכִי עַד אֶעֱבוֹר:

פרק קמב

א: מַשְׂכִּיל לְדָוִד בִּהְיוֹתוֹ בַמְּעָרָה תְפִלָּה:
ב: קוֹלִי אֶל יְהוָה אֶזְעָק קוֹלִי אֶל יְהוָה אֶתְחַנָּן:
ג: אֶשְׁפֹּךְ לְפָנָיו שִׂיחִי צָרָתִי לְפָנָיו אַגִּיד:
ד: בְּהִתְעַטֵּף עָלַי רוּחִי וְאַתָּה יָדַעְתָּ נְתִיבָתִי בְּאֹרַח זוּ אֲהַלֵּךְ טָמְנוּ פַח לִי:
ה: הַבֵּיט יָמִין וּרְאֵה וְאֵין לִי מַכִּיר אָבַד מָנוֹס מִמֶּנִּי אֵין דּוֹרֵשׁ לְנַפְשִׁי:
ו: זָעַקְתִּי אֵלֶיךָ יְהוָה אָמַרְתִּי אַתָּה מַחְסִי חֶלְקִי בְּאֶרֶץ הַחַיִּים:
ז: הַקְשִׁיבָה אֶל רִנָּתִי כִּי דַלּוֹתִי מְאֹד הַצִּילֵנִי מֵרֹדְפַי כִּי אָמְצוּ מִמֶּנִּי:
ח: הוֹצִיאָה מִמַּסְגֵּר נַפְשִׁי לְהוֹדוֹת אֶת שְׁמֶךָ בִּי יַכְתִּרוּ צַדִּיקִים כִּי תִגְמֹל עָלָי:

פרק קמג

א: מִזְמוֹר לְדָוִד יְהוָה שְׁמַע תְּפִלָּתִי הַאֲזִינָה אֶל תַּחֲנוּנַי בֶּאֱמֻנָתְךָ עֲנֵנִי בְּצִדְקָתֶךָ:
ב: וְאַל תָּבוֹא בְמִשְׁפָּט אֶת עַבְדֶּךָ כִּי לֹא יִצְדַּק לְפָנֶיךָ כָל חָי:
ג: כִּי רָדַף אוֹיֵב נַפְשִׁי דִּכָּא לָאָרֶץ חַיָּתִי הוֹשִׁיבַנִי בְמַחֲשַׁכִּים כְּמֵתֵי עוֹלָם:
ד: וַתִּתְעַטֵּף עָלַי רוּחִי בְּתוֹכִי יִשְׁתּוֹמֵם לִבִּי:
ה: זָכַרְתִּי יָמִים מִקֶּדֶם הָגִיתִי בְכָל פָּעֳלֶךָ בְּמַעֲשֵׂה יָדֶיךָ אֲשׂוֹחֵחַ:
ו: פֵּרַשְׂתִּי יָדַי אֵלֶיךָ נַפְשִׁי כְּאֶרֶץ עֲיֵפָה לְךָ סֶלָה:
ז: מַהֵר עֲנֵנִי יְהוָה כָּלְתָה רוּחִי אַל תַּסְתֵּר פָּנֶיךָ מִמֶּנִּי וְנִמְשַׁלְתִּי עִם יֹרְדֵי בוֹר:
ח: הַשְׁמִיעֵנִי בַבֹּקֶר חַסְדֶּךָ כִּי בְךָ בָטָחְתִּי הוֹדִיעֵנִי דֶּרֶךְ זוּ אֵלֵךְ כִּי אֵלֶיךָ נָשָׂאתִי נַפְשִׁי:

ספר תהילים

ט: הַצִּילֵנִי מֵאֹיְבַי יְהֹוָה אֵלֶיךָ כִסִּתִי:

י: לַמְּדֵנִי לַעֲשׂוֹת רְצוֹנֶךָ כִּי אַתָּה אֱלוֹהָי רוּחֲךָ טוֹבָה תַּנְחֵנִי בְּאֶרֶץ מִישׁוֹר:

יא: לְמַעַן שִׁמְךָ יְהֹוָה תְּחַיֵּנִי בְּצִדְקָתְךָ תּוֹצִיא מִצָּרָה נַפְשִׁי:

יב: וּבְחַסְדְּךָ תַּצְמִית אֹיְבָי וְהַאֲבַדְתָּ כָּל צֹרְרֵי נַפְשִׁי כִּי אֲנִי עַבְדֶּךָ:

פרק קמד

א: לְדָוִד בָּרוּךְ יְהֹוָה צוּרִי הַמְלַמֵּד יָדַי לַקְרָב אֶצְבְּעוֹתַי לַמִּלְחָמָה:

ב: חַסְדִּי וּמְצוּדָתִי מִשְׂגַּבִּי וּמְפַלְטִי לִי מָגִנִּי וּבוֹ חָסִיתִי הָרוֹדֵד עַמִּי תַחְתָּי:

ג: יְהֹוָה מָה אָדָם וַתֵּדָעֵהוּ בֶּן אֱנוֹשׁ וַתְּחַשְּׁבֵהוּ:

ד: אָדָם לַהֶבֶל דָּמָה יָמָיו כְּצֵל עוֹבֵר:

ה: יְהֹוָה הַט שָׁמֶיךָ וְתֵרֵד גַּע בֶּהָרִים וְיֶעֱשָׁנוּ:

ו: בְּרוֹק בָּרָק וּתְפִיצֵם שְׁלַח חִצֶּיךָ וּתְהֻמֵּם:

ז: שְׁלַח יָדֶיךָ מִמָּרוֹם פְּצֵנִי וְהַצִּילֵנִי מִמַּיִם רַבִּים מִיַּד בְּנֵי נֵכָר:

ח: אֲשֶׁר פִּיהֶם דִּבֶּר שָׁוְא וִימִינָם יְמִין שָׁקֶר:

ט: אֱלֹהִים שִׁיר חָדָשׁ אָשִׁירָה לָּךְ בְּנֵבֶל עָשׂוֹר אֲזַמְּרָה לָּךְ:

י: הַנּוֹתֵן תְּשׁוּעָה לַמְּלָכִים הַפּוֹצֶה אֶת דָּוִד עַבְדּוֹ מֵחֶרֶב רָעָה:

יא: פְּצֵנִי וְהַצִּילֵנִי מִיַּד בְּנֵי נֵכָר אֲשֶׁר פִּיהֶם דִּבֶּר שָׁוְא וִימִינָם יְמִין שָׁקֶר:

יב: אֲשֶׁר בָּנֵינוּ כִּנְטִעִים מְגֻדָּלִים בִּנְעוּרֵיהֶם בְּנוֹתֵינוּ כְזָוִיּוֹת מְחֻטָּבוֹת תַּבְנִית הֵיכָל:

יג: מְזָוֵינוּ מְלֵאִים מְפִיקִים מִזַּן אֶל זַן צֹאונֵנוּ מַאֲלִיפוֹת מְרֻבָּבוֹת בְּחוּצוֹתֵינוּ:

יד: אַלּוּפֵינוּ מְסֻבָּלִים אֵין פֶּרֶץ וְאֵין יוֹצֵאת וְאֵין צְוָחָה בִּרְחֹבֹתֵינוּ:

טו: אַשְׁרֵי הָעָם שֶׁכָּכָה לּוֹ אַשְׁרֵי הָעָם שֶׁיְהֹוָה אֱלֹהָיו:

פרק קמה

א: תְּהִלָּה לְדָוִד אֲרוֹמִמְךָ אֱלוֹהַי הַמֶּלֶךְ וַאֲבָרְכָה שִׁמְךָ לְעוֹלָם וָעֶד:

ב: בְּכָל יוֹם אֲבָרְכֶךָּ וַאֲהַלְלָה שִׁמְךָ לְעוֹלָם וָעֶד:

ג: גָּדוֹל יְהֹוָה וּמְהֻלָּל מְאֹד וְלִגְדֻלָּתוֹ אֵין חֵקֶר:

ד: דּוֹר לְדוֹר יְשַׁבַּח מַעֲשֶׂיךָ וּגְבוּרֹתֶיךָ יַגִּידוּ:

ה: הֲדַר כְּבוֹד הוֹדֶךָ וְדִבְרֵי נִפְלְאֹתֶיךָ אָשִׂיחָה:

ו: וֶעֱזוּז נוֹרְאֹתֶיךָ יֹאמֵרוּ וגדלותיך {וּגְדֻלָּתְךָ} אֲסַפְּרֶנָּה:

ז: זֵכֶר רַב טוּבְךָ יַבִּיעוּ וְצִדְקָתְךָ יְרַנֵּנוּ:

ח: חַנּוּן וְרַחוּם יְהֹוָה אֶרֶךְ אַפַּיִם וּגְדָל חָסֶד:

ט: טוֹב יְהֹוָה לַכֹּל וְרַחֲמָיו עַל כָּל מַעֲשָׂיו:

י: יוֹדוּךָ יְהֹוָה כָּל מַעֲשֶׂיךָ וַחֲסִידֶיךָ יְבָרְכוּכָה:

יא: כְּבוֹד מַלְכוּתְךָ יֹאמֵרוּ וּגְבוּרָתְךָ יְדַבֵּרוּ:

יב: לְהוֹדִיעַ לִבְנֵי הָאָדָם גְּבוּרֹתָיו וּכְבוֹד הֲדַר מַלְכוּתוֹ:

יג: מַלְכוּתְךָ מַלְכוּת כָּל עֹלָמִים וּמֶמְשַׁלְתְּךָ בְּכָל דּוֹר וָדֹר:

יד: סוֹמֵךְ יְהֹוָה לְכָל הַנֹּפְלִים וְזוֹקֵף לְכָל הַכְּפוּפִים:

טו: עֵינֵי כֹל אֵלֶיךָ יְשַׂבֵּרוּ וְאַתָּה נוֹתֵן לָהֶם אֶת אָכְלָם בְּעִתּוֹ:

טז: פּוֹתֵחַ אֶת יָדֶךָ וּמַשְׂבִּיעַ לְכָל חַי רָצוֹן:

יז: צַדִּיק יְהֹוָה בְּכָל דְּרָכָיו וְחָסִיד בְּכָל מַעֲשָׂיו:

יח: קָרוֹב יְהֹוָה לְכָל קֹרְאָיו לְכֹל אֲשֶׁר יִקְרָאֻהוּ בֶאֱמֶת:

יט: רְצוֹן יְרֵאָיו יַעֲשֶׂה וְאֶת שַׁוְעָתָם יִשְׁמַע וְיוֹשִׁיעֵם:

כ: שׁוֹמֵר יְהֹוָה אֶת כָּל אֹהֲבָיו וְאֵת כָּל הָרְשָׁעִים יַשְׁמִיד:

כא: תְּהִלַּת יְהֹוָה יְדַבֶּר פִּי וִיבָרֵךְ כָּל בָּשָׂר שֵׁם קָדְשׁוֹ לְעוֹלָם וָעֶד:

פרק קמו

א: הַלְלוּיָהּ הַלְלִי נַפְשִׁי אֶת יְהֹוָה:

ב: אֲהַלְלָה יְהֹוָה בְּחַיָּי אֲזַמְּרָה לֵאלֹהַי בְּעוֹדִי:

ג: אַל תִּבְטְחוּ בִנְדִיבִים בְּבֶן אָדָם שֶׁאֵין לוֹ תְשׁוּעָה:

ד: תֵּצֵא רוּחוֹ יָשֻׁב לְאַדְמָתוֹ בַּיּוֹם הַהוּא אָבְדוּ עֶשְׁתֹּנֹתָיו:

ה: אַשְׁרֵי שֶׁאֵל יַעֲקֹב בְּעֶזְרוֹ שִׂבְרוֹ עַל יְהֹוָה אֱלֹהָיו:

ו: עֹשֶׂה שָׁמַיִם וָאָרֶץ אֶת הַיָּם וְאֶת כָּל אֲשֶׁר בָּם הַשֹּׁמֵר אֱמֶת לְעוֹלָם:

ז: עֹשֶׂה מִשְׁפָּט לָעֲשׁוּקִים נֹתֵן לֶחֶם לָרְעֵבִים יְהֹוָה מַתִּיר אֲסוּרִים:

ח: יְהֹוָה פֹּקֵחַ עִוְרִים יְהֹוָה זֹקֵף כְּפוּפִים יְהֹוָה אֹהֵב צַדִּיקִים:

ט: יְהֹוָה שֹׁמֵר אֶת גֵּרִים יָתוֹם וְאַלְמָנָה יְעוֹדֵד וְדֶרֶךְ רְשָׁעִים יְעַוֵּת:

י: יִמְלֹךְ יְהֹוָה לְעוֹלָם אֱלֹהַיִךְ צִיּוֹן לְדֹר וָדֹר הַלְלוּיָהּ:

פרק קמז

א: הַלְלוּיָהּ כִּי טוֹב זַמְּרָה אֱלֹהֵינוּ כִּי נָעִים נָאוָה תְהִלָּה:

ב: בּוֹנֵה יְרוּשָׁלַםִ יְהֹוָה נִדְחֵי יִשְׂרָאֵל יְכַנֵּס:

ג: הָרֹפֵא לִשְׁבוּרֵי לֵב וּמְחַבֵּשׁ לְעַצְּבוֹתָם:

ד: מוֹנֶה מִסְפָּר לַכּוֹכָבִים לְכֻלָּם שֵׁמוֹת יִקְרָא:

ה: גָּדוֹל אֲדוֹנֵינוּ וְרַב כֹּחַ לִתְבוּנָתוֹ אֵין מִסְפָּר:

ו: מְעוֹדֵד עֲנָוִים יְהֹוָה מַשְׁפִּיל רְשָׁעִים עֲדֵי אָרֶץ:

ז: עֱנוּ לַיהֹוָה בְּתוֹדָה זַמְּרוּ לֵאלֹהֵינוּ בְכִנּוֹר:

ח: הַמְכַסֶּה שָׁמַיִם בְּעָבִים הַמֵּכִין לָאָרֶץ מָטָר הַמַּצְמִיחַ הָרִים חָצִיר:

ט: נוֹתֵן לִבְהֵמָה לַחְמָהּ לִבְנֵי עֹרֵב אֲשֶׁר יִקְרָאוּ:

י: לֹא בִגְבוּרַת הַסּוּס יֶחְפָּץ לֹא בְשׁוֹקֵי הָאִישׁ יִרְצֶה:

יא: רוֹצֶה יְהֹוָה אֶת יְרֵאָיו אֶת הַמְיַחֲלִים לְחַסְדּוֹ:

יב: שַׁבְּחִי יְרוּשָׁלַםִ אֶת יְהֹוָה הַלְלִי אֱלֹהַיִךְ צִיּוֹן:

יג: כִּי חִזַּק בְּרִיחֵי שְׁעָרָיִךְ בֵּרַךְ בָּנַיִךְ בְּקִרְבֵּךְ:

יד: הַשָּׂם גְּבוּלֵךְ שָׁלוֹם חֵלֶב חִטִּים יַשְׂבִּיעֵךְ:

טו: הַשֹּׁלֵחַ אִמְרָתוֹ אָרֶץ עַד מְהֵרָה יָרוּץ דְּבָרוֹ:

טז: הַנֹּתֵן שֶׁלֶג כַּצָּמֶר כְּפוֹר כָּאֵפֶר יְפַזֵּר:

יז: מַשְׁלִיךְ קַרְחוֹ כְפִתִּים לִפְנֵי קָרָתוֹ מִי יַעֲמֹד:

יח: יִשְׁלַח דְּבָרוֹ וְיַמְסֵם יַשֵּׁב רוּחוֹ יִזְּלוּ מָיִם:

יט: מַגִּיד דְּבָרָו לְיַעֲקֹב חֻקָּיו וּמִשְׁפָּטָיו לְיִשְׂרָאֵל:

כ: לֹא עָשָׂה כֵן לְכָל גּוֹי וּמִשְׁפָּטִים בַּל יְדָעוּם הַלְלוּיָהּ:

פרק קמח

א: הַלְלוּיָהּ הַלְלוּ אֶת יְהֹוָה מִן הַשָּׁמַיִם הַלְלוּהוּ בַּמְּרוֹמִים:

ב: הַלְלוּהוּ כָל מַלְאָכָיו הַלְלוּהוּ כָּל צְבָאָו:

ג: הַלְלוּהוּ שֶׁמֶשׁ וְיָרֵחַ הַלְלוּהוּ כָּל כּוֹכְבֵי אוֹר:

ד: הַלְלוּהוּ שְׁמֵי הַשָּׁמָיִם וְהַמַּיִם אֲשֶׁר מֵעַל הַשָּׁמָיִם:

ה: יְהַלְלוּ אֶת שֵׁם יְהֹוָה כִּי הוּא צִוָּה וְנִבְרָאוּ:

ו: וַיַּעֲמִידֵם לָעַד לְעוֹלָם חָק נָתַן וְלֹא יַעֲבוֹר:

ז: הַלְלוּ אֶת יְהֹוָה מִן הָאָרֶץ תַּנִּינִים וְכָל תְּהֹמוֹת:

ח: אֵשׁ וּבָרָד שֶׁלֶג וְקִיטוֹר רוּחַ סְעָרָה עֹשָׂה דְבָרוֹ:

ט: הֶהָרִים וְכָל גְּבָעוֹת עֵץ פְּרִי וְכָל אֲרָזִים:

י: הַחַיָּה וְכָל בְּהֵמָה רֶמֶשׂ וְצִפּוֹר כָּנָף:

יא: מַלְכֵי אֶרֶץ וְכָל לְאֻמִּים שָׂרִים וְכָל שֹׁפְטֵי אָרֶץ:

יב: בַּחוּרִים וְגַם בְּתוּלוֹת זְקֵנִים עִם נְעָרִים:

יג: יְהַלְלוּ אֶת שֵׁם יְהֹוָה כִּי נִשְׂגָּב שְׁמוֹ לְבַדּוֹ הוֹדוֹ עַל אֶרֶץ וְשָׁמָיִם:

יד: וַיָּרֶם קֶרֶן לְעַמּוֹ תְּהִלָּה לְכָל חֲסִידָיו לִבְנֵי יִשְׂרָאֵל עַם קְרֹבוֹ הַלְלוּיָהּ:

פרק קמט

א: הַלְלוּיָהּ שִׁירוּ לַיהֹוָה שִׁיר חָדָשׁ תְּהִלָּתוֹ בִּקְהַל חֲסִידִים:
ב: יִשְׂמַח יִשְׂרָאֵל בְּעֹשָׂיו בְּנֵי צִיּוֹן יָגִילוּ בְמַלְכָּם:
ג: יְהַלְלוּ שְׁמוֹ בְמָחוֹל בְּתֹף וְכִנּוֹר יְזַמְּרוּ לוֹ:
ד: כִּי רוֹצֶה יְהֹוָה בְּעַמּוֹ יְפָאֵר עֲנָוִים בִּישׁוּעָה:
ה: יַעְלְזוּ חֲסִידִים בְּכָבוֹד יְרַנְּנוּ עַל מִשְׁכְּבוֹתָם:
ו: רוֹמְמוֹת אֵל בִּגְרוֹנָם וְחֶרֶב פִּיפִיּוֹת בְּיָדָם:
ז: לַעֲשׂוֹת נְקָמָה בַּגּוֹיִם תּוֹכֵחוֹת בַּלְאֻמִּים:
ח: לֶאְסֹר מַלְכֵיהֶם בְּזִקִּים וְנִכְבְּדֵיהֶם בְּכַבְלֵי בַרְזֶל:
ט: לַעֲשׂוֹת בָּהֶם מִשְׁפָּט כָּתוּב הָדָר הוּא לְכָל חֲסִידָיו הַלְלוּיָהּ:

פרק קנ

א: הַלְלוּיָהּ הַלְלוּ אֵל בְּקָדְשׁוֹ הַלְלוּהוּ בִּרְקִיעַ עֻזּוֹ:
ב: הַלְלוּהוּ בִגְבוּרֹתָיו הַלְלוּהוּ כְּרֹב גֻּדְלוֹ:
ג: הַלְלוּהוּ בְּתֵקַע שׁוֹפָר הַלְלוּהוּ בְּנֵבֶל וְכִנּוֹר:
ד: הַלְלוּהוּ בְתֹף וּמָחוֹל הַלְלוּהוּ בְּמִנִּים וְעֻגָב:
ה: הַלְלוּהוּ בְצִלְצְלֵי שָׁמַע הַלְלוּהוּ בְּצִלְצְלֵי תְרוּעָה:
ו: כֹּל הַנְּשָׁמָה תְּהַלֵּל יָהּ הַלְלוּיָהּ: